daring pairings

EVAN GOLDSTEIN

daring pairings

**A Master Sommelier Matches Distinctive Wines
with Recipes from His Favorite Chefs**

Photographs by Joyce Oudkerk Pool

UNIVERSITY OF CALIFORNIA PRESS   BERKELEY | LOS ANGELES | LONDON

The publisher gratefully acknowledges the
generous support of the General Endowment Fund
of the University of California Press Foundation.

University of California Press, one of the most
distinguished university presses in the United
States, enriches lives around the world by
advancing scholarship in the humanities, social
sciences, and natural sciences. Its activities are
supported by the UC Press Foundation and by
philanthropic contributions from individuals and
institutions. For more information, visit www.
ucpress.edu.

University of California Press
Berkeley and Los Angeles, California

University of California Press, Ltd.
London, England

Design by Nola Burger
Photography by Joyce Oudkerk Pool
  with the assistance of Ashley Quintana
Food styling by Pouké
  with the assistance of Christina Milne
Prop styling by Carol Hacker/Tableprop
Copyediting by Erika Búky
Indexing by Thérèse Shere

Text: 10.25/14 Chaparral
Display: Univers and Univers Ultra Condensed
Compositor: Integrated Composition Systems
Printed through: Asia Pacific Offset, Inc.

Library of Congress Cataloging-in-Publication Data

Goldstein, Evan.
  Daring pairings : a master sommelier matches
distinctive wines with recipes from his favorite chefs /
Evan Goldstein ; photographs by Joyce Oudkerk Pool.
    p. cm.
  Includes bibliographical references and index.
  ISBN 978-0-520-25478-7 (cloth : alk. paper)
  1. Cookery.   2. Wine and wine making.   I. Title.
TX714.G647   2010
641.5—dc22   2009037668

Manufactured in China

18 17 16 15 14 13 12 11 10
10 9 8 7 6 5 4 3 2 1

The paper used in this publication meets the
minimum requirements of ANSI/NISO Z39.48–1992
(R 1997) (*Permanence of Paper*).

contents

recipes

ACKNOWLEDGMENTS

I was moved to write this book after I heard from dozens of readers of its predecessor, *Perfect Pairings*, telling me how comfortable they now felt with wine in general but confiding that they still had no idea where to begin when pairing food and wine from unfamiliar grapes, regions, and labels. After the initial inspiration came the heavy lifting, and that took, in the words of the Beatles, "a little help from my friends."

Very special thanks to my wife, Barbara, for her unconditional support and patience as the wine bottles overtook the garage and the countless tastings cut into far too many family dinners. And to my kids, Elena and Adam, for humoring their dad's passion and always happily sampling the recipes.

I thank Connie Shih Cohn, this book's manager, director, and planner, who deftly juggled reams of information about three dozen wines and their wineries, importers, and pricing, always with a smile. And Gary Woo, master recipe tester, whose skill and experienced palate made the food sing. Without his help I would have been frustrated and perhaps made adjustments and tweaks that wouldn't work with the wines or respect the integrity of the chefs' creations.

I thank those thirty-six amazing chefs, my all-star lineup, whose inspired and delicious recipes add color and context to the wines, framing them and bringing out all of their wonderful attributes.

A big thanks to my mother, Joyce, whose familiarity with cookbook structure helped me design a truly balanced set of recipes to accompany a wide range of wines and styles. And to my agent, Eric Lasher, whose clarity, good sense, and guidance are appreciated more than he knows.

I also extend my gratitude to the team at University of California Press: my editor, Blake Edgar, who may be more passionate about these "daring" wines than anyone I know; to Dore Brown and Erika Bűky for their expert fine-tuning of the text; and to Nola Burger, whose design and layout make the book look so good. And once again thanks to Joyce Oudkerk Pool for the amazing and mouthwatering photography.

This book couldn't have come together without the help of the numerous wineries, wine-makers, importers, and wine-business and national trade representatives who provided generous helpings of information, wine, and enthusiasm.

And last, several individuals have been sources of inspiration and motivation and gave me particular help during the writing of this book. Among them is my business partner, Limeng Stroh; I also owe a great deal to the collective generosity of spirit, wisdom, and inspiration of Laura Catena, Chris Fehrnstrom, David Granek, Chet Hutchinson, Youri Korsakoff, Ronn Owens, Kathleen and Michel Rege, Jancis Robinson, Joe Rollo, Allen Shoup, Madeline Triffon, Laura Werlin, and my perennial *vrai ami,* Gilles Deschamps.

As a professional wine educator I travel all over the country and around the world. Wherever I go, I encounter folks who share my passion for wine and food. Living out the premise of Walt Disney's "It's a Small World," I have gone from robust dialogues about the impending harvest in Australia while enjoying German Riesling with street food in Singapore to discussing French wine over takeout Cajun gumbo and Japanese sushi from Whole Foods, washed down with Spanish Garnacha *rosado,* in the suburbs of Austin, Texas. We're fortunate to have access to a dizzying range of world cuisine and wines from dozens of different grapes and in myriad interpretations of these varieties. This is an amazing time to expand one's horizons in wine and food.

Daring Pairings is my way of capturing this pleasure of discovery and sharing it with you. Newly confident consumers may want to step off the main trail and onto a less-traveled path but still feel scared of getting lost. I want to help you overcome that hesitation and to bolster your desire to learn with information that is useful and approachable. As your master sommelier, I want to introduce the approach of "trusted discovery" to your daily wining and dining, at home and in your travels.

In *Daring Pairings,* we move beyond the basic grapes and wines covered in *Perfect Pairings* and venture into a landscape of lesser-known global offerings. Grapes like Albariño, Xinomavro, and Roussanne are as compelling in their own right as Riesling, Syrah, and Chardonnay. Grüner Veltliner may sound like an Austrian sobriety test, but it is increasingly popular in bistros and cafés of many culinary styles. Tempranillo, a key ambassador for Spain's wine industry, is also becoming familiar in non-Spanish restaurants. Most people simply haven't been exposed to many of these emerging varietal wines, but they are worth getting to know.

First I look at how the wine world reached this happy point and examine the various players in the wine industry who have helped to shape it. Then I review the basic principles of tasting wine and pairing it with foods. Finally, I lead you through the maze of grapes. To ensure a more pleasurable voyage, I have selected three dozen of my favorite lesser-known grapes. Some of them you may already know; if you don't, you can expect to hear more about them in coming years. I describe where and how each wine is made, its distinctive characteristics, and other varietal wines that resemble it in some respects. (If you're new to the language of winemaking and wine, you may want to consult the glossary for definitions of winegrowing and tasting terms.)

Because wine is best enjoyed and appreciated with food, each grape profile includes recommendations for pairing with meals and a cheese plate, and also includes a recipe created by a noted chef to complement that grape's unique flavors and attributes. Take thirty-six unsung grapes and thirty-six delicious dishes, and you are on the road to epicurean diversity and discovery! So grab your passport and get ready to journey from A to X, Aglianico to Xinomavro.

THE WINE WORLD AND ITS INFLUENCES

In 2005, according to London's *International Wine and Spirit Record*, the United States became the global leader in wine consumed (by dollar value) as well as the world's biggest market for exporters. The same study points out that sometime between 2008 and 2010, depending on the health of the national economy, the United States will not only spend more on wine but also, collectively, drink more of it than any other country—though it still lags behind traditional wine-drinking nations such as Spain, Italy, and France (and even Malta and Guatemala), in per capita consumption.* Americans are becoming increasingly comfortable with wine, incorporating it more into our daily lives and, as with food, thirsting to learn and broaden our horizons with new tasting experiences. With wine, the proverbial glass is clearly half full.

Imports have reached record levels, now accounting for more than 25 percent of the total U.S. wine market.† Italian and Australian imports dominate, but nations such as Chile, France (whose wine industry has been revitalized), Spain, and more recently, Austria, Argentina, and Greece are also supplying a growing number of the bottles on American store shelves and wine lists. Americans still prefer to drink local: it's just that the definition of *local* has changed over the years. California has more than 2,400 wineries, which constitute 49 percent of all wineries in the United States, but all fifty states are now producing wine commercially. Other key players include Washington State, with more than 550 wineries; Oregon, with more than 370; and New York, with around 270. Quality wines now emanate from states as diverse as Michigan (which has 110 wineries), Maryland (40), and even Montana (11). Combine this range of national diversity with free-trade agreements, competitive market conditions, and a globalized economy and you have perfect conditions for an exciting, dynamic, and healthy market supplying a growing number of well-informed wine drinkers.

Many different factors have helped to create today's climate, in which wine is savored and

* "Per Capita Wine Consumption," California Wine Institute, www.wineinstitute.org/resources/worldstatistics/article44, August 24, 2007.

† Vinexpo/IWSR, www.marketwire.com/press-release/Vinexpo-713461.html, 2007.

respected. As with the individual grape varieties that make up a great red Bordeaux, a complex Champagne cuvée, or a wonderful Spanish Rioja, the whole is greater than the sum of its parts.

North American Winemakers

In the mid-1980s I attended a panel on the future of wine at the Monterey Wine Festival. Most of us listened with no more than polite attention—until the microphone was passed to Randall Grahm.

Grahm, the guiding force behind California's Bonny Doon Vineyard, is considered the ringleader of the wine industry's bad boys. Many of his innovations—his edgy and fun packaging, his decisive switch from corks to screw caps, and his championing of unconventional varieties—have become mainstream. But in the 1980s, his convictions and opinions were new and, to many, sacrilegious. At this panel, Grahm proclaimed that our Mediterranean climate was far better suited to warmer climate varietals (grapes from the Rhône, Spain, and Italy) and that growers would be best served by pulling out the massive acreage planted in Chardonnay and Cabernet and replanting with these other grapes. The rest of the panel visibly moved to distance themselves from this heretical point of view.

I think we are all glad that much of the great stock of California Cabernet Sauvignon and Chardonnay has been left in the magical spots where it was planted. That said, Randall Grahm has contributed greatly to the diversity of wines, grapes, and winemaking styles found in the United States today. An increase in plantings of Syrah and other southern French grapes, a focus on Grenache as more than just a blending grape, and the introduction of unheard-of grapes like Freisa and Teroldego are just a few of his legacies. His latest enterprise, in Washington State, to focus his efforts on Riesling, Grüner Veltliner, and Chenin Blanc has undoubtedly been viewed as quixotic, but time will likely again prove him right.

Of course, many other vintners have taken equally radical stances. Jim Clendenen (of Au Bon Climat) and Bob Lindquist (of Qupé) in Santa Barbara County have experimented effectively with grapes like Vermentino and Arneis, and the importer Bob Haas has successfully planted all of the great Châteauneuf-du-Pape grapes for his Tablas Creek winery's red and white blends and became the primary source of vine cuttings for all serious American producers who crave grapes like Counoise and Vaccarèse. Michael Havens started playing with Albariño at his eponymous winery even before the variety grew beyond its northeastern Spanish roots; Marimar Torres's contemporary efforts with Tempranillo clones in Sonoma County's Green Valley are well documented. And Rudy von Strasser was inspired to plant Grüner Veltliner on Napa Valley's Diamond Mountain.

Such daring does not stop at the California border. Earl Jones of Abacela Winery in Oregon's Umpqua Valley and Doug McCrea of McCrea Cellars in eastern Washington State have challenged the status quo in their regions by offering Rhône and other Mediterranean grapes.

The intrepid efforts of vintners like these have given American wines the panoply of flavors we savor today.

Importers

While North American growers are helping to expand American palates by producing exciting new varieties and blends, many wine importers have also contributed to the effort by supplying an array of great wines from around the world to American stores, restaurants, and dinner tables. In addition, their influence has persuaded some overseas winemakers to tweak the styles of their wines in order to satisfy consumers. Closer to home, good importers can be reliable guides when you're shopping for unfamiliar wines, and I list a number of recommended importers in the back of the book.

Critics

Like them or not, wine critics wield considerable influence over the industry, whether through encyclopedic wine reference books, websites, or the "shelf talkers" in a wine store (those little cards describing a wine). The opinions of the *Wine Spectator,* Robert Parker, Jancis Robinson, Eric Asimov of the *New York Times,* the team of John Brecher and Dorothy J. Gaiter at the *Wall Street Journal,* and Wilfred Wong at BevMo largely determine what we drink—and can make or break wineries.

How seriously should wine drinkers follow their recommendations? My two cents is that the difference between a wine that scores 89 on somebody's scale and one scoring in the low 90s is negligible. Evaluating a wine is like interpreting art or music—it's personal. The critics' palates, however sophisticated, aren't always the best guides to the wines that *you* will enjoy or that will work with your style of dining. You should use wine scores for initial guidance, compare them with your own reactions, and learn to trust yourself as the ultimate judge and jury.

Wine critics do play an indispensable role in seeking out and promoting new grapes, wines, and winemakers. If it weren't for writers like Jancis Robinson, James Halliday, and Steve Tanzer, there are hundreds of wines I would never have tried, regions I might never have explored, and grapes I might never have heard of (much less be able to pronounce). In the dynamic world of wine, we need good guides, arbiters, and chroniclers. Just remember that the opinions of those who write are just that—opinions—and that each of us is entitled to our own views. Becoming a good judge of wine is simply a matter of trusting your own palate enough to determine whether or not you *like* a particular wine. And you really don't need anyone to tell you that, do you?

Consultants

Also influencing the world of wine are consultants, who assist estates and wineries in crafting wines to conform to specific profiles, based on their perceptions of consumer taste and the marketplace.

The moniker *flying winemaker* refers to a small number of talented winemakers who fly all over the world dispensing advice to wineries (for a price). A few big names—Michel Rolland (and his equally gifted wife, Dany), Jacques and François Lurton, and Alberto Antonini, among others—seem to get much of the press, but other powerful consultants include Philippe Melka, Paul Hobbs and Helen Turley in California, Telmo Rodríguez and Alvaro Palacios in Spain, Riccardo Cotarella in Italy, and Stéphane Derenoncourt in France. Because wine quality is now generally quite high overall, consultants focus less on quality control than on specific techniques and strategies to help producers craft wines that will appeal broadly to consumers and critics. These include micro-oxygenation, harvesting grapes at extreme ripeness (resulting in higher alcohol levels), and insisting on very low yields (for greater flavor concentration and greater expression of *terroir*). However, because these strategies are disseminated by the same consultants to winemakers in so many different regions, critics argue that they are causing wines to become homogenized. This is the topic of many wine-geek dialogues and the focus of the documentary *Mondovino* (which is worth watching). The best efforts blend their deftly applied fairy dust with a genuine regard for the appellation and grapes, but the less successful ones result in high-quality products with little distinctive identity. So, in the end, you need to consider each wine on its own merits.

Sommeliers

As a former sommelier myself, I have strong opinions about how important waitstaff and sommeliers are in guiding consumer taste. I used to joke that if I had a dollar for every time I wrote the name of a wine on the back of a business card for a diner, I would have been long retired.

While more wine is sold in stores than in restaurants, most of us are more daring when dining out than when hosting family and friends at home. When entertaining, we have a small repertoire of recipes that we rely on and an equally small range of wines we serve with those dishes. The practical reality is that most of us do not experiment with reckless abandon at home as we are afraid to bomb in front of the people we care about or want to impress. We save our experimentation for dining out.

People choose restaurants for a combination of reasons, including the expertise of those who work there. Sommeliers must be prepared to answer questions such as "What's the best wine for the dish I ordered?," "Can you bring me something great that I don't know?," and even "Can you just pick for me?" All of these questions, when asked of knowledgeable staff, can bring great rewards.

Retailer-client relationships can have the same result, but restaurants and wine bars have an advantage over retail in their ability to sell by the glass, half glass, or even two-ounce pour. (Most places—from an Olive Garden restaurant to Napa Valley's celebrated French Laundry—will even allow you to taste the wine before you commit to the glass, and some restaurants may take the wine back if you don't like it, especially if a server recommended it, preferring that you get something that gives you pleasure.) Wine by the glass has really caught on, representing 65 percent of the restaurant industry's wine sales. Consumers increasingly seem to enjoy trying two or three wines over the course of a meal, which has led to sommelier-selected themed flights—servings of three or more small portions of wines that go together. These flights are fun and easy ways to sample different (and more daring) wines, and the arrangement benefits both buyers and sellers. As I always say, any wine's best friend and best form of advertising is an enthusiastic sommelier!

Retailers

Perhaps the most influential players in the wine trade are the retail buyers, big and small, who determine what sits on their shelves and therefore what ends up on consumers' tables. Almost every American city has at least one specialty wine merchant who is introducing customers to intriguing wines from interesting locales. And even roaming the aisles of Costco or a similar warehouse club can turn up edgy wines from Italy, Spain, and Chile, as well as lesser-known grapes like Barbera, Carmenère, and Grüner Veltliner. It's comforting to know that as people are buying their year's supply of paper towels, they can grab a case of good red wine from the Ribera del Duero while they are at it!

FOOD IN THE U.S.A.

As significant as the evolution of wine has been in America, the food revolution has been even more dramatic. Today, many people are demanding locally and sustainably produced foods. And many aging baby boomers, with their children out of the house, find themselves with extra cash to purchase tastier and better-quality ingredients and more leisure to experiment with new dishes and flavors. These changes are reflected in the popularity of urban farmers markets as well as supermarket offerings. Even in the biggest chain supermarkets you can usually find high-quality products such as range-fed meat and locally grown vegetables. Although organic foods are still perceived by some as an expensive luxury, Wal-Mart's recent entry into the organic grocery market suggests that organics are here to stay.

To me the most significant changes in American cuisine can be symbolized by the following two facts:

- In the 1990s, salsa surpassed ketchup as America's number-one condiment.*

- There are more Chinese restaurants in the United States than there are outlets of Burger King, Wendy's, and McDonald's combined.†

* Donald A. Hodgen, William Bellows, William V. Janis, and Cornelius Kenney, *US Industrial Outlook, Annual, 1993. USA Today,* however, reports that the average American still consumes more than three bottles of ketchup per year (www.usatoday.com/news/nation/2006-06-25-us-population_x.htm, June 25, 2006).
† *Gourmet,* Good Living Section, March 2007.

No longer is the typical American meal a tuna casserole or a pot roast. Today's dinner table is more likely to feature enchiladas, takeout Szechuan, supermarket sushi, or microwavable lemon-pepper chicken. Just a few decades ago, it would have been hard to imagine that tortillas would be a refrigerator staple in more than 40 percent of American households (with Latinos still representing less than 20 percent of the nation's population).* And I suspect that the same holds for soy sauce.

Besides immigration, whose impact is vivid through the introduction of new cuisines to the United States, three other forces have dramatically altered the face of American food: travel, the media, and restaurants.

Travel

I doubt that President Ronald Reagan, the man who once labeled ketchup a vegetable, saw diversifying the American table as a key objective of his plan for the deregulation of air travel, but it was certainly one of the consequences.

Travel has uniquely influenced what we eat. To compete in the global economy, companies send employees around the country and all over the world. Encounters with new foods, be it jambalaya in New Orleans or pad Thai in Bangkok, give business travelers a new perspective on their dining and new dishes to add to their repertoire at home. For those who travel for pleasure, the opportunities to sample new cuisines are even greater and more enjoyable. Many friends of mine have become so smitten after trips to Italy that their diets have shifted from mostly hamburgers and roasts to a dizzying array of pastas and other Italian regional specialties. Epicurean travel has become a recognized pastime, with magazines and guidebooks to support it. Whether you want to travel the back roads of America, guided by Jane and Michael Stern's *Roadfood*, or to sample the offerings at the Michelin-starred restaurants of Paris, it's all possible, and if you plan carefully, such excursions are more affordable than we could have imagined forty years ago.

As travel has expanded our dining habits, businesses and restaurants have adapted to satisfy our diversified tastes. Even going to an amusement park no longer requires gorging on funnel cakes, hamburgers, pizza slices, and French fries washed down with sugary sodas. At Disney's Epcot Food and Wine Festival, an annual celebration, thousands of epicures engage in culinary adventures at food and wine booths offering tastes from around the world. In the course of an hour or so you can meander from Canada and the United Kingdom to Argentina and Japan and finish off with Morocco and France.

The Food Media

The media have played a vital part in this gastronomic revolution. Food and wine media have evolved beyond weekly newspaper food sections and specialty magazines to include websites,

---

* AC Nielsen study, quoted in "Pass the Salsa, Por Favor," http://undercurrents.tmgstrategies.com/2007/04/page/2/, April 24, 2007.

blogs, podcasts, and network and cable television shows. We are tantalized by recipes, wine-tasting notes, and travelogues, many of them available for free. (I list a selection of the best sources in the back of the book.) Vicarious taste and travel adventures can range from the exotic (such as the travels of Bravo's Anthony Bourdain to Vietnam and Brazil) to the purely comfortable (such as the Food Network's Guy Fieri featuring America's favorite diners, drive-ins, and dives). Pick up any traditional epicurean magazine today and compare it to an issue from thirty years back, and you will be astonished at the differences. Long gone are the recipes for chocolate mousse, beef Wellington, and coq au vin that typified aspirational home cooking in the early to mid-1970s. Today they've been replaced with alternatives like lemon-thyme sorbet with summer berries, skirt steak with Moroccan spice rub and yogurt sauce, and Thai chicken stew with potato-chive dumplings. And the wine recommendations have expanded from expensive French bottles to include economical offerings from regions and grape varieties that the late Julia Child might not recognize, such as Argentinean Malbec, Greek Xinomavro, and Italian Vermentino.

Restaurants

Restaurants have played a seminal role as promoters of diversity in American dining. Anyone interested in the place of restaurants in American culture should read *The United States of Arugula* by David Kamp, *The Last Days of Haute Cuisine* by Patric Kuh, or, if you can find it, *America Eats Out* by John Mariani. We've come a long way, baby, as a glance at the restaurant section in your local Yellow Pages will show you. With passionate cooks in your neighborhood who have studied, trained, and traveled around the globe, you no longer need to visit Italy to satisfy a yen for southern Italian food or look to Kuala Lumpur for authentic banana leaf fish.

And lest you think that this simmering excitement exists only in the realm of fine dining, take a look at some of the newer offerings at McDonald's (chicken wraps with chipotle barbecue sauce and Asian chicken salad), Red Lobster (seafood Caesar salad, lobster pizza, and Bayou seafood gumbo), or Applebee's (chicken quesadillas, teriyaki steak skewers, and bruschetta burgers), and you'll see that America's desire to eat more daringly is pervasive. Increasingly advised by celebrity-chef consultants, quick-service restaurants are keenly aware of what drives consumer tastes and are adjusting accordingly. We've moved beyond the world of burgers, fried chicken, and color-coded wines of red, white, and pink.

Admittedly, most folks eating Big Macs aren't thinking about wine (though a ripe Grenache would be a terrific match). But many of us who enjoy the local Greek restaurant, the New England lobster shack by the pier, the Spanish-themed wine bar, or a nearby authentically Roman trattoria are keen to try different wines to complement these new food tastes. And you needn't be a gastronomic daredevil to enjoy an unusual wine: you can also find pleasure in pairing it up with a classic roast chicken or simple lamb stew at home. If you simply enjoy being a little bit adventurous with your wine and food, this book's for you.

CREATING PAIRINGS THAT WORK

To many people, learning about pairing food and wine is like mastering a foreign language. Both require a little study. Both become easier with practice. And with both, you reach a point when your knowledge becomes reflexive.

I feel fortunate to be able to speak fluent French. For years I studied it in school, diligently memorizing verb tenses, vocabulary, and grammar. Then, on arriving in Paris to work, I realized that despite all that study, I was far from being able to communicate, much less speak fluently. Nobody I worked with spoke English, and had it not been for the patience and diligence of the chef with whom I worked on the line (who is still my best friend), I would have been sunk. He taught me *argot* (slang) and, more important, spoke with me, patiently and without judgment, for months as I listened, translated, thought about what I wanted to say, translated it back into French, and spoke the words to him. Five steps, every time. Then one day he said something, and I replied automatically, without translating and retranslating. I had finally begun to think in French. Since then it's been easy.

Learning the "language" of food and wine may feel similarly forced and awkward at first. You may feel as if you are getting things right and wrong without knowing why, and frustrated by the randomness of it all. Trust me, over time it will turn from five steps (reading the recipe or looking at the menu, thinking about your wine selection, tasting the dish, tasting the wine, and deciding whether the pairing works) to two steps (picking a wine that you're confident will pair with the food and then enjoying the match).

It would be self-serving for me to say that the best way to approach wine and food pairing is to read my previous book, *Perfect Pairings*. That said, those of you who have read the book and understand my thinking on pairing will find the process simpler this time around as we explore new grapes, wines, and accompanying recipes. For new readers, I summarize my approach below and adapt it to the grapes, wines, and recipes that follow.

Pairing wine and food is a lot like falling in love. In true love, we may be blind to color, race, religion, and gender, and we find genuine happiness with a lover based on shared values, experiences, interests, and innate attraction. Wine and food come together when the character traits of the wine mesh with the food's personality. The wine doesn't care what the dish is or is not, or where it originates. The food couldn't care less if it's flouting time-honored expectations. For example, an Argentinean Malbec isn't a significantly better match with an *asado* (Argentinean barbecue) than similar-styled wines from other wine-producing grapes, regions, or countries; nor does that delicious Argentinean slow-roasted beef require that the wine come from the same country or even that it be red. What heresy, you say—a white wine with red meat? Depends on the wine; read on.

The bulk of the baggage we bring to wine and food tends to be psychological. As we remove the pressures of emotions and environment (friends, location, and so on), the rationale for most wine and food pairings comes down to our skill at picking out a given wine's identifiable and measurable characteristics and matching them with what we are eating. These wine characteristics are often referred to as primary tastes.

In talking about wine, we need to distinguish between *flavors,* which are subjective and descriptive associations, and *tastes,* which are objective and quantifiable. Although it's wonderful to be able to identify flavors in wine and food, they are not the main basis for successful pairings. After all, what an avocado tastes like to you may not be exactly what it tastes like to me. For some people the flavor nuances of peach versus nectarine can be very difficult to distinguish, and they are certainly not empirically measurable. We can't rate how *porky* a pork chop is or the intensity of orange flavor in an orange. By contrast, there are four classic tastes—sweet, sour, salty, and bitter—and a fifth, recently identified one, umami.* They are pure and primal and can be measured on a scale from nonexistent to high. On this scale, we can express the sourness of a lime, the sweetness of honey, the bitterness of eggplant, the savor of tomato and mushroom, or the saltiness of a good old American hot dog. The role of these tastes and how they work in creating pairings with food follow shortly.

Ultimately, you have to choose whether the food or the wine will be the star of your pairing: only one of the two can take center stage. A "Swiss," or neutral, route is possible, with neither one dominating, but if your goal is to highlight a special bottle of wine, the accompanying food should play second fiddle. If you want to showcase a recipe you've fallen in love with, select a less assertive wine.

Your perception of a wine's flavor and personality when you taste it on its own will be different from when you drink it with a meal. I was always impressed with the short-lived *Wine and Food Companion* newsletter written in the 1990s by David Rosengarten and Joshua Wesson, the authors of *Red Wine with Fish* (1989), still one of the most innovative works on wine and

---

* Umami is the savory taste of substances such as glutamate and monosodium glutamate (MSG), which are found in foods like bouillon, packaged snacks, soups, sauces, and seasonings. Umami is found naturally in such foods as mushrooms, parmesan cheese, tomatoes, sardines, and fish sauce.

food pairing. When they rated wines, they gave two scores. The first was a numeric score for the intrinsic qualities of the wine, much like those assigned by *Wine Spectator, Wine & Spirits,* and *Wine Advocate,* among other publications. But their second score rated the wine's ability to pair with food, from very good (A) through terrible (F). The findings were always interesting and at times surprising. Many highly rated wines showed gorgeously as soloists but failed when paired with food. Learning how to choose between a 94D and an 85A was an eye-opening experience for many sommeliers.

It's accepted today that some wine and food pairings are based on the attraction of opposites. This is why a glass of crisp Pinot Blanc goes sublimely with a basket of deep-fried clams. A squeeze of lemon cuts through the salty, somewhat oily taste and feel of the bivalves. The wine acts the same way by countering the seasoning and preparation of the clams and refreshing the palate.

For me, however, the most obvious and successful wine and food pairings are grounded in shared rather than contrasting characteristics. An off-dry Chenin Blanc served alongside pork medallions with sautéed apples clearly illustrates this type of pairing: the sweetness of the apples complements the slight sweetness of the wine.

At the root of this thinking is the principle that wines and foods share certain basic tastes. Tastes, as I explained earlier, are not flavors. They are omnipresent in food, with most dishes exhibiting various combinations of them. For example, some recipes are founded on plays of salt and sweet, such as crisply fried Vietnamese spring rolls served with an accompanying dipping sauce of sugar, fish sauce, lemon juice, garlic, and chile. Chinese sweet-and-sour pork is an example of the sweet/sour contrast. The new classic dessert, warm bittersweet chocolate cake with a molten center, is an example of the bitter/sweet encounter. In wine, salt is not an element, but the remaining three classic tastes (sweet, sour, and bitter) are the building blocks that define a wine's profile and help us decide how (and with what) it is best served. This interplay of tastes holds what I call the keys to wine and food matching. As I explained in *Perfect Pairings* and repeat here, there are five keys for wine and three for food.

THE KEYS TO UNDERSTANDING WINE

Key 1. Acidity

Understanding the wine's acidity is the single most important factor in pairing wine with food. There are several ways in which acidity—the sourness or tartness factor—figures in wine.

Acidity is the counterpoint to an array of dishes.
If you are seeking to "cut" a dish that is rich, salty, oily, fatty, or mildly spicy, serving it alongside a tart-tasting wine will be effective and refreshing. Think of what I call the "lemon wedge rule": just as a squeeze of lemon juice will accent or cut a rich or salty dish (tempering the

brininess of seafood, for example), an acidic wine will do the same. Foods served with cream- or butter-based sauces, oily or strong-tasting fish or shellfish, mildly piquant dishes, and virtually all deep-fried foods are prime candidates.

Acidic wines are the best wine choices with tart foods.

Tart dishes, such as a green salad dressed with vinaigrette, and sharp ingredients, such as capers, leeks, and tomatoes, harmonize best with wines of similar sharpness. A wine that is less tart than the dish it is accompanying will be thinned out and may taste quite unpleasant. When serving wine with a sharp dish or ingredients, you would be hard-pressed to find a wine that is too tart! Examples of wines that can be too puckery on their own but sing with food include Assyrtiko, Txakoli, and some Pinot Blancs.

Acidic wines lessen the perception of salt.

Again, whites and sparkling wines, as a rule, are inherently sharper and therefore fare better with salty dishes than most red wines do. For example, the zesty bite of acidity from a glass of young Vermentino is a refreshing foil to a deep-fried Italian *fritto misto* or shrimp tempura.

Acidity brings out the integrity of good, simple ingredients.

I like to think of the acidity in wine as the gastronomic equivalent of the yellow highlighter pen. A quick swoosh of the highlighter makes words stand out on a page. A wine's acidity can do the same with food by bringing out the essence of an ingredient. The summer's first sweet corn or vine-ripened heirloom tomatoes, freshly cracked boiled crab or lobster, and farm-fresh mozzarella cheese all take on another dimension when paired with a sharp, uncomplicated wine to make their vibrant and delicious flavor "pop."

A tart wine that may seem too sharp for sipping on its own may work perfectly in conjunction with food. Sometimes an initially sour, unpleasant bottle can turn into liquid magic at the table.

Counterintuitively, perhaps, low-acid wines are more difficult to match with food. It's best to serve them with milder ingredients that contain a touch of sharpness (such as a squeeze of lime or lemon). A flat Trebbiano or Marsanne may perk up if paired with an otherwise mild fish terrine served with a wedge of lemon and a tangy celery-root rémoulade. With some experimentation and exploration, the role and importance of acidity will become clear to you.

Key 2. Sweetness

Wines can be sweet in varying degrees. Dessert wines aside (I address those case by case), wines can be dry (absent any noticeable sugar), off-dry (a little sweet), or semi-dry (medium sweet). We often find a little sweetness in Prosecco, Chenin Blanc, lighter-style Muscats, and some styles of Torrontés.

Sweetness is a great counterbalance to moderate levels of spicy heat.
Fiery Asian preparations, such as Malaysian curry or the archetypal Chinese hot-and-spicy chicken, need not be paired exclusively with beer! Moderate amounts of sweetness in the wine provide a nice foil for the heat and tame its ferocity, even alleviating the burning sensation caused by the peppers.

Sweetness in the wine can complement a slight sweetness in food.
Offering an off-dry Chenin Blanc with a fillet of grouper and a fresh mango salsa is a good example of this observation. Others include pairing sweet wines with dishes accompanied by chutney or sauces made with fresh or reconstituted dried fruit (such as raisins, apricots, and cherries). The fruit flavors resonate well with most off-dry wines.

Sweetness can be an effective contrast to salt.
From Reese's Peanut Butter Cups to Ben and Jerry's Chocolate Chip Cookie Dough ice cream, Americans love salt and sugar juxtaposed. This is the same rationale behind the long-established matches of sweet French Sauternes with salty Roquefort (and other similar blue cheeses) and port with English Stilton. Most successful with Latin and Asian cuisines, this genre of wine and food pairing nevertheless requires some experimenting, as not all of these marriages are happy ones.

Sweetness can take the edge off foods that are too tart.
This type of contrast requires precise balance, or the food can make the wine come across as sour. Many Asian appetizers with vinaigrettes that are at once tart and sweet pair seamlessly with off-dry wines. Green papaya salad, found in the cuisines of Thailand, Vietnam, and Myanmar, is a classic example.

Dessert-style or extremely sweet wines must be sweeter than the dessert itself.
The wisdom of this rule is evident to anybody who has ever attended a wedding and experienced the unfortunate pairing of expensive dry brut Champagne with cake covered in gloppy white buttercream frosting. Your expensive Dom Pérignon suddenly tastes like lemony seltzer water. At a minimum, the levels of sweetness in the wine and the dessert should match, though it's always safer to have the wine's sweetness exceed that of the dessert. With wedding cake, serving a sweeter bubbly (such as the seemingly misnamed, but actually sweeter, extra-dry or demi-sec styles) would be a much better call, as the sweetness of the wine and the cake are better matched. Fruit-based desserts are more compatible tablemates for dessert wines; avoid thick, sweet buttercreams and ganache with bubblies!

Key 3. Tannin
In wine, tannin can be associated with a bitter taste and a somewhat gritty texture. This is the same astringency (from tannic acid) encountered in black tea that has been steeped too long. If you have ever forgotten to cut an overly strong cup of black tea with milk, cream, or lemon,

you have experienced firsthand the taste and mouthfeel of a high level of tannic acid. Tannins in wine come from two sources: fruit tannins generated from the skins of grapes, especially in big, generous red wines; and wood tannins from the oak barrels in which the wine is aged. Longer maceration of wine with its skins amplifies fruit tannins, whereas extended barrel aging, especially in newer barrels, accentuates the wood tannins.

Some thoughts on pairing wine's tannin with food:

Serve bitter foods with tannic wines.

Foods that have been grilled, charred, or blackened are excellent vehicles for showing off bitter-edged wines. Ingredients that are inherently bitter, like arugula, endive, and sautéed broccoli rabe, are great, too. And there's nothing like a charcoal-grilled steak with a full-bodied, tannic Cabernet Sauvignon.

Counterbalance tannins with fat and protein.

This is the fancy way of saying drink red wine with red meat. Those hard and astringent tannins are tamed by pairing with rare to medium-rare red meat (with ample fat and protein) and many cheeses (also chock-full of both). If the wine is too tannic, however, the tannins can still dominate. Also, certain hard, sharp, or pungent cheeses—such as aged Parmesan or Romano, French goat cheeses, aged Spanish Manchego, aged dry English or Vermont Cheddar, or Dutch Gouda—can give the tannic red wines a metallic character, while many of the soft, "stinky" cheeses bring out an unpleasant ammonia flavor in a big-tannin wine. Finally, if you serve a very tannic wine alongside a dish containing little or no protein (a vegetarian entrée, for example), the tannins can react chemically with the available protein (you'll notice it on your tongue and the inside of your mouth) and may well come across as even more tannic.

Tannins can accentuate the perception of salt.

Tannin is an important consideration when serving a salty dish. Particularly when you're serving a rich red wine, tannin will often accentuate the salt in the food, resulting in a match with as much charm as sucking on a salt lick.

Tannin and fish oil usually aren't happy together.

This lesson requires no subtle training of the palate. Generally, all it takes is one bite of fish (or strong shellfish) alongside a rich, tannic wine to provoke the unpleasant "sucking on a penny" reaction between fish oil and tannin. Red wines with less tannin (Gamay is a prime example) fare far better in this challenging pairing of wine and food.

Key 4. Oak

Although plenty of wines are not aged in wood barrels, many winemakers claim it's nearly impossible to create a fine wine without oak. The vanilla and coconut that you may enjoy in Chardonnay as well as some Roussannes and Marsannes, and the smoke and chocolate identifiable in Cabernet Sauvignon, Touriga Nacional, and expensive Malbec don't come from the grapes: the flavors are often due to the extended time spent in oak.

Oaky flavors are accentuated by food.
Food amplifies the oak in wine, making it stand out as a distinct flavor component. Try any extremely oaky wine with virtually any entrée, and lo and behold, you'll have wine, food, and a lumberyard!

Oaky wines need very specific foods to show them at their best.
This is not to say you can't enjoy oak-aged wines with food; you simply need to choose carefully. In addition to its distinctive flavors, most oak imparts tannins (bitterness) that can easily dominate food and need to be balanced. If you want to show off an oaky wine (a youthful Petite Sirah or Nebbiolo, for example), match the oaky flavors in the wine (toast, char or smoke, caramel, and so on) by using cooking techniques, or ingredients cooked with those techniques, that also impart those flavors: grilling, blackening, smoking, caramelizing, and so on.

Lightly oaked or even unoaked wines are the easiest to pair with food.
Most of the time, I prefer to serve wines that are low in oak, well balanced, or unoaked (that is, made and aged in stainless-steel tanks or in very old wooden barrels that impart little or no flavor). Minimizing oak creates a level playing field, allowing you more flexibility in matching your wine with different foods and methods of preparation. An unoaked Pinot Blanc can work with foods ranging from simply sautéed fillet of sole amandine to lamb vindaloo to chicken cacciatore, whereas an oakier version would pair well only with the sole.

Oak adds smoothness and roundness of texture to wines.
Wines that spend little or no time in oak are often austere in texture, whereas wines aged in oak are more mouth-filling and voluptuous. You can play off this added texture by complementing, for example, a silky Roussanne with a dish accompanied by a cream sauce or compound butter. A smooth oak-aged Grenache can be sublime when served with a slow-cooked beef stew or other slow-braised dishes.

Key 5. Alcohol
A wine's level of alcohol is its primary determinant of body and weight. As a rough guide, the higher the alcohol content, the fuller-bodied the wine seems. As with fat content in dairy products, an increase in alcohol content increases the perception of density and texture. A milder wine (7 to 10 percent alcohol) is significantly less weighty and textured on the palate than one of 14 to 15 percent.

Match wines and foods of equal weight.

This principle is somewhat intuitive. You shouldn't crush a gentle Dolcetto with a stick-to-the-ribs lamb stew. Nor should you match a light, simple fillet of trout with an amply textured Marsanne-Roussanne blend, which might obliterate the fish. Try to keep the mouth-weight profiles of the wine and food on a par. For example, a medium-bodied red wine such as a Barbera or Pinotage is successful served with a medium-weight dish such as roast chicken. A rich wine like a barrel-aged Aglianico pairs well with a full-flavored lasagna. As the wine's alcohol content increases, the food-pairing options decrease, and vice versa.

Alcohol is accentuated by salt and pepper.

An abundance of salt in food will make wines seem "hotter" (more alcoholic) than they actually are. This is extremely important to know, because you want the wine to harmonize with the dish, not come across like a shot of vodka. Similarly, if a very powerful wine is paired with spicy dishes, you may feel as though someone poured gasoline on the fire! High levels of spice and heat (from jalapeño, cayenne, and so on) make wine come across as quite hot also. Drinking any full-bodied wine with Texas five-alarm chili almost always leads to heartburn! In general terms, wines with medium alcohol content (11 to 13 percent) and lighter wines are easier to work with at the table.

• • •

Armed with the five wine keys, we can begin to define profiles for wines that are more food-friendly than others. Sparkling, white, rosé, red, and dessert wines that pair well with food have the profiles described in the table below.

FOOD-FRIENDLY WINES

	SPARKLING	WHITE	ROSÉ	RED	DESSERT
ACIDITY	High	Balanced to high	Moderately high	Moderately high	Moderately high to high
SWEETNESS	Dry to balanced off-dry	Dry to balanced off-dry	Dry to balanced off-dry	Dry (ripe fruit, but no actual sweetness)	Balanced with the acid
TANNIN	None	None	None to very low	Balanced	None
OAK	None	None to balanced	None	Balanced	None to balanced
ALCOHOL	Low to balanced	Low to balanced	Low to balanced	Balanced	Low to balanced

Wines that don't fit these profiles aren't necessarily out of bounds or incompatible with food. They do, however, require more effort to pair, and matching options are more limited. A wine with excessive oak or alcohol mandates more careful matching with a dish, and an overtly tannic red requires more thought than one with balanced tannins.

When I taste any wine, and in all of my teaching, I use a technique called *mapping*. Each wine has its own personality, defined by its unique combination of acid, sugar, oak, tannin, and alcohol. When I taste a wine I ask myself how it maps out according to each of these keys. Once I have described a wine's unique fingerprint, I have a better idea of how it will pair up, and then I can choose dishes that will complement it, either from a restaurant menu or in my own kitchen. But, as with a new language, once you gain a little confidence, you'll be on the way to new and exciting discoveries.

THE KEYS TO UNDERSTANDING FOOD

From the food-pairing perspective, the array of grapes covered in this book is challenging. We are not accustomed to tasting them or reading about them, much less pairing them with food. The grapes and wines that we know better—from Chardonnay to Zinfandel—are, by virtue of their popularity and familiarity, easier to match with food, or at least less intimidating.

Moreover, the foods associated with the cultures of many of these more obscure bottles, either by country or region within country, are also less well-known. American diners are not as familiar with Greek, Argentinean, Austrian, and Chilean cuisines as they are with Spanish, French, and Italian. And even in these better-known countries, there are regions with lesser-known cuisines and grapes—the Basque Country, southwestern France, and southern Italy and its islands (like Sardinia), to name a few. Even so, when we use the mapping techniques described above to profile these unfamiliar wines, we find that almost all of them are food-friendly. As a bonus, although they can be harder to find in a store or restaurant, they generally represent great value.

Because most people decide what they are eating before selecting a wine to drink, it's essential that we understand how various ingredients, flavors, and preparation techniques contribute to the taste of a finished dish. It's also important to accept that the wine's personality is fixed: we can't tinker with its tannin, oak, or alcohol levels. But a cook can fine-tune the food to work better with a particular wine. Salt and seasonings can be adjusted, verjus* or citrus juice can be substituted for less wine-friendly vinegar, and desserts can be made less sweet to pair more harmoniously with a dessert wine. In restaurants, the most wine-savvy chefs and food-savvy sommeliers understand these

---

* Verjus is a very acidic juice made by pressing unripe grapes. It is sometimes used by cooks to replace vinegar.

principles and work together to adjust dishes to make them more wine-friendly. That effort is especially important if the goal is to showcase a wine at a dinner or special function. The best chefs, professional and amateur alike, avoid thinking, "It's all about my food, and the wine be damned."

Recipes are as different as we are: it's impossible and frankly not fun to try to pair up every recipe with a single perfect wine. After all, we all have different palates and react in different ways to matches, so it's dangerous to say there's only one match that works. Knowing some guidelines and understanding how interactions work is critical so that ultimately you make your own calls. As with wines, in thinking about any recipe, the rationale remains the same: identify certain basic characteristics. Rather than get caught up in thinking about a dish in all its complexity, it's far easier to look at three key characteristics of food.

Key 1. Ingredients

Many of us have been trained to think about a dish primarily in terms of its core ingredients. This approach allows you to think about wine pairings formulaically: if you know the ingredients, you know the correct wine selection, right? Red meat with red wine, and white meat and fish with white wine. Well, yes—sort of.

Certainly, when you're pairing wine and food, what's cooking is important, and it's often the main consideration. Of course, the wine you choose to accompany snapper will be radically different from what you'd choose to go with venison. However, within the broad "red" and "white" categories of meat, fish, and poultry, there are many shades of pink. For example, some fish are strongly fishy (sturgeon, mackerel, anchovies, and bluefish), while others are mild (rock cod, halibut, sole, and trout).

Red meat can be strong, like lamb, or mild, like a fillet of beef. White meat (pork and veal) is very different from red meat in personality, often acting more like chicken: fairly neutral in character and much influenced by the supporting cast of other ingredients. Poultry also may vary from mild (chicken) to pungent (squab). Then there are other categories, such as offal (sweetbreads, liver, and so on), vegetables, grains, and legumes. So pairing really is more complicated than choosing a red wine for dinner because you're having meat.

Many ingredients are seasonal and will be more or less flavorful at certain times of the year. These variations can also influence your wine and food pairing, especially with fruits, vegetables, and cheeses (yes, cheeses vary seasonally, affected by such factors as the diet of the animal and the amount of aging), as well as some fish, meat, and poultry. Wild ocean salmon caught during the salmon run tastes far richer and more flavorful than farmed salmon. Fresh-picked spring peas and summer corn are far better than any kind of preserved or trucked-in equivalent. Finally, canned, dried, frozen, and fresh ingredients may all react differently in a dish.

A handful of very useful ingredients can strengthen your wine and food pairings. Often referred to as bridge ingredients or wine links, these allow you to play Merlin in the kitchen. See the box on the facing page for a list of "magic" ingredients and their effects.

MAGIC INGREDIENTS AND THEIR EFFECTS

CHEESE AND OTHER DAIRY INGREDIENTS
- Add texture and richness to a dish when used in cooking.
- Can help in pairing salads and vegetable dishes with higher-acid white wines. Try using a small amount of goat cheese, feta, or Gorgonzola.

CURED MEATS
- Prosciutto, bacon, pancetta, and other charcuterie can tilt "white wine" dishes (fish, poultry, veal, pork) toward pairing with red wines. Prosciutto-wrapped fish or shellfish with bacon, for example, can pair beautifully with soft, bright reds and rosés.

GARLIC AND ONIONS, SLOW-COOKED
- Add creaminess and roundness to a dish. When braised, roasted, or sweated, they add sweetness. When caramelized, they add sweetness and smoky flavors.
- Make red or white wines "pop" with riper fruit and slight sweetness.
- Meld nicely with oak-aged and oak-influenced wines.
- Help foods pair with wines that have more weight and texture.
- Provide a link to earthier wines, such as classically styled European wines (this is true of raw and quickly sautéed garlic and onions as well).

HERBS, FRESH OR DRIED
- Fragrant herbs (chervil, dill, tarragon) pair best with whites like Assyrtiko and Arneis.
- More pungent herbs (basil, thyme, rosemary) go best with Verdejo and many reds (especially Carmenère and Cabernet Franc).

LENTILS, BEANS, AND OTHER LEGUMES
- Can pair beautifully with white wines.
- If prepared with herbs, can swing a dish toward white wine; if prepared with meat (bacon, ham, pancetta, sausage), can swing a dish toward red wine.

- Can provide a clean backdrop for fuller-bodied white wines. Waxy white beans are a good example.
- Can enable fish to pair with red as well as white wines. Try serving fish over a bed of green lentils.

MUSHROOMS
- Most mushrooms add earthiness and an affinity for earthy wines.
- Darker mushrooms (especially reconstituted dried mushrooms) make almost all foods red-wine-friendly.
- Creamy and textured light mushrooms (shiitake, chanterelles, oyster, button) help dishes go well with white wines, especially those with texture (Roussanne, oak-aged Pinot Blanc, and Marsanne).

NUTS
- When toasted, chopped or ground, and added to a dish (as a coating on a piece of fish, for example), nuts pick up on the nutty nuances imparted by oak-barrel-aged wines and show off the wines.
- With the skin on, nuts have an inherent bitterness that softens the perception of bitter tannins in red wines and some strongly oak-aged whites. Try using unskinned walnuts and almonds.
- Powdered and used in cooking (as in moles and other Latin and ethnic dishes), nuts make dishes wine-friendly and can favor lightly oak-aged wines.

OLIVES
- Can swing dishes toward pairing with either red or white wines: green olives create a white-wine affinity (especially with Vermentino, Albariño, and unoaked Verdejo), and black olives create a red-wine affinity (especially with Carmenère, Cinsaut, and Mencía).
- With flavored cures (such as those incorporating peppers and herbs), can increase the compatibility of a dish. Strong cures (especially those very high in acid or vinegar) are best rinsed off.

Key 2. Cooking Methods

Although the selection of ingredients is important, it's only one element of the overall plan. And while it's true that the primary ingredient in the food may determine the wine selection, often it's not the only or the main basis for the choice. The preparation of the ingredients just as frequently plays an important role. Savory marinades can transform the taste of the primary ingredient(s), drawing out new or different flavors, and the cooking method may overshadow everything.

Serving ingredients raw (as with a fish crudo, beef carpaccio, tuna sashimi, or unadorned crudités) provides a singular focus for wine because there is no preparation method to influence flavors. Some cooking techniques, such as steaming, poaching, and boiling, impart minimal flavor: I call these *low-impact*. They simply bring out and intensify the flavor of what's being cooked. Others, like smoking, grilling, and blackening, are dominant, high-impact techniques that can transform the flavors in foods. Smoking can add sweet as well as smoky elements. Grilling will impart a bitter, slightly acrid, taste and an outer crust. Sautéing is fairly neutral: it can add mild sweetness, but the flavors in the resulting dish have more to do with the ingredient profile. Deep-frying adds a hint of sweetness and intriguing texture; and braising, roasting, and baking fall somewhere in the middle.

To taste the differences, take three boned chicken breasts, salt and pepper them all in the same way, and prepare one with a low-impact cooking method, one with a medium-impact method, and one with a high-impact method. Then try each with different wines and note how your preference in wine varies with the cooking method.

Key 3. Sauces and Condiments

A sauce is a trump card: it invariably dictates the wine match. Varied in personality, sauces may be cold, room temperature, or hot. They may be vinaigrettes, salsas, chutneys, or reductions. They may contain herbs, spices, fruit, or any combination thereof. Some contain cream or butter; others may be based on stock, flavored infusions, or wine. Some are smooth in texture; others are chunky and coarse. In any form, sauces want to run the show. Every sauce can be analyzed and broken down into its basic taste components, and from that analysis, you can reach an informed choice about wines that will pair with it.

For example, vinaigrette- and citrus-based sauces share the common element of acid. Rather than try to find a wine that works with all the ingredients, it would be wiser to find one that pairs well with sharpness, for that will be the basic personality of the dish. In chutneys, sweetness may dominate, whereas in a salsa, Thai Sriracha sauce, or a hot pepper sauce, the dominant characteristic, and the one that will govern wine choice, is heat.

Matching a wine with the basic tastes and personality of a sauce is a fairly straightforward principle that can also apply to textures. A butter- or cream-based sauce, with its silky and rich texture, may, like emulsified sauces (such as mayonnaise and aioli), pair best with similarly rich-textured wines such as Roussanne, Torrontés, and Grenache.

To demonstrate these principles, try another chicken-breast experiment. This time, sauté three chicken breasts identically and serve them with three very different sauces: salty (soy-based), sweet (such as a fruit chutney), and spicy (incorporating Tabasco, *harissa,* salsa picante, or another hot sauce). Try them with an array of wines. As you work through the permutations, you'll note the dramatic impact of saucing.

DILEMMAS WHEN DINING OUT

We live in interesting times. Travel, food experimentation, and increasingly daring palates, supported by the year-round availability of fresh ingredients from around the world, can create multicultural challenges for wine and food pairings. As in a World Cup opening round, the cuisines of Asia can go up against South America and Europe, all on one plate! I am often astounded by restaurant menus. Not only can these dining establishments lay on the lavish "menu-speak" descriptions, but the dishes themselves may have four to six accompanying items that have personalities as compelling as that of the central item. I have been surprised and at times disappointed to discover that the entrée I ordered had to take a back seat to a more intensely flavored side dish. Surprises like this can wreak havoc on wine choices, so when you're dining out, it's important to read the menu carefully. When you're planning an elaborate meal at home, remember that side dishes and condiments can, like a sauce, influence the wine selection even more than the main ingredient or its preparation. Wasabi-scented mashed potatoes demand more wine attention than a simply roasted quail!

WINE IN COOKING

Having explored how cooking influences wine pairing, we need to look at the use of wine in cooking. There are three fundamental applications of wine in cooking: cooking with or in wine, marinating foods with wine, and macerating foods in wine.

Cooking with Wine

Like your good olive oil and vinegar, your cooking wines should be stored in a cool, dry place—not next to the stove, where so many cooks seem to leave them. Heat detracts from the wine's flavors and accelerates spoilage; the convenience of having the wine right at hand does little to justify the sacrifice of integrity. Also important is what's in the bottle. Hands off any so-called cooking wine from the local market! Such wines are almost always chock-full of added salt and bring nothing to the party. My cardinal rule is never to cook with a wine you wouldn't be willing to drink.

The two most common applications of wine in cooking are as a flavoring component of a sauce (as in a beurre blanc or beurre rouge) and as a cooking or stewing liquid (as in the classic coq au vin or boeuf bourguignon). In both cases, once the wine is cooked (and the alcohol and most of the water evaporated off), what's left bears little resemblance to what was in the bottle. Thus it's generally not worthwhile to try to tie a dish and a wine together by cooking with the same wine that you intend to serve. Here's the making of a lively dinner party conversation: cook down a cup each of two different wines, say an Albariño and a Grüner Veltliner, to a saucelike consistency. Add a touch of butter to emulsify each, and serve the two sauces to all. Ask your guests to identify which is which, and watch the sparks fly.

Wine's transformation is even more pronounced when a dish is stewed for hours. There's no need to pour a sixty-dollar Barolo into your osso buco when a simple but tasty red table wine will do fine.

But surely, people ask, the pedigree of the wine will be revealed in the cooking? In one single case the answer is definitely yes: when the wine is incorporated into the dish or sauce at the last moment, and therefore not cooked. Many recipes either require or suggest this use for wine, and in this instance alone I recommend using a very fine wine or the wine being served with the meal, as its distinctive flavors will come through in the dish.

A couple of other principles are important when cooking with wine. If you cook with an off-dry wine or a sweet wine, the residual sugar can affect the dish. This sweetness may or may not be desirable. High oak and high tannins can add a perceptible note of bitterness: I generally avoid heavily oaked reds and Château Two-by-Four super-oaky whites for cooking, as I don't enjoy the acrid notes.

Marinating and Macerating

Marinating and macerating both use uncooked wine. With marinades, the foods spend time in the wine and are then removed from the wine and cooked. With macerating, the foods spend time in the wine and are generally served in the maceration liquid in the final presentation. As when cooking with wine, most people grab whatever's open and pour in the required quantity, regardless of quality. And although it is true that added seasonings such as chiles, spices, herbs, garlic, and onions may overshadow the flavors of the wine, the wine's quality will nonetheless influence the final dish.

Marinating is a wonderful technique. It creates great complexity of flavor and gives the impression that you slaved over a dish for hours when in fact you might have put the marinade together in twenty minutes yesterday or the day before. In marinades, it pays to use a better wine, as it adds a more complex flavor to the dish. Again, there's no need to pour in an expensive bottle, but don't use rotgut red!

Usually used for meat but often also for fish or fowl, marinades provide layers of flavor while tenderizing and adding texture. The acids in wine act to break down the toughness of the meat, so the higher the acidity of the wine, the more dramatic and effective the marinade will be.

With macerating, too, the quality of the wine has a dramatic effect on the final dish. Two delicious examples of macerating with wine are fresh peaches macerated in Muscat and dried prunes plumped in port.

While using a bottle of fine Barbaresco is not necessary, a tasty, juicy, and appropriately fruity red will make a difference: a local Spanish Rioja *joven,* a zesty Beaujolais, or a plump Italian Dolcetto makes a welcoming base for those cut-up oranges, lemons, and other flavorings for sangria. Similarly, when you're serving a dessert of fresh summer peaches floating in Moscato d'Asti, a cheap, soapy-tasting bottling will take away from the dish; using a better wine will pay off in spades.

TASTE WHILE YOU WORK

I can't overstate the importance of tasting as you are cooking and, if you are truly looking for pairing perfection, tasting the wine as you go along. The number of people who don't do this is surprising. Everyone has a unique mouth and perception of seasoning, and ingredients vary in their flavor intensity. Just because a recipe tells you to add a quarter teaspoon of salt and a dash of pepper doesn't mean that you can blindly measure out these quantities and assume the dish will be perfectly seasoned. Depending on how well a recipe has been tested, on your own palate, and on the variability of ingredients, you may have to increase or decrease ingredients in a recipe. (That jar of cumin that you bought five years ago may have lost its punch.) Taste, taste, and retaste before using honored guests as guinea pigs. And if you intend to serve a specific wine with a dish, test the pairing in the kitchen and adjust the recipe as needed.

■ ■ ■

These past sections are ample and, pardon the pun, meaty. To make the information in this chapter easier to reference, I've created the following cheat sheet summarizing the key points and adding a few other tips.

QUICK REFERENCE (A CHEAT SHEET)

WHEN THE WINE IS . . .

TART

- Select dishes that are rich, creamy, high in fat, or salty to counterbalance the wine.
- Match the wine with tart food (sharp ingredients, vinaigrettes and other sharp sauces).
- Use the wine to cut the heat in mildly spicy dishes.
- Try skipping the lemon wedge that you might otherwise serve with the dish (with fish, chicken, veal, pork, vegetables, and grains).

SWEET

- If you're serving the wine with dessert, choose a dish that's less sweet than the wine, or else the wine will taste sour.
- If the wine is not too sweet (closer to off-dry), try serving it with foods that are slightly sweet to complement it, or dishes that are mildly hot or spicy as a foil.
- Try playing the wine against dishes that are a little salty; you may find some fun combinations, especially with cheeses and many Asian and Nuevo Latino, North African, Floridian/Caribbean, or Hawaiian-influenced "tropical" preparations.

ALCOHOLIC ("HOT")

- Ensure that the dish being served is ample in personality and weight, or it will be overwhelmed.
- Don't serve spicy-hot food, or you'll be sorry!
- Remember that food can make the wine taste somewhat hotter.
- Avoid excessive salt, which will exaggerate your perception of the wine's heat (alcohol).

TANNIC

- Counterbalance the tannins by serving foods that are high in protein, fat, or both.
- Remember that an entrée relatively low in protein or fat may make the wine come off as even more tannic.
- Remember that tannin and spicy heat can clash brutally.

- Serve foods that are bitter (eggplant, zucchini, chard, endive, broccoli rabe, and so on) or prepare ingredients in a way that accentuates bitterness (blackening, cooking over a wood fire, or grilling) to achieve taste symmetry.
- Use pepper (cracked black or white) to counterbalance tannins, as it's somewhat bitter by nature.

OAKY

- Because really oaky wines will always seem "bigger" with food, accompany them with bold recipes.
- Play up the oak through the choice of ingredients (include nuts or sweet spices) or cooking methods (lightly grilling or smoking).
- Remember that oak aging adds rich texture that can be nice with rich and textured sauces and dishes.

AGED AND RED

- Serve rare preparations of meats to fill in the flavor gaps left by the drying out of the youthful fruit that occurs as the wine develops in the bottle.
- Remember that because tannins soften over time, an aged red gives you a broader range of food options than a young wine does.
- Bear in mind that wines become more delicate as they age; choose simpler preparations to show them off rather than make them compete for attention with complex recipes.

AGED AND WHITE

- Serve the wines with dishes that feature similar flavors (nuts, sherry, and dried fruits) to mirror the flavor profile.
- Compensate for the lost acidity in the mature wine with acidity in the dish: a squeeze of citrus, a spoonful of verjus, or a splash of vinegar.

WHEN THE FOOD IS . . .

TART
- Serve a wine that is equally sharp or even more so, or the wine will taste off and shattered.
- Avoid red wines, except those of a sharper nature (Barbera, Xinomavro, Gamay).
- Don't overlook rosés and sparkling wines as options.

SLIGHTLY SWEET
- Make certain that the wine accompanying the food shares its personality traits: choose a wine that is slightly sweet, such as a Chenin Blanc, Prosecco, or Muscat.
- If you really want a dry wine, serve one that's young and very, very ripe.
- Remember that sometimes a wine with oak can work if the wood's *sweetness* mirrors that of the dish; however, success is not guaranteed.

SALTY
- Pick wines with low to moderate alcohol content, as the wine's heat will be exaggerated by the salt.
- Play with wines that have some sweetness; salt and sweet can enjoy each other's company!
- Avoid wines with high levels of oak or tannin.

SPICY OR HOT
- The spicier the dish, the more difficult it is to pair with wine. Select young wines with low to moderate alcohol content, minimal (or no) oak, and, if possible, some residual sugar (for whites and rosés).
- Among still wines, stick to off-dry whites and rosés; sparkling wines can also be nice foils for heat.
- Note that no wine can stand up to Texas five-alarm chili or those Thai, Indian, and Korean dishes that make your hair stand on end. Opt instead for beer and yogurt-based drinks, along with large bowls of rice to temper the heat.

BITTER
- Select wines with bitter components (oak aging, tannins) to complement the personality of the recipe.
- Try wines with high acidity. This doesn't always work, but it's better than the opposite extreme. After all, tannin is an acid.

DOMINATED BY A STRONG SAUCE OR CONDIMENT
- Forget the main ingredient and instead match the wine to the sauce or condiments and side dishes.

SERVED VERY HOT
- Allow the dish to cool off, or it will ruin your enjoyment of the wine and make the alcohol (by heating it) seem overwhelming.
- Serve chilled wines if it's essential that the dish be served very hot.

HOW TO NAVIGATE THE GRAPES

In selecting the grapes to include in this book, I had an obvious starting point. Space limitations meant that I had to omit many classic wine grapes from *Perfect Pairings,* and this was my chance to discuss them. While they are not universal household names like Cabernet Sauvignon and Chardonnay, noble grapes like Tempranillo, Nebbiolo, and Chenin Blanc are well-known, globally important, and often signature varieties in certain countries or regions. Those selections have been augmented by grapes I consider rising stars, such as Grüner Veltliner and Malbec. I've made up the balance by picking a few long shots, like Mencía and Assyrtiko.

These grapes are not the Publix or Safeway superstars, but some of them are far better known in other parts of the world than they are in the United States. For example, significantly more Grenache is planted around the world than Cabernet Sauvignon, Merlot, and Pinot Noir combined. And the acreage planted to Trebbiano dwarfs that of Chardonnay, Sauvignon Blanc, and Riesling.

Many of the grapes here are not what I'd call classic beauties. To enjoy them, you have to appreciate their unique attributes and quirks, like a meaty or feral aroma that is not readily masked by alcohol or French oak. The grapes in this book have a more enigmatic, international profile. Instead of Julia Roberts or Tom Cruise, think Juliette Binoche, Philip Seymour Hoffman, and Javier Bardem.

The Grapes

I introduce each grape by name—with its correct pronunciation—along with other names by which it may be known. I list the types of wine (such as sparkling, red, rosé, or fortified) produced from the grape, and the styles or interpretations that different winemakers may produce (with or without oak, for example). If a grape is usually blended with other varieties, I list them.

Flavor Lexicon

Although the flavors we detect in wine are subjective, there is an accepted working vocabulary for describing them. Rather than give you every evocative term associated with the grape, I provide a handful of the most common flavor descriptors associated with a particular variety or style. Some classic descriptors may seem odd or even insulting but are nevertheless accurate and common. The "burnt rubber" scent of Pinotage is part of the grape's aromatic profile, just as "lentil" describes a typical aroma in Grüner Veltliner, and "wet wool" can be used to describe Verdejo. These terms are loosely grouped into five categories: fruit and vegetable, flower (or herb); earth (or mineral); wood; and other.

Similar Sips

Just as Amazon.com recommends items on the basis of a buyer's previous purchases, this section answers the question, "If I enjoy wine X, what other wines might I enjoy?"

Where It's Grown

This section lists the countries, states, regions, and appellations where the grape is grown and its wines are produced. These lists aren't exhaustive; they emphasize what is commercially produced and widely available.

Vintner's Choices

Here I list the decisions faced by a winemaker that determine the style, taste, and flavor of the wine. Many of these are formulated as choices between two alternatives, such as the use of oak or no oak, blended or 100 percent pure varietal, or barrel rather than stainless-steel fermentation. Traditional, usually Old World, winemaking favors historical methods (less oak, barrel fermentation), while modern-, or international-, style winemaking, generally preferred in the New World, tends to rely on techniques such as the use of new oak barrels and micro-oxygenation that result in cleaner, more fruit-forward and consumer-friendly wines. As *Daring Pairings* is not an encyclopedic wine reference book but is focused on matching food with wine, I don't go into detail about key aspects of wine production. For that information you may want to consult comprehensive wine books such as Tom Stevenson's *Sotheby's Wine Encyclopedia* or Jancis Robinson's *Oxford Companion to Wine*, which offer excellent discussions of grape cultivation and the winemaking process.

Pairing with Food

This section discusses pairing the wine with dishes you're likely to make at home or encounter in a restaurant. Remember, these are just guidelines, not ironclad rules: each of us has an individual threshold for saltiness, bitterness, heat or spice, sweetness, and tartness, and each of us will have a different perception of the interactions of wine and food.

Pairing Pointers

This section lists do's and don'ts for pairing this wine with specific foods and flavors.

The Cheese Plate

I included this section as much for me as for you. Enjoying cheese with wine has come a long way from the orange and white cubes on colored toothpicks still too commonly served at cocktail parties. Today, amazing artisanal cheeses, both imported and domestically produced, are available from specialty cheese and gourmet stores, online cheese merchants, and good supermarkets.

Because cheeses are as varied as wines—they come from several different animals and in a dizzying range of textures, colors, shapes, and tastes—my recommendations are based on seven categories of cheese defined by my friend Laura Werlin, a noted cheese expert and author.

FRESH	Unripened and unaged cheeses like ricotta, mozzarella, and feta.
SEMI-SOFT	Cheeses that give a bit when you squeeze them, like teleme and Havarti.
SOFT-RIPENED	Cheeses that soften (as opposed to hardening) as they ripen, with a higher salt content and edible fuzzy rind. Brie and Camembert fit into this category.
SEMI-HARD	The largest and most wine-friendly category of cheese. They have balanced salt and fat and are very flexible. These cheeses range from basic Cheddar to Gouda, with interpretations that go from buttery to nutty. Those with a washed, inedible rind (including raclette, Emmentaler, and Comté) can be pungent, salty, and firm in texture and are good for shaving.
HARD	Often sharp, salty, and quite firm. Parmesan, aged Cheddar, and dry Jack are examples.
BLUE	Immediately identifiable by their flecks of blue or green mold, these cheeses are salty and strongly flavored. They range from the mildly sweet Gorgonzola dolcelatte to the intense, almost briny Roquefort.
WASHED-RIND	This is the "stinky socks" category in which the rind is washed with brine, wine, or brandy. In fact, these cheeses often smell much stronger than they taste. The rind is edible but strong and off-putting to most people. Taleggio, real Alsatian Munster, and Époisses typify this category.

As with other foods, cheese influences the flavor of the wine more than vice versa. Unless you understand this effect, you may be disappointed when drinking a fine wine with cheese. I recommend categories of cheese that pair best with each grape and wine style and suggest an example or two in each category. Because some styles of cheese are produced in various countries but can taste very different depending on their origin, I recommend examples from specific countries: for example, I may recommend Italian Parmesan rather than U.S. or Argentinean interpretations, and Bulgarian or Greek feta cheese rather than Danish.

The Chef and the Recipe

The most interesting part of writing this book has been pairing each wine with a recipe from a skilled chef. My criteria for selecting chefs were simple: that I know and respect their food, that they know and respect wine, and that they have an innate understanding of pairing wine with food. I began with a list of more than 150 chefs and narrowed it down to 36. For more information on the background of each chef, consult the biographical sketches at the back of the book.

With the recipes, I've tried to strike a balance among appetizers and main dishes; meat, fish, and vegetarian selections; and, of course, desserts. For each grape variety, I decided which course it should accompany, and then paired it with a recipe from a chef whose culinary approach or cultural background complemented the grape. As you can imagine, no single recipe works equally well with all styles of a wine. I picked a representative style for each wine and asked the chef to cater to that style.

I asked the chefs to explain why they created these particular recipes and why they pair well with the assigned wines. I've also added my own comments, pairing tips, and serving recommendations.

Recommended Producers

Following each recipe, I list reliable producers whose wines are consistently made in styles appropriate to the grape. I avoid specifying a particular vintage, vineyard, or bottling because the availability of many wines varies in different areas and from year to year. Instead of listing specific prices, which also vary, I place the selections into three general price ranges:

EVERYDAY $5–15

PREMIUM $16–39

SPLURGE $40 and up

For most varieties, I've tried to give about a dozen recommendations, including some in each price category. In some cases, however, no producers make wines in a certain price category, or I can't recommend any of the available wines: for example, I list no "splurge" Trebbianos.

As always, I have tried to select producers whose wines are reasonably widely available. There is nothing more frustrating than falling in love with a wine and then discovering you can't find it anywhere.

With this road map, you're ready to journey among the grapes!

ALBARIÑO

ARNEIS

ASSYRTIKO

CHENIN BLANC

GARGANEGA

GRÜNER VELTLINER

MARSANNE

MUSCAT

PINOT BLANC

PROSECCO

ROUSSANNE

SÉMILLON

TORRONTÉS

TREBBIANO

TXAKOLI

VERDEJO

VERMENTINO

white

albariño

ahl-bah-*ree*-nyoh

I first tasted a Spanish Albariño in the mid-1980s, when I was running the wine program at Square One, my mom's seminal Mediterranean restaurant in San Francisco. The grape was relatively unknown at the time. I was captivated by its steely acid and sharply defined fruit, perfect for so much of the restaurant's food. A trip to Galicia a few years later expanded my horizons even more, and I've been a walking sandwich board for the grape ever since, preaching its virtues and those of its wine to all who will listen.

Albariño also contributes to the best Vinho Verde in northern Portugal, just across the Spanish border, where it's called Alvarinho.

Alternative Names Alvarinho (Portugal)

Styles Medium-bodied dry white, medium-bodied *pétillant* dry white

Sometimes Blended With Caiño, Godello, Loureiro, Torrontés, Treixadura (Spain); Loureiro, Pederna/Arinto, Trajadura (Portugal)

Flavor Lexicon *Fruit/vegetable:* Apricot, citrus (lemon, tangerine), citrus blossom, fresh grass, nectarine, peach, pear ▪ *Earth:* Mineral ▪ *Other:* Wet wool

Similar Sips Pinot Grigio, dry Riesling, dry Chenin Blanc, lean styles of Viognier

Where It's Grown Australia (Victoria), Portugal (Rios do Minho, Vinho Verde), Spain (Galicia: Rías Baixas), U.S.A. (California, Oregon)

Rumors claim that Albariño is related to Riesling, but so far these are unproven. The name hints at these origins: *alba,* meaning land, and *riño* for the Rhine (in Germany). The spiritual home of this grape, however, is Galicia, especially the appellation of Rías Baixas. This part of Spain looks green and English rather than terra-cotta colored and Spanish, and its proximity to the Miño River in the south and the ocean to the west keeps it cool. There are five subregions, which can be confusing; the best wines come from the Val do Salnés and Condado do Tea. If you find a bottle that says *Albariño,* it's just that—100 percent Rías Baixas Albariño.

Some bottles labeled with the appellation or subappellation, for example Rías Baixas–Sotomayor, may be blends with other grapes, including the aromatic Treixadura or Loureiro grapes, and are markedly more like Gewürztraminer or Viognier in personality.

Though most wine lovers consider Albariño to be uniquely Spanish, the Portuguese have an equal claim to the grape, which is the historic heart and soul of the often-spritzy Vinho Verde, or "green wine," from the Minho region, specifically around the Lima Valley and its best subregion, Monção. These wines are almost always blends: the best wines have ample percentages of Alvarinho. Far more often, however, Alvarinho is an equal player in blends, along with Loureiro, today's hot new grape; Trajadura (Treixadura); and other grapes. Portuguese Vinho Verde lacks the soft richness of texture of the Albariño-based wines coming from Galicia and is noteworthy for its sharpness and a prickle of carbon dioxide on the tongue that stimulates the appetite.

Though a relative newcomer to the United States, the grape seems to perform well when planted in the right spots, which include a number of areas in California—Carneros in the Napa Valley, Clarksburg in Lodi, the northern Central Coast, Santa Barbara, and cooler vineyard sites in southern Oregon. Here the wines more closely resemble their counterparts in Spain, but they often have riper fruit and a slightly fuller body. This variety has enormous unexplored potential in Australia and should be given opportunities in cooler regions such as the Mornington Peninsula, King Valley, and the northern slopes of the Macedon Ranges region (though much of what was thought to be Albariño in Australia has recently been discovered to be Savagnin, a French grape). It would probably also do well in the regions of New Zealand where Riesling is successful.

Vintner's Choices Aged vs. not aged, oak vs. no oak, prefermentation cold soak vs. traditional crush and ferment, single variety vs. blended

Albariño is happy both as a pure, unblended wine (similar to a quality Riesling, Viognier, or Gewürztraminer) or blended with its traditional stablemates. Both interpretations are quite successful; it's really a question of what you prefer. If you are looking for more texture, softer acidity, and a velvety mouthfeel, opt for the blends. Treixadura adds a lychee- or rambutan-like flavor and round body, while Loureiro adds floral notes and a distinct herbal character (*louro* means "laurel") that can tame the leaner and naturally racy Albariño. In Portugal, Vinho Verde blends are increasingly dominated by Loureiro, with Alvarinho as the primary blender, used for its acidity. The blends are all bright, spritzy, and similar to one another. Most examples from the United States and Australia are unblended.

One of the keys to success with this grape is bringing out its delicate flavor. For this reason, fermentations are long and cool (as for Riesling). Some producers let the fruit macerate for several hours on its skins at a very low temperature, inhibiting the yeast's ability to start metabolizing the grape sugar and begin fermentation. This type of cold soak, known as *macéra-*

tion pelliculaire, is intended to extract as much flavor as possible. Others avoid this process because they believe it simply pulls bitter tannins and phenols from the skins.

This is a grape that is easily masked by oak; even older wood is distracting. Though there are successful examples of wood-aged Albariño, they are the exceptions, and most oaked examples simply taste like nice white wine that's been aged in some wood.

Age (or rather youth) is important. In Spain and Portugal, I've tasted many bottlings that have been cellared for a few years, and I've yet to find one that charmed me as much as a fresh current vintage. Albariño is most appealing in its youth—crisp, sharp, and, at its best, penetrating with firm, citrusy acid. This is even more true of the Portuguese examples, which lose their vibrancy within a year or so after release. The bottom line: the fresher the wine, the better.

PAIRING WITH FOOD

If ever there was a perfect connection between the wines and foods of a region, it's on the northeast Iberian coast. The bulk of Spain's seafood (more than two-thirds of the country's catch, it is said) comes from this area. The bounty of the sea is phenomenal, from local crab and octopus to scallops and the local specialty, *percebes,* a type of long barnacle. Whether served with seafood tapas, the local octopus with *pimentón* (Spanish paprika), or straightforward preparations of fish, Albariño is effective in bringing out the flavors and natural sweetness of the seafood while also enhancing them with the grape's lemony acidity. If it swims or clings to a rock, it will be happy with Albariño.

Naturally lemony herbs are great matches with Albariño, from lemon verbena to lemongrass, from lemon mint to Southeast Asian galangal. Also great are starch-based dishes, from paellas to pasta with clams, and northern Asian food, from sushi to stir-fried lemon chicken.

As with Riesling from Germany, Alsace, and Austria, Albariño's deceptively delicate nature belies its ability to pair with rich foods. In both Spain and Portugal, rich stews are common (*caldo gallego* being the classic partner), and this wine cuts through the richness and refreshes the palate amazingly well. Casseroles and rich braises of chicken, sausage, and pork are great with Albariño, especially when studded with garlic and olives and served with cooked greens and potatoes. Of course, this wine is magic with dry chorizo. Salty dishes, too, are cut wonderfully by the grape's natural sharpness and spritz. Just as a sparkling wine refreshes the palate when served with phyllo or puff pastry and deep-fried dishes, prickly Vinho Verde will brighten up a Greek tiropita, a South American empanada, or a local croquette of salt cod (*bacalhau*).

PAIRING POINTERS

Albariño goes well with:
- Most cooked seafood, both fish and shellfish. The grape's citrusy nature, lighter alcohol, and firm acidity make it a natural partner for crab, clams, fish, scallops, and shrimp.

- Raw protein. I love this wine with fish crudo, ceviche, sushi, and carpaccios of tuna, salmon, and even beef, drizzled with olive oil, lemon and a little pepper.
- North Asian fare. It's not that you can't enjoy Albariño with Malaysian, Singaporean, or Vietnamese food, it's just that the pure, clean nature of Japanese, Korean, and northern Chinese dishes is perfect for the wine. For everything from simple Korean tofu to Japanese tempura to milder versions of kung pao chicken, this wine's a great accompaniment.
- Rich white-meat and poultry dishes. Full-flavored and textured stews and braises of pork, chicken, and veal are successful with Albariño, as are Virginia country ham and duck with ginger.
- Deep-fried and richly textured dishes. Albariño's zip cleans and refreshes, so it pairs well with everything from fried oysters to an Italian *fritto* of shrimp and calamari.

Albariño isn't good with:
- Many vegetables. Although I love it with most fish, white meat, and many cheeses, I have found that it's often just okay paired with cruciferous vegetables and root vegetables (parsnips, turnips, rutabagas). It fares less well with greens, such as kale, chard, and spinach, unless you really take the emphasis off the vegetable by preparing and accompanying it with lots of lemon or other acidic flavor.
- Most red meat. Albariño, like most bright wines, can be reasonably successful with a steak drizzled with lemon juice (as is often done in Tuscany), but unless the recipe is designed with a white wine in mind, it's best to avoid this pairing.
- Very spicy dishes. While the wine refreshes, its flavors are often lost behind boldly flavored chiles, spicy sauces, and too much cayenne or Tabasco.
- Boldly flavored dishes. Serving Albariño with a full-flavored Indian curry, Mexican chicken mole, or New Orleans barbecue shrimp simply overwhelms the wine.
- Overtly sweet recipes. The wine tastes dry and puckery when served with foie gras, caramelized or candied fruit, or with puréed fruit sauce (prunes, plums, cherries, black currants, or figs). The same is true when it's paired with butternut squash risotto or duck à l'orange.

THE CHEESE PLATE

FRESH	Chèvre (many countries), mozzarella (Italy, U.S.A.), ricotta (Italy)
SEMI-SOFT	Slightly aged chèvre (many countries), tetilla (Spain)
SOFT-RIPENED	Brie (France), Éxplorateur (France)
SEMI-HARD	Manchego (Spain), queijo de Évora (Portugal)

albariño | STEAMED MANILA CLAMS WITH UDON

LARRY TSE   The House, San Francisco, California

Makes 4 to 6 main-course servings

BROTH
2¹⁄₂ quarts water
1 (4- to 6-inch) square *kombu* (dried kelp)
1 tablespoon instant *hon dashi* (soup stock) granules
3 tablespoons light soy sauce
1 leek, white part only, coarsely chopped
2 cups firmly packed *katsuobushi* (dried bonito flakes)
Salt

4 cups water
3 pounds Manila clams, scrubbed
³⁄₄ pound dried udon noodles
2 (3¹⁄₂-ounce) packages enoki mushrooms,
**   roots trimmed and separated into small bunches**
1 bunch fresh chives, cut into 1-inch pieces
2 sheets toasted nori, cut into 1-by-¹⁄₄-inch strips

To make the broth, in a saucepan, bring the water to just below a boil. Remove from the heat. Lightly wipe the *kombu* with a clean cloth (you don't need to wipe away the white film), and add to the hot water along with the *hon dashi* granules and soy sauce. Let stand for 30 minutes to rehydrate the *kombu*. Return the pan to medium-high heat, add the leek, and bring to a boil. Reduce the heat to low and simmer gently for 15 minutes. Remove from the heat, add the *katsuobushi*, and let steep for 15 minutes. Strain the broth through a fine-mesh sieve into a clean pan. Taste and adjust with salt (it may not need any).

To cook the clams, pour the water into a large, wide pan and bring to a boil over high heat. Add the clams, cover, and steam, shaking the pan occasionally, just until the clams open, about 3 minutes. Remove from the heat. Using a wire skimmer, transfer the clams to a bowl, discarding any that failed to open. Discard the cooking water. Remove the clam meats from their shells and discard the shells. Set the meats aside.

Cook the udon noodles according to the package directions, drain, and reserve.

To serve, bring the broth to a boil, remove from the heat, and add the clams and mushrooms. Divide the noodles evenly among individual serving bowls. Ladle the broth, clams, and mushrooms over the noodles. Garnish with the chives and nori and serve at once.

NOTE Look for *kombu*, instant *hon dashi, katsuobushi,* dried udon, enoki mushrooms, and nori in Japanese or other Asian markets.

LARRY: *I wanted to showcase the sweet, delicate flavor of steamed Manila clams in a simple yet unique preparation. The broth has savory marine flavors from the* kombu *and toasted smokiness from the bonito. The earthy enoki, aromatic chives, and toasted nori add interesting textural components and flavors. The broth is subtle, yet with a hint of richness. I wanted to bring these delicate flavors and textures into harmony to create a "daring pairing" for the crisp, aromatic, and silky Albariño.*

EVAN: *Clean and pure Asian and Asian-inspired food is one of the best ways to show off the equally pure Albariño. The clams are, of course, a natural pairing, but there are daring and edgy aspects to this dish, like the shaved-bonito broth and the seaweed.*

    Some readers may find this match too daring, but I think most will agree that it's a success. The clams are a focal point here and pair seamlessly with the wine. The texture of the udon gives the wine something to cling to while being fairly neutral in flavor. The enoki adds a subtle flavor and a little texture. The leek brings out the underlying minerality of the wine, which is echoed by the seaweed and bonito. These flavors combine with the dashi and light soy to add a salinity that cries out for the wine's inherent acidity as a foil. Even bottles I tried that seemed a bit flat or lacking were revived by pairing with this recipe.

RECOMMENDED PRODUCERS

EVERYDAY	PREMIUM
Adegas Gran Vinum Rías Baixas, Spain	Abacela Umpqua Valley, Oregon
Agnusdei Rías Baixas, Spain	Lusco Rías Baixas, Spain
Casa de Vila Verde Vinho Verde, Portugal	Nora Rías Baixas, Spain
Condes de Albarei Rías Baixas, Spain	Pazo de Señorans Rías Baixas, Spain
Martín Códax Rías Baixas, Spain	Quinta do Ameal Vinho Verde, Portugal
Quinta da Aveleda Vinho Verde, Portugal	Tangent Edna Valley, California

arneis

ahr-nayz

This dry, zippy Italian white is crafted specifically from the Arneis di Roeri grape, which has been grown for centuries in the Piedmont region of Italy. The contemporary interest in modern, nonnative varietals has meant that Chardonnay and other international grapes have begun to supplant local Piedmontese grapes like Arneis (and Erbaluce), but fortunately several committed producers are ensuring that we will have this great grape and its unique wines for years to come. For me, **Arneis is one** of the white wines that really hits its mark, so let's help them spread the word!

Alternative Names Barolo Bianco (Italy)

Styles Medium-bodied dry white

Sometimes Blended With Other local grapes (only occasionally and for locally distributed wines)

Flavor Lexicon *Fruit/vegetable:* Green melon, lemon, lime, pear, raw almond ▪ *Floral:* Anise, flower blossom, fresh herbs ▪ *Earth:* Chalk, mineral ▪ *Other:* Light honey

Similar Sips Pinot Grigio, Sauvignon Blanc without the grassy elements, and Pinot Blanc from Alsace or Italy

Where It's Grown Australia (Victoria), Italy (Piedmont), U.S.A. (California, Oregon)

The Arneis grape is closely associated with its native home of Roero, in Italy's northeast Piedmont region. Here, where it's called Arneis di Roeri, the grape truly shines. An increasing quantity of it is being planted, but it's still dwarfed by the seas of Moscato from nearby Asti and the augmented planting of other grapes. Almost extinct in the mid-1970s, it has found new life as more consumers have discovered its charms: it's a clean, perfumed white wine, void of any pretension. Its unique combination of spring flowers, aromatic herbs, and a distinct minerality can be charming.

Although in Italy Arneis is grown only in Piedmont, the growing global interest in aromatic whites has encouraged winemakers in other countries to experiment with it. A small but increasing number of winemakers in California are vinifying the grape with ripe quince-like fruit and varying levels of acidity, creating a range of wines from good to flabby and occasionally almost off-dry. In Oregon, despite the grape's potential, only one winery, Ponzi Vineyards, seems to be daring enough to bottle it. In Australia, things are more hopeful: more than thirty wineries are planting Arneis, although it's premature to say that it's found a home in any specific area. There seem to be more plantings in Victoria's Mornington Peninsula and King Valley than in other areas.

Vintner's Choices Aged vs. not aged, early vs. late harvesting, oak vs. no oak, sandy vs. clay soil, vineyards at low altitudes vs. high altitudes

Arneis means "difficult" or "stubborn" in Piedmontese dialect, and any winemaker who has worked with this grape probably thinks the name is apropos. For a white grape, it's a relatively late bloomer (ripening at the end of September), and, to add insult to injury, those who are patient are rewarded with consistently low yields. Picking at just the right time to maximize both ripeness and acidity is key because of the grape's naturally low acidity. It is claimed that vineyard location and soil type are critical to maintaining the acidity (and thus the verve of the wine).The best locations tend to be in clay soils, which seem to preserve the acidity, while sandy soils bring out more of the floral aromatics. In practice, most producers are working myriad soil types. Higher-altitude vineyards are also said to be superior.

Although a handful of producers use oak, most believe (as I do) that avoiding oak better maintains the character of the fruit and doesn't push too hard on the wine's structure. Some of the barrel-aged wines I have tasted were oaky and flaccid. The wine's naturally low acidity means that it's best drunk as young and fresh as possible, and not cellared away for your kid's twenty-first birthday.

PAIRING WITH FOOD

The greatest challenge in pairing Arneis with food is coping with its often-underwhelming acidity. The best wines are refreshing and reasonably zippy, but many are barely balanced or lacking. Low-impact cooking methods are best. A pasta tossed with simply blanched peas and a little olive oil and lemon zest or a fillet of fish poached in a court bouillon would be an excellent accompaniment to Arneis. The relatively low alcohol enables Arneis to pair with piquant and often-problematic dishes like Chinese salt-and-pepper shrimp or spaghetti puttanesca, with its olives, anchovies, hot pepper flakes, and tomato. Most fish are a good match—from the simplest of pan-roasted black cod to a good old plate of lightly battered fish and chips, and treatments involving green herbs (such as salsa verde) or a simple wedge of lemon or lime are especially successful. Basic shellfish is also quite happy with Arneis, as are lighter types of poultry, such as Cornish game hen or quail or a simple breast of chicken.

The cuisines of the eastern Mediterranean seem to pair well with Arneis, including Lebanese, Israeli, Turkish, and Greek. Tabbouleh, dolmas, and falafel are all nice options. This variety seems to match up well with many vegetables, though it is less happy with the always-problematic artichokes, asparagus, and Brussels sprouts. Finally, it's not a stretch to have milder charcuterie with Arneis, especially when served with fruit that's not overly sweet (prosciutto with watermelon or Crenshaw melon, as opposed to the traditional sweet, ripe cantaloupe, would be a tasty example).

PAIRING POINTERS

Arneis goes well with:

- A range of starter dishes. It's a wonderful wine to pair with the assortment of flavors and textures in an *antipasto misto,* tapas, and especially Middle Eastern mezes.
- Composed salads. Keep the dressing low in acid (opt for cream- or citrus-based dressings) and have at it. Scallops and grapefruit on mixed greens, almost anything with avocado, and a refreshing couscous salad with lightly grilled vegetables are nice pairings with this wine.
- Almost anything that swims. From fillet of sole to swordfish, most fish, especially milder types, go well with Arneis. Stick to low- to medium impact methods of preparation so as not to overwhelm the wine.
- Dishes with mild, fresh herbs. Rosemary and thyme are too assertive, but sweeter herbs like sweet basil, chervil, and Italian parsley show well with Arneis.
- Mustard, believe it or not. A simple roast chicken with a dab of Dijon mustard, a scaloppine of veal with a light mustard sauce, or a mustard-and-breadcrumb crust on a loin of pork are three treatments that will show the wine well.

Arneis isn't good with:

- Tart dressings and green salads. While fresh and generally bright, most Arneis can't handle acidic vinaigrettes and sharp sauces.
- Heavily smoked or grilled foods. A rich tea-smoked duck or intensely flavored smoked salmon or trout will overpower most Arneis. So will items that have been grilled over powerfully flavored mesquite or other charcoal.
- Very rich dishes.
- Strong spices. Arneis gets lost behind chiles, many Asian spices (five spice, star anise, or garam masala), powdered ginger, and clove, to name a few. If you must include these spices, use a very light hand.
- Very briny shellfish. The wine simply doesn't have the oomph to handle salty oysters, strong clams, or intense *goût de mer* mussels, which make the wine taste off.

THE CHEESE PLATE

FRESH	Burrata (Italy, U.S.A.), chèvre (many countries),
SEMI-SOFT	Slightly aged chèvre (many countries), Havarti (Denmark), stracchino (Italy)
SOFT-RIPENED	Chaource (France), pavé d'affinois (France)
SEMI-HARD	Mild Cheddar (U.S.A., U.K.), Fontina (Italy)
HARD	Ricotta salata (Italy)

arneis | GRILLED SNAPPER WITH ROOT VEGETABLE SALAD

LACHLAN M. PATTERSON   Frasca Food and Wine, Boulder, Colorado

Makes 6 to 8 main-course servings

¾ **cup olive oil**
3 pounds skinless red snapper fillets
Sea salt and freshly cracked black pepper
3 turnips
1 small celery root
3 beets
2 parsnips
1 small head radicchio
1 head flowering kale or small bunch regular kale
2 tablespoons minced shallots
2 tablespoons minced fresh chives
Juice of 4 large lemons (about 1 cup)

Prepare a charcoal or gas grill for direct grilling over a medium fire. Using ¼ cup of the olive oil, rub the fillets on both sides, then season on both sides with salt and pepper. Set aside.

Peel the turnips, celery root, beets, and parsnips. Using a mandoline or a sharp knife, slice the turnips as thinly as possible. Working in batches, stack the slices. Using the sharp knife, shave the stack vertically as finely as possible, or cut into thin julienne. Repeat with the celery root, beets, and parsnips. Alternatively, shred the peeled vegetables in a food processor or on the large holes of a box grater-shredder. Trim the stems from the radicchio and kale and shave or shred the leaves as finely as possible. Place all of the vegetables in a large bowl and add the shallots and chives. Drizzle with the remaining ½ cup olive oil and ¾ cup of the lemon juice and toss well. Season with salt and pepper and toss again. Set aside.

Oil the grill rack. Arrange the fish fillets on the rack and grill, turning once, until nicely marked with grill marks and just opaque in the center when tested with a knife tip, about 3 minutes on each side.

Transfer the fish to warmed plates, and finish each serving with a drizzle of the remaining lemon juice. Serve at once with the salad.

LACHLAN: *Piedmont has a rich tradition of food and wine. Although it's known mostly as a red-wine region with earthy and rich food to match, Mother Nature rounded out its blessings by throwing in a couple of terrific white wines. Arneis, which can be vinified either crisp or rich in style, helps diversify food and wine pairings in Piedmont, and it's complemented by the great local produce of summer and the sensational seafood from the nearby Ligurian coast.*

EVAN: *Northern Italian white wine and Lachlan's food are a match made in heaven. Lachlan's skill at food and wine pairing has been enhanced by his partnership with Bobby Stuckey, a fellow Master Sommelier and a food and wine expert in his own right.*

This is a fun match. The upscale vegetable slaw is refreshing and echoes the freshness in the wine. If you think raw beets are not your thing, this dish may change your mind, and the way the color bleeds into the slaw and blends with the green color of the kale is intriguing. And that's just the slaw! This wine really sings when accompanied with a nice piece of mild white fish.

RECOMMENDED PRODUCERS

PREMIUM

Cascina Bongiovanni Piedmont, Italy	Fontanafredda Piedmont, Italy	Pertinace Piedmont, Italy
Cascina Chicco Piedmont, Italy	Giacomo Ascheri Piedmont, Italy	Ponzi Willamette Valley, Oregon
Ceretto Piedmont, Italy	Marco Porello Piedmont, Italy	Seghesio Sonoma County, California
Damilano Piedmont, Italy	Palmina Southern Central Coast, California	Vietti Piedmont, Italy

assyrtiko

a-seer-tee-ko | ah-*syr*-tih-koh

When we think of Greek white wine, retsina—Greece's inimitable gift to the wine world—typically comes to mind. Known less for its complexity than for its distinctive resiny or anise-like notes, this Greek wine pairs well with fresh fish or octopus in a seaside Greek taverna but generally doesn't add much distinction to the modern international table. Given the rising importance of Greek table wines, I asked a few importers of these wines and fellow sommeliers which Greek white wine excited them most, and they confirmed my belief: Assyrtiko is the most significant white grape cultivated in Greece today, producing wines that are serious and food-friendly.

Alternative Names None

Styles Medium-bodied dry white, medium-full-bodied dessert

Sometimes Blended With Sauvignon Blanc and Chardonnay, as well as indigenous varieties such as Aidani, Athiri, and Savatiano (Greece)

Flavor Lexicon

DRY   *Fruit:* Citrus (lemon, pomelo, kumquat), green apple, green pear, unripe peach, yellow apple ▪ *Earth:* Mineral ▪ *Wood:* Light spice, light smoke

SWEET   *Fruit:* Apricot, candied citrus, marmalade ▪ *Wood:* Cashew, macadamia nut, vanilla ▪ *Other:* Honey, sweet cream

Similar Sips Dry Riesling (especially from Alsace and Australia's Clare Valley), French Muscadet, Austrian Grüner Veltliner

Where It's Grown Greece (Cyclades: Santorini; Peloponnese: Nemea)

This unique grape is native to and grown exclusively in Greece. Although new wines from non-native white grapes (such as Sauvignon Blanc and Chardonnay) have the locals and many wine aficionados excited, this indigenous grape is considered by most to be the source of Greece's finest and most complex white wine. Other grapes, such as Moschifilero and Malagousia, may be flashier and more accessible with their lifted, floral aromatic notes, but Assyrtiko makes the most impressive wines.

Most Assyrtiko is planted on the slopes of the island of Santorini, where it thrives in the steep, stony volcanic soil. At its best, it produces wines that are bright, refreshingly tart, and laced with mineral, zesty lemon, and yellow grapefruit notes. Assyrtiko is difficult to grow at low altitudes because of desiccating summer winds. Santorini growers have met the challenge by wrapping the vines around small baskets placed in hollows in the soil, protecting them from wind. Assyrtiko can also be found farther north, outside Athens, where it is often blended with other grapes to make retsina. While it's not the main grape in retsina, its structure and acidity help carry the wine's resiny personality. In Drama, Kavala, and the Peloponnese in southern Greece, Assyrtiko is commonly blended with international grapes (especially Sauvignon Blanc).

While Assyrtiko is not commercially produced outside Greece, its affinity for food, coupled with the increasing appetite abroad for crisp, refreshing wines like Sauvignon Blanc, Albariño, and dry Riesling, suggest that it's just a matter of time before we start seeing this enjoyable variety made in other countries.

Vintner's Choices Dry vs. sweet, oak vs. no oak, single variety vs. blended, traditional vs. modern approach

Assyrtiko, like Riesling, shows its delicacy best when it is left alone, unblended and unoaked. There are three distinct interpretations of the grape. The most abundant and food-friendly is the lean-and-mean style, with sharp acidity, a tart and citrusy personality, and a signature mineral flavor. Ironically, this style is the most difficult to find outside Greece. The wines most commonly exported are tailored for what producers believe the international market wants: thicker, textured examples with less bracing acid, riper fruit character, and fuller body (higher alcohol). Finally there's a barrel-fermented or barrel-aged style that is age-worthy and complex and can maintain a distinctive Assyrtiko personality if the oak is not too intrusive. While rarer and clearly targeted toward drinkers of Chardonnay and other big white wines, these mature wines nevertheless offer interest at the table.

Not all Assyrtiko is destined for monovarietal bottlings: it can be successfully blended, and Assyrtiko-Chardonnay and Assyrtiko–Sauvignon Blanc blends are becoming more common. Local blends made with Savatiano, Greece's most widely planted white grape, as well as with other Greek grapes, such as Athiri and Aïdani, are becoming available. Assyrtiko also lends acidity to the much softer Savatiano in retsina.

Finally there's a wonderful barrel-aged dessert wine called Vinsanto (not to be confused with Vin Santo, the Tuscan specialty of the same name) which must be at least 51 percent Assyrtiko. The balance is generally a combination of the aromatic Athiri and Aïdani grapes, though other local white grapes can be included. The flavor of this wine is akin to tawny port crossed with a late harvest Riesling, with a hint of cream sherry.

PAIRING WITH FOOD

Assyrtiko is a wonderfully food-friendly grape, and its three styles can be enjoyed with several different types of food.

The lean styles complement the same foods that you would serve with a crisp Italian Pinot Grigio or zesty young Sauvignon Blanc. The bite of acidity makes it a pleasing pairing with many salads and, as in Greece, the freshest and simplest seafood, especially dishes that involve citrus or other tart ingredients, such as capers, olives, and lightly pickled vegetables. Beyond stuffed grape leaves (dolmas), almost anything dressed with yogurt or sour cream is a great match, from fish tacos to vegetable *pakoras* to *tzatziki*, the Greek yogurt, garlic, and cucumber meze.

Assyrtiko blended with other grapes (Sauvignon Blanc, Chardonnay, and the like) can pair nicely with richer preparations, such as seafood risotto, lightly smoked or grilled white meat, fish and poultry, and many pan or oven roasts.

The richer, oak-aged styles should be treated like Chardonnays in pairing. Lobster, scallops, prawns, and shrimp show well with these styles, especially when accompanied by a rich cream- or butter-based sauce.

PAIRING POINTERS

Assyrtiko pairs well with:

- Dishes served with a citrus, creamy, or light vinaigrette, such as a dressed salad or grilled fish, meat, or poultry (especially grilled dishes served at room temperature). Assyrtiko's sharpness can handle tart saucing, but for a softer wine, reduce the acidity of the dressing.
- Dishes that are spicy and moderately hot. Assyrtiko's brighter acidity and lower alcohol cleanse and refresh your palate. Try it with spicier Indian tandoori dishes and fish curries.
- Sharper or more acidic ingredients: citrus, dairy (yogurt, crème fraîche, and sour cream), dill, sorrel, capers, olives, tomatoes, zucchini, and leeks.
- Simply prepared seafood. Try one with a plate of oysters, a shrimp cocktail, a bowl of steamed clams, or grilled trout.
- Fowl and white meat served with a salad. A bottle of Assyrtiko is a lovely match with a simple roast of pork or chicken accompanied by a salad of mixed greens, tossed arugula, or even grilled radicchio.

Assyrtiko isn't good:

- On its own (sometimes). Many people find it too intense for sipping as a predinner drink. It's best to accompany Assyrtiko with some food, even if it's just a bowl of olives or nuts.
- With most traditional red-meat preparations. While the classic Greek roast lamb served with avgolemono, the classic egg and lemon sauce, is sublime, a classic prime rib or grilled venison isn't so successful.
- With savory dishes that border on sweet. An Easter ham, Thanksgiving turkey with prune stuffing, and Chinese chicken with glazed walnuts all require wines with more sweetness and less acidity.
- When you pick the wrong style for a dish. The oaky or blended styles and the crisp, unblended versions can't simply be interchanged.
- With boldly flavored dishes. Assyrtiko's more delicate flavors can be lost if the dish has too strong a personality. Risotto with Gorgonzola, duck with sausage and lentils, or a slathered chili dog are all too much.

THE CHEESE PLATE

FRESH	Chèvre (many countries), feta (Greece, Bulgaria)
SEMI-SOFT	Slightly aged chèvre (many countries), crescenza (U.S.A.), teleme (Italy)
SOFT-RIPENED	Brie (Canada, U.S.A.), tetilla (Spain)
SEMI-HARD	Asiago, pecorino (Italy), raclette (France, Switzerland)—dry; Gouda (Holland, U.S.A.), Gruyère (Switzerland)—dessert

assyrtiko | FILET BEAN AND SCALLOP SALAD

ANNE S. QUATRANO Bacchanalia, Quinones, and Star Provisions, Atlanta, Georgia

Makes 4 first-course servings

**1 pound Nickel filet beans or other small, slender green beans,
   stem ends trimmed**
2 tablespoons Champagne vinegar
1 tablespoon chopped shallots
Few drops of honey
1 tablespoon hazelnut oil
2 tablespoons grape seed oil
Salt and freshly ground black pepper
½ cup hazelnuts
8 sea scallops (about 1 pound total weight), preferably diver
Fresh chervil sprigs for garnish

Bring a saucepan filled with salted water to a boil. Add the beans and boil until tender-crisp, about 30 seconds. Drain and immediately plunge into ice water to halt the cooking. Drain well, transfer to a bowl, and set aside.

To make a vinaigrette, in a small bowl, whisk together the vinegar and shallots. Whisk in the honey, then slowly drizzle in the hazelnut oil and 1 tablespoon of the grape seed oil while whisking constantly. Season with salt and pepper. Set aside.

In a small, dry sauté pan, toast the hazelnuts over low heat, shaking the pan often, just until golden and fragrant, 3 to 4 minutes. Pour onto a cutting board, let cool, then coarsely chop. Set aside.

In a cast-iron skillet, heat the remaining 1 tablespoon grape seed oil over medium heat until hot. Pat the scallops dry on paper towels, then season with salt and pepper. Add the scallops to the hot pan and cook, turning once, until seared on both sides and barely translucent at the center when tested with a knife tip, about 2 minutes on each side.

Place 2 scallops on each warmed plate. Drizzle the vinaigrette over the beans and toss to coat, then scatter the beans randomly over the scallops. Garnish with the hazelnuts and chervil and serve at once.

ANNE: *The buttery scallops play off the richness of the Assyrtiko wine, and toasted hazelnuts are the perfect complement to the wine's residual nutty characteristics. The forward acid of the wine plays nicely with the Champagne vinegar in the vinaigrette, and the mineral finish of the wine adds another dimension to the natural brine of the scallops. The wine and the dish will enliven and brighten each other, complementing rather than contrasting flavors.*

EVAN: *I love Anne and her food. She hasn't locked herself into one specific cooking style, and she always lets the ingredients determine what she does. Knowing Assyrtiko's affinity with salads, I felt that pairing this wine with Anne's food would be a success. The resulting warm salad proved me right!*

Given the richness of the scallops and the natural sweetness of the beans (also known as haricots verts or baby green beans), this dish can handle one of the barrel-aged styles, though it pairs splendidly with any version of dry Assyrtiko, from the pure, zippy stuff to the wines blended with Sauvignon Blanc. The dressing, which is not too sharp, is quite wine-friendly, and the nuts lend texture and a toasty note (which can work with an oak-aged style). The chervil is a lovely bridge element. Both the wine and the dish have long, clean finishes, making you long for more of each!

RECOMMENDED PRODUCERS

EVERYDAY	PREMIUM
Biblia Chora Pangeon, Greece [D]	Argyros Estate Santorini, Greece [V]
Boutari Santorini, Greece [D]	Gaia Estate Santorini, Greece [D]
Domaine Constantin Lazaridi Santorini, Greece [D]	Santo Santorini, Greece [D]
Domaine Evharis Santorini, Greece [D]	Sigalas Santorini, Greece [D]
Greek Wine Cellar D. Kourtakis Santorini, Greece [D]	Spyros Hatziyiannis Santorini, Greece [D]
Pape Johannou Nemea, Greece [D]	Vatistas Santorini, Greece [V]

D = Dry   V = Vinsanto

chenin blanc

shen-ihn *blahn* | *shen*-ihn *blahngk*

There are few grapes that you could build an entire meal around, serving different styles of the same variety—from sparkling to dry to off-dry to sweet and in between. Chenin Blanc is one of them. Its variety is astonishing, though it tends to earn even less respect than Riesling. Still, after decades of advocacy by wine lovers, Riesling has achieved increasing popularity among wine drinkers. Riesling's need for a cool climate constrains supply, as only a small number of regions can grow it successfully. Europe's capacity for producing good Riesling is almost maxed out, and the same is becoming true of Australia, New Zealand, and North America (although Canada has begun producing good examples). The scarcity leaves new fans of quality Riesling craving wines of a similar style. Enter Chenin Blanc.

This grape is grown widely throughout the world (it is South Africa's most important white grape) and in a huge range of interpretations. It's affordable, versatile, and appealing to Riesling lovers. I believe its time is ripe!

Alternative Names Blanc d'Aunis, Confort, Cou-Fort, Franc Blanc, Franche, Gros Pineau, Gros de Vouvray, Pineau d'Anjou, Pineau de Briollay, Pineau de la Loire, Pineau de Savennières, Pineau Nantais, Plant de Brèze (France), Steen (South Africa), Pinot Blanco (South America)

Styles Light- to medium-full-bodied dry white, medium-bodied off-dry white, semi-sweet medium-full-bodied (*moelleux*) white, late-harvest and botrytized medium-full-bodied dessert white, sparkling

Sometimes Blended With Rarely blended, except in sparkling wines

Flavor Lexicon

DRY AND OFF-DRY   *Fruit/vegetable:* Fresh grass, guava, melon, quince, red apple, yellow apple ▪ *Floral:* Chamomile ▪ *Earth:* Chalk, mineral, straw

SWEET	*Fruit/vegetable:* Baked apple, ripe cantaloupe ▪ *Wood:* Vanilla ▪ *Other:* Custard, honey, Juicy Fruit gum
SPARKLING	*Floral:* Citrus (lemon, kumquat), flower blossom, green apple ▪ *Earth:* Chalk, mineral ▪ *Other:* Sour cream

Similar Sips Riesling, in a similar range of styles

Where It's Grown Argentina, Australia (Western Australia), Chile, France (Loire Valley: Anjou, Saumur, Touraine; Languedoc-Roussillon: Limoux), Mexico, New Zealand (Hawke's Bay), South Africa (Coastal Region: Paarl, Stellenbosch, Swartland; Northern Cape: Lower Orange), Uruguay, U.S.A. (California: Central Coast [Lodi], Napa County; Idaho; Oregon; Washington)

Chenin Blanc's reputation and lore come from its native and spiritual home, France's Loire Valley, and specifically the Anjou and Touraine areas. If you like bone-dry whites, then a bottle of the electric and minerally Savennières is your wine. Known for its ability to age for decades, this bright wine picks up nuances of dried flowers, ripe dried apple, and preserved quince as it ages; these flavors are underlined by a chalky earth that gives the wine its extraordinary structure. Other notable examples of the dry style are made in Vouvray: the *sec* (meaning "dry") and Jasnières are similar in profile but less austere in their youth. Winemakers know that to support sweetness in wine, you need acidity to prevent it from becoming cloying. A brilliantly balanced off-dry Vouvray or Montlouis is a case in point, with a kiss of apple or pear and melony sweetness and a lemony-tart streak. This same acidity allows for richer wines, those called *moelleux* (softly sweet; the French term literally means "full of marrow"). In the realm of late-harvest dessert wines (often affected by the "noble rot," *Botrytis*), you can find spectacular, unctuously rich wines with flavors of honey, baked apple, ripe guava, and even a little white truffle. Among these amazing wines are Bonnezeaux, Chaume, and Quarts de Chaume.

Where there's high acid in fruit, you can make fizz, and the Loire Valley's sparkling wines, *méthode traditionnelle* wines made from Chenin Blanc grown in equally chalky soils (locally called *tuffa* soils), make for some of the world's great alternatives to Champagne. In fact, many of the better wineries in the Loire are owned by the Champagne houses, who know that there's only so much true Champagne to meet the almost limitless demand for sparkling wine. Sparklers from Saumur (usually labeled Saumur Mousseux), based on Chenin Blanc, are especially good, but other bottles, simply labeled Crémant de Loire, can also be wonderful. Chenin Blanc performs so well in sparkling wine that it's included in the blend of sparkling wines produced in Languedoc-Roussillon in the appellation of Limoux for their Crémant de Limoux.

France's production of amazing Chenin Blanc, however, is dwarfed by the production of South Africa. There's twice as much of the grape planted there as in France, and although it is decidedly different in flavor profile, it makes very good wines. Still occasionally called Steen (an old name referring to an off-dry style of Chenin Blanc), South Africa's Chenins have the same apple, pear, quince, and melon flavors you find in France, but without the Loire's chalky mineral notes and often with a note of chamomile. Alas, many of South Africa's best Chenin Blanc vineyards, many with vines more than fifty years old, have been pulled up and replanted with other grapes to satisfy the thirst for mainstream white wines such as Sauvignon Blanc and Chardonnay.

Most of the Australian plantings of Chenin Blanc are in Western Australia, near Perth and in the Margaret River (where it's better), but the grape is present all over the country. In New Zealand there are a few wineries producing Chenin Blanc, but the grape is rare there, especially when compared to plantings of other aromatic white varietals, like Riesling and Gewürztraminer.

In the United States, California examples are noteworthy in Lodi's Clarksburg region and in the Napa Valley, where there are still producers dedicated to this grape (Chappellet and Casa Nuestra being two perennial favorites). The wines show a combination of tree fruit and floral blossoms and range from dry to off-dry. Efforts in eastern Washington can be very good (L'Ecole No. 41's is excellent), and there's some in Idaho and Oregon, too.

Although the quality of the wines isn't stunning, the sheer quantity of Chenin Blanc produced in Mexico and South America is worth mentioning. It's more common here to find the wine referred to as Pinot Blanco.

Vintner's Choices Dry vs. off-dry vs. sweet, oak vs. no oak, still vs. sparkling

The ability of Chenin Blanc to balance acid and sweetness is what enables winemakers to produce such a diversity of styles from one grape and to control the sweetness in the wine in all styles. To make sparkling wines, winemakers need grapes of very high acid and lower sugar levels, requiring an earlier picking of the fruit than for table wines. While you can find bottles labeled *pétillant*, which refers to a light, prickly effervescence, most *méthode traditionnelle* wines are made according to the methods of Champagne, resulting in a less fizzy wine. Although blends can be driven by Chenin Blanc, they often incorporate Chardonnay and Cabernet Franc (the last vinified the same way Pinot Noir and Pinot Meunier would be for Champagne, as a "clear white" component—a red grape made into a white wine). The Loire's chalky soil gives the wine a distinct character. Sometimes referred to as "poor man's Champagne," it's considered among the best of France's other sparkling wines.

While oak aging is fairly common in the production of the great sweet dessert wines of the Loire Valley, it's less common in the table wines. When wines are oaked, older, neutral wood is used to minimize its impact. Most Chenins are made in stainless steel vats, with cooler fermentation and no malolactic fermentation. In the dessert wines, the texture and potpourri of spices (vanilla, cinnamon, etc.) that oak introduces into the wine are considered desirable, as in Sauternes and other similarly crafted wines. The introduction of *Botrytis cinerea* is also welcome with Chenin Blanc.

PAIRING WITH FOOD

A good rule of thumb is to treat Chenin Blanc much as you would Riesling. Given the range of styles available, it can pair with an incredible selection of ingredients, from the obvious, including fish (monkfish, halibut, snapper, and rock cod), seafood (scallops, shrimp, lobster, and prawns), and mild poultry (turkey, chicken, game hens, and quail), to the less obvious, including white meat (pork, ham, and veal), rich poultry (duck and goose), and charcuterie (sausages and cured meats). A sweeter Chenin Blanc with a terrine of foie gras is positively orgasmic! Vegetables that are sweet or imply sweetness are lovely with Chenin Blanc, including corn and root vegetables such as sweet potatoes, yams, and slow-roasted turnips or rutabagas. And its hard acid gives it an ability to match with things that seem improbable (as in the recipe that follows). Chenin can also work with creamy or buttery sauces, its implicit sweetness pairing nicely with that of the dairy elements.

Bone-dry Chenin Blanc, electric and refreshing, can pair well wherever a squeeze of lemon or lime would enhance the dish—with a plate of oysters, scaloppine of pork or veal, or a simply poached salmon. It's important to pay attention to the body and weight of the wine, as Chenins from different regions vary considerably. Remember the basic principle of matching the level of alcohol with the richness of the food.

The off-dry interpretations are magnificent at foiling spicy heat (as in an Indian vindaloo or Korean kimchi) or mimicking sweetness (chicken with Calvados, cream, and sautéed apples or deep-fried coconut shrimp). Additionally, off-dry Chenin is sublime with smoked items (especially salmon, trout, and pork) or recipes made with them, like pasta dishes. Moderate levels of salt can also be balanced with these off-dry styles of wine.

The very sweet dessert-style wines are wonderful for pairing with desserts based on white stone fruits (peach and nectarine) and tree fruits (pear and apple, especially in tarts), or with custards such as crème brûlée. Finally, the botrytized versions are super with recipes that include honey. As always, ensure that the dessert is less sweet than the wine.

PAIRING POINTERS

Chenin Blanc goes well:

- With many different dishes. As long as you are willing to adjust the style, from dry to sweet, sparkling to dessert, you'll almost always find a wine to work with the food you are preparing. Thank you, Chenin Blanc!
- Where you'd serve Champagne. At a fraction of the price but with many of the same flavor characteristics, a quality sparkling wine based on Chenin Blanc can allow you to splurge on the dish and spend less on the bottle. Corn blinis with a spot of caviar and a little crème fraîche or sour cream served with a *crémant* from the Loire are very nice. You might even try it with a bag of popcorn sprinkled with your favorite topping, from Parmesan to Cajun spice.

- With fruit-based desserts. Perhaps more than any other dessert wine, late-harvest Chenin works superbly with recipes ranging from a classic apple tart served with a dollop of whipped cream to a honey-infused mousse accompanied by a compote of ginger-scented pears and quince.
- With slightly sweet entrées and appetizers. There's so much sweetness in food today, from the complex coconut curries of Thailand and the Indian state of Kerala to a plate of grilled chicken slathered with mild Texas barbecue sauce, that off-dry Chenin Blanc comes into its own where many wines would be diminished.
- With cheese. With Chenin's versatility, it makes sense that there's a Chenin to pair with almost any wedge, wheel, or shaving of cheese from the cow, goat, or sheep.

Chenin Blanc isn't good:

- When you pick the wrong style. Basic common sense should prevail. Don't pair a dry Chenin Blanc with a dessert, nor a *moelleux* style with your pan-roasted halibut with lemon-caper butter.
- With dishes that are too fiery. A heavy hand with the cracked black pepper or the Scotch bonnet or jalapeño chiles will overpower most dry Chenin Blancs, though off-dry examples and lower-alcohol sparkling versions will fare better.
- With most green vegetables, unless they are slightly sweet (like snap peas with a slightly sweet Asian sauce). Bone-dry examples may work on occasion, but it's tough to pair Chenin with basic sautéed zucchini, Swiss chard, or spinach.
- With traditional red-meat dishes. Easter ham, yes; prime rib with Yorkshire pudding, no. And don't even think about strong foods like calves' liver.
- With desserts based on chocolate, coffee, or mocha. These ingredients bury the subtlety of the wine.

THE CHEESE PLATE

FRESH	Chèvre (many countries)—dry; fromage blanc (France), ricotta (Italy, U.S.A.)—off-dry
SEMI-SOFT	Slightly aged chèvre (many countries), teleme (U.S.A.)—dry
SOFT-RIPENED	Boursault, Brie (France)—dry
SEMI-HARD	Cantal (France), Iberico (Spain)—sparkling
HARD	Parmesan (Italy)—sparkling; aged Cheddar (U.K., U.S.A.)—sparkling, *moelleux*, dessert
BLUE	Cambozola (Germany), Gorgonzola dolcelatte (Italy)—*moelleux*, dessert
WASHED-RIND	Taleggio (Italy)—dry, off-dry; Morbier (France)—off-dry, sparkling

chenin blanc | MUSHROOM SALAD WITH WARM GOAT CHEESE TOASTS

LORETTA KELLER   COCO500 and the Moss Room, San Francisco, California

Makes 4 salad-course or first-course servings

6 ounces white button mushrooms, trimmed
½ cup crème fraîche
6 drops fresh lemon juice
¼ teaspoon grated lemon zest
Sea salt and freshly ground black pepper
1 celery stalk

4 slices coarse country bread
2 tablespoons extra virgin olive oil
1 clove garlic, halved
½ pound fresh goat cheese, at room temperature

HERB SALAD
1 tablespoon fresh tarragon leaves
1 tablespoon finely sliced fresh chives
¼ cup fresh chervil leaves
¼ cup fresh flat-leaf parsley leaves
1 tablespoon coarsely chopped fresh dill
½ cup small-leaf arugula
1 cup mâche
2 tablespoons extra virgin olive oil
2 teaspoons fresh lemon juice

Using a mandoline or a sharp knife, thinly slice the mushrooms, then place in a bowl. Add the crème fraîche, lemon juice, lemon zest, and a pinch each salt and pepper. Gently combine the ingredients, being careful not to break up the mushrooms. Set aside.

Using a vegetable peeler, remove the strings from the celery stalk, then thinly slice the stalk crosswise with the mandoline or knife. Add to the mushrooms and toss gently to mix.

Toast the bread slices, and brush one side of each slice with the olive oil. Drag the cut sides of the garlic clove across the oiled side of each bread slice once or twice. Spread one-fourth of the goat cheese on each slice of toast.

Working quickly now, make the herb salad. In a bowl, combine all of the herbs, the arugula, and the mâche. Drizzle with the olive oil and lemon juice and toss to mix. Season with salt and pepper and toss again.

Divide the mushroom salad evenly among 4 plates. Scatter the herb salad over the top, and place a slice of warm goat cheese toast on the side. Serve immediately.

LORETTA: *A dry Chenin Blanc is a fantastic vehicle to showcase minerality and terroir. The mushroom-and-chèvre combination is perfect with these wines. Some of my favorites come from the Loire Valley appellations of Montlouis and Savennières.*

EVAN: *I have known Loretta for more than fifteen years, and, my mom aside, she's one of the only chefs I know whose palate is in intuitive harmony with my own. I would cheerfully order anything off her menu and be certain that it will all go beautifully with wine. She may be a great chef, but she's a sommelier at heart.*

Chenin's acidity craves more acidity, and goat cheese's naturally sharp personality is a perfect vehicle for it. A soft, young, and less salty feta would probably also work well in a pinch. The mushrooms pick up beautifully on the chalky minerality of an Old World (French) style of Chenin. If you're serving a New World Chenin, skip the garlic on the toast and downplay the herbs in the salad. The core of the recipe still pairs well. If your wine is off-dry, ensure your goat cheese is fresh and mild; you might even substitute fresh ricotta or a ricotta–goat cheese blend, again leaving the garlic off the bread and focusing on the mushrooms, the toast, and a small smattering of dressed herbs (I might substitute lemon basil for the tarragon). An off-dry pairing is daring for sure; some will enjoy it, while others may not.

RECOMMENDED PRODUCERS

EVERYDAY	PREMIUM	SPLURGE
Bouvet Saumur, France [Sp]	Casa Nuestra Napa Valley, California [D]	De Trafford Stellenbosch, South Africa [D, Sw]
Domaine Pichot Vouvray, France [D, O]	Domaine Vincent Carême Vouvray, France [Sp]	Domaine des Baumard Quarts de Chaume, France [Sw]
Dry Creek Vineyard Sonoma County, California [D]	Huet Vouvray, France [D, O]	
Kanu Stellenbosch, South Africa [D, O]	Pierre Soulez Savennières, France [D, O]	
Man Vintners Coastal Region, South Africa [D, O]	Raats Stellenbosch, South Africa [D, O]	

D = Dry   O = Off-Dry   Sp = Sparkling   Sw = Sweet

garganega

gahr-*gah*-neh-gah

When I first began exploring Italian wines in the late 1970s, the selection of Italian white wine was poor: aside from the signature Verdicchio in the fish-shaped bottle and a few token bottles of Pinot Grigio, my exposure was limited primarily to Soave and its principal grape, Garganega.

The great challenge facing Soave, and thus Garganega, was its own popularity: many producers fell into the same trap as makers of Pouilly-Fuissé and Vouvray in the 1970s and 1980s, which was to blindly satisfy the skyrocketing demand by overcropping and compromising quality. Sadly, all three of these wines have suffered as a result. But ambitious and committed producers have worked to bring the grapes and their wines back to the quality they deserve, and Garganega's return has perhaps been the most significant.

Alternative Names Gargana, Lizzana, Ostesona (Italy)

Styles Medium-bodied dry white, medium- to medium-full-bodied dessert white

Sometimes Blended With Chardonnay, Trebbiano (Italy)

Flavor Lexicon

DRY *Fruit/vegetable:* Fresh ginger, jicama, lemon, white peach ▪ *Floral:* Freesia, jasmine ▪ *Earth:* Mineral, steel ▪ *Wood:* Almond, cashew, pine nut

SWEET *Fruit:* Golden raisin, marmalade ▪ *Wood:* Hazelnut, nougat, spice ▪ *Other:* Candied banana, honey

Similar Sips Pinot Grigio, Pinot Blanc (Pinot Bianco) with a nutty edge

Where It's Grown Italy (Friuli–Venezia Giulia; Lombardy; Umbria; Veneto: Soave)

Wines from the Veneto's Soave appellation are virtually the only Garganega wines found outside Italy. When it's good (as more and more of it is), it achieves a balanced richness and is redolent of citrus and fresh ginger, with faint notes of white peach and nectarine. It can be quite floral and, with balanced cropping, yields mildly mineral overtones of chalk and wet stone. When these wines are good they are very, very good; but when they are bad, they are awful. There's still a lot more Garganega that is dilute, unappealing, and not worth its rising price.

There are two effective strategies for enjoying Garganega. First, look for wines from Classico. This is the heart of the Soave region, where all of the best vineyards are located, and unquestionably where the best wines are made. (The term *cantina* on a label identifies the wine as a cooperative bottling. In this system, which is common in this part of Italy and responsible for 80 percent of most Soave, growers sell their grapes to co-ops, which then make the wine. Historically, this has not resulted in a high-quality product, but the Soave co-op wine is getting better all the time.) Second, ask your retailer if the wine is 100 percent or nearly all Garganega. Garganega is to Soave what Touriga Nacional is to port, or Tempranillo is to Rioja—the primary and quality-driving grape, but not necessarily the only variety in the wine. It is legal to blend other grapes into Soave, and they can affect the overall quality. A second Venetian wine, Bianco di Custoza, often includes Garganega in the blend and can be refreshing, lightly herbal, and enjoyable.

Garganega is Italy's sixth most widely planted white wine grape; it is also grown in Friuli–Venezia Giulia, Umbria, and on the border of and in adjoining Lombardy.

Vintner's Choices Aged vs. not aged, balanced crop vs. high yield, dry vs. sweet, oak vs. no oak, single variety vs. blended

This grape does not take well to being overcropped. It's usually grown on pergolas, cement structures that lift the vines off the ground to a height of about six feet so that air can circulate around them and the sun can ripen the grapes more readily; these structures also make the crop easy to harvest, creating ideal circumstances for overcropping. This is a temptation with all grapes, as most growers are paid by yield, and Soave suffers demonstrably when the vine is asked to do too much. The best producers manage their yields and keep crop levels in check.

Unblended, the grape is remarkable, with fresh fruit and floral flavors and racy acidity, which are even better when yields are properly managed. Soave must be no less than 70 percent Garganega, with the balance most often being Trebbiano; changes in the laws now permit the use of Chardonnay as well. Most Soave is of the everyday sort and is likely to contain the maximum permitted amount of Trebbiano, allowing producers to harvest riper Garganega grapes and balance the resulting sweetness with the local Trebbiano, known as Trebbiano di Soave (which is actually Verdicchio, as Jancis Robinson points out in her renowned *Oxford Companion to Wine*). Chardonnay can contribute texture and some additional flavor components. But the more Garganega and the less Trebbiano in the blend, the better the Soave will be.

Many of Soave's most vocal proponents and winemakers advocate judicious use of oak, and some favor new oak *barriques*. Oak can add body but can also overwhelm the fruit. As with many grapes that can integrate oak in small doses, wood in Soave is fine as long as you don't really taste or notice it; if you do, you know that the oak has masked the fruit. That said, there are a number of examples of oak-aged Soave that are stellar.

Garganega is at its best when young, with a fragrant and aromatic flavor profile framed by rapier-like acidity. Aged for a couple of years, well-made wines take on a more saline and chalky mineral and often nutty character. Whether this appeals to you is a very personal matter.

Lastly, some producers make a wonderful dessert wine out of Garganega called Recioto di Soave, a luscious *passito*-style wine that is defined by its flavors of honey, orange marmalade, and spice and is said to be the perfect accompaniment for panettone, the Italian dessert bread studded with candied fruit.

PAIRING WITH FOOD

The appeal of well-made Soave is in its approachability, its balanced to sharp acidity, and its complexity of flavors. Its freshness calls out for all the bounty that summer brings—flavorful tomatoes and melons, and dishes for picnics and other alfresco events. Unoaked Soave can be splendid with seafood: Garganega's moderately rich texture makes it an especially good match with crab. Yet it's also very happy served with a fillet of fish wrapped in a grape leaf, lightly grilled, and served with a slight squeeze of lemon, or a brochette of prawns with garlic butter.

White meat and poultry can be brilliant: a whole chicken roasted and stuffed with lemon and onion chunks, for example, would be perfect. And here's a wine that can stand up to many egg preparations, like a leek and goat-cheese quiche or a mixed-vegetable frittata. Pastas and risottos can be lovely, especially when they incorporate crab, and even a plate of tomatoes and fresh mozzarella accompanied by a little pesto is sublime. Speaking of pesto, its ingredients— pine nuts, olive oil, and basil—seem to have a natural affinity for Garganega. Almost anything drizzled with pesto and paired with Garganega-based wines is successful.

Oak-aged examples with more texture can stand up to slightly richer sauces. A compound butter on a piece of fish, a light rosemary-infused cream sauce napped on a breast of chicken, or a simple stock reduction are three good examples.

Last, the dessert styles are great with simple cakes, like an almond or vanilla pound cake, especially when served with fruit, either fresh or slightly cooked. A marmalade or pear and frangipane tart would be another tasty pairing. And of course there's always that panettone!

PAIRING POINTERS

Garganega goes well with:

- Most treatments of shellfish, especially crab. With classic Maryland crab cakes or a steamed Dungeness crab served with a basil aioli, Garganega hits the spot. It's also nice with shrimp and lighter treatments of scallops. Stay away from the heavily oaked examples with shellfish unless the sauce has a butter base.
- Simple preparations of fish, poultry, and white meat. A basic roast loin of pork, a piece of swordfish, or poached or lightly sautéed chicken is quite lovely with Garganega, especially when served with a risotto or pasta scented with lemon zest.

- Anything with pesto! Okay, maybe not everything, but Garganega is magic with this very useful sauce.
- Marinated vegetables. Garganega is a nice match with an assortment of antipasti, roasted red and green peppers, or even lightly pickled asparagus or garlic cloves (really!).
- Egg-based dishes. Few wines go with eggs, and even fewer go with plain shirred eggs or eggs over easy; Garganega can handle the match. A frittata or a quiche with green vegetables and cheese can be very good with Garganega-based wines.

Garganega isn't good:
- With extremely rich dishes. Though its acidity can cut through almost anything rich, the subtlety of the wine is lost.
- With mushroom dishes. Try as I might, I've found that morels, porcini, and other more pungent brown fungi simply don't pair well with Garganega. And basic chanterelles and other white mushrooms aren't all that successful even if sautéed with garlic, fresh herbs, and other bridge ingredients.
- With most red-meat preparations. Though a beef stew with olives and herbs can be nice alongside a Soave, dishes like classic boeuf bourguignon and a lasagna Bolognese, made with a rich meat and tomato *ragù*, are ill suited.
- With very spicy dishes. Garganega works with ample spice flavor, but not with fiery heat. Most curries, regardless of origin, and powerful smoked preparations with spicy rubs tend to overwhelm the wine.
- When you pick the wrong one. Recioto di Soave is a late-harvest dessert wine made from Garganega. You'll regret pairing it with your fish crudo appetizer.

THE CHEESE PLATE

FRESH	Chèvre (many countries), feta (Bulgaria, Greece)—dry
SEMI-SOFT	Boursin (France), stracchino (Italy)—dry
SOFT-RIPENED	Brie (France, U.S.A.), pavé d'affinois (France)—dry
SEMI-HARD	Mild white Cheddar (U.S.A., U.K.), Fontina (Italy)—dry
BLUE	Cambozola (Germany), Gorgonzola dolcelatte (Italy)—sweet

garganega | GRILLED BRANZINO WITH HEIRLOOM-TOMATO PANZANELLA

ETHAN STOWELL   Union, Tavolàta, and How to Cook a Wolf, Seattle, Washington

Makes 6 first-course servings

3 (1-pound) whole branzino, filleted with skin intact (see note)
Extra virgin olive oil for brushing
Salt and freshly ground black pepper

PANZANELLA
½ pound day-old ciabatta or other crusty coarse country bread,
    cut into 1-inch cubes (about 3 cups)
2 large heirloom or other good-quality tomatoes (about ½ pound each),
    cut into 1-inch cubes
½ cup peeled, seeded, and diced cucumber
2 tablespoons finely diced red onion
½ cup extra-virgin olive oil
¼ cup red wine vinegar
10 fresh basil leaves, torn into small pieces
Salt and freshly ground black pepper

Prepare a charcoal or gas grill for direct grilling over a medium fire. Rub the 6 fish fillets on both sides with olive oil and season with salt and pepper. Set aside.

While the grill is heating, make the *panzanella*. In a bowl, combine the bread, tomatoes, cucumber, onion, olive oil, vinegar, and basil and mix well. Season with salt and pepper. Set aside for 5 to 10 minutes to allow the flavors to develop and the bread to soak up the oil and vinegar.

Oil the grill rack. Place the fillets, skin side down, on the rack and grill until the skin is crispy, 3 to 4 minutes. Carefully the turn the fillets over and continue to grill just until opaque in the center when tested with a knife tip, 2 to 3 minutes.

Divide the *panzanella* evenly among 6 plates, and place the fillets on top. Spoon any dressing remaining in the bottom of the bowl over the fish. Serve at once.

NOTE Ask your fishmonger to fillet the fish for you. Check the fillets carefully for pin bones and remove any the fishmonger missed. If you cannot find branzino, a type of Mediterranean sea bass, substitute six 4-ounce halibut fillets.

ETHAN: *I'm not the type of person who tries to find the perfect wine and food pairing. I try to match food dishes with types of wine that make sense. To me, a glass of Soave and a nice piece of grilled fish sounds great. Throw in some awesome tomatoes that have a nice juicy and sweet bite to them, and I'm in heaven. Garganega is a great grape for the food that I like to eat: clean, refreshing, and light.*

EVAN: *Ethan is a self-taught chef who is inspired by fresh ingredients and simple, straightforward flavors. Like a sailor who can navigate by the stars, he has an innate intuition about food that produces tasty results. And being based in Seattle, Ethan knows his fish.*

Fish is a natural and obvious pairing, not a truly daring one. But what pulls this dish together for me is the panzanella, *with its crusty toasted bread, the tart-sweet tomatoes, the heat and sweetness of the red onion, the sharpness from the dressing, the freshness from the crisp cucumber, and the little bite of the basil, which never hurts with Garganega. The toasted bread allows you to pair the dish with an oak-aged or slightly bottle-aged wine. Resist the temptation to enjoy the salad on its own, and ensure you get an ample piece of fish with each bite for maximum enjoyment.*

RECOMMENDED PRODUCERS

EVERYDAY	PREMIUM
Allegrini Veneto, Italy [D]	Anselmi Veneto, Italy [D, Sw]
Corte Gardoni Veneto, Italy [D]	Coffele Veneto, Italy [D, Sw]
Corte Giara Veneto, Italy [D]	Gini Veneto, Italy [D, Sw]
La Cappuccina Veneto, Italy [D]	Pieropan Veneto, Italy [D, Sw]
Marcato Veneto, Italy [D]	Suavia Veneto, Italy [D, Sw]
Santi Veneto, Italy [D]	Tamellini Veneto, Italy [D, Sw]

D = Dry   Sw = Sweet

grüner veltliner

groo-ner *felt*-lih-ner

It's apropos that this fashionable wine goes by the sobriquet "Groo-vee" when ordered by wine and food lovers in chic restaurants. Riesling never got this much respect! This grape has been around for a while, but only of late has it been treated like the "It" girl just off the plane from Vienna. But given how well Grüner Veltliner pairs with an extensive range of food, this girl seems like she'll be around for a while, like Catherine Deneuve, rather than being a one-hit wonder, like RuPaul.

Alternative Names Grüner, Grunmuskateller, Manhardrebe, Mouhardsrebe, Weissgipfler (Austria), Veltlin Zelene (Czech Republic), Veltini (Hungary)

Styles Medium- to medium-full-bodied dry white, medium- to medium-full-bodied off-dry white, medium-full-bodied dessert white

Sometimes Blended With Except in generic table wines and sparkling wines (*Sekt* in Austria), this grape is not blended.

Flavor Lexicon *Fruit/vegetable:* Cardoon, celery or celery root, citrus (lemon, yellow grapefruit), cucumber, green bean, green melon, lemon rind, lentil • *Floral:* Caraway • *Earth:* Mineral • *Other:* Musk, white pepper

Similar Sips Dry Riesling, or a spicy version of Vernaccia, Verdicchio, or other Italian wine of similar quality. Off-dry interpretations are similar to late-harvest German Rieslings.

Where It's Grown Austria (Donauland, Kamptal, Kremstal, Wachau, Weinviertel), Czech Republic, New Zealand (Central Otago), U.S.A. (California: multiple appellations)

The wine gods got it right when they set Grüner Veltliner in Austria. Not only does it perform well throughout Austria's many wine regions (except Styria), but it represents one-third of all grapes grown in that country. Long enjoyed in Vienna's *Heurigen*, or wine taverns, it is being consumed increasingly in restaurants everywhere. Fortunately there's plenty to go around, and most of it is well made. The best wines come from the Wachau, Kamptal, and Kremstal, though it would be splitting hairs to identify any one of these regions as the best. The wines share a wonderful combination of flavors, which can range from lemon cucumber to green bean, brown lentil to white pepper, framed by lemony acid and balanced alcohol. It's unique and very appealing: once you've tasted a good example, you'll always recognize the wine, much like a Gewürztraminer from Alsace. Region and vineyard are key factors in the wine's complexity, as is the ripeness of the fruit. As with German wines, Grüners are categorized and labeled by these criteria, so picking out a wine that appeals to your tastes should be easy— once you've brushed up on your German vocabulary!

Grüner is only now gaining popularity outside Austria. Though it's been produced for a long time in neighboring countries like the Czech Republic and Hungary, far less is planted outside Europe. There have been only a few efforts in the New World, chiefly in New Zealand and in California's Napa Valley (Rudy von Strasser grows it on Napa Valley's Diamond Mountain). Given its growing popularity, though, I expect we'll be seeing more of it soon.

Vintner's Choices Aged vs. not aged, dry vs. sweet, grown anywhere in the vineyard vs. in a specific site, harvested when ripe vs. less ripe, oak vs. no oak

Grüner Veltliner can range in style from lean and mean to full and fat. At its best it's somewhere in between, a wine of elegance and refinement. It has the focused quality of a great European or Australian dry Riesling and is as subtly complex. Most GV is dry (*trocken*). As with German wines, these wines are broken into three categories: *Tafelwein* (table wine), *Qualitätswein* (wine of quality), and *Prädikatswein* ("certified" wine). The last two categories are determined by the higher sugar content of the grape must (unfermented grape juice). Also as with German wines, sweeter styles are categorized, from *Kabinett*, for which the perception of sugar is likely to be just off-dry, to *Spätlese*, to *Auslese* and *Trockenbeereneauslese*, which are really darn sweet. Austria has a unique category called *Ausbruch*, which lies somewhere between *Auslese* and *Trockenbeerenauslese*. In wines from the Wachau region, three other terms are used: *Steinfeder* for the lightest examples of the variety; *Federspiel* for the more developed and elegant interpretations, with more viscosity and focus; and *Smaragd* for the ripest and most expressive examples. As a rule, the more information you see on the label, the more sense of place you can expect the wine to have. The best wines can be traced to a specific vineyard, and, if you know the vineyard, even more specific parcels within it.

As with Riesling and other similar aromatic white varietals, some vintners age their wines in small oak barrels to add texture and flavor. You'll know them when you taste them, and the label will likely give some warning (the word *barrique* is a giveaway). As with all wines, oak-aged Grüners need special attention in pairing with food.

As GV ages, it picks up layers of complexity and a deeper, more complex mineral character but still maintains its unique flavor profile. I prefer my Grüners young and vibrant, but they are quite interesting after some time in the bottle, and the best ones do age gracefully.

PAIRING WITH FOOD

Even more appealing than Grüner's distinctive flavor profile is its versatility at the table. There's little that Grüner doesn't go with, and a whole assortment of foods with which it can pair where many other grapes can't. Want a wine to go with asparagus? Artichokes? Strong-flavored fish and shellfish? This is it. For a wine to go with bitter greens like escarole or collard greens, look no further. But Grüner is not simply a wine for taming belligerent food: it can pair with many other dishes.

Just about every Asian restaurant with some ambition in its wine list carries at least one GV. It's as happy with the correctly chosen Chinese dishes as with Indian, Vietnamese, or Indonesian food. The core herb and spice profiles of these countries—from Thai basil to tamarind, cardamom to coriander—pair well with the inherently spicy and aromatic nature of the wine. So many sommeliers pair Vietnamese spring rolls with a young GV that it's becoming almost as established a match as French Chablis and oysters—and equally wonderful!

Grüner is just as enjoyable with rich white meats, fowl, and charcuterie. If you've had a plate of schnitzel and potatoes served with a balanced Grüner, you'll believe in the old saying about wines and foods growing up together. But GV can also be sublime with a sweet, spiced boudin blanc or similar white sausage (say, bratwurst) and is lovely with a simple chicken breast grilled with a North African seasoning based on caraway and cumin.

Finally, Grüner is great with legumes, with which it shares personality traits. Lentil stew with pork and sausage, a southwestern chili made with white beans and green chile, and a bowl of lima beans and ham are all superb when matched with a balanced GV.

PAIRING POINTERS

Grüner Veltliner goes well:

- With aromatic and distinctive marinades or sauces. Off-dry Grüner plays especially well with sweet and sour (yes, here's a good wine for sweet-and-sour pork!), sweet and salt, and sweet and spicy aromatics (chiles).
- With most styles of Asian food. From Indian to Indonesian, this wine is almost always able to connect the dots. In addition to the pairing with Vietnamese spring rolls, try GV with noodle stir-fries, wok-charred vegetables, and even tofu.
- With salads and vegetables. These dishes, often posing challenges in matching with wine, are easy for Grüner. This wine will stand up to asparagus (both green and white) as well as artichokes. Also, most composed green salads, Asian or European inspired, fare quite nicely. And GV is a wine that can handle shiso and other pungent leafy greens as well.
- With beans and lentils. Lentils of all colors (green, brown, pink, or red), are great with Grüner, so if you feel like drinking white wine with your sausage and lentils, you're golden. The same is true for a loin of rabbit served with fava beans with bacon.

- As a counterbalance to rich, salty meats and meat treatments—ham, sausage, charcuterie, and the like. Grüner is quite content alongside a plate of Italian salumi, French charcuterie, or German Wurst. And is there truly a better match than the classic local pairing of Grüner Veltliner and schnitzel?
- With many exotic and flavorful spices. Try GV with foods seasoned with curry, cardamom, cinnamon, clove, mace, star anise, cumin, and turmeric.

Grüner Veltliner isn't good:
- By itself. Many will disagree with this statement, but, with a few exceptions, Grüner simply craves food. Even pairing it with a little sushi or a dish of olives is more interesting than having it solo.
- When you pick the wrong one. A sharp, dry, and puckery GV is great with a plate of briny oysters, but an off-dry and luscious interpretation will be much less successful.
- With traditional red-meat dishes. While a sauce or a long braise could steer the dish the right way, Grüner is not at its best with simply sautéed or roasted lamb, beef, or venison.
- With dishes that are too rich and dominant. Most Grüners are penetrating but still subtle, and asking this wine to hang in there with a thick, cream-based sauce is simply not fair.
- With overtly sweet dishes. I am happy to have a cumin-studded poppadum dipped in a little apricot chutney and served with a Grüner Veltliner if the chutney isn't drowning the poppadum and the wine style is apropos. If the dish is too sweet, dry GV or even off-dry GV, unlike Riesling, will struggle. And if you match the sweetness of the food with a sweet wine, the entire match may be too cloying. Experiment by all means, but be forewarned.

THE CHEESE PLATE

SOFT-RIPENED	Chaource (France), pavé d'affinois (France), robiola (Italy)—dry, off-dry
SEMI-HARD	Garrotxa (Spain), Gruyère (Switzerland)—dry, off-dry
HARD	Aged Cheddar (U.K.), mimolette (France)—dry, off-dry, sweet
BLUE	Cabrales (Spain), Cambozola (Germany)—off-dry, sweet
WASHED-RIND	Époisses, Munster (France)—dry, off-dry, sweet

grüner veltliner | VEGETABLE POT-AU-FEU WITH TOASTED SPICE BROTH

FLOYD CARDOZ   Tabla, New York City, New York

Makes 6 main-course servings

18 small shallots or pearl onions, unpeeled
1 head garlic, separated into cloves, unpeeled
3 tablespoons canola oil
Salt and freshly ground black pepper
18 baby turnips, peeled and halved
3 carrots, peeled and cut into $\frac{1}{2}$-inch cubes (about 3 cups)
$\frac{3}{4}$ pound fingerling potatoes

SPICE BROTH

3 cloves garlic, lightly crushed
1-inch piece fresh ginger, peeled and thinly sliced across the grain
1 cup diced, peeled butternut squash ($\frac{1}{2}$-inch dice)
$\frac{1}{2}$ cup pink lentils, picked over, rinsed, soaked in cold water to cover
    for 30 minutes, and drained
2 quarts vegetable stock

SPICE MIX

1 tablespoon coriander seeds
1 teaspoon black peppercorns
$\frac{1}{2}$ teaspoon cumin seeds
$\frac{1}{4}$ teaspoon mace blades
2 whole cloves

TO FINISH THE BROTH

1 tablespoon canola oil
1 tablespoon black mustard seeds
2 cups shelled *edamame*
Juice of 1 lime
$\frac{1}{2}$ cup fresh cilantro leaf chiffonade

Steamed rice for serving

Preheat the oven to 350°F. Place the shallots and garlic cloves on a sheet of aluminum foil. Drizzle with 1 tablespoon of the canola oil and season with salt and pepper. Bring up the sides of the foil and secure closed. Place the turnips and carrots on a small rimmed baking sheet. Drizzle with the remaining 2 tablespoons canola oil, season with salt and pepper, and toss to coat. Place the foil packet and the baking sheet in the oven and roast until all the vegetables are tender, about 25 minutes. Remove from the oven. Set the turnips and carrots aside. Unwrap the shallots and garlic, let cool, peel, and set aside.

In a saucepan, combine the potatoes with lightly salted water to cover. Bring to a boil, reduce the heat slightly, and cook until tender when tested with a knife tip, about 20 minutes. Drain and, when cool enough to handle, cut into quarters. Set aside.

While the vegetables are in the oven, begin making the broth. Heat a heavy, 4-quart skillet over medium heat. Add the garlic and ginger and dry roast until lightly colored, about 10 minutes. Add the squash, lentils, and stock and simmer until the squash and lentils are tender, about 40 minutes.

Meanwhile, make the spice mix. In a small skillet, combine the coriander, peppercorns, cumin, mace, and cloves and toast over low heat, shaking the pan often, until all the spices are fragrant and have taken on color, 3 to 5 minutes. Pour onto a plate and let cool, then transfer to a spice grinder and grind finely.

When the lentils and squash are ready, add the ground spices to the broth and simmer for 10 minutes to blend the flavors. Remove from the heat and let cool slightly. Working in batches, transfer to a food processor and pulse until the consistency of oatmeal, then pass through a coarse-mesh sieve into a clean saucepan. Discard the contents of the sieve. Taste the broth and season with salt.

To finish the broth, in a small skillet, heat the canola oil over medium heat just until it smokes. Add the mustard seeds and heat until all the seeds start to pop, about 30 seconds. Be careful because a few seeds will pop almost instantly. Add the contents of the skillet to the broth.

Place the broth over medium-high heat, add the shallots, garlic cloves, turnips, carrots, potatoes, and *edamame*, and bring to a simmer. Cook just until all the vegetables are heated through. Add the lime juice and cilantro and stir well.

Transfer the vegetables and broth to a warmed serving bowl. Serve at once with the rice.

FLOYD: *This dish is based on a south Indian vegetable stew called* sambhar. *Adding the butternut squash to the broth gives it a very meaty body. Toasted spices give a nice warmth to the dish. It stands up to Grüner and enhances its flavor.*

EVAN: *Given Grüner Veltliner's affinity for Indian food and for produce, Indian cuisine's championing of vegetables, and Floyd's unique Western adaptation of Indian flavors to the Western kitchen, this pairing is an ideal meeting of flavors, cultures, and talent.*

This recipe is a perfect showcase for both the wine and the vegetables. The individual personalities of each shine through, but they also come together in a very harmonious way. I especially like the way the flavors of the wine pick up on the exotic spices and delicious and slightly spicy broth (the heat comes from the ginger), while the wine's ripeness is echoed by the sweetness of the carrots and squash. Don't be afraid to choose a sweeter wine with this dish. GV's bright green acidity brings out the flavor of all the ingredients like a highlighter pen.

RECOMMENDED PRODUCERS

EVERYDAY	PREMIUM	SPLURGE
E. & M. Berger Kremstal, Austria [D]	Johann Donabaum Wachau, Austria [D]	F. X. Pichler Wachau, Austria [D]
Gritsch Mauritiushof Wachau, Austria [D]	Nigl Kremstal, Austria [D, Sw]	Prager Wachau, Austria [D, Sw]
Koenigsegg Burgenland, Austria [D]	Rudi Pichler Wachau, Austria [D]	
Kurt Angerer Kamptal, Austria [D]	Schloss Gobelsburg Kamptal, Austria [D]	
Winzer Krems Kremstal, Austria [D]	Weingut Bründlmayer Kamptal, Austria [D, Sw]	

D = Dry   Sw = Sweet

carmenère | **FRANK STITT'S LENTIL SOUP WITH**
FENNEL SAUSAGES PAGE 192

cinsaut | **MOURAD LAHLOU'S DUCK BASTEEYA** PAGE 199

gamay | **CHARLIE TROTTER'S SALAD OF CORNISH GAME HEN WITH SHIITAKE MUSHROOM VINAIGRETTE** PAGE 216

mourvèdre | **CINDY PAWLCYN'S BARBECUED TURKEY SKEWERS WITH CARAMELIZED SAGE ONIONS** PAGE 248

nebbiolo

NATE APPLEMAN'S BRAISED DUCK LEG IN RAGÙ WITH CHESTNUT POLENTA AND GREEN OLIVES PAGE 257

petite sirah | **CHRISTOPHER GROSS'S MIXED GRILL** PAGE 265

marsanne

mahr-*san*

With siblings there are always comparisons: Bobby is smarter than Johnny, and a better athlete as well. Such is the relationship between Marsanne and its sibling, Roussanne: Marsanne is Johnny. Of the two grapes, Marsanne is produced in greater quantity, in large part because of its more consistent yields and more predictable vinification. However, it's less aromatic than Roussanne and often produces wines that are big in alcohol but short on complexity. This reality leads many wine drinkers to declare that it's the underachiever. Nevertheless, well-made Marsanne is a real treat and can be wonderful with food.

Alternative Names Avilleran, Grosse Roussette (France), Ermitage Blanc, Hermitage (Switzerland)

Styles Full-bodied dry white, sparkling, medium-full-bodied dessert white (not widely available)

Sometimes Blended With Clairette, Rolle, Roussanne, Syrah, Viognier (France), Grenache Blanc, Roussanne, Viognier (Australia, U.S.A.)

Flavor Lexicon

DRY *Fruit:* Melon, orange, pear, ripe lemon, tangerine, tropical fruit (dragon fruit, guava, papaya) ▪ *Floral:* Wildflower ▪ *Wood:* Almond, spice ▪ *Other:* Honey

SWEET *Fruit:* Dried apricot, raisin ▪ *Floral:* Herbs ▪ *Wood:* Caramel, marzipan, vanilla

Similar Sips Mild, full-bodied Chardonnay, lighter-flavored Viognier

Where It's Grown Australia (Victoria), France (Languedoc-Roussillon, Rhône Valley), Switzerland, U.S.A. (California: Southern Central Coast, Napa County, Sierra Foothills [Amador County])

This grape, which is native to France and likely specific to the northern Rhône Valley (the town of Marsanne sits near the city of Montelimar), produces very rich, waxy-textured wines that, at their best, can explode with flavors ranging from white flowers to soft tropical fruit (guava, dragon fruit), sweet spice, and raw nuts. Alas, it's often overcropped and made into wines with a generic white-fruit character and an obvious, whopping kick of alcohol. In the northern Rhône, where it's at its best, it is combined with Roussanne to constitute up to 20 percent of the blend in red Hermitage, where it helps hold and fix the Syrah color and add floral components and roundness; but it is more often found, again blended with Roussanne, in white wines from St.-Joseph, Crozes-Hermitage and, relatively rarely, Hermitage. A little farther south in the Rhône Valley, Marsanne is a key component in St.-Péray, as both a still and a sparkling wine. In the southern Rhone Valley, it's allowed in the basic Côtes du Rhône white wines but is not permitted in Châteauneuf-du-Pape (five other white-wine grapes are permitted, including Roussanne). Here it's usually blended and makes enjoyable wines with flavors less pronounced but similar to those from the north. More and more Marsanne is being planted in Languedoc-Roussillon in southwestern France, where it is blended with Roussanne, Viognier, and Rolle, as in the Côtes du Rhône.

In the Valais canton of Switzerland, where it is called Ermitage, Marsanne produces light, dry wines and complex sweet wines. Sadly, we see very little of either in the United States. Australia is said to possess some of the world's oldest Marsanne vineyards, notably in the Goulburn Valley in Victoria, where the wines are distinctively citric and (in my opinion, which is the minority) quick to age.

Led spiritually by Randall Grahm and practically by other producers, including Alban and Tablas Creek, the California Rhône-wine movement has been advocating this variety for several years. The resulting wines share the grape's tendency toward flab and need to be well managed; when they are, they achieve a combination of beeswax, white flowers, and tropical fruit.

Vintner's Choices Aged vs. not aged, balanced vs. high yield, dry vs. sweet, oak vs. no oak, single variety vs. blended, sparkling vs. still

Marsanne's strength is also its Achilles heel. Grape growers love vines that crop vigorously and consistently. For this reason, Marsanne is a staple in the Rhône Valley and the Southwest. But high production can lead to dilute flavors and lower acidity, and the result is wines for which the most complimentary terms you can use are *Rubenesque* or *zaftig,* but which are likely to be flabby and banal. Today, with many producers managing yields more carefully, the resulting wines are better balanced and structured. Put Marsanne on a treadmill, make it lose some weight, and it can perform quite well!

Except for a few efforts in Australia and California, most Marsanne wines are actually blends. Marsanne's fleshiness and texture are always welcomed, but its flavor profile is often uninspiring. More often than not this deficiency is remedied by adding Roussanne to the blend, though other grapes, like the Viognier, which is employed both in France's Southwest and in California, are also included to add pop.

Rarely do we speak of oak and Marsanne in the same sentence. Old, large vats are sometimes used, but they serve as vessels for the wine rather than for adding wood notes. The gradual oxidation that results from using wood vats can add a nutty nuance to the wine, but because this grape has an inherent tendency to oxidize, the process needs to be carefully managed. New oak overwhelms this grape, which can already be bland.

In the middle Rhône, St.-Péray produces tasty, Champagne-styled sparkling wines, of which Marsanne is one component. These wines tend to be slightly fuller in body than your typical sparkling wine and, though not ultra-complex, are often very enjoyable. Finally, in Switzerland dessert wines are made from Marsanne, which, at their best, are full of notes of light green herbs, apricots, vanilla, and golden raisins.

PAIRING WITH FOOD

Most of the Marsanne available in the United States is dry, so I focus on pairings with that style here. The dessert wines can be treated much like late-harvest Sémillons, and the sparkling wines share much in common with other dry bubblies, though the higher alcohol level of the St.-Péray offerings should be taken into account, especially if you're preparing spicy foods.

Food pairings need to accommodate Marsanne's smooth texture and chubbiness. Sauces that contain cream, butter, or reductions of stock are very successful with a Marsanne-based blend, as they mimic the character of the wine. Likewise, richer ingredients like duck, scallops, lobster, and even roasted root vegetables are seamless matches. A classic local dish like *brandade*, the Provençal preparation of puréed salt cod and potatoes, is an exceptionally good match; the wine can handle the cod's salt quotient without coming off as too alcoholic. (You can hedge your bets by selecting a less alcoholic example of the wine.) Seafood lasagna or a mild Thai coconut curry are also good companions.

Because Marsanne tends to be alcoholic to begin with, too much spicy heat can make it taste and feel like grappa if you're not careful. Use red pepper flakes and chiles sparingly, and opt for examples with alcohol levels closer to 13 percent than 14.5 percent. A spicy Szechuan dish and Marsanne could result in a gastronomic combustion and a run for the Rolaids.

A little bit of bottle age can bring out a distinctly nutty tone in most Marsanne and Marsanne-based wines. Play this up by using nuts as an accent in the food, as in chicken with hazelnuts, cream, and sweet spices or macadamia-crusted fish. And don't overlook the sweet-citrus nature of this variety. Adding a little orange or tangerine zest is a natural bridge for this wine, whether you're making a risotto, a marinade, or even the crust for a savory tart, which can work nicely with many Marsanne-based wines.

Marsanne goes well with:

- Most seafood—the richer the better. From a mild Cajun crayfish étouffée to simply broiled lobster, these dishes pair well with the rich texture of Marsanne without the flavors fighting too hard. With aged wines, think about richer cooking or saucing techniques that pick up on the nutty character of the wine—a fish *en croûte* (wrapped in pastry) or scallops in a brown-butter sauce, topped with toasted breadcrumbs.
- Many rich first courses. I could drink a bottle of Marsanne with a plate of hamachi sashimi almost any day of the week. The smooth and creamy texture and lightly nutty flavor of my favorite sushi fish is magic with Marsanne. A mild cheese soufflé or a cream of potato soup also works. Rich but mild is the key here.
- Pastas and risottos with creamy sauce. As pasta and rice are both blank canvases onto which we paint flavors, they are perfect backdrops to many Marsanne-based wines. A risotto of shrimp, peas, and lots of butter is lovely, as is a bowl of spaghetti served with chicken, lemon zest, olives, and a sauce of reduced chicken stock.
- Rich vegetables. I adore Marsanne (and Roussanne too) with most squash and squash-based dishes. A plate of butternut-squash ravioli and a bowl of pumpkin soup are great examples of dishes that pair well. And with sautéed plantains—yum!
- Exotically spiced dishes. Marsanne's ripe-fruit character is a reasonably neutral backdrop; like many other aromatic white wines, it pairs nicely with curry powder, cinnamon, cumin, and mace, among other spices.

Marsanne isn't good with:

- Very spicy dishes. Hot spices increase your perception of alcohol, and Marsanne tends to be high in alcohol. Use a soft touch with your hot salsa, favorite chile sauce, or shaker of red pepper flakes. Don't attempt to pair hot Asian cuisine with a rich Marsanne blend unless you enjoy heartburn.
- Lighter preparations. Given the full-bodied nature of this wine, it's easy to squash and lose simple dishes behind its girth. It's gentle, but still a giant.
- Very smoky foods. Marsanne can be overwhelmed by mesquite-grilled meats, slowly smoked chicken, or a smoked-salmon terrine. The wine may still work, but it will lose any nuance of harmony with the dish.
- Very sharp dishes. This warning may seem counterintuitive, as you might expect the dish's acid to fill in the gaps in the wine, but it usually just takes out what's left. Avoid sweet and sour treatments, acidic sauces and ingredients (vinaigrettes, eggplant, zucchini), and even ceviche, unless you have a reasonably tart example of the wine.

- Artichokes, asparagus, and other problem children. The low acidity of Marsanne means it can't compete with these difficult vegetables. Try a glass of white St.-Joseph with a steamed artichoke and you'll see what I mean.

THE CHEESE PLATE

SEMI-SOFT	Havarti (Denmark, France), tetilla (Spain)—dry
SOFT-RIPENED	Brillat-Savarin (France), Camembert (France)—dry
SEMI-HARD	Emmentaler (Switzerland), tomme de Savoie (France)—dry
HARD	Aged Asiago (Italy), aged white Cheddar (U.S.A., U.K.)—sparkling
WASHED-RIND	Munster (France), Serra (Portugal)—dry

marsanne | VEAL CHOPS WITH ALIGOT

PHILIPPE JEANTY   Bistro Jeanty, Yountville, California

Makes 4 main-course servings

VEAL CHOPS
4 veal chops, 1 inch thick (see note)
¾ cup olive oil
4 fresh sage sprigs
4 fresh thyme sprigs
4 cloves garlic, crushed
Salt and freshly ground black pepper
2 tablespoons unsalted butter

ALIGOT
2 cups mashed cooked potatoes (see note)
1 cup grated Cantal or *tomme* cheese
¼ cup Marsanne or other dry white wine
½ clove garlic, finely chopped

Place the veal chops in a shallow glass baking dish. Coat them well on both sides with ½ cup of the olive oil. Press a sage and a thyme sprig and a garlic clove into each chop. Cover and marinate overnight in the refrigerator.

Preheat the oven to 350°F. Remove the chops from the refrigerator, and remove the garlic and herbs and discard. Season the chops on both sides with salt and pepper.

In an ovenproof, nonstick skillet large enough to accommodate the chops without crowding, heat the remaining ¼ cup olive oil over medium heat. When the oil is hot, place the chops in the pan and add the butter. Cook the chops, turning once, until golden brown on both sides, about 3 minutes on each side. Transfer the pan to the oven and roast for about 10 minutes for medium. Transfer the chops to a rack, tent loosely with aluminum foil, and let rest for a few minutes before serving.

When you put the chops in the skillet, begin making the *aligot*. Place the potatoes in a heavy saucepan over medium-low heat. Add the cheese and stir with a wooden spoon until the cheese melts and potatoes are the consistency of cheese fondue, about 5 minutes if the potatoes were warm when they were added to the pan, or 10 to 15 minutes if they were cold.

Add the wine and garlic and cook, stirring, until the potatoes have a good elasticity, a few minutes longer.

Divide the potatoes evenly among 4 warmed plates. Place the chops atop the potatoes and serve at once.

NOTE Traditionally, the potatoes for this fonduelike preparation from the Auvergne are cooked in butter, but the home cook can use a favorite mashed potatoes recipe, made with Kennebec or russet potatoes, and yield an excellent result. Be sure the potatoes are mashed perfectly smooth for this dish. You can adjust the amount of cheese, increasing or decreasing it depending on your taste. Also, you can substitute 1-inch-thick pork chops for the veal chops. You can dress up the veal or pork version of the dish by topping the chops with a spoonful of sautéed fresh porcini, morels, and shiitakes.

PHILIPPE: *This dish is unusual in that you use white wine as the liquid in the mashed potatoes. If you like cheese fondue, you will love this dish. It is rich and bright in flavor and goes well with Marsanne. We sometimes serve these potatoes at Bistro Jeanty with a porcini-rubbed flatiron steak—yummy!*

EVAN: *Philippe is a consummate pro and the chef's chef. I can't tell you how many of my culinary friends, after several days of wining and dining in the Napa Valley, always ask to finish up at Bistro Jeanty for a classic, comforting meal. Nobody does that as well as he does. Marsanne is all about café and bistro food for me, so this was an ideal and obvious match.*

This recipe is a classic, and classic is good. These potatoes are about as perfect a vehicle for showing off Marsanne as you can get. Like the wine, they have rich texture, but they don't overwhelm. The natural acidity of the wine used in the dish is balanced, regardless of what type of wine you cook with, and the cheese is mild enough not to steal the stage. The veal is a great match for the wine as well, rich and flavorful but not overpowering. I bet you'll cook this combination again and again.

RECOMMENDED PRODUCERS

EVERYDAY	PREMIUM	PREMIUM
Cline Sonoma County, California	Domaine Bernard Gripa Rhône Valley, France [D, Sp]	Qupé Southern Central Coast, California
Mas Carlot Languedoc, France	Domaine Chèze Rhône Valley, France	Rosenblum Cellars Sonoma County, California
Rutherglen Estates Victoria, Australia	J.C. Cellars Sonoma County, California	Stevenot Winery Calaveras, California
	Krupp Brothers Napa Valley, California	Tahbilk Victoria, Australia
		Yves Cuilleron Rhône Valley, France [D, Sp]

D = Dry   Sp = Sparkling

muscat

muhs-kat | *muhs*-kuht

Muscat is the most difficult variety to write about in this book. Given the range, the sheer number of selections, and the diversity of wine styles, it deserves a book of its own. The Muscat family reminds me of *My Big Fat Greek Wedding*—a gathering of hundreds of distinctive characters. The bride's family, the Muscat Blanc à Petits Grains grape, is Greek in origin, as well as traditional, noble, social, and gregarious. The groom's family, the Muscat of Alexandria grape, is foreign (from Egypt), also numerous, but less extroverted than the future in-laws. Together they make up a large, diverse, and flavorful clan. Muscat is so tangy, distinctive, and easy to enjoy that it's no wonder it's found in every country!

Alternative Names

Petits Grains: Frontignac, Muscat d'Alsace, Muscat de Beaumes de Venise, Muscat Frontignan (France); Brown Muscat, Frontignan (Australia); Goldmuskateller, Moscato Bianco, Moscato Giallo, Moscato Rosa, Rosenmuskateller (Italy); Moscatel de Grano Menudo, Moscatel Menudo Blanco, Moscatel Dorado (Spain); Muskadel (South Africa), Moscatel Branco (Portugal); Muscat Blanc, Muscat Canelli, Muscat Frontignan, White Muscat (U.S.A.)

Alexandria: Chasselas Musqué, Muscat Romain (France); Lexia, Muscatel, Muscat Gordo Blanco (Australia); Hanepoot (South Africa); Zibibbo (Italy); Moscatel, Moscatel de Málaga, Moscatel Gordo Blanco, Moscatel Romans (Spain); Moscatel de Setúbal (Portugal); Moscatel de Alejandria (Chile)

Ottonel: Muskotály (Hungary); Muscadel Ottonel (South Africa)

Styles Medium- to medium-full-bodied dry white, medium-full-bodied off-dry white, light- to medium-bodied slightly sparkling off-dry white, light- to medium-bodied off-dry to sweet sparkling, full-bodied late-harvest sweet, full-bodied fortified sweet

Sometimes Blended With Almost always unblended, except in southwestern France, where Muscat Blanc à Petits Grains and Muscat of Alexandria are blended together and with other grapes (mostly Grenache Blanc), and in Jerez and Málaga in Spain, where it is sometimes blended with Pedro Ximénez

Flavor Lexicon

DRY	*Fruit:* Green apple, unripe apricot, yellow apple ▪ *Floral:* Dried flower blossom ▪ *Earth:* Mineral ▪ *Wood:* Spice
SPARKLING	*Fruit:* Fresh grapes, lychee, melon, nectarine, peach, tropical fruit (guava, mango, jackfruit, rambutan) ▪ *Floral:* Flower blossoms
LATE-HARVEST	*Fruit:* Candied citrus ▪ *Floral:* Chamomile, fresh ginger, white tea leaf ▪ *Other:* Honey, lemon drops
FORTIFIED	*Fruit:* Candied citrus peel, prunes, raisins ▪ *Wood:* Butterscotch, caramel ▪ *Other:* Maple syrup

Similar Sips Ranges stylistically from a tangy late-harvest Riesling with a musky edge to an off-dry Champagne to a raisiny tawny port

Where It's Grown

Petits Grains: Australia (South Australia: Barossa Valley; Victoria: Rutherglen), France (Languedoc-Roussillon: Banyuls, Maury, Rivesaltes; Rhône Valley: Beaumes de Venise, Die), Greece (Aegean: Samos; Ionian Islands: Cephalonia; Peloponnese: Patras), Italy (Piedmont: Asti; Trentino–Alto Adige), U.S.A. (California: multiple appellations)

Alexandria: Australia, Chile, France (Languedoc-Roussillon: Muscat de Lunel, Muscat de St.-Jean-de-Minervois, Rivesaltes), Greece (Aegean: Limnos), Italy (Sicily: Moscato di Pantelleria), Portugal (Setúbal), South Africa, Spain (Alicante, Jerez, Málaga, Valencia)

Ottonel: Austria (Burgenland, Wachau), France (Alsace), Hungary, Romania (Transylvania)

It's more logical to explore each grape in the family individually rather than survey all plantings by country. Muscat Blanc à Petits Grains has its roots in Greece, and you would still be hard-pressed to find nobler examples of this grape and its wines than those from Greece. The wines are at their best in the Aegean appellation of Samos, where they explode with intense pineapple, apricot, and cinnamon flavors and are sweet but not cloying. The remaining Greek wines made from Petits Grains come from Patras and Cephalonia, where they are often concentrated by being made with sun-dried grapes. They are best enjoyed young and fresh, when they are explosively spicy. Redolent with flavors of raisins, citrus peel, dried flowers, and caramel, the examples from Cephalonia and Patras are less intense and more minerally than those from Samos.

In Southwest France, the grape is responsible for the great *vins doux naturels* (VDNs) that dominate the Roussillon region. The wines of Banyuls, Rivesaltes, and Maury, among others, are blends of two types of Muscat (Petits Grains and Alexandria) with Grenache Blanc. They make extraordinary wines that are different in style from but just as enjoyable as the famous fortified red wines from these regions, which are based on Carignan. However, most Muscat wines here are late-harvest styles, like those from Greece; they are meant to be enjoyed fresh, and they carry the varietal name on the label. Muscat de Rivesaltes and Muscat de St.-Jean-de-Minervois are scented with citrus and floral sweetness and perfectly balanced. In the Rhône Valley, Muscat de Beaumes de Venise is a superb expression of the Petits Grains selection and explodes on the palate with honeyed tangerine, spicy pear, and lychee, usually with a nuttiness on the finish. Farther north, in Die, Petits Grains is often blended with Clairette in the local sparkling wines.

Most of the world knows the Petits Grains grape (Moscato Bianco) through Italy's massive production of Piedmontese sparkling and semi-sparkling wines, Asti Spumante and Moscato d'Asti. These delightful wines are often criticized for their overt grapey flavors and not considered serious wines. The best have splendid tropical flavor and can be marvelous with the right desserts. If you're looking for a substitute for Champagne, don't pick these wines; but if you want a wine to match with summer's bounty of fruit, look no further. In the Alto Adige, the grape is vinified both dry and off-dry.

California's efforts have been inconsistent, though the recent examples from wineries in the coastal regions are exciting, particularly from the Central Coast, Napa Valley, Sonoma, and parts of the Anderson Valley.

Any conversation about Petits Grains must include a few words on Australia. The fabled liqueur Muscats of Victoria's Rutherglen are sensational. Usually labeled as being made of Brown Muscat, they are treated somewhat like sherry to maximize their complexity. Differently aged wines from a system of different barrels are carefully blended. The wines in the Barossa, which are in the traditional late-harvest style, tend to be fresher and grapier in their flavor profile.

Although Muscat of Alexandria has its roots in Egypt, it's rarely seen anywhere in that country today. Its plantings worldwide dwarf those of the more interesting Petits Grains, and much of the production is used not for wine but for raisins, table grapes, and grape concentrate. Wines from this grape, although important, lack the complexity of those made from Petits Grains and tend to be simple, sweet, and grapey. In France, it's used as a blending grape with Petits Grains. In Italy, the grape, known as Zibibbo, is grown in Sicily and its offshore islands, specifically Pantelleria, where the wines are made in a *passito* fashion and brim with maple syrup, candied ginger, and golden raisins. Zibibbo is also made into a dry table wine and plays a role in the production of Marsala.

This grape is perhaps most important in Spain. Muscat of Alexandria is planted in Alicante in Valencia and other regions for various uses but is most significant in Jerez for Muscat sherries and in Málaga for its celebrated Moscatel de Málaga. These wines can be excellent, especially when pure and not blended with Pedro Ximénez (or PX): they are complex and not too sugary. The Setúbal region of Portugal produces Muscat de Alexandria (here called Moscatel de Setúbal) as a VDN, resulting in wines that ooze with ripe candied orange, chamomile, and golden raisins. In the United States, this grape is most often grown for table fruit and grape concentrate. In Australia, most of the ample plantings of Muscat of Alexandria meet a similar fate, though many inexpensive, blended box wines incorporate this grape. In Chile and in South Africa (where it goes under the name of Hanepoot), it plays a similar blending role.

Muscat Ottonel is perhaps the least known of the Muscat family. Developed by a French vine grower in the 1800s, it is a cross of Chasselas with a clone of Loire Valley Muscat. It's not known for its complexity or any real classic Muscat personality: perhaps its main virtue is that it thrives in cooler weather, which explains why so much of it is grown in Alsace. It makes mostly dry wines, though it is also used in late-harvest and dessert wines. In Austria, Ottonel is widely planted and makes some excellent wines (mostly sweet); it's also found in Hungary and Romania, where again it produces wines ranging from dry to sweet.

I can't end this section without a tip of the hat to a couple of more distant relatives of the Muscat family: Orange and Black Muscat. Orange Muscat is not really Muscat per se, but it exhibits some similar traits. It is found in California and Italy (where it's known as Moscato Fior d'Arancio) and produces, as you might expect, orange-tasting Muscat-ish wine. Black Muscat, also known as Muscat Hamburg or Black Hamburg, is found in California and throughout Europe, mainly as a table grape.

Vintner's Choices Choice of clone or selection, dry vs. off-dry vs. sweet, fortified vs. not fortified, oak vs. no oak, still vs. sparkling or *frizzante*, vintage vs. age-blended

Lots of choices must be made in producing wine from this big family of grapes. Long before the first grapes are harvested, the winemaker has to choose which part of the family to marry into! In some places the choice is mandated by tradition and history, in concert with laws governing production and appellations, but it also depends on growing conditions and the desired style and complexity of the wine. You couldn't make the extraordinary wines of Beaumes de Venise, Asti, or Samos, for example, with the Muscat of Alexandria grape. A table wine made from Petits Grains might be interesting, but the Muscat wines of Alsace, made from the Ottonel selection of which the Alsatians are proud, wouldn't be the same vinified from Petits Grains. Blending the different strains, as is done in the fabled VDNs of Roussillon in France, is the stuff of family feuds.

Around the world, the Petits Grains and Alexandria selections are made exclusively into sweeter, dessert-style wines, except in Greece, where some table wines are made from both. Muscat Ottonel is most frequently made into dry table wine—in Alsace, Austria, and Central Europe. It can be made off-dry (as with the *vendage tardive,* or VT, wines in Alsace) or sweet (like the *selections de grains nobles,* or SGNs, in Alsace, and the *Beerenauslese* and *Trockenbeerenauslese* dessert wines in Austria and Hungary).

The sparkling Muscat-based wines of Italy's Piedmont, Asti Spumante and Moscato d'Asti, can be a real pleasure to drink and don't deserve the scorn they elicit from many wine snobs.

When well made, they explode with flavors of lychee and white peach. The slightly less fizzy Moscato d'Asti may be the world's greatest picnic wine.

The elders of the family, the fortified VDNs, are unique in the world of wine, idiosyncratic but delightful. They can be a bit heady (alcoholic) and too intense for some people's tastes; you have to try for yourself. I love Beaumes de Venise, which for me represents the quintessence of the Petits Grains grape, though some examples from Samos and Patras are equally distinctive. Among the VDNs made from Muscat of Alexandria, my favorite is Moscatel de Setúbal. Muscat sherries from Spain differ from VDNs: they are also fortified, but not until the winemaking process is complete. Also rather than being dated by vintage, as most wines are, they are crafted by fractional blending of wines of different ages, along the lines of aged Scotch or tawny port. Liqueur Muscats from Australia's Victoria are made in a hybrid manner, starting off as VDNs but then undergoing long barrel aging and fractional blending.

Decisions about wood are significant. Many styles of Muscat, from Asti Spumante to the fresh Muscats of Roussillon and Alsace, never see any wood. Others spend ample time in wood, including the liqueur Muscats, Muscat sherries, and both dry and sweet examples from Greece. These decisions are driven by location, tradition, and desired result, and the winemaker always faces a challenge in balancing the wood with the inherently sweet and delicious character of the Muscat grape.

PAIRING WITH FOOD

The different styles of Muscat demand different approaches to pairing with food.

DRY TABLE WINES

My approach with these wines is a hybrid of the approaches I'd take with Grüner Veltliner and Riesling. The acidity of most dry Muscats is on the sharp side. That promises synergy with Asian food as well as rich white meats, fowl, and charcuterie. Pairing local wines with local foods—Ottonel wines with the traditional foods of Alsace and Austria—works brilliantly. And, as you'd expect, many fish and shellfish dishes shine.

SPARKLING WINES

Asti Spumante and Moscato d'Asti are great with food. Most of us think first of pairing them with desserts. Simple preparations of stone fruit or tree fruit (such as poached pears), served with or without a light sauce, are delightful with sweet sparkling wines. Lighter mousse- or yogurt-based desserts (Greek yogurt drizzled with honey and nuts—scrumptious!) can also pair well with these wines, especially if accompanied with fresh fruit. And going naked—serving perfectly ripe, unadorned fresh fruit (peaches, nectarines, cherries, and berries) is a great option. But these wines can also work with appetizers and main courses: they offer a savory foil to aromatic levels of heat, as in tandoori shrimp.

Here, too, Muscat's fresh and lively personality calls out for white stone fruit—peaches, apricots, and nectarines. With botrytized wines, the dessert can include honey, vanilla, and more texture. The rich texture of a custard or mousse can handle richer wines, including wood-aged examples. Though I am not a huge fan of white chocolate, it pairs very well with this genre of Muscat wines.

FORTIFIED WINES

High in body and alcohol, these interpretations can overwhelm lighter desserts. Recipes based on reconstituted dried fruit (dried apricots poached in wine, or a tea-leaf-scented compote of dried apples, pears, and prunes) work well. Nut- and caramel-based desserts pair nicely with aged fortified wines (especially Muscat sherry and Málaga) and with many liqueur Muscats from Australia. Accenting with a little chocolate (bitter is best unless the wine is very sweet) helps to bring out the wine's rainbow of flavors.

PAIRING POINTERS

Muscat goes well with:

DRY TABLE WINES

- Asian-edged dishes, especially vegetables, chicken, fish, or shellfish. Try dry Muscats with a stir-fry of chicken, cashews, and crunchy vegetables, or deep-fried prawns with ginger and garlic. A bit of sweetness—from peanut, hoisin, or sweet soy sauce—pairs nicely without making the wine seem sour.
- Rich white meats and poultry. One of my favorite pairings with dry Alsace Muscat is classic French *blanquette de veau*. A simple roast duck served with the starch and vegetables of your choice is another great option.
- Lots of cheeses. Nominally dry Muscats can often border on the sweet (as with the *vendage tardive* style). These are among the most versatile of wines with a large range of cheeses.

SPARKLING WINES

- Fresh summer fruit. At a picnic, a backyard barbecue, or the kitchen table, a glass of fizzy Muscat with grilled peaches or prosciutto and melon is sublime.
- Light mousses and gelées: A buttermilk tart with berries and a bowl of whipped, vanilla-scented mascarpone cheese with a drizzle of berry purée are two excellent ways to show off a sparkling Muscat. Floating a few strawberries in a slightly sweet fruit gelatin is perfect with a Moscato d'Asti.
- Tropical fruit. Muscat has a natural affinity for exotic tropical fruit, particularly mango, lychee, and rambutan. Serving those fruits with Asian black sticky rice is a great match with Asti Spumante, or you can pair them with a *panna cotta* or light custard.

- Fresh fruit and cream. The renowned wine-and-food pairing pro Fiona Beckett is a staunch proponent of strawberries and cream served with Muscat de Beaumes de Venise, and indeed the wine and food create a wonderful synergy. If you don't want a wine quite as rich and heady, this dessert is equally lovely with a Muscat de Lunel or Muscat de Rivesaltes.
- Cheesecake. I've played with this pairing quite a bit, and with the exception of dense chocolate cheesecakes, it is the bomb! Dense New York–style cheesecake works well, because you can change the accompanying sauces or serve it on its own and make lots of people happy. Try some of the more edgy flavors—from pumpkin to lemon ricotta to *dulce de leche*—for a little daring with your pairing.
- Fruit crisps and cobblers. These desserts provide a nice balance between the fruit flavors and the added complexity of the nuts, brown sugar, oats, and other ingredients in the toppings. Peaches are my favorite, but many fruits work well.

FORTIFIED WINES

- Nuts, caramel, and a nuance of chocolate. Many of these wines have some degree of toasted- and roasted-nut character and a more pronounced toffee or caramel character. Rich tortes that include those ingredients are generally quite successful matches, and these wines can also stand up to some chocolate. So a quick run to Godiva, See's, or Ghirardelli is in order!
- Rich and flavorful desserts. Serve a liqueur Muscat with butterscotch pudding or sautéed bananas drizzled with warm caramel sauce and toasted almonds for a truly decadent dessert course.
- Blue cheeses, from the mild to the pungent. Pairing local wines with local cheeses works well here: Moscato di Pantelleria with Gorgonzola, Muscat sherry and Málaga with Spanish Cabrales, and Beaumes de Venise with a bleu d'Auvergne.

Muscat isn't good with:

DRY TABLE WINES

- Sweet foods. Any savory dish with a distinctively sweet component will kick the stuffing out of the wine and compromise your enjoyment.
- Overly spicy dishes: A little heat is nice to set off this wine's fruit, especially if the wine verges on the sweet anyway, but if the dish is too hot, the wine's charm will be destroyed. Avoid spicy salsas and hot sauces unless the wine is borderline sweet; even then, be careful.
- Rich red meats. While these wines pair beautifully with pork and veal, they have a far more difficult time with lamb loins and rib-eye steaks.

SPARKLING WINES

- Many savory items. Though the drier versions can pair well with combinations of salt and sweet (such as prosciutto and melon), most lean toward the sweet and taste out of place when matched with entrée dishes that have no sweetness at all.

- Heavy desserts. Though their effervescence can refresh the palate and cut richness, these wines are easily trampled by dense buttercreams and thick custards.
- Chocolate. Ouch. You might get away with fresh fruit served with a tiny accent of chocolate.

LATE-HARVEST WINES

- Very light desserts. The wine's rich character and assertive personality can dominate lighter and simpler desserts. They won't taste bad; they'll just be weighed down.
- Many savory dishes. Though you can find some good matches if you work hard, most often pairing these wines with entrée dishes is challenging.
- Simple, fresh fruit. This pairing can sometimes work: some of the fresher-tasting wines can mirror the flavors of fresh fruit wonderfully. Others, especially those that have been aged in wood, need more complex treatments of fruit—tarts, compotes, cobblers, clafoutis, and similar dishes.

FORTIFIED WINES

- Many desserts. This category of wines requires thoughtful pairing with sweet dishes. Because the wines tend to be alcoholic, fiery, and intense, they can dominate or clash with many desserts. I'd avoid fresh fruits, simple tarts, and basic poached fruit, for example. I often drink these types of wines by themselves or enjoy them with good conversation and a token cookie or two, or a plate of cheese.
- Most savory dishes. I'm still looking for a reliable pairing.

THE CHEESE PLATE

FRESH	Mascarpone (Italy, U.S.A.), ricotta (Italy, U.S.A.)—sparkling
SEMI-SOFT	Slightly aged chèvre (many countries), teleme (U.S.A.)—dry
SOFT-RIPENED	Brillat-Savarin (France), Camembert (France, U.S.A.)—dry, off-dry, late-harvest
SEMI-HARD	Gruyère (France), raclette (Switzerland)—dry, off-dry, late-harvest
HARD	Aged Cheddar (England, U.S.A.), Piave (Italy)—sparkling, fortified
BLUE	Bleu d'Auvergne (France), Cabrales (Spain), Gorgonzola dolcelatte (Italy), Maytag (U.S.A.), Roquefort (France)—late harvest, fortified
WASHED-RIND	Époisses (France), Munster (France), Serra (Portugal)—off-dry, late-harvest; Taleggio (Italy)—dry, off-dry, late-harvest

muscat | ALMOND CAKE WITH A WARM
RED BERRY–VANILLA COMPOTE

EMILY LUCHETTI   Farallon and Waterbar, San Francisco, Nick's Cove, Marshall, California

Makes 8 servings

ALMOND CAKE

1¼ cups all-purpose flour
½ teaspoon baking powder
⅛ teaspoon kosher salt
½ cup plus 2 tablespoons unsalted butter, at room temperature
5 ounces almond paste, at room temperature
¾ cup sugar
3 large eggs
1 teaspoon pure vanilla extract

RED BERRY–VANILLA COMPOTE

½ cup fresh orange juice
1 teaspoon fresh lemon juice
1 tablespoon sugar, or as needed
Large pinch of kosher salt
1 vanilla bean, halved lengthwise
4 tablespoons unsalted butter, at room temperature
1 pint strawberries, hulled and quartered if small
   or cut into eighths if large
1 pint raspberries

To make the cake, preheat the oven to 350°F. Butter a 9-inch round cake pan and line the bottom with parchment paper.

Sift together the flour, baking powder, and salt onto a piece of parchment paper or into a bowl. Set aside.

Using an electric mixer on medium speed, beat together the butter and almond paste until smooth and malleable, about 1 minute. Add the sugar and beat until smooth, 2 to 3 minutes. Add the eggs, one at a time, mixing well after each addition. Stir in the vanilla extract. On low speed, add the dry ingredients and beat until combined. Transfer the batter to the prepared pan and smooth the top.

Bake until a skewer inserted into the center comes out clean, about 35 minutes. Let cool in the pan on a wire rack to room temperature. Run a thin-bladed knife along the inside edge of the pan to loosen the cake sides. Invert a large plate on top of the pan and invert the plate and pan together. Lift off the pan and carefully peel off the parchment paper. Transfer the cake, top side up, to a serving plate and set aside.

To make the compote, in a large sauté pan, combine the orange and lemon juices, 1 tablespoon sugar, and salt. Using a knife tip, scrape the seeds from the vanilla bean halves into the pan. Place over medium-high heat and heat, stirring occasionally, for 1 minute. Add the butter and heat until the butter melts, about 30 seconds. Add the strawberries and raspberries and heat, stirring gently, just until heated through, about 1 minute. Taste for sweetness and add a little more sugar, if necessary. Do not overcook or the berries will break apart.

Cut the cake into wedges and place on individual plates. Add a spoonful of the warm compote to each wedge and serve.

EMILY: *Trying to create a dish that bridges the wide range of Muscat-based wines is hard. In this recipe, the aromatic and flowery qualities of Muscat complement the berry compote and are also enhanced by the almond flavor in the cake.*

EVAN: *Emily is one of my favorite people, and it just so happens that she's one of America's most accomplished pastry chefs. As a chef who thinks about pastry as carefully as I do about the wines that go with pastry, she has worked at many, many events with me over the years, and we know each other's approaches and palates well. (Plus we share the same birthday, so we're obviously culinary soulmates.)*

Given the breadth, range, and sheer volume of options available with the Muscat grape, this may be one of the most difficult pairings in the book. Emily nailed it with a dish that pairs with all styles except the driest examples. The almond cake adds a texture and richness that is dense enough for the VDN and fortified styles but light enough for late-harvest interpretations. The inclusion of berries is a good call, as their higher acidity and fresh, bold flavors can work with sparkling wines, yet they have enough sweetness to show off many styles, even a Black Muscat such as Quady Winery's Elysium, from California. Finally, the texture of the compote adds elements that will work with thicker styles of wine, especially if you add (as I did while testing the recipe) a dollop of whipped cream.

RECOMMENDED PRODUCERS

EVERYDAY	PREMIUM	SPLURGE
Bonny Doon Ca' del Solo Santa Cruz, California [O]	Chambers Victoria, Australia [Sw]	Jorge Ordóñez and Co. Andalucía, Spain [Sw]
Bottega "Petalo" Veneto, Italy [Sp, Sw]	Coppo Asti, Italy [Sp]	Klein Constantia Coastal Region, South Africa [Sw]
Martin & Weyrich Southern Central Coast, California [Sp]	Domaine Ostertag Alsace, France [O]	
Muscat de St.-Jean-de-Minervois Vignerons du Val d'Orbieu Languedoc, France [Sw]	Marcel Deiss Alsace, France [D]	
Terre di Orazio Basilicata, Italy [Sw]	Paul Jaboulet Rhône Valley, France [Sw]	

D = Dry   O = Off-Dry   Sp = Sparkling   Sw = Sweet

pinot blanc

pee-noh *blahn* | *pee*-noh *blahngk*

When I think about Pinot Blanc I am reminded of the classic TV show *What's My Line?* and its trademark line, "Will the real X please stand up?" It's very difficult to identify or characterize Pinot Blanc, which goes under many aliases in different parts of the world. Although it's often referred to as "poor man's Chardonnay," Pinot Blanc in fact has little in common with Chardonnay. The bottles labeled Pinot Blanc in France's Alsace are usually blends consisting of as much of the local Auxerrois grape as of Pinot Blanc. And most of what is bottled in California as Pinot Blanc is in fact a completely different grape, Melon de Bourgogne, the variety that gives us France's Muscadet. However, "real" Pinot Blanc is a wonderfully food-friendly, tasty wine worthy of shelf space in any epicure's refrigerator.

Alternative Names Clevner, Klevner (France); Klevner, Weissburgunder, Weisser Arbst, Weisser Ruländer (Germany); Klevner, Weissburgunder (Austria); Borgogna Bianco, Chasselas Dorato, Pinot Bianco (Italy); Féherburgundi (Hungary); Roučí Bílé, Rulandské Bílé (Czech Republic, Slovakia)

Styles Light- to medium-full-bodied dry white, medium-bodied sparkling, late harvest medium- to medium-full-bodied dessert and ice wines

Sometimes Blended With Auxerrois, other local grapes (France), Welchsriesling (Austria), Chardonnay (U.S.A.)

Flavor Lexicon *Vegetable:* Raw almond ▪ *Floral:* Citrus (lemon, yellow grapefruit), green apple, melon, unripe pineapple, yellow apple ▪ *Earth:* Mineral ▪ *Other:* Yogurt

Similar Sips Unoaked Chardonnay, ripe and slightly fleshy Pinot Grigio

Where It's Grown Austria (Styria), Canada (British Columbia: Okanagan Valley, Vancouver Island), Czech Republic, France (Alsace, Burgundy), Germany (Baden, Mosel, Nahe, Pfalz), Italy (Friuli–Venezia Giulia, Trentino–Alto Adige, Veneto), U.S.A. (California: Central Coast, Napa County; Oregon)

Pinot Blanc is a long-ago mutation of Pinot Noir that is genetically similar to Pinot Gris, but Pinot Gris has more sweet versions and a stronger reputation. Like Pinot Gris, Pinot Blanc is most closely associated, by reputation and volume of production, with Alsace in France. But unlike Pinot Gris, which has texture and richness and is considered one of the noble varieties in that region, Pinot Blanc is merely delicious, with the best examples showing notes of pear and mineral. Moreover, if you drink a bottle of Pinot Blanc in Alsace, you are likely consuming as much, if not more, Auxerrois, a less noble white grape that brings little to the party. Adding to the confusion, these bottles are locally labeled as Clevner or Klevner. Much of the Pinot Blanc of Alsace ends up in a local blend, Edelzwicker, an assemblage of several white wine grapes that yields a white table wine that is often quite good. Pinot Blanc is also a key grape in Alsace's regional sparkling wine, Crémant d'Alsace. Unblended, Alsatian Pinot Blanc can be on the viscous side, not unlike Pinot Gris, and can be quite good. But more often, especially when it's blended with Auxerrois, it's perceived as a distinctly bland, white-bread wine.

Other regions, however, demonstrate that Pinot Blanc can also be brioche, pumpernickel, or sourdough! The few bottlings in Burgundy emanate mostly from Morey-St.-Denis and sometimes achieve greatness. Much of the harvest, however, is just blended into the local Bourgogne Blanc, a generic white wine. Italy does a nice job with Pinot Bianco, as it's called—creating wines that are moderately rich in body and with racy acidity and clean fruit, ranging from green and yellow apple to unripe pineapple and green melon flavors. Most is planted in the northeast, but it's found all over the country. The best examples come from Friuli–Venezia Giulia and the Veneto.

Germany and Austria hold this grape in high esteem and make noteworthy wines out of it, sold mostly under the pseudonym Weissburgunder, or white burgundy. The examples from Baden and the Pfalz are rich and concentrated, whereas those from the Nahe and Mosel are more elegant. In Austria, the wines from Styria, the only examples that I have tried, are noteworthy. In other regions it's made into dessert-style wines that can attain the quality of *Auslese*, *Ausbruch*, and *Trockenbeerenauslese* bottlings. Eastern Europe produces abundant Pinot Blanc under a host of monikers, and it can be tasty, especially in the Czech Republic, Slovenia, and occasionally in Hungary.

New World examples of Pinot Blanc are most remarkable for the fact that they aren't always Pinot Blanc. In California, most plantings are actually the Melon grape used to make Muscadet, which explains the often vapid personality of the wines, usually masked by excessive oak aging. True Pinot Blanc is found farther north in Oregon and in Canada, in British Columbia's Okanagan Valley and on Vancouver Island; the wines here are more like Alsace examples and varietally correct and include some fine ice wines. In South America, specifically in Chile, there are sizable plantings of a grape called Pinot Blanc, though there's some question about what it actually is.

Vintner's Choices Aged vs. not aged, malolactic fermentation vs. no malolactic fermentation, oaked vs. unoaked, still vs. sparkling vs. dessert wine

Though it may seem obvious, ascertaining that you have a wine made from Pinot Blanc grapes is job number one. As mentioned above, California vintners use the grape Melon de Bourgogne, which originated in France's Muscadet region and which is, at best, neutral and uninteresting. To counter this blandness they often use techniques such as oaking to bolster flavor, which transforms the wine into something it isn't—usually a Chardonnay wannabe. This can be a rude awakening if you were anticipating a true Pinot Blanc.

Classic unoaked Pinot Blanc is delicate, fresh, and clean, like dry Riesling, unoaked Chardonnay, and, at times, Pinot Grigio. Producers will occasionally trade some of its fresh floral and citric flavors for a smoother texture and a kiss of butterscotch or Indian ghee, the result of malolactic fermentation. It can age gracefully, but many wine drinkers prefer it in a more youthful state.

PAIRING WITH FOOD

Most Pinot Blanc found in the American market comes from Alsace, the U.S.A. (Oregon and California), and Italy, although you can find Canadian wines if you look hard. Because the first three are the most prevalent, they're the ones I discuss here.

More than 90 percent of these wines are clean and unoaked. Any oak-scented Chardonnay wannabes should be treated exactly that way, as barrel-aged, oaky Chardonnays. However, a good Pinot Blanc is actually a far more flexible food wine. It loves good, clean flavors that match its own personality, and it shines when highlighting the simple. A plate of oysters or a mild crawfish boil is a great match; so is a grilled trout with lemon butter or a dish of deep-fried popcorn shrimp. In the words of those corporate consultants, KISS (keep it simple, stupid).

Richer examples (from Alsace, Oregon, and California) can handle slightly richer but still straightforward recipes. A moderately rich Pinot Blanc shines with a simple white pâté (made with chicken or a mix of chicken and pork), savory mousse (made with fish or scallops, say), or basic crab cakes with a little aioli. It's also one of the most flexible wines with respect to cooking methods. The lighter-styled and brighter examples from Italy are great with sashimi or a whole steamed fish with ginger, while the richer versions can handle dishes that are sautéed (such as a fillet of sole amandine), deep-fried (tempura), grilled (brochettes of chicken or prawns), and even smoked (salmon, trout, and the like).

I love Pinot Blanc with sophisticated takes on otherwise homey dishes. A BLT with seafood added (such as shrimp or lobster), fish tacos made with a nice cut of fish, and even macaroni and cheese are three good pairings.

Last, don't overlook the agility and flexibility of Crémant d'Alsace, which is one of the great underrated sparkling wines, along with Spanish Cava and Italian Prosecco.

Pinot Blanc goes well with:

- Salads. Pinot Blanc has excellent structure, and because of that brightness it pairs well with light, wine-friendly composed salads (using ingredients and dressing that match the wine's acidity) and salads that stress seafood (deep-fried soft-shell crabs on greens) or chicken.
- Picnic foods. I always pull out a Pinot Blanc for a good alfresco dining experience. With everything from sandwiches to crudités, fresh fruit to cold roast chicken and pork, this wine sings. Although I prefer the Italian Pinot Bianco style here, others work well, too.
- Deep-fried foods. These work best with more austere examples of Pinot Blanc. Deep-fried calamari, *panko*-crusted or batter-coated fish, fried chicken, and savory prawn fritters are all good with both the bubbly Crémant d'Alsace and a lemony, zippy version from Italy.
- White pastas and risottos. A cream-based risotto or pasta is quite good with most Pinot Blanc: the rich wines pair well with the rich texture, and the light, more refreshing examples cut through the richness.
- Most fish. I struggled to think of a fish that does *not* go with Pinot Blanc. The wine's clean flavor profile plays a wonderful supporting role for most sweet fish (black cod, halibut, sole) and the texture of the fuller-bodied wines works well with others (swordfish, Chilean sea bass, monkfish). The sharper eastern European and Italian styles provide an acidic foil for mackerel, anchovies, and sardines.
- Dishes made with a variety of cooking methods. Some grapes' personalities limit the cooking styles they can pair with. Pinot Blanc's personality allows it to work well with dishes that range from raw (sashimi) to grilled (chicken, fish, or vegetables).

Pinot Blanc isn't good:

- When you choose the wrong style. Despite the wine's general affinity with most recipes, it's possible to go wrong. A light, less flavorful wine will get lost behind a bowl of hearty New England clam chowder, while a rich example from California or Oregon, especially one that's spent time in oak, might trample over a simply baked snapper.
- With red meat. Although I once had a rich Alsace Pinot Blanc served with smoked beef tenderloin that made a very nice pairing, generally this is not the wine for lamb, venison, beef, or richer offal (calves' liver or steak and kidney pie).
- With strong spices. Recipes that are defined by bold spices (cumin, curry masala, turmeric, and smoked paprika) can easily overwhelm the delicate nature of Pinot Blanc.
- With spicy-hot dishes. Though Pinot Blanc's bright acidity can work as a foil to some dishes with very mild heat, most hot dishes just knock it out, and you're left with a mere ghost of a wine. This doesn't mean you can't have a Pinot Blanc with a bowl of Texas chili or andouille-

studded Creole gumbo if you really want to; but you can expect that the wine will bring little to the party and get lost behind the dish. I'd prefer a wine that adds something to the pairing or at least has a reason to be there.

THE CHEESE PLATE

FRESH	Chèvre (many countries), feta (Greece, Bulgaria)—dry
SEMI-SOFT	Slightly aged chèvre (many countries), Port Salut (France), tetilla (Spain)—dry
SOFT-RIPENED	Brie (France, U.S.A.), Éxplorateur (France)—dry, sparkling
SEMI-HARD	Gruyère (France), aged provolone (Italy)—sparkling
BLUE	Fourme d'Ambert (France), Gorgonzola dolcelatte (Italy)—sweet

pinot blanc | HAWAIIAN BURGER
WITH PINEAPPLE–MACADAMIA NUT RELISH

HUBERT KELLER   Fleur de Lys and Burger Bar, San Francisco, California, and Las Vegas, Nevada

Makes 4 main-course servings

PINEAPPLE–MACADAMIA NUT RELISH

1 cup finely diced pineapple

$\frac{1}{2}$ cup finely diced mango

2 tablespoons fresh or canned finely diced water chestnuts

2 tablespoons coarsely chopped toasted macadamia nuts

1 tablespoon chopped fresh flat-leaf parsley

$\frac{1}{4}$ cup olive oil

1 tablespoon balsamic vinegar

Salt and freshly ground black pepper

2 pounds skinless, boneless chicken thighs or
   ground dark-meat chicken

3 tablespoons unsweetened coconut milk

2 tablespoons chopped fresh cilantro, plus leaves for garnish

1 tablespoon finely grated, peeled fresh ginger

1 clove garlic, finely chopped

Juice of 1 lime

Salt and freshly ground black pepper

1 tablespoon olive oil

4 sesame buns, split

Lettuce leaves

4 large tomato slices

Toasted unsweetened flaked coconut for garnish (optional)

To make the relish, in a bowl, gently mix together the pineapple, mango, water chestnuts, macadamia nuts, parsley, olive oil, and vinegar. Season with salt and pepper. Cover and refrigerate until chilled.

If using chicken thighs, cut into cubes, place in a food processor, and pulse until coarsely chopped, or chop by hand.

In a large bowl, combine the chopped or ground chicken, coconut milk, chopped cilantro, ginger, garlic, and lime juice and mix well. Season with salt and pepper. Cover and refrigerate for 30 minutes.

Prepare a charcoal or gas grill for direct grilling over a medium fire. Divide the chicken mixture into 4 equal portions, and shape each portion into a patty about $\frac{3}{4}$ inch thick. Brush the patties on both sides with the olive oil.

Oil the grill rack. Place the burgers on the rack and grill, turning once, until golden on both sides and cooked through when tested with a knife tip, 4 to 5 minutes on each side. Place the buns, cut side down, on the rack to toast for the last 1 to 2 minutes.

Place the bottom of each bun, cut side up, on a plate. Layer each bottom with a lettuce leaf, a tomato slice, and a burger. Add a spoonful of the relish, a few cilantro leaves, and a sprinkle of coconut. Close with the tops of the buns and serve at once.

HUBERT: *The delicious fruits and nuts of Hawaii always inspire me. For this recipe, I marinated the chicken in coconut milk and then added a colorful and crunchy relish of pineapple and macadamia nuts that demonstrates a wonderful yet simple combination of ingredients. It shows Pinot Blanc off beautifully.*

EVAN: *It seemed only logical to pick a chef from the spiritual home of Pinot Blanc, Alsace, but I had a great many Alsatian chefs to choose from. There are more Michelin-starred restaurants in Alsace than in any other region in France, and a number of Alsatian chefs have brought their craft to the United States. Hubert, more than most, remains true to his roots, as the menu at Fleur de Lys shows, but he can also be open and whimsical, as he shows in the fare at the Burger Bar.*

Pinot Blanc loves a good sandwich, and it loves twists on classic dishes. And who doesn't love a good burger? Here the use of chicken rather than beef creates a perfect match for Pinot Blanc. The accompanying ingredients, from the rich but mild and crunchy macadamias to the faintly sweet coconut milk and tart-sweet pineapple, pick up on all facets of Pinot Blanc's complex personality. And who said you needed a beer to go with a burger? Try this one with a bottle of Crémant d'Alsace.

RECOMMENDED PRODUCERS

EVERYDAY	PREMIUM
A to Z Wineworks Willamette Valley, Oregon	Alois Lageder Alto Adige, Italy
Byron Southern Central Coast, California	Jermann Friuli, Italy
Girlan Alto Adige, Italy	Paradise Ranch Okanagan Valley, Canada [Sw]
Hugel Alsace, France	Schiopetto Friuli, Italy
Kuentz-Bas Alsace, France	Tangent Southern Central Coast, California
Pierre Sparr Alsace, France [D, Sp]	WillaKenzie Willamette Valley, Oregon

D = Dry   Sp = Sparkling   Sw = Sweet

prosecco

proh-*sehk*-koh | praw-*sehk*-koh

Despite its recent popularity as a sort of soda pop among celebrities, Prosecco is a tasty, fun, affordable sparkling wine. This enjoyable drink has surpassed Asti Spumante as Italy's number-one exported sparkling wine—and there's a lot of Asti Spumante in the world. Happily, most of us have been embracing Prosecco for what it is—an enjoyable, food-friendly effervescent sipper—and not as a fashion statement to be sipped through a fluorescent-colored straw.

Alternative Names Balbi, Glera, Serprina, Tondo (Italy)

Styles Light- to medium-bodied dry white, rosé (relatively rare), dry to sweet sparkling

Sometimes Blended With Bianchetta, Pereza, Pinot Bianco, Verdiso

Flavor Lexicon *Fruit:* Apple, citrus rind, pear ▪ *Floral:* Citrus blossom, honeysuckle, narcissus ▪ *Other:* Bitter almond, honey

Similar Sips Fruit-forward sparkling wines, such as those from California, but with a touch more sweetness; drier, less overtly fruity versions of Asti Spumante

Where It's Grown Argentina, Italy (Friuli–Venezia Giulia; Veneto: Cartizze, Conegliano-Valdobbiadene)

Prosecco's phenomenal success has created a legion of critics. Most claim that it can't compete with Champagne, California sparkling wine, or anything else with bubbles. I reply that they are missing the boat and overthinking the issue. Prosecco is about food and enjoyment, not bubble size, *tirage* time, or chalky soils.

   Native to Italy's Veneto region and said to have originated in the town of Prosecco (now a sub-urb of burgeoning Trieste), Prosecco is the name of the grape, the region, and the wine. This doesn't happen often: France's Muscadet is the only other example I can come up with offhand. Cava, the popular Spanish sparkling wine, comes from Spain's Cava region in Catalonia, but it incorporates grapes that don't share the Cava name. But Prosecco has other things in common with Cava: although it's not produced by the *méthode traditionnelle* as Cava is, it's much closer in personality to Cava than to Champagne.

In the Veneto, most Prosecco is made into basic sparkling wine. The best comes from an appellation called Conegliano-Valdobbiadene, which accounts for 25 percent of the region's production. Within this appellation is a subappellation called Cartizze, which is considered to produce the best wines of all. Look for these names on the label: they make a big difference. Conegliano-Valdobbiadene may appear as a single name, or either Conegliano or Valdobbiadene may be listed separately. Bottlings from Cartizze are labeled *Superiore* and tend to be a little sweeter, as their structure can carry it so well. Conegliano wines are thought to be bigger and richer, while those from Valdobbiadene are more aromatic and racy; but for most of us that's splitting hairs. It's all delicious!

As of August 1, 2009, all Prosecco wine must be internationally designated as *denominazione di origine protetta,* meaning that there will no longer be any generic Prosecco. Check for authentic Proseccos labeled DOC or DOCG (in the case of the historic areas of Conegliano, Valdobbiadene, and Colli Asolani). The new law limits production to certain areas of northeastern Italy and should put an end to the proliferation of poor-quality Prosecco imitations from other European countries.

It's worth keeping a few other names in mind from other areas of the Veneto: Montello e Colli Asolani, Colli Trevigiani, and Marca Trevigiana, in that order. Prosecco is also grown in Friuli, where it's made into both still and sparkling wines. No Prosecco of note is found anywhere else in the world except for a tiny amount in Argentina, reflecting the heritage of twentieth-century Italian immigrants. Italian Prosecco should not be confused with Dalmatian Prosecco, or Prošek, a sweet dessert wine made out of dried grapes.

Vintner's Choices Aged vs. not aged, bulk fermentation vs. *méthode traditionnelle*, dry vs. off-dry vs. sweet, single variety vs. blended, sparkling vs. still, vintage vs. nonvintage

The Prosecco grape is an early ripener, which makes it ideal for sparkling wines. The few still wines that are made from the grape can be lovely, bursting with the same floral and fruity opulence and framed by a distinctive wildflower aroma.

The sparkling-wine category is divided into two styles: the less aggressive *frizzante* style, which prickles the tongue like a Moscato d'Asti and represents about one-third of the Prosecco sparkling production, and *spumante,* or effervescent sparkling wine. Both are made by the Charmat or bulk method. After the base wines are made, a mixture of yeast and sugar is added, and this causes a secondary fermentation that takes place in a pressurized, closed tank (rather than in the bottle as in the *méthode traditionnelle*). This technique is less expensive than the *méthode traditionnelle* and better preserves the fruit character in the grapes. A few Prosecco wines are made according to the *méthode traditionnelle* (or *metodo tradizionale*), notably

Valdo's Numero 10 and Bellanda's SC 1931, but they are the exceptions, because aging the wine in bottles suppresses the primary-fruit character that is the hallmark of this wine.

Many winemakers employ only the Prosecco grape in their wines, though the law requires only 85 percent Prosecco, with the balance made up of the early-ripening Bianchetta, the aromatic Perera, and the sharp and acidic Verdiso. The blend is less critical than the final style of the wine, which falls into one of three categories of sweetness: brut (driest), extra dry, and dry (sweetest). As with Champagne, there's some overlap in the sugar levels in these categories, so you can theoretically have a brut that's sweeter than an extra dry. I discuss below how to pair these different categories with food.

Prosecco's charm, like that of Asti, is the freshness of its fruit. It's best to drink it soon rather than to cellar it as you might a good bottle of Champagne or sparkling wine. Unless you are having a party or hedging the value of the euro, there's no need to stash cases in your basement. For similar reasons, it's probably not worth hunting for vintage-dated Prosecco. Although most Prosecco is made from the wine of a single harvest, it's rarely vintage-dated. It's best for the wine (and for the winery's finances) to get the bottles to market as quickly as possible. When wineries do produce a vintage-dated Prosecco, the primary reason is so that they can charge more for it, trading on the popular assumption that a vintage wine is always better and worth a higher price. With Prosecco, this isn't the case.

PAIRING WITH FOOD

If ever a wine was created to harmonize with the food of its home region, it is Prosecco. It pairs beautifully with the famed specialties of the Veneto, especially wild game, spit- or oven-roasted or cooked into stews accompanied by polenta. Further enriching the local cuisine are mushrooms: porcini (or *cèpes*, as the French call them), the *chiodino* or honey mushroom, and various members of the chanterelle family. These mushrooms are often paired with sweet chestnuts. The fleshiness of the mushrooms and the texture and sweetness of the chestnuts enhance the fruit character of the Prosecco.

Don't think of Prosecco as a cheap alternative to Champagne. Prosecco shares Champagne's bubbles and food-friendliness but little else. Champagne is all about toast and chalk, lean citrus, and long, expansive finishes. Many of its complex signature notes derive from autolysis, the process of the spent yeast breaking down in the bottle after secondary fermentation. Prosecco is more about a balance of ripe fruit and sweetness than about complexity and nuance.

I'd guess that most Prosecco is enjoyed at the beginning of a meal, a decision that suits the wine just fine. It's very good with snack foods, from roasted almonds to Chex Mix (really!), and from sweeter sushi to basic antipasti or salumi. You've got a wide choice of appetizers, too, as Prosecco is a solid match with dishes ranging from crab and shrimp salads to Chinese pot stickers and Argentinean empanadas. Further into the meal, you can enjoy Prosecco with shellfish, sweet treatments of white meat or fowl (cured slow-cooked pork belly, roast chicken served with chutney), or rich vegetable preparations like a butternut squash stew or a gratin. And, given its often-sweet nature, Prosecco can be dynamite with many desserts, especially those stressing fruit and nuts, alone or in combination.

PAIRING POINTERS

Prosecco goes well with:

- Many Asian cuisines. Its fruit-forward and off-dry nature make a naturally good match with Japanese sushi and teriyaki; Chinese deep-fried dishes, seafood dishes, and some poultry; Thai crepes, fish cakes, and some coconut milk–based curries; and Indian curries, *biryanis,* and samosas.
- Salty, greasy, and deep-fried foods. Prosecco with fried chicken is *so* good.
- Many Latin dishes (such as empanadas, ceviche, and mole) and the cuisines of Florida, the Caribbean, and Hawaii. A little spice is not a bad thing; try Prosecco with Hawaiian poke, that tasty raw-fish salad with just a kick of heat and sesame oil, for a refreshing and enjoyable pairing.
- Rustic or coarsely textured foods: polenta, pesto, hummus, and baba ghanoush. Indeed, Prosecco pairs nicely with Middle Eastern foods in general.
- Dishes that suggest sweetness (or have slightly sweet condiments or treatments). From prosciutto-wrapped persimmons to a ketchup-slathered hamburger, Prosecco picks up on the sweetness.

Prosecco isn't good with:

- Extremes. Dishes that are intensely rich or flavorful squash its subtlety. Dishes that are too spicy take the middle out of the wine.
- Dishes that are too sweet (unless they are paired with the sweeter styles of wine). Prosecco is often thought to be the perfect match with desserts, as most examples do have some sweetness. The key, however, is just that—*some* sweetness. If the dessert is far sweeter than the wine, you won't be happy. Say yes to an apple galette, no to rich buttercream.
- Strong-tasting fish, other strong flavors, and certain vegetables, especially bitter vegetables (broccoli rabe, kale, and eggplant), which can make the wine taste metallic.
- Rich red meats. Although there are rosé styles of Prosecco that may work, more often than not, it's not a successful match, unless your accompanying sauce or side dishes have personalities that overshadow the meat. One possible pairing is a filet mignon with a port reduction sauce, accompanied by sweet roasted pearl onions and a rich potato gratin.

- Caviar. Ouch. This is a train wreck in the mouth. Just because it has bubbles doesn't mean it will go with caviar. Prosecco can pair with a little salmon roe on top of scrambled eggs with a dollop of sour cream, but that's about the only fish-egg and Prosecco match I've had that worked.

THE CHEESE PLATE

FRESH	Cassatella (Italy), feta (Greece, Bulgaria)—brut
SEMI-SOFT	Crescenza (U.S.A), teleme (U.S.A.)—brut, extra dry
SOFT-RIPENED	Brillat-Savarin (France), Saint-André (France)—brut, extra dry
HARD	Aged Cheddar (U.S.A.), Parmesan (Italy)—brut

RECOMMENDED PRODUCERS

EVERYDAY	EVERYDAY	PREMIUM
Collalto Veneto, Italy	Nino Franco Veneto, Italy	Aneri Veneto, Italy
La Marca Veneto, Italy	Rive della Chiesa Veneto, Italy	Canella Veneto, Italy
Le Bellerive Veneto, Italy	Sommariva Veneto, Italy	Desiderio Bisol & Figli Veneto, Italy
Mionetto Veneto, Italy	Zardetto Veneto, Italy	Ruggeri & Co. Veneto, Italy

roussanne

roo-*sahn*

Roussanne is a grape that you should definitely know. Sadly, this rich, honeyed grape is quickly disappearing from the vineyards of Hermitage and other appellations in the northern Rhône Valley where it once held court. It is difficult to ripen and grow, and its tendency to oxidize provides vintners with challenges at every turn. Amazingly, even though it comes off as rich and exotic, with an apparent lack of structure that makes it seem as if it's falling apart, it can hold that pose for years, even decades. A permitted component of white Châteauneuf-du-Pape, Roussanne is sharper and more flamboyant than its sibling Marsanne, which it is paired with in the northern Rhône but separated from in the south.

Alternative Names Barbin, Bergeron, Grefon, Picotin Blanc, Rebelot (France), Rosana (Italy)

Styles Medium-full to full-bodied dry white, medium-bodied sparkling (not widely available)

Sometimes Blended With Bourboulenc, Clairette, Grenache Blanc, Marsanne (France), Trebbiano (Italy), Chardonnay, Marsanne, Viognier (Australia, U.S.A.)

Flavor Lexicon *Fruit:* Citrus rind, white cherry, yellow apple, yellow pear ▪ *Floral:* Fresh herbs, green coffee beans, herbal tea, honeysuckle, sweet citrus blossoms ▪ *Other:* Honey

Similar Sips Viognier, full-bodied fruit-forward Chardonnay, rich Sémillon-Chardonnay blends

Where It's Grown Australia (Victoria), France (Languedoc-Roussillon, Provence, Rhône Valley, Savoie), Italy (Liguria, Tuscany), U.S.A. (California: Sierra Foothills, Sonoma County [Russian River], Southern Central Coast [Paso Robles]; Washington: Columbia Valley)

Like its sibling Marsanne, Roussanne is native to France's Rhône Valley. Roussanne is a more difficult grape to grow and thus has fallen out of favor with growers who seek a predictable crop. It is used, like Marsanne, in small percentages as a blending grape for some of the key northern Rhône reds, like Hermitage, and as a component of the lovely white wines of St.-Joseph and Crozes-Hermitage. It is also the essential component in the rare but captivating Hermitage Blanc. Roussanne has a rich and exotic aroma reminiscent of white cherries, chamomile tea, and fresh herbs, with nuances of bitter citrus peel. It is enchanting and intoxicating when ripe and well made, and it adds aromatics to Marsanne's textured but less showy personality. In St.-Péray, it is a component of the appellation's medium-bodied sparkling wines, though it's far less prevalent than Marsanne. Roussanne's aromatics can add a lot to these otherwise well-made but often uninspiring wines. In the southern Rhône, Roussanne is a key component of white Châteauneuf-du-Pape, contributing its unique perfume to this often underappreciated white wine. So good can this grape be that it's occasionally bottled locally as a varietal wine, which can be stunning, especially when the grapes come from older vines.

In Provence, a specific clone of the variety, Roussanne du Var, produces a wine that's more blush than deep straw yellow, but the wines are lackluster, and it's really just a blending grape. Roussanne should not be confused with the Provençal grape Roussette, which is a different variety. In the mountainous Savoie region, where it's known as Bergeron, Roussanne can make very aromatic wines. It is also found in France's Southwest and can add intrigue to the white wine blends of this vast region.

In Italy, Roussanne is grown in Liguria and blended with Trebbiano in the white Montecarlo Bianco. In Australia, Roussanne, like Marsanne and Viognier, performs quite well in Victoria, where it is made into a varietal wine and also forms a part of a white Rhône-style blend. This approach is similar to that in California, where growers in the Central Coast's Paso Robles and Santa Barbara areas have done a magnificent job with the grape. Blends of Roussanne and Viognier produce wines with captivating floral and fruit aromatics.

Vintner's Choices Oak vs. no oak, single variety vs. blended, still vs. sparkling, young vs. old vines

Sexy as it is by itself, unblended Roussanne is relatively rare. However, it is occasionally vinified into a varietal wine, like that produced by Château de Beaucastel in Châteauneuf-du-Pape. It is sometimes exposed to oak to emphasize its unique personality, which is all the more evident in grapes from older vines. However, oak aging and old vines remain unusual in Roussanne production. Some California producers are experimenting successfully with newer oak in Roussanne-based blends.

Traditionally Roussanne has been blended with Marsanne, as in the northern Rhône, or with three other grapes—Grenache Blanc, Clairette, and Bourboulenc. New World producers, however, are experimenting with blends that incorporate the very forward Viognier and even a little Chardonnay. These exciting wines are explosive and food-friendly, being rich as well as aromatic. The sweet-spice profiles of oak can benefit these evocative wines. Younger vines are the rule in California; in Australia, some very old Roussanne vines survive in Victoria. Curiously, the older the vines, the greater the wine's capacity to age. Although its rich, fragrant relatives (Marsanne and Viognier) are comparatively short-lived, Roussanne seems to be capable of aging gracefully if produced from old vines and well stored.

PAIRING WITH FOOD

When Roussanne sings with food—and it sings often—it reminds me of Viognier. As with Viognier, Roussanne's food-friendliness is underrated. The best wines are rich, silky and balanced, with a panoply of unique flavors. I love Roussanne with exotic dishes, from North African *tagines* to pork marinated in cumin and ginger. If the flavors in your dish are less exuberant, use textures that will pick up on the richer texture of the wine. Thick and creamy soups, slow-cooked root vegetables (like parsnips and carrots), rich cream- and butter-infused pastas and grains (risotto and polenta), oily nuts (especially macadamias and cashews), and richer preparations of fish and white meats, such as veal, are all great tablemates for Roussanne and Roussanne-based blends.

Roussanne matches well with rich shellfish, as the texture and ripe fruit bring out the sweet flavors of scallops, crab, and lobster. Few wines match better with crab cakes than Roussanne. And bring on the butter and cream, because this wine can both match them in texture and, with its balanced acidity, cut through their richness.

With aged bottles from older vines, opt for recipes that incorporate nuts, reconstituted dried fruit, and white meat, rather than seafood or fish.

PAIRING POINTERS

Roussanne goes well:
- By itself. Roussanne is mouthfilling and not overly acidic; it can be a refreshing change from the ubiquitous preprandial glass of Chardonnay, though its similar texture will appease Chardonnay loyalists.
- With rich-textured root vegetables, tubers, and winter squashes. Roussanne is very good with yams, mashed potatoes, roasted turnips and rutabagas, and savory dishes of manioc and tapioca. Something like a buttery fennel gratin or butternut squash ravioli with sage and chopped, toasted hazelnuts can also rock.
- With many traditional holiday foods, especially goose, turkey, and honey-glazed ham (even when studded with cloves and served with pineapple and cherries!).
- With rich, unctuous purées (soups or vegetables), especially those enriched with cream or butter. Blends that contain Marsanne are especially good, as Marsanne adds baby fat to the wine's texture.
- With the exotic. With dishes from Thai curries to Indonesian satays and from mild Jamaican jerk chicken to North African chicken with apricots and almonds, Roussanne and Roussanne blends are seamless pairings.

Roussanne isn't good with:

- Dishes that are charcoal- or pan-grilled or pan-blackened, as smoky and seared foods overwhelm and detract from the wine's charm.
- Too much heat. Roussanne is high in alcohol, and serving it with chiles or Sriracha sauce makes the wine seem more alcoholic while crushing its enjoyable flavors.
- Very light recipes. Very simple sand dabs or plain roasted quail can be crushed by a viscous, oak-aged example of this wine. If the wine is full, the dish needs to be full as well.
- Foods that are overly sweet. Roussanne's ability to pair with the exotic leads some cooks to go over the top. A little hoisin sauce, for example, can pair well with the wine, but too much can make it taste thin and bitter.
- Strong-flavored fish. Especially with a round and fruit-forward blend, stay away from pungent fish such as sardines, anchovies, and mackerel, as well as fish sauces like the intense Southeast Asian *nuoc mam*.

THE CHEESE PLATE

FRESH	Fromage blanc, Petit-Suisse (France)—dry
SEMI-SOFT	Crescenza (U.S.A.), young Mahón (Spain)—dry
SOFT-RIPENED	Camembert, Éxplorateur (France)—dry
SEMI-HARD	Fontina (Italy), vacherin fribourgeois (Switzerland)—dry
HARD	Mimolette (France), aged St. George (U.S.A.)—sparkling
WASHED-RIND	Époisses (France), Taleggio (Italy)—dry

roussanne | LOBSTER CIOPPINO

RICHARD VELLANTE   Legal Sea Foods, Boston, Massachusetts

Makes 4 main-course servings

BROTH
1 celery stalk, finely diced
1 carrot, peeled and finely diced
½ yellow onion, finely diced
1 tablespoon olive oil
1 clove garlic, minced
1 cup diced canned tomatoes with juice
1 cup bottled clam broth
2 cups chicken stock
Kosher salt and freshly ground black pepper
1 bay leaf
1 teaspoon chopped fresh thyme

ROUILLE
½ cup chopped roasted red bell pepper
1 teaspoon chopped garlic
1 teaspoon chopped fresh flat-leaf parsley
1 teaspoon fresh lemon juice
½ teaspoon paprika
¾ cup mayonnaise
Kosher salt and freshly ground black pepper

2 tablespoons olive oil
8 littleneck clams, scrubbed
1 pound mussels, scrubbed and debearded
1 cup Roussanne or other dry white wine
2 (1½-pound) live lobsters
4 sea scallops
8 large shrimp, peeled and deveined
2 tablespoons fresh basil leaves, torn into pieces
Kosher salt and freshly ground black pepper
Coarse country bread for serving

To make the broth, in a heavy saucepan, combine the celery, carrot, onion, and olive oil over low heat and cook, stirring occasionally, until the vegetables have softened, about 5 minutes. Add the garlic and continue to cook for 1 to 2 minutes. Add the tomatoes, clam broth, and chicken stock, bring to a simmer, and simmer for 5 minutes to blend the flavors. Season with salt and pepper, add the bay leaf and thyme, and simmer for 5 minutes longer. Remove from the heat, and remove and discard the bay leaf. (The broth can be made up to 3 days in advance, covered, and refrigerated.) You should have at least 3 cups broth.

To make the rouille, in a food processor, combine the red pepper, garlic, parsley, lemon juice, and paprika and process until smooth. Add the mayonnaise and continue to process until fully incorporated. Season with salt and pepper. Transfer to a small bowl, cover, and refrigerate until serving.

In a soup pot, heat the olive oil over medium heat. Add the clams and sauté for 2 minutes. Add the mussels and wine, cover, and cook, shaking the pan occasionally, until the clams and mussels open, 3 to 5 minutes. Using a slotted spoon, transfer the clams and mussels to a bowl, discarding any that failed to open, and cover to keep warm.

Continue to simmer the wine uncovered over medium heat until it is reduced by half, about 3 minutes. Add the 3 cups broth and bring to a simmer. Add the lobsters, cover, return the broth to a simmer, and cook just until the lobsters begin to turn red, 8 to 10 minutes. Add the scallops and shrimp and simmer until they are just cooked through, 3 to 4 minutes longer. Stir in the basil and season with salt and pepper. Remove from the heat.

Remove the lobsters from the pot, and cut each lobster in half lengthwise. Divide the clams and mussels evenly among 4 warmed large soup plates, arranging them around the edge of each bowl. Divide the broth, scallops, and shrimp evenly among the bowls. Place a lobster half in the center of each bowl and serve at once with the bread. Pass the rouille at the table for diners to add to their bowls.

RICHARD: *A regional fish stew made from the catch of the day, cioppino is said to have been developed by Italian fishermen who settled in San Francisco in the 1800s. The name can be traced to the stories of wharf cooks calling out in their heavy Italian accents for everyone to "chip in" some of their catch to the communal soup pot.*

Roussanne, an underappreciated grape variety, has a minerally, layered character. This style blends well with the natural mineral flavors of the shellfish. The addition of the rouille really balances out the broth and offers a touch of creaminess that aids the pairing.

EVAN: *I love Roussanne with lobster; it's a favorite combination. And when I think of lobster, I immediately think of Rich, as he's the expert on preparing New England's beloved crustacean.*

Lobster, with its rich texture, is a natural pairing with Roussanne, and this rendition of cioppino is given a decidedly New England accent with the inclusion of the beautiful Maine lobster, which is cooked in a fragrant broth with shrimp and scallops. Unlike the traditional San Francisco versions that are based on tomatoes and soft heat, both of which could hurt the Roussanne, this interpretation accentuates the seafood. If your clams are very salty, you may want to limit them, as too much salt can spike the wine's alcohol and diminish the fruit. I recommend lots of crusty bread and rouille to provide a textural backdrop for the wine. I also mix the rouille directly into the broth, as in a bouillabaisse, to add richness, which works well for the wine. The bread allows for a slightly oak-aged version of the wine.

RECOMMENDED PRODUCERS

EVERYDAY	PREMIUM	SPLURGE
Château de Campuget Southwest France	Anglim Winery Southern Central Coast, California	Alban Southern Central Coast, California
Eberle Southern Central Coast, California	d'Arenberg McLaren Vale, Australia	Château de Beaucastel Rhône Valley, France
	L'Aventure Southern Central Coast, California	Clos Solène Southern Central Coast, California
	Yves Cuilleron Rhône Valley, France	Giaconda Victoria, Australia
	Zaca Mesa Southern Central Coast, California	Jean-Luc Colombo Rhône Valley, France

sémillon

seh-mee-*yohn*

Sémillon shows two faces to the world. The principal variety in the wine that most connoisseurs consider the finest expression of great dessert wine, Château d'Yquem of Sauternes, is the same one that makes the racy and dry table wines ordered by the glass in hundreds of fashionable restaurants from Sydney to Seattle.

Many people erroneously think it's Sauvignon Blanc that drives the great sweet wines of Sauternes and its satellite appellations. In fact, it's Sémillon that provides the highest percentage of fruit in the blend, the rich color, and the velvety texture, and is most strongly affected by the *Botrytis* that defines the wine. Sémillon is also blended frequently with Sauvignon Blanc to make Australia's wildly popular SSB (Sémillon–Sauvignon Blanc) and is often vinified and blended with and aged similarly to Chardonnay in both Australia and Washington State, with similar results, under the hybrid name SemChard.

Alternative Names Blanc Doux, Chevrier, Colombier, Málaga (France), St.-Émilion (Romania), Hunter Valley Riesling (Australia), Green Grape, Wyundruif (South Africa)

Styles Medium- to medium-full-bodied dry white, medium-bodied dry sparkling (not widely available), medium-full-bodied dessert

Sometimes Blended With Muscadelle du Bordelais, Sauvignon Blanc, Ugni Blanc (France), Chardonnay, Sauvignon Blanc (Australia, U.S.A.)

Flavor Lexicon

DRY   *Fruit:* Apple, citrus (Meyer lemon, tangelo), green fig, olive, quince ▪
        Wood: Butterscotch, caramel, hazelnut—aged versions ▪ *Other:* Beeswax

SWEET   *Fruit:* Apricot, baked pear, marmalade, peach ▪ *Wood:* Caramel, vanilla ▪
        Other: Honey, yogurt

Similar Sips Rich but muted Chardonnay, full-flavored Pinot Gris blends, unctuous dessert wines

Where It's Grown Argentina, Australia (New South Wales: Hunter Valley, Riverina; South Australia: Adelaide Hills, Barossa Valley; Western Australia), Canada (Okanagan Valley), Chile, France (Bordeaux: Sauternes and other satellite appellations; Southwest France), Hungary (Lake Balaton), New Zealand, Romania (Dealul Mare), South Africa (Coastal Region: Paarl, Franschhoek), U.S.A. (California: Napa County, Northern Central Coast [Livermore Valley], Sonoma County, Southern Central Coast [Santa Barbara]; Washington State: Walla Walla Valley, Yakima Valley)

One of the most prominent white varieties of France, Sémillon was once among the most widely planted grapes in all Bordeaux, and with good reason. It's a vigorous vine that is resistant to most diseases, mildews, and rot. The most substantial Sémillon plantings in the world are still in France, mostly in Bordeaux and the Southwest. The grape, although regal in Sauternes, the Graves, and the surrounding area, can suffer elswehere from being flaccid, heavy, and viscous. Because of these attributes, in Bordeaux it's frequently blended with the more crisp and expressive Sauvignon Blanc and, in smaller quantities, the very aromatic Muscadelle du Bordelais.

The most stellar examples of dry Sémillon in France are the blends found in the Graves and Entre-Deux-Mers regions, while the best sweet wines are found in and around Sauternes, Barsac, and the nearby appellations of Ste.-Croix-du-Mont, Cadillac, and Loupiac. The surprise for most is that Sémillon is also part of the blend in Crémant de Bordeaux, which employs the *méthode traditionnelle* to make an enjoyable, though not frequently exported, sparkling wine.

Elsewhere in Europe, Sémillon is vinified in Hungary, Romania, and parts of the former Yugoslavia, though these offerings are rarely found in the American market. Instead, most Sémillon sold in the United States is imported from Australia, where it is extensively grown, most widely in New South Wales. It flourishes in the Hunter Valley north of Sydney, where for a long time it was known as Hunter Valley Riesling. There are four styles of Sémillon-based wines made here: a popular dry style, often blended with Chardonnay or Sauvignon Blanc; a sweet style patterned after Sauternes; a complex, minerally, early-picked style that is released soon after the harvest; and a variation on the early-picked style in which the wine is aged in oak or in the bottle. Most examples of the bottle-aged Hunter Sémillons exhibit a deep yellow color and complex brioche and honey aromas and flavors, with a long but moderately soft finish. Cooler-vintage Hunter Sémillons seem to be among the most highly sought after of the oak-aged wines, with some of the late 1970s and 1980s bottlings still drinking well. Large volumes of Sémillon made in Riverina, the New South Wales equivalent of California's irrigated Central Valley, find their way into generic blends. In Western Australia, the best stuff comes out of the Margaret River; in South Australia, the strongest producers are in the Barossa Valley and Adelaide Hills. Sémillon from these regions is frequently made into SemChards—blends of roughly equal parts of Sémillon and Chardonnay, with delicious notes of quince, pear, and white peach—as well as the chic and quite tasty SSBs, which are racy and redolent of tangy lime, green olive, and yogurt.

In South Africa, this grape variety once represented a large portion of all Cape vines but now accounts for less than 1 percent. Most of the remaining Sémillon is planted in Paarl and Franschhoek. Even with this decline, Sémillon produces pleasant, soft wines and is often used in blends. Some outstanding oaked varietal wines have also been produced. In New Zealand, though there's not much planted, Gisborne and Hawke's Bay make nice dry blends as well as sweet examples.

In the United States, as a dry wine, Sémillon is more volumetrically important in California but more interesting in Washington State, where it's made as both a varietal wine and, as in Australia, a lovely blend with Chardonnay. Both Washington and California make excellent dessert wines based on Sémillon. In both states, the dry wines tend to be lean and citrusy when young and develop a waxy, ripe-fig character as they age. California's most successful dry Sémillons usually end up in Sauvignon Blanc blends. Farther north, there's Sémillon in British Columbia's Okanagan region in Canada: to the south, large volumes of relatively nondescript Sémillon are produced in Chile and a small quantity in Argentina.

Vintner's Choices Aged vs. not aged, oak vs. no oak, single variety vs. blended, sparkling vs. still vs. dessert

Sémillon lends itself to a range of styles. It can be found in delightful sparkling wines (especially in Australia) and wonderful still wines made as both a single variety and a blend with Sauvignon Blanc (notably the SSB and SBS wines from Down Under) or Chardonnay (in Washington State and, again, Australia). However, the grape may be most regal as a dessert wine, either in a pure, late-harvest Sémillon or, more likely, as the largest component of a classic Bordelais in Sauternes and its surrounding regions, where it is blended with Sauvignon Blanc, some Muscadelle du Bordelais, and, if you are lucky, a good dose of *Botrytis* to make a succulent, honey scented, and unctuous wine with notes of sweet spice, poached or baked pear, and soft apricot. Sémillon dessert wines are almost always oaked, which adds texture, creaminess, and some of the vanillin and sweet spice flavors that these wines are renowned for. Some Sémillon table wines are oaked too, but this treatment is rare, as most believe the charm of the dry wine, on its own and blended, lies in the purity of its fruit. Some of the Sémillon-Chardonnay blends are oaked, but it's increasingly unusual to find varietal Sémillons, SSBs, or SBSs with much wood influence. As with many white grapes, the dry versions of these wines are most interesting in their youth and become more of an acquired taste as they get older and lose some of their roundness and charm. However, Sémillon and Sémillon blend dessert wines can age gracefully for decades, with the fruit becoming more candied and marmalade-like as the wines evolve.

PAIRING WITH FOOD

The two extremes of Sémillon's personality require separate treatment in pairing, although a few dishes can work with both the dry and sweet styles.

For the dry wines, I consider first the richer versions, either monovarietal or blended with Chardonnay. These styles, predictably, love seafood: pasta with shrimp, lemon zest, and cream or scallops served with a purée of creamed parsnips. Those with a modicum of oak are lovely with butter, mild mushrooms (chanterelles, oyster mushrooms, and basic button mushrooms), and grains like couscous, *farro,* or even pilafs with white rice and wild rice. Textured dishes like savory soufflés, white lasagnas, and creamy risottos are also good calls. I also like to play off the fruit character that the wine can show. A roast chicken with a savory fig jam or a roast loin of pork with sautéed apples are good examples of this type of pairing. Slower-cooked dishes, like chicken fricassee or a veal stew with spring vegetables, are also nice with this style of wine.

The SSBs work best if treated like other bright, zippy whites and paired with fresh seafood, appetizers, and composed salads, which let the acidity of the wine highlight the ingredients. At a Western Australian wine tasting I attended, where the focus was on SSBs, I enjoyed a range of dishes, from Southeast Asian spring rolls to raw oysters to goat-cheese crostini.

The intriguing bottle-aged Sémillons from the Hunter Valley deserve special consideration. They have a distinct toasty, light mineral, and dry honeyed finish. Opt for elements that can pick up on the toastiness (gratins, breadcrumb toppings, toasted nuts), a little bit of sweet spice (cinnamon, nutmeg, and allspice), and lightly smoked or grilled white meats and poultry, especially those with a sweet-salt glaze (honey mustard, honey and soy, and the like).

Sweet Sémillons and Sémillon blends are an entirely different story. The new classic of foie gras with Sauternes or a similar-styled wine does work, as long as the wine's sweetness is not over the top. Opt for late-harvest rather than botrytized examples for successful pairings. Tropical fruit and Sémillon are a lovely combination. Incorporating mango, banana, and cherimoya (custard apple) into a savory preparation can make a nice bridge for a sweet wine. A simple entrée salad of roast chicken, mango, and coconut rice would be a nice pairing with a sweet, but not overly sweet, Sémillon blend.

Most sweet Sémillon lovers, however, will want to pair the wine with desserts. Fruit desserts, especially pears, peaches and figs, are delicious, and those with nuts or streusel toppings work well with oak-aged wines. Finally, picking up on the texture of these wines is always a good approach. Top a dessert with a dollop of sweetened whipped cream, serve a small ladle of vanilla-scented crème anglaise alongside a tart wedge, or accompany fruit cookies with a rich, honey-scented mousse, and you'll be a happy camper.

PAIRING POINTERS

Sémillon goes well with:

- Rich, textured dishes. Sémillon's waxy texture provides a great backdrop for dishes with buttery and creamy textures. As a wine ages, its texture increases and its acidity generally decreases, so pay attention to the balance. Try a creamy fish bisque, scaloppine of veal with a light mustard cream, or even a buttery risotto of scallops and peas.
- Greens and vegetables. Not all Sémillons work well with produce, but the very popular Australian SSBs are excellent with recipes ranging from spanakopita and vegetable *pakoras* to grilled asparagus, leek and potato soup, and vegetable *tagines*.
- Seafood. Although the range of Sémillons is not as vast as the range of seafood, there's usually a Sémillon-based wine for everything from rich shellfish (textured Sémillon or Sem-Chards) to briny oysters (SSBs) to plank-roasted halibut or sea bass (oak-aged examples) to sweet and sour whole fish (a slightly sweeter version).
- Desserts. Sauternes and Sauternes-style wines and other unoaked, late-harvest Sémillons are wonderful with desserts. They work across a range of fruits, especially stone fruit and tree fruit. I noted in the Muscat chapter that my friend Fiona Beckett loves strawberries and cream with Muscat-based dessert wines; they're great with Sauternes as well. For oak-aged wines, good choices are recipes that pick up on the wine's vanilla, caramel, and sweet-spice flavors, as well as dishes featuring butterscotch, caramel, toffee, or crème brûlée.
- Cheeses. The range of styles provides many options in pairing Sémillon with cheese (see below). There are few better matches in the world than the traditional pairing of Sauternes with Roquefort.

Sémillon isn't good:

- When you pick the wrong one. Obviously, you don't want to pair overtly sweet Sémillons with very savory dishes, but you have to be careful with the other interpretations as well. An aged, nutty Sémillon isn't a great match for an Asian chicken salad or Peruvian ceviche.
- With very salty dishes. Sauternes with Roquefort aside, most dry Sémillon-based table wines can't handle excessive salt. Avoid all but the sharpest examples with clams or mussels, chunks of Parmesan cheese, or a pizza with pancetta and sun-dried tomato.
- With red meats. This caveat seems obvious, but it's worth restating. White meats work, and even offal (sweetbreads and Sémillon are fabulous together), but most lamb, aged beef, and venison should be avoided.
- With bitter foods. With the exception of zingy SSBs, most Sémillon and Sémillon blends struggle when matched with dishes containing ingredients like radicchio, endive, and bitter melon.
- With chocolate or mocha. Chocolate is a very difficult pairing with sweet wines, except as a very minor accent to a fruit- or custard-based dessert. It overpowers and dominates the wine. Mocha, with its coffee accents, can work better, but it's still not a perfect match.

THE CHEESE PLATE

FRESH	Chèvre (many countries)—dry; feta (Bulgaria, Greece)—dry, sweet
SEMI-SOFT	Butterkäse (Germany), crescenza (U.S.A.)—dry
SOFT-RIPENED	Éxplorateur, Saint-André (France)—dry, sweet
SEMI-HARD	Cheddar (U.K., U.S.A.), Gouda (Holland)—dry
HARD	Aged Cheddar (U.K., U.S.A.), Parmesan (Italy)—off-dry, sweet
BLUE	Fourme d'Ambert, Roquefort (France)—off-dry, sweet
WASHED-RIND	Red Hawk (U.S.A.), Taleggio (Italy)—dry, off-dry

sémillon | SHERRY-ROASTED FIGS
WITH CRISPY STREUSEL AND CRÈME FRAÎCHE

KATE ZUCKERMAN   Author of *The Sweet Life: Desserts from Chanterelle*

Makes 6 servings

STREUSEL

2 tablespoons granulated sugar

2 tablespoons firmly packed light brown sugar

½ cup all-purpose flour

¼ teaspoon salt

4 tablespoons cold unsalted butter, cut into ¼-inch cubes

12 Black Mission figs

⅓ cup plus 2 tablespoons granulated sugar

¾ cup medium-dry sherry

2 orange peel strips, each about 3 inches long

Crème fraîche for serving

Preheat the oven to 400°F. To make the streusel, line a rimmed baking sheet with aluminum foil or parchment paper. In a small bowl, combine the granulated sugar, brown sugar, flour, and salt and toss with a fork to mix well. Scatter the butter over the top and, using 2 knives, cut in the butter until it is coated with the dry ingredients and is the size of peas or smaller. Spread the mixture on the prepared baking sheet, and allow it to dry out while you prepare the figs.

Trim off the stems from the figs, and cut each fig in half lengthwise. Lay the fig halves, cut side up, in a single layer in a nonreactive baking pan just large enough to accommodate them. In a small bowl, combine the ⅓ cup granulated sugar and the sherry, stirring with a spoon until the sugar is dissolved. Add to the roasting pan along with the orange peel.

Place the figs in the oven and roast for 10 minutes. Remove from the oven and baste the figs with the pan liquid. Sprinkle 1 tablespoon of the granulated sugar evenly over the figs and return to the oven. Roast for 10 minutes longer, then repeat the basting and sprinkle with the remaining 1 tablespoon granulated sugar. Return the figs to the oven and roast for 10 minutes longer. They should be very tender but not falling apart. Remove from the oven, and remove and discard the orange peel. Leave the figs in the pan in their cooking liquid and set aside at room temperature. (Or let cool, cover, and refrigerate for up to 1 day.)

Reduce the oven temperature to 350°F. Place the streusel in the oven and bake for 15 minutes. Remove from the oven and toss the streusel crumbs with a metal spatula or 2 knives, breaking up any large clumps. Return to the oven and bake until lightly browned, 10 to 15 minutes. Remove from the oven, toss the crumbs again, breaking up any clumps, and bake for 5 minutes longer. Remove from the oven and let cool completely. (The streusel can be made up to 3 days in advance and stored in an airtight container at room temperature.)

To serve, if you have turned off the oven, preheat it once again to 350°F. Return the figs to the oven until hot, about 10 minutes. Place 4 fig halves, cut side up, on each plate, and spoon 1 tablespoon of the cooking syrup over each serving of figs. Place a dollop of crème fraîche on each plate, and then sprinkle each plate with a generous spoonful of the crispy streusel. Serve at once.

KATE: *A Sémillon dessert wine is not too sweet, slightly viscous, with a more off-dry, acidic note than full-on sweet dessert wines have. To match it, a dessert needs to modulate its sugar carefully—too much and you won't taste the complexity in the wine. This dessert of roasted figs served in their own roasting liquid is part of a larger repertoire of roasted fruits, a technique of dessert making that I love and which also seems approachable for a home cook. Fresh figs, at the height of the season, have an earthiness that offsets their innate sweetness. The addition of sherry restores the natural acidity that is lost in the cooking process. Topped with tangy crème fraîche and streusel, this combination makes for a simple, straightforward dessert that marries well with the fruity, citrus, and honey notes in the wine.*

EVAN: *Once I decided to go for a sweet rather than a savory pairing for Sémillon, asking Kate to take up the challenge was an obvious decision. As the former executive pastry chef at Chanterelle in New York, she's one of America's real masters in the world of desserts. After two quick conversations, we'd settled on this stunning recipe. All I can say is yum!*

Kate understands wine and food matching at an entirely different level from almost any pastry chef I've ever worked with. Her notes above are spot-on. This dessert accommodates the gamut of dessert-styled Sémillon wines. There's honey to pair with any Botrytis, sweet spices and streusel topping for oak (the oak pairing is further enhanced by the reduction of the liquid, which adds a caramel-like quality), fig for the core fruit profile of the grape, and crème fraîche to pick up on the silky-smooth texture. The sherry adds sophistication and complexity. This is a pairing that's sure to please everyone.

RECOMMENDED PRODUCERS

EVERYDAY	PREMIUM	SPLURGE
Chateau Ste. Michelle Columbia Valley, Washington [D]	Beringer Napa Valley, California [Sw]	Boekenhoutskloof Franschhoek, South Africa [D]
Peter Lehmann Barossa Valley, Australia [D]	Château Roques Mauriac Southwest France [Sw]	Château Giraurd Sauternes, France [Sw]
Plantagenet Western Australia [D]	L'Ecole 41 Columbia Valley, Washington [D]	Château Rieussec Sauternes, France [Sw]
Brokenwood New South Wales, Australia [D, Sw]	Tyrrell's New South Wales, Australia [D]	De Bortoli New South Wales, Australia [Sw]

D = Dry   Sw = Sweet

torrontés

tohr-rohn-*tayss*

Over and over in food and wine publications, I've read that Torrontés is the next Malbec. While I agree that Torrontés's time is a-coming, about all it has in common with Malbec is that they are both staple grapes of Argentina. One is white, the other is red; one has its roots in Argentina, and the other is clearly imported from France. And although they both have their place at the table, they are unlikely ever to be served with the same dishes.

This explosive white wine is intoxicating, with aromas reminiscent of a Brazilian fruit stand and Hawaiian leis made of plumeria or other intensely perfumed tropical flowers. When fresh, Torrontés is a captivating and very food-friendly wine.

Alternative Names Albariño Francés, Aris (Argentina); Moscatel de Austria, Torontel (Chile)

Styles Medium- to medium-full-bodied dry white

Sometimes Blended With Chardonnay (Argentina), Albariño, Treixadura (Spain)

Flavor Lexicon *Fruit:* Apricot, passion fruit, mango, yellow apple ▪ *Floral:* Honeysuckle, jasmine, plumeria, tuberose ▪ *Wood:* Spice

Similar Sips Medium-full-bodied aromatic whites like Viognier and Gewürztraminer, with explosive exotic fruit

Where It's Grown Argentina (Catamarca, La Rioja, Mendoza, Rio Negro, Salta, San Juan), Chile, Spain (Galicia: Rías Baixas, Ribeiro)

The provenance of Argentina's most widely planted white wine grape is complicated. To get a grip on its puzzling regional differences, DNA testing was undertaken by the wine experts at the University of California, Davis. They demonstrated that Torrontés Riojano, the most common and finest of the three different Torrontés varieties in Argentina, is actually a cross between Muscat of Alexandria and the local Criolla Chica, which we know in North America as the Mission grape. These flamboyant parents have produced a fragrant, rich, and explosive offspring. Additional studies have confirmed that Torrontés Riojano is related to Torrontés Sanjuanino, another commercial strain of the variety. A third selection, Torrontés Mendocino, may be genetically different, and indeed it looks different, with smaller, tighter bunches of darker-yellow grapes.

Not yet seen in many other countries, Torrontés is also grown in Chile, but the output there is of moderate quality and employed largely for the production of Chilean *pisco,* a distilled spirit.

Though genetically different from its South American counterparts, a white-grape variety of the same name can be found on the plains of Galicia, in northwest Spain. The Spanish version of Torrontés traces its lineage to the Malvasia family, which is responsible for its perfumed aroma. It originates in Ribeiro in northern Spain, just east of Portugal, where it is most often blended with the local Treixadura and less often with Albariño. Spanish Torrontés is usually expressive, with aromatics that are similar in style and weight to those of Muscat and Gewürztraminer. It is used in local wines and Albariño blends.

Vintner's Choices Aged vs. not aged, choice of clone or selection, low-altitude vs. high-altitude vineyard, single variety vs. blended, skin contact or no contact

The single most important factor determining the quality of Torrontés is vineyard altitude. The grapes from higher altitudes ripen in a more balanced fashion and seem to maintain better acidity. This difference is most evident in wines from Argentina's northernmost region, Salta, considered the finest for Torrontés.

The selection or strain of Torrontés that a vintner employs is also critical. The Mendocino selection is less forward and more restrained than the preferred Riojano or Sanjuanino selections (the latter coming from the region of San Juan). As with other aromatic white grapes, such as Viognier and Gewürztraminer, managed skin contact *(macération pelliculaire)* is used. Because grapes have much of their flavor packed into their skins, macerating the skins with the wine maximizes the flavors. With the flavors, however, come tannins, which can be bitter and can reduce the shelf life of white wines. Given the naturally low acidity of this grape (which is often adjusted during winemaking), most people don't try to cellar Torrontés-based wines. In fact, it's best to drink them as fresh as possible. The wines are released from the wineries often just a few months after harvest, and that's when they're at their best. Anything more than about a year old will taste tired and lacking.

Though most often consumed as a monovarietal wine, Torrontés can be successfully blended. In Argentina blending is rare: when it is done it's usually because a producer has an eye on the American market and has blended some Chardonnay into the wine. I have had a couple of these blends, and they can be quite good. In Spain, the local Torrontés is almost always blended with other local grapes.

PAIRING WITH FOOD

André Soltner, the former chef of Lutèce in New York, was once asked when he most enjoyed drinking Gewürztraminer, a similar varietal to Torrontés. He replied, "When I am mowing my lawn." He had a point. Torrontés, like Gewürztraminer, can be surprisingly hard to pair with food, as it can overwhelm and dominate, compete for attention, or have all of its beguiling fruit knocked out if it's paired with the wrong dishes.

Torrontés is well matched with shellfish, as the rich, almost oily texture and ripe fruit bring out the basic sweet flavors of scallops, crab, or lobster. The wine mirrors the viscosity of butter and cream and in some cases has enough balanced acidity to cut through their richness. Given its exuberant fruit profile, it makes sense that you can pair it with dishes that have some sweetness, real or implied: a puréed carrot and ginger soup, mild Indian or Southeast Asian curries, or even a classic Waldorf salad. Other ingredients that work seamlessly with this grape include rich-textured, slow-cooked root vegetables (like yams and carrots), pasta and grains (risotto and polenta), oily nuts (especially macadamias and cashews), mild white mushrooms, and rich fish and white meats.

Torrontés does well with preparations and cooking techniques that bring out its ripe fruit and perceived sweetness. So slow-roasting pork belly, caramelizing onions or garlic, smoking a poussin or Cornish game hen (which brings out a subtle, sweet edge), and even deep-frying in batter are all excellent ways to show off this grape.

PAIRING POINTERS

Torrontés goes well with:

- Sweet-sour dishes. The play between acid and fruit in sweet and sour pairings works well with most Torrontés and Torrontés-based wines. With classic Chinese sweet-and-sour pork, a traditional sauerbraten, or short ribs glazed with pomegranate molasses, balsamic vinegar, and a little thick soy sauce, this wine can find harmony.
- Exotic and ethnic dishes. Though a great Torrontés and Argentinean meat-and raisin-stuffed empanadas sing together, other South American dishes can also be great with this wine. A coconut-based Brazilian *mariscada* (fish stew) or *muqueca de peixe* is superb, as is a Caribbean nut-encrusted fish or Cuban fried plantains in *mojo* sauce—a delightful blend of orange and lime juice, black pepper, garlic, and cumin.
- Rich dishes and cream sauces. These wines have an inherently viscous, almost fatty texture that allows for great pairings with richer foods. Sautéed shrimp in a rich lemon-and-chive cream and butter-poached lobster are good examples, as are most dishes featuring coconut milk.
- Combinations of fruit and sweet spice, including Indian mango chutney, Chinese plum sauce, and a tangy fruit-based barbecue sauce.

- Most Southeast Asian foods. Though they originate thousands of miles apart, Torrontés mixes happily with the cuisines of Vietnam, Malaysia, Indonesia, and Singapore. Try it with classic dishes like Hainanese chicken rice, Vietnamese spring rolls, Indonesian satay, and Malaysian *ikan bakar,* a dish of grilled fish wrapped in banana leaves.

Torrontés isn't good with:
- Recipes that involve heavy grilling or blackening. The resulting flavors detract from the wine's charm, especially if mesquite or charcoal is used.
- Salty foods. Too much salt mutes and tightens up the otherwise zaftig fruit character of the wine.
- Heat. Hot spices have the same effect on the wine as salty foods, but for a different reason, and often with accompanying heartburn.
- Dishes that are too sweet. The fruit-forward character of the wine invites cooks to be daring, but if the dish is overly sweet, the wine will reveal a hidden bitter character.
- Subtle dishes. More subdued foods can be squashed by these sometimes assertive wines. If your recipe seems tame, it's better to go with a less-dominating wine.

THE CHEESE PLATE

FRESH	Neufchâtel (U.S.A.), ricotta (Italy)
SEMI-SOFT	Port Salut (France), tetilla (Spain)
SOFT-RIPENED	Brie (France), robiola (Italy)
SEMI-HARD	Young Idiazábal (Spain), provolone (Italy)
WASHED-RIND	Chaumes, Morbier (France)

torrontés | PERUVIAN SEAFOOD CHOWDER

MICHELLE BERNSTEIN   Michy's and Sra. Martinez, Miami, Florida

Makes 4 to 6 main-course servings

2 pounds extra-large shrimp in the shell (about 24)

SHRIMP STOCK
1 tablespoon olive oil
Reserved shrimp shells
3 cups water
1 cup dry white wine
2 bay leaves
3 or 4 black peppercorns

6 tablespoons olive oil
½ cup finely chopped red onion
¼ cup finely chopped red bell pepper
¼ cup finely chopped fennel
3 cloves garlic, minced
¼ teaspoon minced habanero or Scotch Bonnet chile
1 cup dry white wine
½ cup evaporated milk
Salt and freshly ground black pepper
½ cup corn kernels (from about 1 ear)
½ cup finely diced, peeled sweet potato
¼ cup finely diced tomato with juice
¼ cup coarsely chopped fresh cilantro leaves and stems
4 large eggs, at room temperature, lightly beaten

Peel and devein the shrimp, reserving the shells, and refrigerate the shrimp until needed.

To make the stock, in a heavy saucepan, heat the olive oil over medium-high heat until almost smoking. Add the shrimp shells and cook, stirring often, until deep red, 2 to 3 minutes. Add the water, wine, bay leaves, and peppercorns and bring to a boil. Reduce the heat to medium-low and simmer gently for about 20 minutes to draw out the flavor from the shells.

Strain the stock through a fine-mesh sieve, pressing down on the shells with the back of a spoon to extract as much flavor as possible. You should have 4 cups stock. If you have less, add enough water to make 4 cups. Set aside.

In a wide, heavy saucepan, heat 2 tablespoons of the olive oil over medium heat. Add the onion, bell pepper, fennel, garlic, and chile and cook, stirring often, until the vegetables have softened but are not brown, about 4 minutes. Pour in the wine, bring to a simmer, and cook, stirring to dislodge any browned bits from the bottom of the pan, until the liquid is reduced by half, about 3 minutes.

Add the 4 cups stock, bring the mixture to a simmer, and simmer over medium heat until the liquid is reduced by about half, 10 to 15 minutes. Stir in the milk and simmer until the mixture thickens, 3 to 4 minutes. Season with salt and pepper, and remove from the heat. Keep warm.

In a large, heavy sauté pan, heat 3 tablespoons of the olive oil over medium-high heat. Add the shrimp, season with salt and pepper, and cook, shaking the pan occasionally, until the shrimp are firm and pink, about 2 minutes. Using a slotted spoon, transfer the shrimp to a bowl and keep warm.

Return the sauté pan to the stove top over medium-high heat and add the remaining 1 tablespoon olive oil. Add the corn and sweet potato and cook, stirring and tossing, for 2 minutes. Stir in the reserved broth and heat, stirring to loosen any flavorful bits cooked onto the bottom of the pan. Bring to a simmer and return the shrimp to the pan, along with the tomato and cilantro. Season with salt and pepper and stir until the tomato is heated through.

Remove the pan from the heat and slowly pour in the eggs while stirring constantly. The eggs will set, forming long ribbons in the hot liquid, in about 1 minute.

Ladle the stew into warmed shallow bowls and serve at once.

MICHELLE: *This dish is one of my favorites from Peru. I have made it in my own style, but the flavors that I fell in love with in Peru are all in the stew; these are the flavors that I truly believe match with this somewhat unknown wine, Torrontés. The spiciness of the chiles, the sweetness of the corn and sweet potatoes, and the bite of the cilantro make a beautiful combination with the crispness of the Torrontés. The variety also has a history of going well with Latin dishes and seafood. The wine's heady floral and herbal notes bring out all these flavors and make the dish even better!*

EVAN: *Few chefs in the "Mango Gang" (the collective of South Florida culinary talents who came up in the 1980s) are as intuitively connected to their Latin roots as Michelle. Her thorough understanding of pan-Latin seasoning and skillful touch with seafood made this pairing one of the book's most obvious. And the Jewish connection? Well, the dish's generosity speaks for itself.*

If there's a better dish to show off Torrontés, I have yet to taste it. This wonderful pairing owes a lot to Michelle's understanding of her Latina heritage and her talent for bringing out the best in a wine. This chowder has texture (from the evaporated milk and sweet potatoes), sweetness (from the shrimp, corn, and milk), and just enough heat to bring out but not diminish the wine's fruit. The added slight resistance of the vegetables is a nice contrast to the wine's waxy, almost oily texture.

RECOMMENDED PRODUCERS

EVERYDAY

Alta Vista Salta, Argentina	Bodegas Etchart Salta, Argentina	La Riojana Coop La Rioja, Argentina
Andeluna Cellars Mendoza, Argentina	Michel Torino Salta, Argentina	Santa Julia Mendoza, Argentina
Bodega Colomé Salta, Argentina	Pascual Toso Mendoza, Argentina	Tamari Mendoza, Argentina
Crios de Susana Balbo Salta, Argentina	Valle de la Puerta La Rioja, Argentina	Zolo Mendoza, Argentina

trebbiano

treb-*byah*-noh | treh-bee-*ah*-noh

Trebbiano owes its importance to the world of distilled spirits as much as to the world of wine. The ubiquitous grape variety of Italy, providing the source of the great majority of Italian white wines, it's also the basis for France's great brandies, Cognac (for which the grape is known as Ugni Blanc) and most Armagnac (for which it's known as St.-Émilion). Estimates indicate that Trebbiano vines produce more wine than any other variety in the world, even though the Spanish Airén grape is planted on more acreage. And yet it is still more often distilled than vinified as a table wine.

As a wine, it has the reputation of being, at best, inoffensive, and more often boring and flavorless. However, there are always exceptions. And because of the grape's poor reputation among wine aficionados, a good Trebbiano can be a great value. The question is how to find one.

Alternative Names Many, including Clairette Ronde, Rossola (France), Procanico (Italy), St.-Émilion (Argentina, France, U.S.A), Thalia (Portugal, Bulgaria), Ugni Blanc (France, South Africa), White Hermitage (Australia)

Styles Light- to medium-bodied dry white, medium- to medium-full-bodied dessert

Sometimes Blended With Garganega, Malvasia, grapes in the Sangiovese family, Verdicchio (Italy), Colombard, Folle Blanche, Rhône and Provençal white grapes (France)

Flavor Lexicon

DRY   *Fruit:* Green apple, green pear, lemon, lime, white grape ▪ *Other:* Light spice, nuts

SWEET   *Fruit:* Orange zest, persimmon, raisin ▪ *Other:* Fruitcake, gingerbread, maple syrup

Similar Sips Uncomplicated white wines, lighter styles of Pinot Grigio, Muscadet, and Pinot Blanc

Where It's Grown Argentina, Australia (New South Wales, South Australia), Brazil, Bulgaria, France (Bordeaux; Cognac; Provence; Rhône Valley; Southwest: Armagnac), Greece, Italy, Mexico, Russia, Uruguay, U.S.A. (California: Central Valley)

Much as you might like to, you can't dismiss Trebbiano completely: it's simply too important a grape. In Italy, its native home (along with France's Southwest), it's responsible for about one-third of the total white-wine production. On the official Italian website www.agriline.it, Trebbiano is referenced in more appellations regulations than any other variety. While much of it is bland stuff, many examples are quite tasty. It's worth sampling bottles of Trebbiano d'Abruzzo, Orvieto (a blend with mostly Trebbiano, specifically the Procanico clone), and Frascati (ditto). You can also appreciate what it adds to a good bottle of Verdicchio (as part of the blend) and the occasionally intriguing bottle of Est! Est! Est! from Montefiascone. The best examples display notes of just-ripe white pear, light green herbs, and raw nuts and have a clean citrus finish. Overall, Trebbiano is not spectacularly complex, but it can be tasty, refreshing, and enjoyable.

Trebbiano is one of two white wine grapes permitted in basic Chianti (the other is Malvasia). The better wines, those that bear the designation DOCG (the highest quality rating in Italy) are banned from using it. And increasingly, winemakers aspiring to better quality are moving away from this grape. More important is the role that Trebbiano plays in the lovely dessert wine Vin Santo. Made from a blend of late-harvest Trebbiano and Malvasia grapes that have been further desiccated on straw mats, and then barrel-aged, Vin Santo can be a wonderful and not stupefyingly sweet way to finish a meal or enjoy an afternoon—with a few biscotti, of course.

In France, the bulk of the Trebbiano crop is distilled, and with good reason. Most table wines made from the grape are low in alcohol, lean, acidic, and essentially devoid of any redeeming social value—until they're distilled. In an alembic still, they're magically transformed into outstanding brandy. In the Cognac and Armagnac regions, the local saying is that the meaner the wine, the better the spirit.

Elsewhere in France, the grape is important in terms of volume but not quality. It's found, under various local pseudonyms, in Provence and the Rhône Valley and contributes, with other local grapes, to generally unremarkable blended white wines. There's Trebbiano on the island of Corsica and, elsewhere in Europe, in Bulgaria, Portugal, Greece, and Russia.

In the New World, Trebbiano is a workhorse grape, producing large volumes of wine for generic blends in California, Australia, and Latin America, particularly in Argentina and Mexico. In Mexico, however, much of the crop is distilled to make the universally popular Mexican brandy.

Vintner's Choices Aged vs. not aged, dry vs. sweet, single variety vs. blended, vinified vs. distilled

Trebbiano is not a complex varietal, and the choices about what to do with it are pretty straight-forward. Meticulous handling is paramount, for the relatively clean profile of the grape, and the absence of any oak, malolactic fermentation, or tannin to hide behind, means that it will reveal any fault in production or storage more readily than most varieties. When it's successful, as with a well-made Trebbiano d'Abruzzo or an Orvieto from Umbria, the wine displays pristine fresh citrus, green apple, and table grape (Thompson Seedless) character with balanced to high acidity and a palate-cleansing finish.

More often, Trebbiano is a supporting grape in a blend. Again, poor winemaking techniques will be evident in the resulting wine. A Verdicchio or Soave with poor quality Trebbiano as a significant component is simply not a very good wine. But when the Trebbiano is good, it helps bring out the wine's flavors.

Vin Santo can be a lovely wine and a nice change from the usual end-of-meal offerings. Along with Malvasia, Trebbiano is the key grape in the Tuscan versions that dominate the popular market.

PAIRING WITH FOOD

Trebbiano's weakness is also its strength. Being a clean and relatively neutral wine, it goes with just about everything that white wines traditionally pair with, from seafood to poultry, from white-wine-focused pastas to vegetarian dishes. Unless you've got a bad bottle, the wine won't fight the recipe or overwhelm the dish, and it doesn't have any of the characteristics that make for difficulty in pairing—excessive oak, tannins, or alcohol. I like to have some Trebbiano around the house for those nights when I want a tasty wine but I don't want to think too hard about the choice. If, at the end of a busy day, I've thrown a chicken in the oven, sprinkled on a little salt, pepper and *herbes de Provence,* and made the kids an accompanying wild rice pilaf because that's what they want, a Trebbiano's perfect for me. And if my wife opts for a piece of broiled fish and wok-fried vegetables instead, the Trebbiano will work with that too. It's an easy, flexible, and malleable wine.

For Vin Santo, stick to desserts and cheeses: my experience in pairing the wine with savory dishes has been less than compelling. Because most of the good examples are barrel-aged for a considerable period, nut-based desserts are great for showing them off, especially when set off by dark raisins or other rich brown ingredients like caramel, butterscotch, maple syrup, or molasses. Almond or hazelnut biscotti with Vin Santo are something of a cliché: they do pair nicely, but I'd opt for those that are classic and simple, maybe with a touch of citrus peel. Avoid those that are overly sweet: definitely don't serve biscotti that are essentially half chocolate! And don't dip them in the wine: rather, enjoy each for its own unique attributes. For other dessert options, again, avoid anything overly sugary; Vin Santos are generally not excessively sweet. Cheeses can be quite nice matches, and I've recommended a few below.

PAIRING POINTERS

Trebbiano works well:

- When it can show off the integrity of the dish. Trebbiano's clean and refreshing nature will bring out the flavors and tastes of good-quality ingredients and snap them into focus.
- With almost any dish that a basic white wine would pair with. Given its high acid, moderately ripe fruit, and low oak, tannin, and alcohol, most Trebbiano will pair seamlessly with a host of recipes.
- With light cream sauces and stock reductions. The key with this wine is not to overwhelm it but take advantage of its straightforward personality. It can hang in there with mildly rich cream sauces and reductions of poultry, veal, or even fish stock.
- With dishes that include fruity and nutty flavors. A Waldorf salad with grapes, apples, walnuts, and cheese is great, as is trout stuffed with plumped golden raisins, lemon zest, and lightly toasted breadcrumbs or pine nuts.
- With many rice and pasta dishes. Maybe it's the Italian connection, but a good Orvieto or Frascati with a pasta primavera or a straightforward risotto with melted cheese and a little prosciutto is excellent.

Trebbiano isn't good:

- When the wine isn't good—and there are lots of mediocre examples out there. No dish will bring out the best in the wine if the best simply isn't there. Make an effort to seek out wines from the better producers and appellations.
- When the recipe overwhelms the wine. Charcoal grilling, lots of curry or spice, or any other strong flavoring has the potential to blow the wine away. Simple is best with Trebbiano.
- With really rich preparations. As a rule, the Trebbiano-based wines have only moderate acidity. Thus it's easy to crush the wine under an entrée that's simply too much. Rich moussaka, dense cream-sauced veal loin, or a rib-sticking turkey chili, even if they are mild in flavor, will be too much for most Trebbiano wines.
- With red meats. Not a lot to add here. A preparation geared to pair with white wine, such as an herb-marinated loin of lamb served at room temperature with a salsa verde, could work with a bold example of the wine, but most pairings of red meat and Trebbiano are a stretch.
- If the dessert is too sweet for the wine. Many people lump Vin Santo in with most other dessert wines and are surprised to find that it's less sweet. Long barrel aging leaches out sweetness from a wine (as with tawny port or aged Madeiras). Opt for moderately sweet dishes focusing on nuts, light caramel, and nougat.

THE CHEESE PLATE

FRESH	Young brindamour (France), queso fresco (Mexico), ricotta (Italy)—dry
SEMI-SOFT	Young Mahón (Spain), young pecorino (Italy)—dry
SOFT-RIPENED	Brie (U.S.A., France), Camembert (U.S.A., Canada)—dry
SEMI-HARD	Cheddar (U.K.), Fontina (Italy)—dry, Vin Santo
BLUE	Gorgonzola (Italy), young Stilton (U.K.)—Vin Santo
WASHED-RIND	Reblochon (France), young Taleggio (Italy)—dry

trebbiano | LOUISIANA POPCORN RICE AND WILD RICE PILAF WITH CRABMEAT, ALMONDS, AND LEMON

SUSAN SPICER   Bayona, New Orleans, Louisiana

Makes 4 to 6 main-course servings

1 cup wild rice

3 cups water

Salt and freshly ground black pepper

3 tablespoons unsalted butter or olive oil

1 yellow onion, finely chopped

2 celery stalks with leaves, stalks finely diced and leaves chopped

Grated zest and juice of 1 lemon

1 bay leaf

2 cups Louisiana pecan rice (see note)

1 pound jumbo lump blue crabmeat or Dungeness crabmeat, picked over for shells and cartilage

$1/2$ cup Trebbiano or other light-bodied white wine

$2^{1}/_{2}$ cups chicken stock, vegetable stock, or water

$1/4$ cup sliced almonds, lightly toasted

1 bunch green onions, including tender green tops, thinly sliced

Rinse the wild rice in 2 or 3 changes of water. In a saucepan, bring the water to a boil over high heat. Add the wild rice and a pinch of salt, stir well, cover, reduce the heat to medium, and simmer until the kernels split open and are tender but still slightly chewy, 25 to 40 minutes. Remove from the heat and drain off any excess water. Keep warm.

When the wild rice is about half cooked, heat 2 tablespoons of the butter in a shallow, wide, heavy saucepan over medium-high heat. Add the onion, diced celery stalks, lemon zest, and bay leaf and sauté until the onion is softened and translucent, 3 to 5 minutes. Add the pecan rice and stir to coat the rice thoroughly with the vegetables and butter. Carefully stir in half of the crabmeat, then add the wine, stock, half of the lemon juice, and $1/2$ teaspoon salt. Bring to a boil, reduce the heat to low, cover, and cook until the liquid has been absorbed and the rice is tender, about 15 minutes. Stir in the cooked wild rice and season with salt and pepper. Remove and discard the bay leaf.

In a small sauté pan, heat the remaining 1 tablespoon butter over medium-low heat. Add the remaining $1/2$ pound crabmeat and heat gently until hot. Season with salt and the remaining lemon juice.

Divide the pilaf evenly among warmed plates. Top with the warm crabmeat, dividing it evenly, and sprinkle with the celery leaves, almonds, and green onions. Serve at once.

NOTE Louisiana pecan rice, also known as popcorn rice, is an aromatic long-grain white rice. Look for Ellis Stansel or Konriko brand. If you cannot find pecan rice, substitute basmati rice. If you like, you can prepare the pecan rice as directed up to the point the pan is covered, then transfer the covered pan to a preheated 350°F oven and cook until the liquid is fully absorbed and the rice is tender, about 15 minutes.

SUSAN: Once, while I was drinking a glass of Trebbiano at home, I was snacking on some sesame rice chips, which went quite well with this particular wine. The combination got me thinking about rice and toasty, nutty flavors, and I remembered a wild-rice salad I had made in the past. I thought the addition of the crab, lemon, and Louisiana rice would pair well with the freshness and acidity of the wine and would make a tasty, light entrée, topped off with the almonds and green onions. A simple green vegetable would complete the menu.

EVAN: I met Susan a good decade or so ago, when we teamed up to run a food and wine seminar (she covered the food, I handled the wine) at the New Orleans Wine and Food festival. Though I knew her by reputation, I hadn't had the pleasure of working with her. That seminar turned out to be one of the most memorable wine events I've been involved with. Susan's ability to take basic ingredients and make them shine without demanding attention, all the while harmonizing with the wine, made her the ideal chef to create a recipe to pair with a grape that can get lost behind elaborate fare.

This recipe is a perfect vehicle to show off a good Trebbiano. Susan's comments about toastiness and nuttiness are spot-on. The crab adds a natural sweetness, which picks up on the fruit character of the wine. The lemon brings out the flavor of the rice salad while lifting the personality of the wine ever so slightly—a deft touch. The green onions and almonds add a nice bite and texture. Overall, the dish is balanced and brings out the wine's qualities without crushing its straightforward nature.

RECOMMENDED PRODUCERS

EVERYDAY	PREMIUM
Camillo Montori Abruzzo, Italy	Avignonesi Tuscany, Italy [V]
Domaine du Tariquet Southwest France	Bruno Nicodemi Abruzzo, Italy
Falesco Abruzzo, Italy	Fattoria di Felsina Tuscany, Italy [V]
Farnese Abruzzo, Italy	Isole e Olena Tuscany, Italy [V]
Rocca delle Macie Umbria, Italy	Marramiero Abruzzo, Italy
Tenuta le Velette Umbria, Italy	Masciarelli Abruzzo, Italy

V = Vin Santo

txakoli

cha-koh-*lee*

In public speaking, you're advised never to start off your presentation with an apology. Nevertheless, I am sorry. I am sorry that I have made the decision to present the grape Hondarribi Zuri in this book not by the name of the grape but rather by the Basque name of the far better-known wine made from it, Txakoli. The reason is simple: the name Hondarribi Zuri is unlikely to appear on any wine labels, front or back. If you don't want blank looks from a store clerk, ask for Txakoli.

Including this wine here, as with Assyrtiko, is a bit of a stretch. Many other wines discussed in *Daring Pairings* are far more widely available and established. And I don't suspect that we'll be seeing Txakoli explode in popularity any time soon. However, I passionately believe that this wine has the potential to excel in the United States, and not just because it sounds so good rolling off your tongue. It goes really well with food. Read on.

Alternative Names Chacolí, Txakolina (Basque region, Spain)

Styles Light-bodied dry white, light-bodied dry *frizzante* white

Sometimes Blended With Folle Blanche, Gros Manseng, Hondarribi Beltza, Petit Courbu, Petit Manseng (Basque region, Spain)

Flavor Lexicon *Fruit:* Citrus (lemon, lime), green papaya, jackfruit ▪ *Earth:* Mineral ▪ *Other:* Yeast

Similar Sips Young Albariño, Italian Pinot Grigio, Vinho Verde

Where It's Grown Spain (Basque region: Getariako Txakolina, Bizkaiko Txakolina, Arabako Txakolina)

The Hondarribi Zuri grape, responsible for close to 80 percent of all Txakoli wines, and its kissing cousin, the red Hondarribi Beltza, are both native to the Spanish Basque country. Known best for its unique language, extraordinary food, and the amazing Guggenheim Museum in Bilbao, the Basque region sits in the northeast of Spain, along the Bay of Biscay. The city of San Sebastián, home of the best tapas bars in all of Spain (in my humble opinion) and many great restaurants, is where most Txakoli is consumed, and a few days here will establish your love for this delightful wine.

On my first trip to this corner of the world, I naively thought all Txakoli was the same. A sommelier in Bilbao explained to me that there are three appellations in the region. Getariako Txakolina is the most important, though it's small by Spanish standards. Bizkaiko Txakolina is an even smaller appellation in the Vizcaya area around Bilbao. Arabako Txakolina is the smallest and newest. Though I'd certainly have difficulty identifying differences between these appellations in a blind tasting, the locals, over several *pintxos* (the Basque term for tapas) and an equal number of glasses of Txakoli during a *txikiteo*, or tapas crawl, swear that they exist. More exploration is clearly in order.

Vintner's Choices Aged vs. not aged, single variety vs. blended, still vs. *frizzante*

Txakoli is a fairly straightforward wine. You pick the grapes, you make it, you drink it. As most of the wines are made using the Hondarribi Zuri grape, it's safe to assume that many are monovarietal wines. When the red Hondarribi Beltza grape is used, either in a blend or solo, it is vinified as a *vin clair*, a clear (white) wine, in the same manner that Pinot Noir and Pinot Meunier are made into white wines in the production of Champagne or sparkling wine. Within the appellations, Bizkaiko Txakolina uses Folle Blanche as its secondary grape, which makes for sharper and greener wines. The Arabako Txakolina uses mostly Hondarribi Zuri and Hondarribi Beltza, with smatterings of Petit and Gros Manseng and Petit Courbu, all three of which have their roots on the other side of the border in France.

Txakoli's charm lies in its vibrant and zesty, youthful nature. Freshness is key, as its shelf life is not long; I wouldn't keep a bottle around for more than a few months. As with the Portuguese Vinho Verde, made with the Albariño grape, many wines are bottled with the objective of keeping a little carbon dioxide in the wine so that it's slightly spritzy and prickly on the palate. This slight effervescence stimulates the appetite, making it a very effective accompaniment to tapas.

PAIRING WITH FOOD

Txakoli is light in alcohol, which means that it's food-friendly, and you can enjoy it with less worry about getting tipsy. My wife, Barbara, loves it because she can have it at lunchtime and then get back to work. I like Txakoli because I can enjoy more than one glass without feeling sated. The fact that it's always unoaked simplifies pairing with food, and the effervescence refreshes the palate.

Of course Txakoli and tapas are a match made in heaven. Txakoli isn't perfect with all types of tapas, but its range is amazing, from slices of dry chorizo to crunchy deep-fried fish, from stuffed crab to olive oil–sautéed peppers and multiple *bocadillos* (small sandwiches).

Seafood is a safe bet. Txakoli has excellent structure and acidity and will bring out the flavor of the seafood while mitigating any excess saltiness. In Spain, seafood means squid, crab, and salt cod, whereas in the United States it might mean fresh oysters, steamed clams or mussels, or crab prepared in all sorts of different ways.

This may sound wacky, but I think of Txakoli as going well with the same foods I would enjoy with a crisp pilsner or blond lager beer. Like these beers, Txakoli is light, effervescent, and refreshing. So I'd pair this wine with anything from beer nuts and nachos to sushi and sandwiches. And if you'd like to spice up your Chinese takeout, Txakoli can be a tasty alternative.

Finally, Txakoli has a way of going with foods that are intrinsically sour. Vinaigrettes, pickled items, and tart vegetables and herbs (like leeks, sorrel, and lemongrass) seem to hold up nicely without overpowering the wine.

PAIRING POINTERS

Txakoli goes well with:
- Almost anything from the sea. Txakoli has a natural affinity for fish and shellfish. Though most people drink it with hors d'oeuvres and tapas, it carries well further into the meal, especially if the fish or shellfish is treated simply.
- Somewhat salty recipes. While Spain's local *bacalhau,* or salt cod, is a great example, it's not commonly found in the United States. Items such as deep-fried calamari and olives are excellent. Roasted Marcona almonds with sea salt are equally happy alongside a glass of this wine.
- Tapas. Too easy? Maybe, but let's stretch the definition of tapas to include other small plates: Italian antipasti, Middle Eastern meze, Chinese dim sum, and Japanese bento boxes. Txakoli can pull together a wider range of flavors and textures.
- Asian food. At the risk of overgeneralizing, many of the foods of China, Vietnam, Japan, and Thailand pair nicely with Txakoli, from Japanese gyoza to ginger-steamed fish, Vietnamese spring rolls, or pad Thai.
- Dishes that go well with light lager and pilsner beers. Though it tastes very different from beer, Txakoli can be a lovely and much tastier stand-in for a cold one. It works with dishes from chicken wings to pizza, grilled chicken to Malaysian satays.

Txakoli isn't good:
- If you want a wine that will change your life. Txakoli is as much about enjoyment, context, and good company as it is about gourmet pairings. If you're looking for an epiphany, try a Grand Cru Montrachet instead.
- With thick, rib-sticking dishes. The wine's low alcohol means that it can be easily crushed by rich preparations. Simple, light dishes are better calls than thick stews and soups.

- With smoky-flavored foods. Long-smoked meats and fish overwhelm this straightforward and light wine.
- As a substitute for sparkling wine. Even though some Txakolis are spritzy, the effect is just a little prickle, not full-on bubbles. Txakoli pairs better with foods that accompany bright still wines than with those intended for serving with sparkling wines.
- With items that are more sweet than savory. Txakoli does well with accents of sweetness, but not all-out sugar. Prosciutto and melon, yes; oven-roasted stuffed dates, no.

THE CHEESE PLATE

FRESH	Chèvre (many countries), feta (Greece, Bulgaria)
SEMI-SOFT	Brie (France), tetilla (Spain)
SEMI-HARD	Gouda (Holland), Mahón (Spain)
HARD	Aged Manchego (Spain), Parmesan (Italy)

txakoli | WHITE BEAN AND SALT COD STEW WITH GUINDILLA PEPPERS

GERALD HIRIGOYEN   Piperade and Bocadillos, San Francisco, California

Makes 4 first-course servings

$^1\!/_2$ pound salt cod fillet

$^1\!/_4$ cup extra-virgin olive oil

$^1\!/_2$ cup diced yellow onion

2 tablespoons thinly sliced garlic

2 cups drained, cooked or canned cannellini beans
     or other large white beans

$1^1\!/_2$ cups bean cooking liquid or chicken stock

Kosher salt and freshly ground black pepper

1 tablespoon sherry vinegar

GARNISHES

Olive oil for frying

4 cloves garlic or shallots, sliced lengthwise paper-thin

4 guindilla chiles (see note)

Fresh flat-leaf parsley leaves

Place the salt cod in a bowl, add cold water to cover, and refrigerate for 24 hours, changing the water 2 or 3 times. Drain the salt cod.

Heat a *cazuela* (stove-top terra-cotta casserole) or deep sauté pan over medium heat. Add the olive oil and heat until it ripples. Add the onion and garlic and cook, stirring occasionally, until the onion is softened and translucent but has not colored, about 4 minutes. Lay the cod on top of the onion and garlic and cook, turning once, for 5 minutes total. Using a slotted spoon or spatula, transfer the cod to a plate.

If using canned beans, rinse under cold running water and drain. Add the beans and the cooking liquid (or stock if using canned beans) to the *cazuela* and sprinkle with a little salt and pepper. Cover, reduce the heat to maintain a low simmer, and cook for 20 minutes to blend the flavors.

Scoop out about $^3\!/_4$ cup of the beans, place in a small bowl, and mash roughly with a spoon. Return the mashed beans to the *cazuela* and add the cod, breaking up the fish into large flakes with a spoon and discarding any errant bones. Cook for 5 minutes to heat through. Using pot holders, pick up the *cazuela* with both hands and rotate it, swirling the contents several times, until the elements are blended and the mixture has thickened. Season with salt and pepper and stir in the vinegar. Keep warm.

While the beans are cooking, prepare the garlic garnish. Pour olive oil to a depth of $\frac{1}{4}$ inch into a small saucepan and heat over medium heat until hot. Add the garlic and cook, adjusting the heat if necessary to prevent it from browning too quickly and burning, until golden brown and crisp, 2 to 3 minutes. Using a slotted spoon, transfer to paper towels to drain.

To serve, ladle the stew into warmed soup plates. Garnish each serving with the fried garlic chips, a chile, and a scattering of parsley leaves. Serve at once.

NOTE The guindilla, a long, slender, medium-hot green Spanish chile, is sold pickled in jars. Italian *peperoncini* may be substituted.

GERALD: *I cannot think of two more distinctive elements of the Basque terroir and traditions than salt cod and Txakoli. A green, fizzy, clean, and uncomplicated wine, it marries well with the great supply of seafood and shellfish offered by the Cantabrian Sea.*

EVAN: *Gerald and I go back a long way, to when he was cooking mostly traditional French food. At that time I was struck by his talent. But it was when he gradually rediscovered his Basque roots that he really came into his own, and I've been a vocal advocate of his cuisine ever since. His understanding of the food and traditions of the Basque region make this a great recipe for accompanying Txakoli.*

What I enjoy about this recipe and the pairing is that it's at once authentically Basque (the salt cod being a classic local pairing with Txakoli) and Americanized by making it into a stew with beans and the accent of the peppers. It's a bacalhau recipe that you'll embrace as a way to turn your friends on to this neat wine. By adjusting portion size, you can serve it as either an appetizer or an entrée. Bacalhau is easily ordered online if you can't find it locally.

RECOMMENDED PRODUCERS

PREMIUM

Ameztoi Getariako Txakolina, Spain	Gurrutxaga Bizkaiko Txakolina, Spain	Talai-Berri Getariako Txakolina, Spain
Arregi Getariako Txakolina, Spain	Itsas Mendi Getariako Txakolina, Spain	Txomin Etxaniz Getariako Txakolina, Spain
Doniene Bizkaiko Txakolina, Spain	Nicolas Ulacia e Hijos Getariako Txakolina, Spain	Uriondo Bizkaiko Txakolina, Spain
Finca Jakue Getariako Txakolina, Spain	Roque Eizaguirre Getariako Txakolina, Spain	Xarmant Arabako Txakolina, Spain

verdejo

vehr-*day*-hoh

The arrival of Verdejo in the United States from Spain in the mid-1980s greatly boosted the reputation of Spanish white wines. Vinified most often in stainless steel vats and fermented cool, Verdejo offers up dry citrus and pear-flavored white wines that pair well with food. Its success paved the way for the arrival of Albariño on the market a few years later.

Although they sound the same, don't confuse Verdejo with Verdelho. Verdelho (or Verdello) is a great, somewhat dry grape that's closely associated with the Portuguese island of Madeira. It produces fortified wines with crisp acidity and unusual lime flavors as well as lovely dry table wines in Australia, but it's quite different from Spanish Verdejo.

Alternative Names Planta Fina, Verdejo Palido (Spain)

Styles Medium- to medium-full-bodied dry white

Sometimes Blended With Palomino, Sauvignon Blanc, Viura (Spain)

Flavor Lexicon *Fruit/vegetable:* Fresh grass, grapefruit, green herbs, green olive, green pear, kiwifruit, kumquat, lime ▪ *Wood:* Nuts ▪ *Other:* Light honey, wet wool

Similar Sips Sauvignon Blanc and Sauvignon Blanc blends with flavors leaning more toward tree fruit than citrus or herbs

Where It's Grown Spain (Castilla-León: Cigales, Rueda, Toro; Castilla–La Mancha: Valdepeñas)

Verdejo is unique to Spain. Native to the appellation of Rueda in the region of Castilla-León, south of the city of Valladolid, Verdejo has a long history in the region. In the middle of the nineteenth century, the wines were essentially imitations of sherry. Over time, the desire to produce more interesting wines drove some of the vintners in the region to consult Émile Peynaud, the famed enologist from Bordeaux. He advised them to make white table wines using cool fermentation, stainless steel, and judicious blending to accentuate the grape's inherent fruit. Domains such as the Marqués de Grinon took this advice to heart, and a new style of white wine was born in Spain. Hooray!

Although the grape is at its best in Rueda, you can find Verdejo planted elsewhere in Spain, notably in the appellations of Valdepeñas in La Mancha, nearby Almansa, Toro, and Cigales, which happens to be fairly near Valladolid. In these other regions it's incorporated into blended wines, and when those wines are good, the credit is due in large part to the role of Verdejo.

Vintner's Choices Aged vs. not aged, low-altitude vs. high-altitude vineyard, oak vs. no oak, single variety vs. blended, unfortified vs. fortified

Most Verdejo-based wines, regardless of appellation, are blends. In Rueda the grape is generally blended with Sauvignon Blanc, which accentuates similar qualities in the Verdejo; with Viura (sometimes called Macabéo); or, in sherry-styled wines, with Palomino, the primary grape of sherry. The blending of Verdejo with Sauvignon Blanc is said to result from further advice from Émile Peynaud, who, when asked what other grapes he would plant in Rueda in case Verdejo did not perform well as a dry white wine, recommended Sauvignon Blanc. In general, the higher the percentage of Verdejo in the blend, the better the wine. Rueda's top category of wine, Rueda Superior, must, by law, include at least 60 percent Verdejo; the very best wines are almost always pure monovarietal bottlings. Verdejo grown at higher elevations is the best and most concentrated, and can therefore handle oak and bottle aging. More barrel-aged wines are now being produced, as well as examples that are aged in the bottle before they are released for sale. The traditional sherry-style wine produced in Rueda from Verdejo grapes can be quite good, though it is not often seen outside the local area.

PAIRING WITH FOOD

The simplest approach with Verdejo is to treat it like a slight twist on Sauvignon Blanc. Some Rueda wines have a distinctive fruit-basket character on top of their signature herbal notes. With these wines, the fruit notes—grape, light peach, and nectarine—should be taken into consideration in pairings, especially if the winemakers have left a little sweetness in the wine to pop the fruit.

The hallmarks of Verdejo are vivid flavor and crisp acidity. Like the herbal and grassy styles of Sauvignon Blanc, these wines pair well with many salads, vegetarian dishes, and the freshest and simplest fish. They're also well matched with most shellfish and light poultry and show beautifully with white meats (pork and veal) prepared in a manner that spikes Verdejo's flavors (with citrus, capers, garlic, olives, and ginger). Try it with ceviche; smoked trout salad with endive and grapefruit; a pasta with chicken, sun-dried tomatoes, roasted peppers, and cream; and pan-seared tuna with a lemon-pesto butter. A Verdejo can highlight a recipe without masking its character. Additionally, it pairs well with many cheeses.

The richer oak-aged styles, fuller in flavor and texture, are better treated like a mildly oaked Chardonnay. Pairing with nuts accentuates the light oxidation that occurs with bottle aging. Crostini, with different toppings, are also lovely with these wines.

If you come across a Verdejo made in a sherry style, treat it like sherry and pair it with the kinds of things you'd serve with dry sherry: olives, nuts, semi-hard cheeses, seafood, and brothy soups.

PAIRING POINTERS

Verdejo goes well with:

- Vegetables, especially green-vegetable soups. Verdejo can pair with some bitter greens too difficult for other wines to handle, such as watercress, sorrel, and spinach. Minestrone, purées, and many bisques are also good matches.
- Almost anything emphasizing or enhanced with fresh herbs, such as a Greek salad, chicken breasts grilled with or over rosemary or lemon thyme, or a dish served with salsa verde, herb pesto—or one of my favorites, citrus-spiked guacamole.
- Sharp and racy ingredients. Verdejo is defined by its bright and vibrant structure. Vinaigrette is often the enemy of wine, but with Verdejo, a vinaigrette-dressed salad, or grilled fish, meat, or poultry drizzled with a vinaigrette (especially served at room temperature), can be a solid match.
- Pure and clean ingredients. Try a Verdejo with a tuna poke or a crawfish boil, simply grilled swordfish with garlic-caper butter, or an asparagus salad with toasted walnuts and goat cheese.
- Dishes that are spicy and hot. Verdejo's bright acidity and low alcohol help cleanse and refresh your palate. And if you can find a wine with ripe fruit and a hint of sweetness, all the better.

Verdejo isn't good:

- On its own (sometimes). Some people find it too intense for sipping before a meal. I prefer to drink it with food.
- With sweet dishes. With the exception of a few Verdejo wines that are perceptibly off-dry, most examples don't pair well with the likes of Chinese orange chicken or honey-glazed ham.
- With rich red meats. Although preparing the meat with spices or herbs can work by playing down the meatiness (a lamb brochette with an herbal marinade is quite good), prime rib or a cowboy steak is not the best match.
- With salty dishes. Too much salt kills the fruit and leaves the wine tasting quite tart. And blue cheese is a no-no.

- With earthy dishes. Dishes with ample garlic, onions, or mushrooms can make Verdejo, especially the more fruit-forward examples, seem disjointed.
- With extremely rich dishes. This grape pairs best with leaner foods, and very rich or creamy dishes can make the wine taste tart.

THE CHEESE PLATE

FRESH	Chèvre (many countries), feta (Greece, Bulgaria)
SEMI-SOFT	Teleme (U.S.A.), tetilla (Spain)
SOFT-RIPENED	Boursault, Brie (France)
SEMI-HARD	Provolone (Italy), Roncal (Spain)
HARD	Aged chèvre (many countries), aged Edam (Holland)

verdejo | SHRIMP TARTINE WITH FAVA BEAN, ALMOND, AND MINT PESTO

DAVID KINCH   Manresa Restaurant, Los Gatos, California

Makes 6 first-course servings

FAVA BEAN, ALMOND, AND MINT PESTO
1 cup shelled young fava beans (about 50, from 1 pound unshelled)
1 clove garlic
10 fresh mint leaves
Sea salt and freshly ground black pepper
1 olive oil–packed anchovy fillet, finely chopped
10 almonds, lightly toasted and salted
3 tablespoons grated Parmigiano-Reggiano cheese
About ½ cup extra virgin olive oil
Few drops of fresh lemon juice (optional)

36 large shrimp in the shell (1½ to 2 pounds)
12 slices coarse country bread, toasted, preferably over a wood fire
Extra virgin olive oil for drizzling
Freshly ground black pepper

First, make the pesto, which is best started in a mortar and finished in a food processor. If you don't have a mortar, a food processor can be used for the whole process. Bring a saucepan filled with salted water to a boil. Add the fava beans and blanch for about 30 seconds. Drain immediately and immerse in cold water to cool completely. Squeeze each bean to free it from its tough outer skin. Set aside. (This can be done up to 1 day in advance; cover and refrigerate until needed.)

Using a mortar and pestle, crush together the garlic, mint, and a pinch of salt until a rough purée forms. Add the anchovy, followed by the almonds and continue to crush and pound the ingredients until a paste forms, then transfer to a food processor. If you don't have a mortar and pestle, combine the garlic, mint, anchovy, almonds, and pinch of sea salt in a food processor and pulse until coarsely chopped. If the chopping is labored, add 1 tablespoon of the olive oil.

Add the fava beans to the processor and pulse until well combined but some texture remains. Be careful not to overwork the mixture, as you want it to have some texture. Add the cheese and pulse until well mixed. Then, with the motor running, very slowly add the olive oil in a fine stream until the mixture is the consistency of a pesto. Season with salt and the lemon juice, transfer to bowl, and set aside.

Bring a large saucepan of salted water to a boil. Drop in the shrimp, then immediately remove the pan from the heat, cover the pan, and let stand until the shrimp turn pink and are opaque throughout, 3 to 5 minutes. Drain the shrimp in a colander, and peel and devein while still warm.

To assemble, spread each slice of toasted bread with a generous amount of the pesto and top with 3 warm shrimp. Drizzle with a little olive oil, and then top with a grind or two of pepper. Arrange on a platter or individual plates and serve at once.

DAVID: *When I think of Verdejo, I think of a pleasant "green" character that seems a great match with vegetables, especially in the springtime, and also of nuts and an acidity that stands up to great seafood. The mortar sauce made with almonds and the season's first young fava beans is a perfect flavor match as well as a visual one: the color of the sauce reminds me of the qualities of the wine. The mint leaves and the subtle amount of anchovy also fit in well. Simply boiled shrimp and even the yeasty quality of the grilled bread make their contributions to this simply yet elegantly flavored dish. The mortar sauce is versatile, going well with pasta and even spring lamb as well as other seafood.*

EVAN: *Manresa is named for an inland town in the province of Barcelona. David's food, while not classically Iberian, is inspired and Spanish in soul. David is hugely talented in the world of haute cuisine and a very wine-savvy chef.*

Quintessential is the word I would use to describe this pairing. David has come up with a dish that bridges just about every interpretation of Verdejo imaginable (even the sherry-like styles). His twist on pesto is creative and successful, while the bread, the texture of the spread, and the slight saltiness from the anchovies provide weight and balance to counter the bright acidity of the wine. The shrimp bring out the natural sweetness in the wine. Brilliant.

RECOMMENDED PRODUCERS

EVERYDAY	PREMIUM
Hermanos Lurton Rueda, Spain	Agrícola Castellana Rueda, Spain
Marqués de Irún Rueda, Spain	Aura Rueda, Spain
Sitios de Bodega Rueda, Spain	Buil & Giné Rueda, Spain
Sueño Rueda, Spain	Crianza Castilla la Vieja Rueda, Spain
Tapeña Castilla-León, Spain	Martinsancho Rueda, Spain
Telmo Rodríguez Rueda, Spain	Naia Rueda, Spain

vermentino

ver-mehn-*tee*-noh

The wine industry of southern Italy has emerged from the shadows of its central and northern neighbors. No longer looked upon as curiosities, the local red grapes, led by Aglianico and Primitivo (a grape that is identical to Zinfandel), have caused a stir with their deep, full-bodied wines exploding with spice, parched-earth notes, and concentrated, ripe black fruit. Equally intriguing are the region's new white wines. Tasty white blends from Sicily are derived from both indigenous and international varieties, and Sardinia is producing vibrant and delicious wines from the newly fashionable Vermentino.

The Vermentino grape is grown widely on Sardinia, in Liguria on the Italian Riviera (where it makes some lovely wines to sip while you're gazing at the beautiful people), and on the island of Corsica, which, although adjacent to Sardinia, is part of France. The grape is also grown on the French mainland, in Provence and Languedoc-Roussillon. Although the winemakers may speak different languages, they all agree that Vermentino makes wines you should know about.

Alternative Names Favorita, Pigato, Varresana Bianca, Vennentino (Italy), Malvoisie de Corse, Rolle (France)

Styles Light- to medium-full-bodied dry white

Sometimes Blended With Grenache Blanc, Marsanne, Roussanne, Ugni Blanc, Viognier (Italy, France)

Flavor Lexicon *Fruit/vegetable:* Fresh grass, green or white-fleshed melon, green tea, herbs (lemon thyme, sweet basil), sweet lemon, lime, orange, or tangerine ▪ *Floral:* Citrus blossom ▪ *Earth:* Mineral ▪ *Other:* Bitter almond

Similar Sips Austere Viognier, aromatic Pinot Grigio, very light Gewürztraminer

Where It's Grown Australia (Victoria: Murray Darling; South Australia: McLaren Vale), France (Corsica, Languedoc-Roussillon, Provence), Italy (Liguria, Piedmont, Sardinia, Tuscany), U.S.A. (California: Southern Central Coast)

Depending on whom you ask, Vermentino is said to have originated in Italy or in France. Others believe that it came to these regions by way of the Spaniards who, if you recall your European history, were giving the orders in Corsica from the fourteenth to the eighteenth century.

Americans familiar with Vermentino most likely know it from the crisp, flavorful bottles that emanate from Sardinia, specifically from Gallura, its lone appellation and the source of the most expressive examples. Preferring warmer climates, the Vermentino grape contributes body and balanced acidity to wines. When the ripeness is well managed to avoid flabbiness, Vermentino wines, like Gewürztraminers, are defined by their lifted aromatics. However, their fragrance is nothing like Gewürztraminer's: it consists less of exotic white flowers and pear than of fresh blossoms, green tea, and ripe, sweet citrus. Vermentino's bold, aromatic profile has led many to believe that it is related to Malvasia, and the Corsican name for the grape, Malvoisie de Corse, pays homage to this possibility.

In Liguria, Vermentino (called Pigato locally) produces wines that are lighter and crisper than the Sardinian versions. You can enjoy some really delightful wines from the areas around Imperia, La Spezia, and Savona. In neighboring Tuscany, Vermentino is responsible for the appellation wines of Candia dei Colli Apuani in Massa-Carrara and the lovely Bolgheri Vermentino from Livorno. Genetically the same grape, Piedmont's Favorita is so named because it was the favorite white-wine grape in the region a century or so ago. As white wines have fallen sadly out of favor in Piedmont, it can no longer lay claim to that distinction.

Vermentino is by far Corsica's most widely planted white-grape variety and is the variety in white Patrimonio, the celebrated appellation wine from the north of the island. All Patrimonio white wines are made pure, with blending strictly forbidden. Corsican Vermentino tends to be full and low in acidity.

In Provence, the grape is now known as Rolle and is used for the production of the dry seaside wines of Bellet, while farther west, in Languedoc-Roussillon, it contributes to many local blends, along with other local French varieties such as Viognier, Roussanne, Marsanne, and Grenache Blanc.

Vermentino has recently been embraced in Australia with astonishingly solid results, especially in the Murray Darling area of Victoria and in McLaren Vale in South Australia. In the United States the grape is also new and again quite promising. Although winemakers are still experimenting with several styles (I tried wines that ran the gamut from austerely dry to definitely off-dry), the ripe fruit and aromatic profile of Vermentino is clearly consistent with America's new interest in perfumed whites.

Vintner's Choices Aged vs. not aged, harvested when ripe vs. less ripe, oak vs. no oak, single variety vs. blend

Vermentino can be tricky to work with. Ripeness is vital to bring out the aromas and flavors of the grape, but the grape has a tendency to lose acidity quickly when the fruit gets too ripe and subsequently becomes flabby and far less interesting. Some winemakers redress this imbalance artificially, but in my experience with Vermentino, you really notice the intervention, as the sharpness tastes separate from the rest of the wine, at times almost gritty.

Most of the Vermentino of note in Italy is unblended; the most expressive examples come from Gallura in Sardinia. In southern France, it's more commonly blended. Because it's often sharing the stage with other aromatic whites like Viognier and Roussanne, it can be difficult to ascertain what the Vermentino is bringing to the wine.

This is not a wine for cellaring. Like many other aromatic whites, it's best consumed as soon after release as you can find it. Unlike Riesling, Grüner Veltliner, and even Gewürztraminer, Vermentino-based wines tire quickly and lose their youthful splendor. But ever-hopeful, some vintners are beginning to experiment with wood aging in large, neutral vessels.

PAIRING WITH FOOD

Vermentino is aromatic, and you should think of it as you might a Viognier or Gewürztraminer. Some interpretations can be more austere, perhaps closer to Garganega (Soave) or Arneis, while still other versions have the texture of a good Alsace Pinot Gris and the flavor profile of a warmer-climate, Old World Sauvignon Blanc. So what's the best way to approach this grape? Its hallmarks are balanced to occasionally racy acidity, ripe perfumed fruit, and soft to somewhat austere texture. These make it best suited to pairing with hors d'oeuvres and snacks, selected salads and appetizers, and fish, fish and more fish. Richer examples, like many from Gallura and the Patrimonio wines from Corsica, can pair with pork and even veal. But seafood is usually where I start.

From the raw—salmon carpaccio, sashimi, and even richer tuna tartare—to the cooked—scallop brochettes, shrimp risotto, or pan-roasted halibut—anything fresh and simple is likely to work. Avoid bold and pungent preparations, as the wine gets lost behind them. Similarly, avoid heavy spices and excessive heat and salt. A little miso paste in a dressing or marinade can be nice, but too much will overpower.

Vermentino likes blank canvases: pasta, risotto, *farro,* and potatoes. I find that using the sweeter fingerling potatoes or baby Yukon Golds is a great way to bring out Vermentino's fruit. It follows that a preparation of yam or sweet potato, not too sugary, would also work, as would oven-roasted parsnips, rutabagas, and even corn.

On the meat and poultry side of things, try straightforward dishes that allow the wine to star. In general, it's easier to plan dishes that will show off the Vermentino than vice versa: this makes it an anomaly among the aromatic whites, which usually show off food so well. A plate of mild salumi or charcuterie served up with a little bread and some not-too-briny green olives is a great way to start an evening.

PAIRING POINTERS

Vermentino goes well with:

- Raw fish and shellfish. Vermentino is one of the best wines to pair with fish carpaccio and tartare as well as sashimi.
- Simply cooked preparations of fish and shellfish. Basic whole fish and fish fillets, grilled or oven-roasted and served with potatoes, are great for showing off a Vermentino-based wine. Pastas can pair very well too: fettuccine with shrimp, olive oil, and garlic; penne with squid, Italian parsley, and butter; or a bowl of penne served with clams, peas, and cream.
- Slightly salty dishes. Because Vermentino is moderate in alcohol, it can handle dishes that have a pop of salt. Deep-fried dishes are especially good, such as fresh anchovies finished with a little sea salt or an appetizer portion of *panko*-crusted shrimp.
- Coconut, in moderation and without too much sweetness. Try a side of toasted coconut rice with a breast of chicken, a light and mild coconut curry, or ceviche dressed with coconut milk to soften the bite of the acid.
- Salads. Vermentino is a wonderful wine to pair with main-course salads. Try one with a Caesar salad with shrimp, an Asian chicken salad, or a pasta salad with fresh vegetables and scallops. Avoid sharp dressings.

Vermentino isn't good with:

- Strong flavors. It's better to pick a dish that can highlight the Vermentino than to have it fight unsuccessfully for attention. Pungent curries, flavorful spices, and bold sauces (tamari, oyster sauce) overwhelm its subtlety.
- Very rich dishes. In addition to being subtle and easily overwhelmed, Vermentino's balanced acidity can't compete with dense cream sauces, hearty soups and chowders, or intense stock reductions.
- Dishes that are too sweet. This is a tightrope walk because many Vermentino-based wines, especially those that are ripe and round, can pair nicely with mildly sweet dishes. With too much sweetness, though, the wine will become disjointed. A Thai crepe or butternut-squash gratin can be nice, but sweet mango chutney and candied yams are over the top.
- Very briny or acidic ingredients. Again, most Vermentino-based wines lack the crisp acidity required to pair well with fresh oysters or the sampling of pickled side dishes, *banchan*, which precedes most Korean meals.
- Very earthy flavors. Beets, brown mushrooms, squab, and pungent cheeses are tough on these wines.

THE CHEESE PLATE

FRESH	Burrata (Italy), chèvre (many countries)
SEMI-SOFT	Bel Paese (Italy), Havarti (Denmark)
SOFT-RIPENED	Brie (U.S.A., Canada), pavé d'affinois (France)
SEMI-HARD	Cantal (France), Mahón (Spain)
HARD	Semi-aged chèvre (many countries), dry Monterey Jack (U.S.A.)

vermentino | PAN-ROASTED HALIBUT WITH MELTED LEEKS AND MEYER LEMON–CAPER BUTTER

CRAIG STOLL   Delfina Restaurant and Pizzeria Delfina, San Francisco, California

Makes 4 main-course servings

6 leeks
Kosher salt
4 tablespoons unsalted butter
2 tablespoons brined capers
½ cup olive oil

BEURRE BLANC
2 cups dry white wine
1 tablespoon Champagne or white wine vinegar
4 shallots, sliced
¼ bunch fresh tarragon
1 fresh thyme sprig
1 fresh or 2 small dried bay leaves
6 black peppercorns
2 Meyer lemons
¼ cup heavy cream
¾ cup plus 2 tablespoons (7 ounces) unsalted butter, at room temperature, cut into 2-inch cubes
Kosher salt

4 (6-ounce) halibut fillets
Kosher salt
1 tablespoon unsalted butter
¼ bunch fresh chives, finely chopped

To prepare the leeks, cut off and discard the green leaves, reserving only the white part. Cut off and discard about ¼ inch from the root end of each leek. Cut each leek in half lengthwise, then cut each half in half again lengthwise to create strips about ¾ inch wide. Cut across the strips at ¾-inch intervals to produce ¾-inch squares. Place the leek squares in a large bowl of cold water and mix vigorously by hand. Allow the water to settle for 5 minutes; the leek squares should float to the top of the water. Gently scoop the leeks out of the water, being careful not to disturb the sand and other sediment at the bottom of the bowl.

Place the leeks in a 10-inch sauté pan and add water just to cover and a pinch of salt. Bring to a boil over high heat, reduce the heat to medium, and simmer vigorously until about $1/2$ inch of water remains, 10 to 15 minutes. Add the butter and toss, mixing well. If the leeks still have some crunch at this point, add a little more water and simmer for a few minutes until the water is almost evaporated. If the leeks are creamy and have a "melted" texture, remove from the heat and set aside.

Blot the capers dry on paper towels. In a small saucepan, heat the olive oil over medium-high heat until the surface begins to shimmer. Drop in the capers and fry until they puff up and are crisp, 1 to 2 minutes. Using a slotted spoon, transfer to paper towels to drain. Set aside.

To prepare the beurre blanc, in a 2-quart nonreactive saucepan, combine the wine, vinegar, shallots, half of the tarragon (stems and all), the thyme, the bay leaf, and the peppercorns. Grate the zest from the lemons and set aside. Halve the lemons, and set aside 1 lemon half. Squeeze the other 3 lemon halves into the saucepan and then toss in the spent rinds. Place over high heat and bring to a boil. Reduce the heat to medium and simmer until almost dry, 15 to 20 minutes. Add the cream and cook until reduced by half, 5 to 10 minutes. Reduce the heat to low and add the butter, a cube or two at a time, whisking constantly until emulsified after each addition. Always keep the heat low so the butter will melt but the mixture will not boil. When all of the butter has been incorporated, remove the pan from the heat and strain the contents through a fine-mesh sieve into a clean bowl.

Pick the leaves from the remaining tarragon sprigs, discard the stems, and finely chop the leaves. Stir the chopped leaves into the sauce along with about half of the capers and all of the lemon zest. Taste and adjust the seasoning with salt and squeeze in a little of the juice from the reserved lemon half for balance if necessary. Place the bowl over (not touching) hot water in a saucepan and put in a warm spot. Do not allow the butter sauce to get too hot or it will break.

To cook the halibut, preheat the oven to 325°F. Season the halibut well on both sides with salt. In a heavy, ovenproof sauté pan, melt the butter over medium heat. Add the fillets and transfer the pan to the oven. Roast just until the fish is cooked through, about 15 minutes. To test for doneness, gently press on a fillet. It is done if it seems ready to separate into large flakes.

Just before the fish is cooked, bring the leeks to a boil over medium-high heat. Add half of the chives and cook, stirring occasionally to prevent scorching, until the remaining water evaporates but the leeks are still moist. Spoon one-fourth of the leeks onto each warmed plate and top with a piece of halibut. Ladle on some warm beurre blanc and garnish with the remaining fried capers and the chives. Serve at once.

CRAIG: *This is a dish that can be prepared all year long but is at its best in winter, when Meyer lemons are in season. The simple flavors in the dish support the star ingredient, halibut, and pair beautifully with all styles of Vermentino.*

EVAN: *Craig is an extraordinarily talented chef and one who really connects with Italian food. Delfina is often the restaurant of choice in my family for birthday meals, largely because of Craig's deft hand with all kinds of fish, and fish and Vermentino are magic.*

This is a sublime pairing at many levels. Halibut's natural sweetness works especially well with the wine's fruit. The Meyer lemon echoes this sweet citrus character, while the creamed leeks match beautifully with the wine's often velvety texture. The dish is clean and flavorful but does not overwhelm the wine.

RECOMMENDED PRODUCERS

EVERYDAY	PREMIUM
Argiolas Sardinia, Italy	Antinori Tuscany, Italy
Bruni Tuscany, Italy	Cantina Santadi Sardinia, Italy
Casamatta Tuscany, Italy	Clos Teddi Patrimonio, Corsica
Rocca Sardinia, Italy	La Pietra del Focolare Liguria, Italy
Sella & Mosca Sardinia, Italy	Pala Sardinia, Italy
Uvaggio Lodi, California	Tablas Creek Southern Central Coast, California

AGLIANICO

BARBERA

CABERNET FRANC

CARIGNAN

CARMENÈRE

CINSAUT

DOLCETTO

GAMAY

GRENACHE

MALBEC

MENCÍA

MOURVÈDRE

NEBBIOLO

PETITE SIRAH

PINOTAGE

TANNAT

TEMPRANILLO

TOURIGA NACIONAL

XINOMAVRO

red

aglianico

ah-*lyah*-nee-koh

Italy boasts three great red grapes: Nebbiolo, from Piedmont, in the north; Sangiovese, from Tuscany in central Italy; and Aglianico, from the south. Sadly, although Nebbiolo and Sangiovese are well established, Aglianico is little known or appreciated outside a small group of fans.

The most complex grape of southern Italy, Aglianico has thick, chewy, black or dark cherry fruit and a lively personality along with ample, sometimes massive tannins that are balanced by sharp acidity. Although not for the faint of heart, it is a wonderful wine for lovers of robust reds and for wine collectors. The best Aglianicos age for decades and often outlast the famous wines from farther north in Italy because of their balanced complexity. With the world's climate getting a little warmer every year, I suspect we'll be soon seeing a lot more of this grape outside southern Italy.

Alternative Names Aglianicone, Aglianicuccia, Agliano, Agliatica, Ellanico, Ellenico, Fiano Rosso, Uva dei Cani (Italy)

Styles Medium-full- to full-bodied dry red, medium-bodied dry rosé (not widely available)

Sometimes Blended With Cabernet Sauvignon, Merlot (Italy), other red grapes (California)

Flavor Lexicon *Fruit:* Blackberry, black cherry, black plum ▪ *Earth:* Graphite, mineral ▪ *Wood:* Dark chocolate, dark roast espresso, smoke, spice ▪ *Other:* Dried porcini, tar

Similar Sips Zinfandel, Syrah, and rustic interpretations of Petite Sirah

Where It's Grown Australia (Victoria, South Australia), Italy (Taurasi, Campania; Basilicata), U.S.A. (California: Sierra Foothills [Amador County], Southern Central Coast [Paso Robles])

This grape was reputedly brought to Italy by the Greeks in the sixth century B.C.E. and planted around the Greek colony of Cumae, close to present-day Avellino in Campania. However, the recent DNA profiling work by Attilio Scienza of Milan University found no connection between Aglianico and any known Greek grape variety.

After nearly being wiped out by phylloxera in the nineteenth century, Aglianico has made a comeback over the past few decades, thanks to the relentless advocacy of Campania's Antonio Mastroberardino with his Taurasi and Taurasi Riserva appellation wines. He has almost single-handedly elevated the grape from a curiosity to a universally heralded red grape capable of producing bottles that can rival Barolo, Barbaresco, and Brunello, Italy's other long-lived red wines. Today, Aglianico is an important grape throughout Campania and down into Basilicata, whose Aglianico del Vulture DOC is one of southern Italy's best red wines.

Given Aglianico's ability to thrive in warmer climates, it's curious that it hasn't spread around the globe as Primitivo (Zinfandel), southern Italy's other main player, has done. So far only a handful of producers have taken to growing Aglianico in any quantity outside Italy. Efforts in Australia are encouraging, especially those in Victoria's Murray Darling region. In California, Caparone Winery in Paso Robles led the charge beginning in the early 1990s, and others are now experimenting with it, notably in Amador County.

Vintner's Choices Early vs. late picking, micro-oxygenation vs. traditional tannin management, red vs. blush (rosé/*rosato*/*rosado*), single variety vs. blend, traditional vs. modern approach

Aglianico is a late-ripening variety that boasts inky-black depths of color, ferocious tannins, a firm structure, and aromas and flavors that can be harsh and bold. Despite the often-torrid heat of the south, this grape takes its sweet time ripening and can be at risk of rain and frost if it pushes into winter. It's not unusual to be picking Aglianico as late as November to allow full maturation of the grapes and a softening of the bitter and astringent tannins. Picking too early generally results in hard, green, astringent wines that lack charm and rip up your palate.

Modern winemaking has made young Aglianicos more approachable by incorporating New World methods such as using new oak, shorter barrel aging, and winemaking techniques that preserve fresher fruit. Some winemakers may also be using micro-oxygenation, but few advertise the fact. The same battle of modern versus traditional approaches that persists with Sangiovese in Tuscany and Nebbiolo in Piedmont is also being waged in southern Italy. Only you can decide which style you prefer.

The fundamental decision governing wine style is whether to make a dry red wine or a rosé (called *rosato* in Italy). Winemakers argue that bleeding off some of the fruit juice early in the winemaking process concentrates the remaining red wine, giving Aglianico its hallmark concentration and density. The bled-off must, fermented to make a dry wine, makes a lovely, spicy rosé.

As a red wine, Aglianico is most often not blended, though some modernists have taken to blending the grape with other grape varieties (generally Cabernet Sauvignon and Merlot) to add complexity, balance the tannins, and lend smoothness to this sometimes rough grape and its wines.

My tasting experience indicates that Aglianico grows better in poor, volcanic soils, as fewer nutrients make the vines work harder and result in greater acidity and balance. The finest examples are the Taurasi in Campania and Aglianico del Vulture in Basilicata.

PAIRING WITH FOOD

Aglianico is one of those grapes meant for lovers of colossal red wines, and it demands robust dishes as accompaniments. For pairing, it's important to know whether the wine is made in a traditional or a modern style. Traditional wines tend to be harder, with drier black fruit, intense spice, gritty tannins, and balanced but biting acid; unless you're a bit of a masochist, these are unpleasant by themselves or with lighter fare. The more modern renditions of Aglianico are smooth, rich wines with ripe rather than desiccated fruit flavors and oak and spice nuances; they have mellower tannins and acidity, affording more flexibility in food pairings.

Classic companions are rich stews, grilled meats, and hearty preparations of offal (liver, kidneys, and full-flavored treatments of sweetbreads). Many Aglianico-based wines, traditional or not, will kick the stuffing out of light and simple dishes and suppress the flavor of a straightforward risotto, pasta, or baked fowl. The more gripping and astringent the tannins, the richer and heavier in fat the recipe needs to be. Young Taurasi or Aglianico del Vulture call for full-flavored rustic dishes, such as pastas, roasts, and stews—the less highfalutin the better. Dishes like braised lamb shanks and osso buco are perfect fare with almost all Aglianicos, as are sausage and bean stews, grilled chops, and large steaks. As Aglianico ages and the tannins soften, you can more successfully pair it with veal and pork, which a younger wine can overpower. The same is true of simpler pastas and many semi-hard cheeses. But avoid fish with any Aglianico—the pairing isn't fun for either the *vino* or the *pesce*.

PAIRING POINTERS

Aglianico goes well with:

- Rich and ample meat dishes. The richer the wine, the richer the dish must be. Braised Asian short ribs and thick stews and daubes are ideal.
- Flavorful, rustic dishes, from osso buco to oxtails to braised lamb shanks. As the cartilage and connective tissue around the bones break down, adding their smooth fatty collagen to the sauce, you enter Aglianico country!
- Tomato *in* a sauce, but not *as* a sauce. Some disagree with me here, but a pure tomato sauce tends to remove the texture from a lot of Aglianico because it is too acid. Tomatoes in a sauce, especially fire-roasted or sun-dried, help bring forward the fruit in the wine, as long as the sauce's acidity is balanced.
- Bean and meat dishes: From Brazilian *feijoada* to good old meat and bean chili, there's something about a hearty stew or sausages and lentils that cries out for a young Aglianico.

- Thick pastas and risottos. Baked ziti, pasta with a rich meat *ragù,* risotto with brown mushrooms and Parma ham, or equally ample dishes conjured from your leftovers will all harmonize with Aglianico.

Aglianico isn't good:
- By itself. The wine is almost always too big and tannic if served without food.
- With fish. Even rich and strong-tasting fish will collide with the tannins in the wine, causing the unpleasant sensation of sucking on a penny. If you must serve an Aglianico with fish, go very light (a potential oxymoron) or, better still, choose a *rosato.*
- With light recipes. Very light or simple dishes can be overwhelmed by the wine's personality and flavor. If you want to serve an Aglianico, opt for a fuller recipe; if not, choose a less full-bodied wine.
- With very spicy dishes. If you're seeking to elevate flavors like dry-rubbed barbecue spices, then your chances of a pleasant match are reasonably good. But if you're serving a piquant habanero chile sauce alongside your meat, the flavors will clash, not resonate; again, go for a *rosato* or pick a different variety.
- With most poultry. The full frontal assault of Aglianico can create perfection with a rich duck, goose, or squab but is too much for all but the most robust preparations of quail, chicken, or Cornish game hen.

THE CHEESE PLATE

SEMI-HARD	Gouda (Holland, U.S.A.), pecorino (Italy)
HARD	Aged Manchego (Spain), Roncal (France)
WASHED-RIND	Chaumes (France), Taleggio (Italy)

aglianico | LASAGNA WITH NEAPOLITAN RAGÙ

JOYCE GOLDSTEIN Chef, Author, and Consultant, San Francisco, California

Makes 8 main-course or 12 first-course servings

NEAPOLITAN RAGÙ
⅓ cup olive oil
1½ pounds beef brisket or boneless chuck, in one piece
½ pound boneless veal shoulder, in one piece
½ pound boneless pork shoulder, in one piece
Salt and freshly ground black pepper
1 small yellow onion, chopped
½ cup dry red wine
2 (28-ounce) cans plum tomatoes with juice, hand chopped or pulsed in a food processor
Small pinch of chile pepper flakes (optional)
Meat stock or water, if needed

BASIC CREAM SAUCE
½ cup unsalted butter
½ cup all-purpose flour
4 cups whole milk or half-and-half, heated
Salt and freshly ground black pepper
Freshly grated nutmeg

½ pound dried or 1 pound fresh lasagna noodles
1 cup grated Parmesan cheese
Unsalted butter, at room temperature, cut into bits for topping

To make the *ragù*, in a Dutch oven, heat the olive oil over medium-high heat. Add the beef, veal, and pork and sprinkle with salt. When the meats have given up their juices, after about 15 minutes, add the onion and stir well. Reduce the heat to medium and cook, stirring the onion and turning the meats occasionally, until the meats are browned and the onion is golden. This might take as long as 15 minutes.

Add the wine and continue to cook over medium heat until the wine is absorbed into the meats, about 10 minutes. Add the tomatoes and the chile pepper flakes and stir well. Cover partially, reduce the heat to low, and simmer, stirring often, for 2½ hours. Check from time to time to see if more liquid is needed, adding stock if necessary to prevent scorching. At this point, the sauce should be thick enough to coat a spoon and the meats should be very tender.

Using a slotted spoon or tongs, remove the meats and chop into small pieces. Return the meats to the sauce, and season the sauce with salt and pepper. Set the *ragù* aside.

To make the cream sauce, in a heavy saucepan, melt the butter over low heat. Add the flour and cook, stirring, until it is well incorporated with the butter, about 3 minutes. Do not let the mixture color. Slowly whisk in the milk, raise the heat to medium-high and bring almost to a boil. Reduce the heat to low and cook, stirring often, until the sauce is quite thick and the flour has lost all of its raw taste, about 8 minutes. Remove from the heat and season with salt, pepper, and nutmeg. Set aside.

Preheat the oven to 350°F. Butter a 9-by-12-by-3-inch or a 10-by-13-by-3-inch baking dish.

Bring a large pot of salted water to a boil. Add the lasagna noodles, stir, and cook until nearly al dente, about 3 minutes if using fresh pasta or according to package directions if using dried. If using fresh pasta, lift the noodles from the boiling water with a wire skimmer or large slotted spoon and immerse in a large bowl of cold water to halt the cooking. If using dried pasta, drain in a colander. Lay the cooked fresh or dried noodles flat on kitchen towels.

Spread a thin layer of *ragù* on the bottom of the prepared dish. Add a layer of noodles, overlapping them slightly. Top with another layer of *ragù,* and then a layer of cream sauce. Sprinkle with some of the Parmesan. Repeat the layers, beginning and ending with a layer of noodles, until you have used up both sauces, the noodles, and the cheese. Dot the top with butter.

Bake until heated through and bubbling at the edges, 45 to 60 minutes. Remove from the oven and let rest for 10 minutes, then cut into squares to serve.

NOTE The *ragù* can be made up to a day or two in advance, covered, and refrigerated. The cream sauce should be used as soon as possible after making, as it thickens if it is left standing. If you are not using it immediately, thin it with a little milk or half-and-half before using. The lasagna can be assembled up to a day before baking, covered, and refrigerated. Bring to room temperature before baking, or add 10 minutes or so to the baking time.

JOYCE: *Most of us are familiar with the classic* lasagna alla bolognese, *with its rich meat sauce (containing little or no tomato), velvety cream sauce, and Parmesan, all layered with fresh, tender pasta. In Campania, the lasagna is a luxurious dish that uses dried pasta, creamy ricotta instead of* besciamella *(cream sauce), and a substantial amount of tomato. I typically like to pair a wine with a dish from its region, which for Aglianico would be the Campanian lasagna. Instead, I have blended the two great lasagna traditions, using the* besciamella *of Bologna with the tomato of Naples, and have offered the option of fresh or dried pasta. (To be even more equitable, you can cut the cream sauce recipe in half and combine the sauce with 2 cups ricotta cheese.) Because Aglianico is a full-bodied robust wine with firm tannins and balanced acidity, it can stand up to the tomato component in the sauce. This lasagna is rather formidable, so it needs a wine of similar fortitude.*

EVAN: *Could I do a book without a recipe from my mother? Seriously, those of you who know my mom know that she's one of this country's great Italian chefs, immensely knowledgeable and true to tradition in a contemporary context. She was presenting Wednesday Regional Italian meals in the 1980s at Square One long before regional Italian was the rage. Aglianico is one of her very favorite grapes.*

This is a dish that you will make over and over again: it is as simple and easy to cook as it is delicious, comforting, and brilliant with most Aglianico and Aglianico-based blends. The tomato's challenging acidic bite is tempered by the addition of meat and cream. The lasagna is rich enough to pair with the most generous of wines, and it's versatile: it has both a smoothness that works well with the more modern interpretations of the grape and a rusticity that's perfectly paired with the traditionalists. Buon appetito!

RECOMMENDED PRODUCERS

EVERYDAY	PREMIUM	SPLURGE
Cantina di Venosa Basilicata, Italy	De Conciliis Campania, Italy	Alois Campole Campania, Italy
Caparone Southern Central Coast, California	Feudi di San Gregorio Campania, Italy	Aminea Balardo Campania, Italy
Di Majo Norante Molise, Italy	Mastroberardino Campania, Italy	Basilisco Basilicata, Italy
Terredora Campania, Italy	Tormaresca Apulia, Italy	Elena Fucci Basilicata, Italy

barbera

bar-*beh*-rah

In the Piedmont region of northern Italy, they say Barolo and Barbaresco (made from Nebbiolo grapes) are for selling, and Barbera is for drinking. Piedmont's most widely planted red grape, Barbera comprises nearly half of the red-wine grapes planted in northern Italy. But the Italians have no monopoly on this wonderful grape, which is cultivated successfully in many other countries.

One of the most remarkable aspects of the grape is its climatic range: it is the world's sixth most widely planted red-wine variety. It's also versatile in the bottle. Depending on the age of the vines and the amount of oak aging, Barbera can be light and tart or hearty and robust. While most wine drinkers think of it in its unblended form as an everyday wine, it can be a serious if not especially age-worthy wine, either blended or on its own.

Alternative Names Called Barbera everywhere in Italy and identified by its place of origin—Barbera d'Asti, Barbera d'Alba, Barbera Monferrato—or occasionally by style—Barbera fina, Barbera forte, and so on.

Styles Medium- to fairly full-bodied dry red wine; light- to medium-bodied, slightly *pétillant* red wine; medium-bodied dry *rosato* (not widely available)

Sometimes Blended With Bonarda, Croatina, Nebbiolo, other local grapes (Italy), Bonarda (Argentina), various red grapes (U.S.A.)

Flavor Lexicon *Fruit:* Black cherry, black fig, plum, raspberry, red cherry, red currant ▪ *Wood:* Cacao, spice ▪ *Earth:* Dust, stones ▪ *Other:* Red licorice

Similar Sips Bright, sharp reds with some body, such as ripe, full, high-acid Pinot Noir or Gamay

Where It's Grown Argentina (San Juan), Australia (New South Wales: Hunter Valley, Mudgee; Victoria: Mornington Peninsula, King Valley; South Australia: McLaren Vale), Brazil, Italy (Piedmont: Alba, Asti, Monferrato; Lombardy: Oltrepò Pavese; central and southern regions), Uruguay (Canelones), U.S.A. (California: Central Valley [Lodi], North Coast [Lake County], Sierra Foothills [Amador County], Southern Central Coast [Paso Robles])

Along with Sangiovese and Montepulciano, Barbera is one of the most widely planted red varieties in Italy, and for good reason. It provides growers with excellent yields while imparting deep color, soft to balanced tannins, and (unusual for a warm-climate red grape) high levels of acid. The Barbera from the Piedmont region of northwestern Italy, the area widely accepted as the grape's birthplace, is the best. Once it was thought of as simply a good local wine for washing down the region's rich cuisine, but today many winemakers have reconsidered Barbera and are making it into a delightful though perhaps not serious wine. Although Barbera is ubiquitous in Piedmont, the commonest examples outside Italy are still Barbera d'Asti and Barbera d'Alba. The latter can come from any of more than fifty municipalities (called *comuni* in Italy) in the area, with the best being Monforte d'Alba, Novello, and Serralunga d'Alba. The best areas in Asti, to the east of Alba, include Castiglione Tinella, Santo Stefano Belbo, and Rocchetta Belbo. Asti is considered real Barbera country, as the best vineyard sites there are set aside for the variety, whereas in Alba the best sites are generally planted with Nebbiolo. Perhaps because of this vineyard selection and *terroir,* the Barberas from Asti are riper and more powerful than those from Alba, which are more restrained and elegant.

Elsewhere in Italy, Barbera is grown as much for its propensity to ripen predictably and produce abundantly as it is for its quality. In Lombardy's Oltrepò Pavese, it's made both as a pure varietal wine (ranging from the pedestrian to the pretty good) and as a blended wine incorporating the Bonarda and Croatina varieties. In Emilia-Romagna's Colli Piacentini, it is again blended with Bonarda. It's also grown and produced in the Bologna and Parma hills, the Colli Bolognesi and Colli di Parma, where it tends to produce a light varietal wine and is often made in a *frizzante* style. Almost everywhere else in Italy, Barbera plays a minor role in blends featuring the local varieties.

Barbera likely arrived in California with the Italian immigrants who established themselves as vintners. It is a very important grape throughout the Central Valley, where most of it ends up in generic table reds; quality improves farther north, in the Sacramento River delta near Lodi, and in the Sierra Foothills, including Amador County. Although the wines tend to lack the electricity of their Italian counterparts, they can be full bodied and well balanced when yields are controlled and care is taken in the winemaking process. Nice examples also come from Sonoma County's Dry Creek Valley and from the Southern Central Coast around Paso Robles and Santa Barbara.

Not every Italian immigrant went to North America; plenty went south. Argentina has a substantial amount of Barbera planted, especially around San Juan, and it is often blended with the local Bonarda (which is not to be confused with Italian Bonarda). Barbera is also planted in Brazil and in Uruguay's impressive Canelones region.

Australia is also a source of good Barbera. It's a widely planted grape (grown in no less than seventy-five wineries across the continent), with the best examples coming from the Hunter Valley and Mudgee in New South Wales (which has some of the oldest plantings Down Under), South Australia's McLaren Vale, and Victoria's Mornington Peninsula.

Vintner's Choices Balanced vs. high-yield, oak vs. no oak, red. vs. *rosato*, single variety vs. blend, still vs. *frizzante*, traditional vs. modern approach

Barbera ripens relatively late. Its most notable attribute is its high level of natural acidity even when fully ripe, which has increased its popularity as a grape for hot climates. In these areas (including California's Central Valley and much of central and southern Italy), the grape is grown for its high yields. It is used in blended table wines with the hope that its acidity will enliven the blend, though that's rarely a successful strategy. There's far more mediocre and poor Barbera around than good stuff, so choose carefully. Fortunately for drinkers in the U.S.A., most of what's brought in from Italy is awfully good and often a good value, too.

Although most Barbera is made into still table wines, in Italy it is also made into a slightly sparkling *frizzante*-style wine that is a wonderful counterbalance to rich food, from salumi in Emilia-Romagna to hearty risottos in Piedmont. If you get the opportunity to try one, please do: you'll forget about all but the best Lambruscos!

The main style choice among makers of Barbera is whether to take a traditional or a modern approach. The traditionalists—as embodied by Agostino Pavia, Bruno Giacosa, and Giuseppe Rinaldi—advocate more and older wood, longer aging, and less bright extracted primary fruit. Modernists favor small French *barriques*, new wood, shorter aging, and powerful primary-fruit flavors. These wines are designed to appeal to the modern "international" wine lover. Producers like Giacomo Bologna (with his trendsetting Bricco dell'Uccellone), Angelo Gaja, and Tenuta Garetto are prominent advocates of the modern style. A few, like Michele Chiarlo and Luca Currado of Vietti, are right in between.

Although I believe the best Barberas to be unblended, Barbera can contribute to successful blended wines. Piedmont's Barbera d'Alba cannot legally be blended with any other varieties. In wines from Monferrato (rarely seen in the U.S.A.) and Asti, blending is permitted, and both regions produce some very good examples. Finally, there are some "super wines" that are blends of Barbera with Nebbiolo; these can be quite good, as can playful blends of Barbera with Dolcetto. Barbera can also make a nice *rosato* (rosé), which is produced in Italy mostly for domestic consumption.

PAIRING WITH FOOD

Barbera has all the hallmarks of food-friendliness—high acid, low to medium tannin, balanced alcohol, and usually not too much wood. It goes down easily, and because of its high acidity, it makes a good start to a meal before you move on to bigger red wines with later courses. In

Piedmont you might have a few initial courses (antipasti, pasta, etc.) with Barbera before switching to a Barolo or Barbaresco. And the *frizzante* styles, although difficult to find, are particularly good accompaniments to rich food.

Even more than Sangiovese from Chianti, Barbera is considered the quintessential wine to accompany dishes with "red" sauces. Though both grapes have high acidity, which is critical when matching with tomatoes and tomato sauces, Barbera's bright fruit can help make the flavors of a dish "pop." But it can also pair happily with recipes ranging from veal chops to grilled halibut, and from simple roast lamb to mixed antipasti. Try it with grilled portobello mushrooms stuffed with sausage or dishes with pronounced Asian flavors—*char siu* (roast pork), tandoori chicken, or Vietnamese shaking beef. And in my humble opinion, there are few wines that are better with pizza, or even burritos.

Mushrooms and Barbera have a special affinity—from Piedmont's truffles, if you can afford them, to cultivated mushrooms like portobellos and cremini. Slice and sauté them and serve them over pasta, alongside a steak, or on top of toasted slices of bread as crostini. When pairing with more traditional or earthy wines, try adding a bit of garlic or herbs to tie the flavors together.

Some of the modern-style bottlings tend to be quite oaky, which is a key consideration when pairing with food. If the oak is smoky and sweet, play to that by grilling with mesquite or other charcoal, and char the meat to meld with those characteristics. If the wine is fleshy and smooth from the oak, opt for richer preparations. Above all, remember that not all Barberas are the same.

PAIRING POINTERS

Barbera goes well with:

- Comfort foods. I don't know what magnetic force it has, but the bottles of Barbera I've had with burgers, pizzas, meat loaves, and burritos over the years could fill a small wine cellar several times over.
- Charcuterie, cold cuts, and salumi. This match is a tradition in northern Italy for a good reason. Barbera's high acidity cuts through the richness of salami, *soppressata,* mortadella, bologna, prosciutto, and *lardo.* It's also a nice counterbalance for French pâté and rustic terrines.
- Mushrooms. Put them on veal chops, burgers, and crostini, toss them with pasta, or add them to a risotto. Most kinds will work, from morels to portobellos, porcini to truffles.
- Mild and meaty fish. If you want to break out and serve red wine with fish, Barbera is a great choice. Its high acid, low tannins, and balanced flavors work well with grilled tuna, swordfish, or even shark. Add a tomato vinaigrette, basic puttanesca (with tomato, olives, anchovies, and red pepper flakes) or tapenade, and smile.

- Thick stews and rich meat dishes. When the big meat dishes come out, Barbera is often shunted aside in favor of Barbaresco, Barolo, or even a Tuscan Brunello. But a full-flavored Barbera can hold its own against a lamb stew, traditional osso buco milanese, or classic steak au poivre. If you want a serious wine, try a modern-style, oak-aged Barbera rather than a Nebbiolo-based wine.

Barbera isn't good:
- When you select the wrong one. The range of Barbera is dizzying, from big and oaky to light and *frizzante*. Consider the dish and the wine style before you pop the cork.
- With strong-flavored fish. In spite of its high acidity, Barbera's flavor profile and tannins clash with Chilean sea bass and sturgeon, among others. It will work with milder finned creatures, such as trout, sole, or rock cod.
- With most shellfish. Fins are fine, but avoid the mollusks. You need to be very deliberate in your recipe selection to pair Barbera (except *rosato*) with most shellfish, lobster, or crab.
- With very spicy foods. Chili, curry, or fiery Buffalo wings generally overwhelm most Barberas, although much lighter or *rosato* Barberas might stand up to them, especially if they are chilled.
- With sweet dishes. Though Barbera may offer the impression of sweetness with its ripe fruit and (frequently) oak, most will taste too austere alongside pronounced and obvious sugar, such as a sweet-and-sour sauce, a fruit compote with a roast, or a tropical-fruit salsa.

THE CHEESE PLATE

FRESH	Burrata, mascarpone (Italy)
SOFT-RIPENED	Camembert (France, U.S.A.), robiola (Italy)
SEMI-HARD	Comté (France), pecorino (Italy)
HARD	Mimolette (France), aged Piave (Italy)

barbera | JUNIPER-SCENTED CHICKEN LIVER PÂTÉ ON CROSTINI

EVAN KLEIMAN   Angeli Caffe, Los Angeles, California

Makes 4 to 6 hors d'oeuvre servings

CROSTINI
1 baguette or Italian *filone*
Extra virgin olive oil for drizzling (optional)

CHICKEN LIVER PÂTÉ
1 pound chicken livers
¼ cup extra virgin olive oil
1 thin slice prosciutto, minced
3 tablespoons tomato sauce
1 or 2 juniper berries, crushed in a mortar
Salt and freshly ground black pepper

To make the crostini, preheat the oven to 350°F. Thinly slice the bread, and arrange the slices on a rimmed baking sheet. Drizzle with olive oil. Place in the oven and toast the slices just until they begin to color, about 5 minutes. Do not leave them until they have darkened so much they become hard. Let cool completely, then use immediately, or store in a zippered plastic bag at room temperature for up to 3 or 4 days.

To make the pâté, using a sharp knife, clean the livers, trimming away any fat, membrane, or green spots. In a sauté pan, heat the olive oil over medium heat. Add the livers, prosciutto, tomato sauce, and juniper berries, season with salt and pepper, and sauté, stirring occasionally with a wooden spoon, just until the livers start to firm up, 5 to 8 minutes. Do not overcook the livers or they will be bitter. Use the edge of the spoon to cut into 1 or 2 livers to check for doneness. A touch of pink should be visible in the center. Remove the pan from the heat and allow the mixture to cool for a few minutes.

Using a slotted spoon, transfer the warm mixture to a large cutting board, and chop with a chef's knife to form a rough purée. Taste and adjust the seasoning with salt and pepper.

Scrape the warm liver mixture into a small, colorful serving bowl, place in the center of a platter, and surround with the crostini. Or, smear a little of the warm liver mixture atop each crostino and arrange the crostini on a platter. Serve at once.

EVAN: *This is not your bubbe's chopped liver. The secret to a sweet, creamy result is not to overcook the dish. Try to serve the mixture slightly warm, which will make the livers luscious in texture. Juniper berries add a cleansing sparkle to the earthy liver, and the tomato sauce helps it all hang together. Making this dish is a messy job, but it's quick and always gets a rave review.*

EVAN: *Evan Kleiman has been an advocate and proponent of great Italian food for decades, and her Angeli Caffe was a pioneering establishment in Southern California. She and I share a love for all things epicurean and Piedmontese. Her recipe is a great pairing with Piedmont's most abundant red wine.*

This dish illustrates the principle of serving Barbera early in the meal with antipasti, pastas as primi piatti, *and other starter dishes. Chicken liver crostini is a perfect match with Barbera of almost any style. Its richness is cut by Barbera's acidity, while the meatiness cries out for the dense fruit character and tannin of a red. A* frizzante *style can hold up just as well as the still wines do. Even those modern, oaky interpretations have the smooth, silky richness and spice profile to pick up on the juniper and the sweetness coming from the tomato sauce.*

RECOMMENDED PRODUCERS

EVERYDAY	PREMIUM	SPLURGE
Monteviña Amador County, California	Conterno Fantino Vignota Piedmont, Italy	Campè della Spinetta Piedmont, Italy
Prunotto Piedmont, Italy	Coppo Piedmont, Italy	Giacomo Bologna Piedmont, Italy
Villa Giada Piedmont, Italy	Elio Altare Piedmont, Italy	Michele Chiarlo Piedmont, Italy
	L'Uvaggio di Giacomo Lodi, California	
	Palmina Central Coast, California	
	Pio Cesare Piedmont, Italy	

cabernet franc

ka-behr-nay *frahn* | *ka*-behr-nay *frahngk*

As a former kids' sports coach, I think a lot about team dynamics. Steady rather than a superstar, Cabernet Franc is a key player on any blended red-wine team. I love to have players like Cabernet Franc on my squad—consistent, productive, and easygoing. Not nearly as demanding as Cabernet Sauvignon, and more predictable than Merlot, Cabernet Franc quietly makes many wines shine; yet when the pressure is on it to perform solo, as it does in many Loire Valley appellations, it proves itself equal to the job.

Cabernet Franc brings an herbal note to a wine, ranging from slightly tobacco-flavored to pungently leafy. It is used in Bordeaux, notably in St.-Émilion and Pomerol, but it is also important in the Médoc as a blending grape, and it features in other blends around the world. Some regions produce a wine that is 100 percent Cabernet Franc: the best comes from Chinon in the Loire Valley and its neighbor Bourgueil.

Alternative Names Bouchet, Bouchy, Breton, Carmenet (France), Bordo, Cabernet Frank (Italy)

Styles Medium- to full-bodied dry reds, dry or off-dry rosés (not widely available), dry to off-dry sparkling wines (not widely available), late-harvest medium- to full-bodied dessert and ice wines

Sometimes Blended With Cabernet Sauvignon, Merlot (France), grapes from the Cabernet family (U.S.A., Italy, Australia, and other countries)

Flavor Lexicon *Fruit:* Currant, raspberry, strawberry ▪ *Floral:* Bay leaf, mint, violet ▪ *Wood:* Smoke, toast, vanilla ▪ *Earth:* Dust, graphite, humus ▪ *Other:* Black licorice

Similar Sips Cooler-climate Merlot or Cabernet

Where It's Grown Argentina, Australia (northeastern Victoria; South Australia: Clare Valley, McLaren Vale), Canada (British Columbia: Okanagan Valley; Ontario), Chile, France (Bordeaux: Fronsac, Pomerol, St.-Émilion; Loire Valley: Anjou, Bourgueil, Chinon,

Saumur, and others; Southwest France: Bergerac, Madiran), Hungary, Italy (northwest: Friuli–Venezia Giulia, Veneto), New Zealand, Slovenia, South Africa, Spain (Catalonia: Penedès), U.S.A. (California: Central Coast, Napa Valley, Sonoma County; Michigan; New York: Long Island; Virginia; Washington State: Columbia Valley)

It has now been proved that the lofty Cabernet Sauvignon grape is actually the progeny of Cabernet Franc and Sauvignon Blanc in France, and not vice versa, as previously believed. Cabernet Franc is fairly widespread throughout its home region of Bordeaux, but it stars on the right bank in the wines of St.-Émilion (where it is the foundation of great wines like Château Cheval Blanc and Château Ausone) and Pomerol, famed for its Merlot (though these wines often have a percentage of Cabernet Franc blended in), as well as less-celebrated areas like Fronsac. On the left bank and in other nearby areas like Bergerac, Cabernet Franc takes a back seat to Cabernet Sauvignon. Even so, the often overly austere and closed nature of Cabernet Sauvignon benefits from blending with complementary varieties like Cabernet Franc and Merlot. In France's Southwest, Cabernet Franc tends to be less deeply pigmented and more aromatic. There it is punctuated by berry fruit (black currant, raspberry) and blue flowers (violet and lavender) and framed by a signature dusty herbal aroma and cool mintiness, the latter flavor being most evident in St.-Émilion and Pomerol. In Madiran, the grape is used to help restrain the local Tannat's massive personality in the same way it's used in the Médoc region with Cabernet Sauvignon.

The other standard example of Cabernet Franc, perhaps more representative because it's usually unblended, comes from the central Loire Valley, specifically the appellations of Chinon, Bourgueil, and St.-Nicolas-de-Bourgueil. Here Cabernet Franc, known locally as Breton, makes leaner, fresher styles of wine, generally intended for earlier consumption. Pure and full of black raspberry, bay leaves, and violets, these wines are quintessential Cabernet Franc. Also in the Loire Valley, in Anjou, it is made as an off-dry rosé table wine (Cabernet d'Anjou) that's enjoyed locally but rarely exported. Elsewhere in Europe, Spain produces Cabernet Franc in the Penedès region of Catalonia, where it's used in blends. It's also found in Italy, where it's commonly blended with Cabernet Sauvignon as an easy-drinking, licorice-scented wine often just labeled as Cabernet. Most prominent in the northeastern regions of the Veneto, Friuli, and Trentino–Alto Adige, the grape (known also as Bordo or Cabernet Frank) can be, like the local Merlot, quite green and stalky. Finally, there's plenty of Cabernet Franc planted in central Europe, most of it in Hungary and Slovenia.

The grape has had a rough go of it in the United States. California's efforts have been hit and miss. Here, as in Bordeaux, Cabernet Franc is at its best in blends with Cabernet Sauvignon and Merlot. There are a few noteworthy examples of unblended Cabernet Franc, but most tend to be overoaked and show minimal varietal character. I have enjoyed varietally expressive Cabernet Francs from New York (Long Island), Virginia (Monticello), and Michigan (Leelanau). The grape has been very successful in the cooler climates of Canada's Okanagan region in British Columbia, and in Ontario, where it is made as both a still table wine and a dessert wine, especially as an ice wine. In Australia, Cabernet Franc is grown extensively and used in both blends and unblended varietal wines, notably in the Clare Valley and in McLaren Vale. There are small plantings in New Zealand and South Africa and more in Argentina, especially in Mendoza, and Chile, where it's used mostly for blending.

Vintner's Choices Aged vs. not aged, dry vs. off-dry vs. sweet, oak vs. no oak, old oak vs. new oak, single variety vs. blend, small barrels vs. casks, still vs. sparkling

To me Cabernet Franc is at its best when blended with other members of the Cabernet family. A great Chinon or St.-Nicolas-de-Bourgueil may convince you that the grape can stand on its own, but those examples are exceptions. Even varietal wines in the United States (wines that must contain at least 75 percent of the stated grape on the label) still contain some percentage of other grapes, and that's usually a good thing. Cabernet Franc on its own can be thin, green or weedy in flavor, and lacking in body and texture. But when melded with Cabernet Sauvignon in a Bordeaux blend or used simply as a flavoring agent in a Cabernet Sauvignon or Meritage it adds complexity. Most quality Cabernet Franc spends some time aging in wood, usually oak. Many of today's more international-style wines, especially from the New World, tend to be oak bombs. However, oakiness is a matter of taste.

Oak, along with other factors, can enhance a wine's ability to age. Cabernet Franc, though not always a long keeper on its own, matures gracefully in the company of other grape varieties, as in wines from Bordeaux. Most Cabernet Franc is made into dry table wine, either blended or unblended, but it's also found as an element in sweet wines (especially ice wines in Canada and late-harvested dessert wines) and sparklers such as Crémant de Loire.

PAIRING WITH FOOD

Cabernet Franc is a food-friendly grape. Pairings are largely dictated by the particular style of wine. A classic pure Cabernet Franc, such as one from Chinon, is different from a big, rich, oak-aged bottling from California. And a late-harvested wine from Ontario is quite a different animal from a sumptuous and smooth St.-Émilion from France.

Of course, wines made with this grape still share some signature characteristics. Because Cabernet Franc is inherently herbal, leafy, and a little green, preparing dishes with herbs and herbal marinades and cooking with herbs are good bets. Even throwing a few branches of rosemary onto your grill with the charcoal can bring out the herbal qualities in the wine. Its balanced to high acidity and moderately hard tannins make it a flexible accompaniment to food.

The most significant challenge in pairing with this wine is level of oak. Many Cabernet Franc varietal wines are dominated by caramel, chocolate, and vanilla flavors, giving them limited application at the table. Still, oak is an equal-opportunity challenge: cooks face the same pairing problems with Cabernet Sauvignon, Tempranillo, and Barbera. The solution: if you've got oak, play to the oak.

The off-dry wines can be difficult to find but, when well made, they are great with food. The ripe red fruit, ranging from raspberry to red cherry, with a little kick of sweetness, makes for great pairings with slightly hot Asian or Latin fare and can bring out the best in a ketchup-slathered burger with pickle relish. The sweeter dessert wines can be tasty with chocolate desserts and dishes accented with berry fruit or jam (a Linzertorte, jam cake, or fruit-topped sundae).

PAIRING POINTERS

Cabernet Franc goes well with:

- Green herbs and herbal-scented recipes. Especially good partners for Cabernet Franc include rosemary, thyme, marjoram, and sage. Veal saltimbocca (with sage and prosciutto), a brochette of rosemary-marinated pork, or a classic meat stew garnished with fresh herbs would pair well, as would a risotto or pasta with herbs, onions, garlic and a little pancetta, Canadian bacon, or sausage.
- Cooked tuna. Though not happy with sashimi, sushi, or tuna tartare, Cabernet Franc, especially from the Loire Valley, is a nice accompaniment to a piece of seared tuna or similarly textured fish. Serve it up with a little sautéed spinach, and you've got a winning combination.
- Goat cheese. I enjoy Cabernet Franc with dishes that incorporate mild goat cheese, with its higher acidity and slight piquancy, in the preparation. Pasta with goat cheese, greens, and toasted walnuts is a winner, as is a phyllo pie stuffed with goat cheese and spinach.
- Enchiladas and other Mexican fare. Sometimes accidents are quite fortuitous. After completing a tasting of many Cabernet Francs one afternoon, we brought in some Mexican food. Most of it matched up well, but the enchiladas were dazzling. The sauce, with a traditional red chile, garlic, and tomato base, pulled it all together; the *enchiladas suizas,* with green chile sauce, were also very tasty with the wine.
- Chocolate. This works mostly with the sweeter wines, accompanying moderately to intensely chocolaty desserts—especially when set off by red berries. A ripe and oaky dry example with a chicken mole is also nice.

Cabernet Franc isn't good:

- When you pick the wrong one. When the dish craves a leafy, green French wine and you select a coconut-chocolate macaroon masquerading as an oaky Cabernet Franc from California, the results are rarely pleasant.
- With rich shellfish. The flavor bridges between protein and most Cabernet Franc–based wines are pungent herbs and green vegetables (such as leafy greens, sautéed bell peppers, and broccoli). Because few shellfish recipes include these ingredients, pairing prepared shellfish with most Cabernet Francs is tough.

- With strongly flavored fish. Leaving aside the classic Bordeaux blend or the rich oaky examples, which obviously won't work, even the leaner, greener styles don't show well with catfish, mackerel, or fresh sardines.
- With sweet entrées. Unless you are opting for a fruit-bomb wine (and some Cabernet Francs like this do exist) or working with a style that is actually a little sweet (a rosé or even a red with a lot of new wood), even slightly sweet dishes are tough to match up with these wines.
- With delicate and subtle dishes. Regardless of style, most Cabernet Franc wines are forward and expressive. Subtle or understated dishes are easily overwhelmed.

THE CHEESE PLATE

SOFT-RIPENED	Chèvre (various countries), Neufchâtel (France)—dry
SEMI-HARD	Garrotxa (Spain), Gloucester (U.K.)—dry
HARD	Aged Gouda (Holland), Parmesan (Italy)—dry
BLUE	Cambozola (Germany), Gongonzola dolcelatte (Italy)—sweet
WASHED-RIND	Capriole Farmstead goat cheese (U.S.A.), chaumes (France)—dry

cabernet franc | PENNE WITH ASPARAGUS, PROSCIUTTO, AND PEPPERS

MICHAEL ROMANO Union Square Cafe, New York City, New York

Makes 4 to 6 main-course servings

2 red bell peppers
2 yellow bell peppers
1 pound asparagus spears
4 tablespoons unsalted butter
1 teaspoon minced garlic
1½ cups chicken stock
¾ pound penne
1½ tablespoons minced fresh thyme
2 ounces thinly sliced prosciutto, cut into ¼-inch-wide strips
⅔ cup grated Parmigiano-Reggiano cheese
1 teaspoon kosher salt
⅛ teaspoon freshly ground black pepper

Preheat the broiler. Arrange the red and yellow peppers on a rimmed baking sheet, and place under the broiler. Broil, using tongs to turn the peppers as needed, until blistered and charred on all sides, 12 to 15 minutes. Transfer to a shallow bowl, cover, and let cool for about 10 minutes. The peppers will steam as they cool, which helps loosen the skin. Using your fingers, peel away the charred skin. Then, split each pepper open, remove and discard the stem and seeds, and dice the flesh. Set aside.

Cut or snap off the tough end from each asparagus spear. Using a vegetable peeler, thinly peel the skin from each spear to within about 2 inches of the tip. Cut the spears crosswise on the diagonal into 2-inch lengths.

In a large skillet, melt 2 tablespoons of the butter over medium heat. Add the asparagus and cook, stirring, until tender and lightly browned, 2 to 3 minutes. Stir in the diced peppers and garlic and toss to heat through, about 1 minute. Add the stock, bring to a boil, and remove from the heat. Set aside.

Bring a large pot filled with salted water to a boil. Add the pasta, stir well, and cook until not quite al dente, about 8 minutes. Drain the pasta.

Return the skillet to medium heat, add the drained pasta and thyme, and stir to combine. Cook, stirring occasionally, until the pasta is al dente, 5 to 7 minutes. Stir in the prosciutto, $^1/_3$ cup of the cheese, the remaining 2 tablespoons butter, and the salt and pepper, mixing well.

Transfer to a warmed serving bowl, sprinkle with the remaining $^1/_3$ cup cheese, and serve immediately.

MICHAEL: *Stir-frying asparagus in butter gives it a nutty taste, and the prosciutto adds a complementary "porky" flavor. In this recipe, partially cooked penne is finished in the reduced stock, enriching the sauce with its starch.*

EVAN: *Michael is a gifted chef with a great sensitivity to wine and the unique characteristics of different varieties. Sure, asking Michael, noted for his Italian cuisine, to provide a recipe for an Italian varietal wine would have been easy, but knowing how well he understands pairings, I asked him for an Italian recipe (a pasta) to go with a grape that's not classically Italian.*

This pasta matches well with a wide range of Cabernet Franc styles. The varietal cues (asparagus, thyme, and roasted peppers) are soulmates in the skillet and pair seamlessly with the wine. Oaked examples benefit from the nuttiness provided by the butter. Prepared with dried pasta, the dish is a very good match for fuller-bodied styles. When I prepared it with a fresh pasta, it paired nicely with lighter-bodied wines.

RECOMMENDED PRODUCERS

PREMIUM	SPLURGE
Couly-Dutheil Loire Valley, France	Charles Joguet Loire Valley, France
Lang & Reed Napa Valley, California	Château Cheval Blanc Bordeaux, France
Marc Brédif Loire Valley, France	Clos des Jacobins Bordeaux, France
Philippe Alliet Loire Valley, France	Crocker Starr Napa Valley, California
Truchard Napa Valley, California	Owen Roe Columbia Valley, Washington
Wolffer Long Island, New York	Peller Estates Ontario, Canada [Sw]

Sw = Sweet

carignan

kah-ree-*nyahn*

Carignan (sometimes spelled with an *e*, as *Carignane*) can boast that it's the second most planted red wine grape in the world after Grenache and in the top ten of all wine grapes planted globally. This would be quite an accomplishment if it were planted for the right reasons, which is unfortunately not the case. Great Carignan, still and dry as a red or rosé table wine, or sweet and fortified as a splendid dessert wine, can be delicious, balanced and, in the best cases, suitable for cellaring. But not all Carignan and Carignan-based wines are great.

Carignan is celebrated more for its high volume than for its distinction. It is planted mostly in France, where its primary use is as a blending grape, and it is rarely labeled as a varietal wine. But don't skip to the next chapter yet; there are many good Carignan-based wines, and there is even a website devoted to it: www.closdugravillas.com/carignanrenaissance.htm.

Alternative Names Carignane (U.S.A.), Carignano (Italy), Cariñena, Mazuelo (Spain)

Styles Medium-full- to full-bodied dry red wine, medium-bodied dry rosé, full-bodied fortified dessert wine

Sometimes Blended With Cabernet Franc, Cabernet Sauvignon, Cinsaut, Grenache, Syrah, Merlot, Mourvèdre (France), grapes in the Cabernet family, Garnacha, Tempranillo (Spain)

Flavor Lexicon

RED   *Fruit:* Blackberry, black olive, plum ▪ *Wood:* Baking spice, bitter chocolate, carob ▪ *Other:* Black pepper

ROSÉ   *Fruit:* Orange, rhubarb, sour cherry, strawberry, tangerine, watermelon

SWEET   *Fruit:* Dried cherry, plum, prune, raisin ▪ *Wood:* Vanilla ▪ *Earth:* Gravel, mineral, stone ▪ *Other:* Fruitcake, leather, white pepper

Similar Sips Zinfandel or Petite Sirah in a sharp and tart style, or lean and rustic versions of Pinot Noir or Barbera

Where It's Grown Algeria, Argentina, Australia (South Australia: Barossa Valley), Chile, France (Languedoc-Roussillon: Aude, Banyuls, Corbières, Hérault, Minervois), Israel, Mexico, Morocco, Spain (Catalonia: Priorat; Rioja), Tunisia, Uruguay, U.S.A. (California: Central Valley [Lodi], Sonoma County [Alexander Valley, Dry Creek Valley], Mendocino County; Texas)

Carignan is the workhorse grape of southwestern France's Languedoc-Roussillon, the country's most productive winemaking region. It is planted in vast amounts in the south of France, where most of it is used for basic table wine (sold inexpensively and generically by the liter) and the rest is distilled and used for government-subsidized industrial purposes. Most of the plantings are based in the larger Languedoc departments of the Aude and the Hérault. There the grape is ample in acidity, tannins, and pigment. These traits make it a prime candidate for blending, which is unquestionably the best use for Carignan. The natural bitterness of its acid-tannin profile generally makes for less interesting unblended wines. The best varietal efforts—dark, concentrated, and full of peppery spice—come from very specific appellations and should be sought out. These include Corbières (generally the best), Minervois, Collioure, and Fitou, all blends that have large components of Carignan. There are also excellent red fortified dessert wines, based on Grenache blended with Carignan, from Banyuls, near Collioure, and surrounding appellations.

Although the grape is supposedly from Spain, it is far rarer in Spain than in France. In Spain it is known as Cariñena, which is both the name of the town where the grape is said to have originated and a modern-day appellation with which the grape is essentially unaffiliated today: the variety is grown all around the country. Carignan is at its best in Catalonia, where it's usually blended with Cabernet family grapes. This is well illustrated in Priorat, where old vine Carignan and Grenache are key components of the bold reds of the area. Carignan is most important in Rioja, where it goes under the pseudonym Mazuelo and is used to add complexity and a spicy, almost floral character to the reds of this prestigious region. The producers who use Mazuelo/Cariñena tend to make more interesting wines; most vintners attribute much of this complexity to the minor but important role of this grape.

Carignan is planted widely in Algeria and to a lesser extent in Morocco and Tunisia. Again, it is usually found in blends, which can be quite tasty. You're more likely to find it in Parisian couscous houses (like the popular Chez Bebert) than in American restaurants, but if you do find one, it's worth trying. The wines tend to have a rustic quality, with ample, peppery spice and desiccated, almost pruny fruit. Italy quietly does a nice job with Carignano, especially in Sardinia, where it's a specialty. Here it has notes of plum and black olive, with balanced tannins and pointed or sharp acidity.

The New World also has wide plantings of Carignan. In California, it does well in Lodi, in Sonoma County's Alexander and Dry Creek Valleys, and in Mendocino, among other places. I am especially fond of the Lodi stuff, much of which comes from very old vines with deep plum and berry concentration and an appealing bite. It's also planted in Texas and south of the border in Mexico and farther south in Argentina, Uruguay, and Chile.

Decades ago, Carignan was popular in Australia and often blended with such varieties as Shiraz, Grenache, Cinsaut, and Mourvèdre, but in the 1980s fervor of expanding the wine industry, much of it was pulled up in favor of other varieties (a practice which is also gathering steam in southwestern France). I was surprised and pleased to taste a few Israeli bottlings, which, although idiosyncratic in style, nevertheless showed varietal character.

Vintner's Choices Carbonic maceration vs. traditional red fermentation, dry vs. sweet, fortified vs. not fortified, low vs. balanced yield, oak vs. no oak vs. oak alternatives (staves, wood chips), red vs. rosé, single variety vs. blend, young vs. old vines

Carignan is driven by its strong personality—pronounced in acidity, tannins, and extracted magenta color and framed by an accompanying bitterness. Not only is it rare to find varietal Carignan, especially in France, but the unblended versions do not show it at its best, often resulting in an unpleasant combination of bitter tannins, high acid, and high alcohol. The most successful uses of Carignan feature it as the driving variety in a blend such as Corbières or Fitou or as an accent grape. In Rioja, it plays an important third fiddle to Tempranillo and Grenache (Garnacha). Carignan thrives in hot climates, exploding with flavors of smoked pepper, dark berry, and plum. It crops fruitfully but rarely has much character when cultivated for high yields. However, when grown for more restricted yields and on better soil, the grape thrives. Vine age also seems to be important. Most vines produce better-balanced fruit as they mature and root systems are established. As vines age, their yields drop, achieving even more flavor concentration in the fruit produced. While the optimum vine age varies among varieties, most red grapes hit their stride at between fifteen and thirty years of age, with yields dropping after fifty years. Carignan seems to excel with vines on the higher end of this range.

Carignan, like Grenache and Syrah, needs only light oak. Unless the fruit can really handle the full force of new wood, it's wasted, and many producers would argue that it masks the fruit. If any wood is used, the vessels are likely to be larger, older, and relatively neutral (that is, used several times over so as to provide light oxidation and texture but not affect flavor). Most oak flavor and impact are achieved though wood alternatives such as inner staves (staves of wood immersed in a tank), oak chips (like large teabags filled with oak), or even wood dust (effective and less expensive). Because most Carignan is consumed young, vintners have attempted to soften its hard tannins and sharp acidity while popping the often-weaker fruit with techniques such as carbonic maceration. In this process, which has been perfected in Beaujolais in France, grapes are essentially crushed and fermented by stacking whole clusters on top of each other. The weight crushes and breaks the grapes on the bottom, and the remaining grapes begin to ferment inside their skins in the presence of carbon dioxide: this results in wines with vibrant magenta color, soft red berry and banana fruit, and very soft or no tannins. When the same technique is used with Carignan, it achieves similar results. Finally, there's a small but significant amount of Carignan that finds its way into Grenache-driven fortified red-wine blends made by the VDN process. These wines can be spectacularly complex and for many wine aficionados are the best way to finish a meal with cheese and a chocolate dessert.

PAIRING WITH FOOD

There are several different pairing approaches to take with Carignan, depending on the style. The bulk of the rosé is generic and forgettable, so I won't address it or advocate that you spend much time shopping for it. Most of the quality wines are dry reds with abundant acidity, balanced to astringent tannins, deep color, and peppery fruit.

These bottles are best with fuller-flavored dishes, those that contain tannin-canceling proteins and fat, and those that have a rustic edge to them. Whether served with a French cassoulet, a double-cut pork chop grilled and served with mashed potatoes, or a rich soup such as Italian *ribollita* (a hearty soup enriched with bread), good-quality Carignan-based reds will shine. If the tannins are more pronounced, you need to increase the fat: for example, serve that pork chop with cheesy grits or polenta instead of mashed potatoes, or grate some Asiago cheese over the *ribollita*. It's always safe to play to the spice and pepper in these wines, and a peppercorn-rubbed steak grilled to perfection will show you why. Finally, full-flavored vegetarian dishes, often enriched with cheese, are worthy tablemates: vegetarian lasagna, Greek moussaka, or macaroni and cheese enhanced with any goodies you like, such as truffles or roasted garlic.

For those wonderful fortified wines from Banyuls and other nearby regions, there's no better match than chocolate. Even the most partisan port lovers will agree that this pairing is sheer heaven. I prefer chocolate recipes that are more bitter than sweet and aren't too creamy, as most of these wines, although sweet, aren't sugary. They pair beautifully with those edgy, savory chocolate treatments popular in restaurants today, like chocolate with chile or green herbs. And they rock with cheese, especially blue cheeses.

PAIRING POINTERS

Carignan works well with:
- Rich, rustic dishes. Thick, rib-sticking stews, grilled chops and steaks, or hearty pastas are great accompaniments for a peppery, full-bodied Carignan blend.
- Meat and dried-fruit preparations. In playing with pairings like this, I found the best combinations in dishes that provided texture, "sweetness," and richness, such as veal stew with prunes, and sausage and lamb with apricots and North African spices.

- Composed salads. Not all Carignan-based wines are monsters. Some of the medium-weight versions with higher acidity and balanced tannins pair well with salads combining protein (such as cheese or smoked poultry), peppery greens (arugula is great with Carignan), and balanced, not too sharp dressings.
- Chocolate. From a simple flourless chocolate cake with a molten bittersweet center to a plum tart served with warm chocolate sauce and bitter chocolate wafers, it's all good with a Carignan-accented Banyuls! Avoid heavy, creamier sweets, and opt for dark-chocolate recipes.
- An array of cheeses. Even the drier wines suggest sweetness, with opulent plum and berry fruit. You have to select well, but I have finished many a bottle of Carignan with a plate of cheese, some crusty bread, and a few dried figs.

Carignan isn't good:
- If you pick a bad example. Be very judicious in your selections, as Carignan is a less forgiving grape than Cabernet Sauvignon or Gamay. The good are good, the not so good . . . well, they're definitely not so good.
- With most fish. The oilier the fish, the more difficult the match. Most Carignan-based wines have assertive tannins, which will hurt the fish and vice versa.
- With light and delicate dishes. These wines pair better with full-flavored, rustic preparations. Haute cuisine, simply roasted poultry, or an unadorned veal loin will be blown away by the ample blends. The same is true of fresh and mild cheeses.
- With spicy-hot foods. The capsaicins create a storm by exaggerating the perception of the wine's alcohol while also accentuating the bitter and astringent nature of the tannins.
- With many fresh-fruit desserts. As a fortified dessert wine, Carignan loves chocolate, mocha, many nuts, and dried fruits (raisins, dates, and prunes). It's less successful with fresh white and yellow stone fruit (peaches and nectarines) and apples and pears, unless you incorporate chocolate in a creative way (say, peach Melba with a dose of bitter chocolate sauce).

THE CHEESE PLATE

SEMI-HARD	Mahón (Spain), Petit Basque (France)
HARD	Mimolette (France), Parmesan (Italy)
BLUE	Cabrales (Spain), Cambozola (Germany)—dessert wines
WASHED-RIND	Beaufort (France), Red Hawk (U.S.A.)

carignan | WARM KABOCHA SQUASH SALAD
WITH DANDELION, BACON, RONCAL, AND PECANS

SUZANNE GOIN   Lucques, A.O.C., and The Hungry Cat, Los Angeles, California

Makes 6 first-course servings

1 kabocha squash, about 1³⁄₄ pounds
6 tablespoons plus 1 teaspoon extra virgin olive oil
Kosher salt and freshly ground black pepper
1 tablespoon fresh thyme leaves
¹⁄₂ cup pecan halves
²⁄₃ pound apple wood–smoked bacon, in a single piece
3 tablespoons sherry vinegar
¹⁄₂ pound young dandelion greens
¹⁄₄ cup thinly sliced shallots
¹⁄₄ pound Roncal, Manchego, or pecorino cheese

Preheat the oven to 475°F. Cut the squash in half through the stem end. Scoop out and discard the seeds and fibers, then, using a sharp knife, peel off the skin. Cut each half lengthwise into wedges ¹⁄₂ inch thick.

Mound the squash on a rimmed baking sheet, drizzle with 4 tablespoons of the olive oil, and sprinkle with 2 teaspoons salt, a few grinds of pepper, and the thyme. Toss to coat evenly, then lay the squash wedges flat and in a single layer on the pan.

Roast the squash wedges, turning them over about halfway through cooking, until tender when pierced with a knife tip, about 20 minutes. Remove from the oven and keep warm. Reduce the oven temperature to 375°F.

Spread the pecans in a pie pan or on a small rimmed baking sheet, place in the oven, and toast, stirring once or twice, until they have a nutty fragrance and have darkened slightly, about 10 minutes. Transfer to a bowl, add the 1 teaspoon olive oil and a pinch of salt, and toss to coat evenly. Set aside.

While the nuts are toasting, cut the bacon into slices ³⁄₈ inch thick. Divide the slices in half, and then neatly stack each half. Cut each stack crosswise into lardoons ³⁄₈ inch wide. (The rectangular strips should be a uniform ³⁄₈ inch on each side.)

In a small bowl, whisk together the vinegar, the remaining 2 tablespoons olive oil, and ¹⁄₄ teaspoon salt to make a vinaigrette. Place the dandelion greens in a large salad bowl.

Heat a large sauté pan over high heat for 1 minute. Add the bacon and cook, stirring occasionally, just until it begins to brown but is still tender and chewy, about 5 minutes. Discard all but 2 tablespoons of the fat from the pan. Reduce the heat to medium, add the shallots, and toss to combine with the bacon. Remove the pan from the heat and swirl in the vinaigrette to warm it.

Add the warm squash and the contents of the pan to the dandelion greens, season with $\frac{1}{4}$ teaspoon salt and a pinch of pepper, and toss gently to coat all the ingredients evenly with the vinaigrette. Taste and adjust the seasoning with salt and pepper.

Arrange half of the salad on a large platter. Using a vegetable peeler, shave about half of the cheese over the salad, then sprinkle with half of the nuts. Top with the remaining salad, shave the remaining cheese over the salad, and then sprinkle with the remaining nuts. Serve the warm salad at once.

SUZANNE: *Carignan can be a tricky variety to work with in general, and especially for a salad course. My objective here was to contrast the bitterness of the greens and the natural sweetness of the squash with the grape's earthiness for an engaging palate match. The cheese adds texture, enabling you to serve a richer wine.*

EVAN: *Suzanne is one of America's great chefs. We first met at Aspen, when she was named one of* Food & Wine's *ten best new chefs in 1999. At the time, she was just coming into her own. Suzanne understands and loves wine and has a penchant for more daring varieties. I challenged her to come up with a salad dish to pair with Carignan, and she responded with this delicious recipe.*

Carignan comes in many forms, and clearly one dish can't match well with all of them. This salad, although fabulous, is not a perfect match with a very tannic and overly dense blend, but it does pair well with other styles. Carignan needs a foil for its higher acidity (hence the wine-friendly sherry vinaigrette), its tannins (balanced by the cheese), and the alcohol (the squash adds the necessary richness and texture). The wine's personality may demand that you adjust the seasoning a little (using more or less pepper) and perhaps add a little more cheese, but that's an individual choice. It's a really wonderful match for most of the Carignan-based wines available in the market.

RECOMMENDED PRODUCERS

EVERYDAY	PREMIUM
Castelmaure Southwest France	Agly Brothers Roussillon, France
Cline Cellars Contra Costa County, California	Domaine d'Aupilhac Southwest France
CoVilalba Catalonia, Spain	Domaine du Mas Blanc Languedoc-Roussillon, France [Sw]
Domaine de Fontsainte Southwest France	Frick Mendocino County, California
Domaine de Nizas Southwest France	Les Clos de Paulilles Languedoc-Roussillon, France [Sw]
Santadi Sardinia, Italy	Tenute Sella & Mosca Sardinia, Italy

Sw = Sweet

carmenère

car-men-*ehr*

The story of Carmenère is a bit like the tale of the ugly duckling. Banished from France's Bordeaux, it was quietly transported to Chile, where it was previously unknown but embraced and subsequently confused with Merlot. And it thrived. When the grape was later discovered by accident to be Carmenère, a Chilean swan emerged.

Although Carmenère is not indigenous to Chile, it might as well be, as it performs better there than anywhere else on earth. Chileans take pride in this grape, much as Argentineans do with Malbec and New Zealanders do with Sauvignon Blanc.

Alternative Names Cabernelle (France), Carmenelle, Carméneyre, Grand Vidure (France, Chile)

Styles Medium- to medium-full-bodied dry red wine

Sometimes Blended With Grapes from the Cabernet family (Chile, France)

Flavor Lexicon *Fruit/vegetable:* Blackberry, plum, tomato leaf ▪ *Floral:* Black tea leaf, herbs (fresh rosemary, thyme, and tarragon), sarsaparilla ▪ *Wood:* Bitter chocolate, smoke, spice ▪ *Other:* Cinzano (red)

Similar Sips Cabernet Franc, herbal examples of Merlot and Mencía

Where It's Grown Australia (Victoria: Geelong, King Valley), Chile (Aconcagua; Central Valley: Cachapoal Valley, Colchagua Valley), France (Bordeaux), Italy (Friuli–Venezia Giulia, Veneto), U.S.A. (California)

Was there really a sixth Jackson (Janet) in the Jackson Five? Well, Carmenère could have been Janet, related to but not included in the nuclear family of Cabernet Sauvignon grapes—Merlot, Cabernet Franc, Malbec, and Petit Verdot. Carmenère made some significant contributions to the early wines of Bordeaux. Never a star, it was used to produce full red wines used for blending, in the same way Petit Verdot is used today. But Bordeaux was a cooler environment then, and Carmenère requires a lot of heat to ripen. The grape fell out of favor and was banished when the area was replanted after France's phylloxera epidemic in the late nineteenth century. It is still grown in Bordeaux, where it is still used for blending, but it is becoming increasingly rare.

Instead, today the wine world associates Carmenère with Chile, where it was brought from France in the mid-1800s. It's not surprising that Chileans initially confused it with Merlot, because the vines look very similar and produce similar-flavored grapes. It wasn't until 1994 that the French ampelographer Jean-Michel Boursiquot unmasked the ugly duckling. Today, under the name Carmenère, it is a very important grape in Chile that exhibits strong regional differences. In the Central Valley's Cachapoal area, where 80 percent of the grapes are red, styles are classic, balancing a deep, ripe black fruit with the grape's characteristic smoky and slightly herbal tones. In the newer winegrowing area of nearby Colchagua, Carmenère takes on deeper bitter-chocolate and spicy, smoky tones. The cooler part of the region is especially known for an elegant and austere style of wine. Farther north, in the Aconcagua Valley, where the climate is drier and warmer, Carmenère is a newcomer, and the wines appear to be marked by a fresh fruit and less intensity.

Carmenère is still rare in the United States, though some vintners in warmer climates are excited about its possibilities. The warm climates of Australia would also seem to offer a good home for it, but it really hasn't caught on outside the King Valley and Geelong in Victoria. More of it is grown in Italy, where the grape, again initially mistaken for another variety (Cabernet Franc), is used successfully for blending with Cabernet family grapes.

Vintner's Choices Cool vs. warm-climate vineyards, micro-oxygenation vs. traditional tannin management, young vs. old vines

Carmenère is a risky grape. It can be heroically unforgiving if not managed well, and it's a bit like Goldilocks in needing growing conditions that are just right—ample water in winter, gentle spring weather for budding, and long, hot summers for maturing. Without plentiful warmth to ripen the grapes, drinking cool-climate Carmenère is like sucking on dill pickles (this is the great challenge of growing Carmenère in Bordeaux). The other challenge is achieving high enough acidity to ensure that the wine is balanced rather than flabby. Tannins can be harsh and gritty, so judicious micro-oxygenation is increasingly being practiced to round out the texture and create a supple mouthfeel. Most winemakers I have spoken with also say that blending the variety correctly (since it's rarely made as an unblended wine), is essential. Some add Petit Verdot (for acidity and bite); others add Syrah (Shiraz) for fruit. Most blends tend to be classically Bordelais, with varying amounts of Merlot and Cabernet Sauvignon to add complexity and smooth out the rough edges and compensate for potential deficiencies. Finally, many growers and vintners believe that harvesting from vines over twenty years old is a key to quality.

At its best, Carmenère can produce full-bodied, full-flavored, deeply pigmented wines that combine some of the best qualities of Cabernet Franc and Merlot, with balanced tannins and the ripe herbal notes that Cabernet Franc wines display in a wine like Chinon. Modern winemaking is giving us more wines like this and far less pickle juice.

PAIRING WITH FOOD

I generally approach Carmenère much the same way I do the better Merlots. Under most circumstances, both grapes have an underlying green and lightly herbal character. It's always a good strategy to play to these elements. Carmenère pairs well with meat dishes containing olives (a Provençal stew of lamb with black olives and fresh thyme), and herbal treatments (marinades, accompaniments like a *salsa verde,* or condiments like *gremolata*). Vegetables that can be hard to pair with many other red wines, including Swiss chard, eggplant, radicchio, mustard greens, broccoli rabe, and spinach, can pair nicely with Carmenère's green character. And virtually anything prepared with lentils is a slam dunk.

Much like a Cabernet Franc, Carmenère in lighter, less oaky versions is a wonderful partner for tuna and swordfish. Unlike Cabernet Franc, Carmenère works nicely with prawns or scallop dishes (for example, wrapped in roasted or grilled bacon or prosciutto or sautéed with sun-dried tomatoes). Because of Carmenère's naturally smoky personality, it works nicely with hardwood-smoked foods, and of course grilling is an option. Even wok smoking on the stove top is a great cooking method to show off a Carmenère.

PAIRING POINTERS

Carmenère goes well with:

- Smoked foods. One of the hallmark flavors of Carmenère is smokiness, so go with it. Smoked salmon may be a stretch for all but the lightest of Chilean examples, but smoked chicken, pork shoulder, and even beef brisket all match up well with these wines.
- Herbs and sauces. More than almost any other red grape, Carmenère pairs well with herbs because of its own herbal notes. An herbal *salsa verde* or a classic lemon, garlic, and parsley *gremolata* on a piece of grilled meat is perfect. A rolled and tied lamb loin with fresh rosemary, slowly roasted, would also be sublime.
- Gamy recipes. This grape stands up well to strongly flavored poultry, offal, and red-meat dishes. I enjoy Carmenère with squab, calves' liver, lamb, and venison.
- Pasta. Carmenère can pair well with a tomato and meat sauce over penne, a spaghetti puttanesca, or a traditional amatriciana sauce with bacon, red wine, tomato, onions, and a kiss of hot pepper.
- Eggplant. This is my top choice of wine to serve with eggplant—moussaka, eggplant lasagna, baba ghanoush, and more.

Carmenère isn't good with:

- Dishes that border on sweet. Most Carmenère is very dry, herbal scented, and smoky, so unless you are entertaining with an oaky-sweet and heavily ripened international interpretation, the wine will clash with perceived or actual sweetness in food.
- Simply prepared fish. Tuna and swordfish aside, most simple fish dishes don't pair well with Carmenère. With oily fish, Carmenère will take on an unpleasant metallic accent, and most white-fleshed fish will be overwhelmed, especially if the wine is big and tannic. A basic fish stew, like cioppino, could work if you leave out the mussels and clams (see below).
- Most bivalves and mollusks. Oysters, clams, mussels, and sea snails are awful with Carmenère. The wine tastes coppery or tinny, as does the shellfish.
- Delicate and subtle dishes. Like Cabernet Franc or Sauvignon, most Carmenère is just too bold for lighter dishes.
- Many cheeses. Semi-hard and harder cheeses will work; very strong cheeses, like Époisses, will not. Carmenère overwhelms soft-ripened and fresh cheeses, too.

THE CHEESE PLATE

SEMI-HARD	Caciocavallo (Italy), Comté (France)
HARD	Aged Cotija (Mexico), aged provolone (Italy, U.S.A.)
WASHED-RIND	Chaumes (France), Taleggio (Italy, U.S.A.)

carmenère | LENTIL SOUP WITH FENNEL SAUSAGES

FRANK STITT Bottega, Chez Fonfon, and Highlands Bar and Grill, Birmingham, Alabama

Makes 6 main-course servings

3 tablespoons extra virgin olive oil
1 large Vidalia or other sweet onion, cut into ¼-inch dice
2 carrots, peeled and cut into ¼-inch dice
2 red bell peppers, seeded and cut into ¼-inch dice
½ fennel bulb, trimmed and cut into ¼-inch dice
1 clove garlic, crushed
1 dried chile
2½ cups Le Puy lentils or brown lentils, rinsed
Bouquet garni of several fresh thyme sprigs, 1 leek top (optional),
    and 2 bay leaves, tied in a cheesecloth bundle
2 quarts spring water or chicken stock
Salt
2 fresh fennel sausages
½ cup Carmenère or other dry red wine
Fruity extra virgin olive oil for serving
Chopped fresh flat-leaf parsley, thyme, or marjoram for garnish

In a large soup pot, heat 2 tablespoons of the olive oil over medium heat. Add the onion, carrots, bell peppers, and fennel and cook, stirring occasionally, until the vegetables have softened, about 10 minutes. Raise the heat to high, add the garlic and chile, and cook until the garlic is softened, 1 to 2 minutes. Add the lentils, bouquet garni, and water, season with salt, and bring to a boil. Reduce the heat to medium-low and simmer, uncovered, until the lentils are very tender, about 45 minutes.

While the soup is simmering, in a heavy sauté pan, heat the remaining 1 tablespoon oil over medium heat. Add the sausages and cook, turning as needed, until golden on all sides, 6 to 8 minutes. Add the wine, cover, reduce the heat to low, and cook until the sausages are cooked through, about 10 minutes. Remove from the heat and keep warm.

When the soup is ready to serve, remove and discard the bouquet garni. Slice the sausages and add them, along with any wine left in the sauté pan, to the soup. Stir to mix, then taste and adjust the seasoning. Ladle the soup into warmed bowls and top each serving with a drizzle of fruity olive oil and a scattering of chopped herbs. Serve piping hot.

FRANK: *I like the dusty, herbal, mineral quality of the Carmenère with the rustic flavor of lentils and sausages. Lentils add a pleasing green character and a texture that works beautifully with the wine, while the sausage adds the necessary meatiness.*

EVAN: *Frank's food is soulful and authentic. Although he is one of the pioneering great chefs of the American Deep South, he's much more than a southern chef. Frank's roots, as the recipe attests, are in Europe. (And as I don't cover Scuppernong in this book, I can't really test how well his recipes pair with traditional local southern wines.)*

You'd have a hard time coming up with a dish to show off Carmenère any better. The pairing with lentils is perfect. I especially like the addition of fennel sausage, as the spice works nicely with the wine. If you opted for smoked sausage instead, that flavor would link with the smokiness in the wine. There's enough richness and texture in this soup or meal in a bowl for even those turbo-charged, high-alcohol international interpretations, and the oak will be countered by the lentils' personality.

RECOMMENDED PRODUCERS

EVERYDAY	PREMIUM	SPLURGE
Inacayal Mendoza, Argentina	Carmen Maipo Valley, Chile	Apaltagua Colchagua, Chile
MontGras Colchagua Valley, Chile	Concha y Toro Colchagua Valley, Chile	Casa Lapostolle Colchagua, Chile
Santa Rita Rapel Valley, Chile	Cono Sur Colchagua Valley, Chile	Hacienda Araucano Colchagua Valley, Chile
Terra Noble Colchagua Valley, Chile	Miguel Torres Central Valley, Chile	Viña Errázuriz Aconcagua, Chile

cinsaut

san-soh

Cinsaut (or Cinsault) is most familiar not for itself, but for its role as one of the two parent grapes of the often-maligned Pinotage. Nevertheless, it is a grape to be reckoned with. It's one of France's most prolific producers (ranked as high as fourth in the late 1970s). With the focus on sexier, more-complex grapes with higher pedigrees, however, Cinsaut has fallen out of favor. It is still used as a blending grape in southern France and is an important component in one of the world's greatest rosés, from Tavel in the southern Rhône Valley. In fact, this red grape is almost always at its best as a rosé. But it's worth looking at all of the styles and interpretations of the variety before our recipe leads us to one of these great pink wines.

Alternative Names Blue Imperial, Bourdales, Cinq-sao, Cinsault, Hermitage (South Africa), Oeillade (Australia), Ottavianello (Italy), Picardin, Prunella, Salerne (France)

Styles Medium- to full-bodied dry rosé; medium- to full-bodied dry red

Sometimes Blended With Other grapes from the classic Châteauneuf-du-Pape blend, including Grenache, Mourvèdre, Syrah, Counoise, Vaccarese, and Clairette; grapes from the Cabernet family (France)

Flavor Lexicon

RED   *Fruit:* Blueberry, plum, prune ▪ *Wood:* Cinnamon, toasted almond ▪
    Earth: Farmyard ▪ *Other:* Meat, white pepper

ROSÉ   *Fruit:* Raspberry, sour cherry, strawberry, watermelon ▪ *Floral:* Tea leaf ▪
    Earth: Dust ▪ *Other:* Pink peppercorn

Similar Sips Xinomavro, lighter Pinotage, lighter Grenache-driven Rhône and red or rosé blends

Where It's Grown Algeria, Australia (South Australia: Barossa Valley, McLaren Vale; Western Australia: Geographe), France (Corsica, Languedoc-Roussillon: Aude, Hérault, Provence, Rhône Valley), Lebanon, Morocco, South Africa, U.S.A. (California: Sierra Foothills [Calaveras County], Sonoma County [Dry Creek Valley]; Washington: Walla Walla Valley)

Cinsaut has historically been an important grape in the south of France. Like Carignan, it is both very productive and drought-resistant. It was widely grown until the recent focus on higher quality led to its being replaced with other grapes. Rarely found on its own as a red wine, Cinsaut is known for producing softer, fruit-forward, aromatic wines that are simply not all that interesting in isolation. It has deep color and gushes with fruit: in this respect it resembles Grenache, which is often blended with Cinsaut. Moreover, like Grenache, it's flexible in being able to contribute to blended dry red wines, dry rosés, and even, in small quantities, some Roussillon *vins doux naturels* (VDNs). It's clearly at its best as a component of wines such as Châteauneuf-du-Pape, where it's admittedly a bit player, and in the great blush wines of Tavel, a rosé-only appellation in the southern Rhône region just north of Avignon. With Tavel's status a benchmark for the increasingly popular category of dry rosés, Cinsaut has started to be appreciated for what it brings to the mix. Indeed, all-Cinsaut rosés are becoming increasingly visible. Cinsaut is still produced in large quantities in the Languedoc, especially in the larger Aude and Hérault departments. It is also grown in Provence, as a blending grape, and in Corsica.

Although Cinsaut's popularity has been fading in many parts of France, it's still viable in North Africa. It forms the base of Morocco's red and rosé wine industry; it is less important in Algeria. Cinsaut plays an important role in Lebanon's wine industry, as it has for centuries, although here too it is losing acreage to better-known grapes: it is a vital component of Serge Hochar's great Château Musar.

Known as Ottavianello in Italy, it plays a part in many basic red wines. In South Africa, where it was once the most widely planted red variety, Cinsaut plantings have decreased, but it is still found as a varietal wine or blended with Cabernet Sauvignon. My tastings confirmed that many of the best examples of Cinsaut as a red table wine come from South Africa. They tend to be smoky, fruit-forward, defined and balanced; their approachable tannins are characteristic of the grape. As in other places, Cinsaut is also used in South Africa for easy-drinking red wine blends and for rosés. And without Cinsaut, there would be no Pinotage.

Cinsaut doesn't play a major role in the Americas: about the only sightings worth mentioning are in California, where it's made in a Rhône style, as both a red and a rosé, and in Walla Walla, Washington, where several Rhône-wine devotees have planted it to use in their blends. In Australia, where it's known mostly as Oeillade, it's not a prominent grape: the most noteworthy plantings are in South Australia's Barossa Valley and McLaren Vale.

Vintner's Choices Balanced vs. high yield, pure vs. blended, red vs. rosé

The greatest challenge with Cinsaut, as with Carignan or Grenache, is to keep yields in balance. Winemakers may be tempted to get greedy and allow the vines to put out lots and lots of fruit. Ironically, high yields have minimal effect on the color of the grapes, which is why it's appealing to let it go. But when the vines produce exuberantly, the fruit becomes increasingly dilute. Its tannins, already relatively low, drop further as yields are extended, lowering the life expectancy of the wine. All of these factors call for blending the grape with other varieties, and it is often cast in a supporting role. It's known for adding a rustic, fruity, or meaty character to wines, with nuances of pepper (these can be hard to distinguish if it's blended with Mourvèdre or Syrah) and various spice notes. For the finest examples of Cinsaut as a red wine, seek out South African and Lebanese versions. However, Cinsaut's fruit character is best shown off in a rosé—especially in Tavel, but also throughout Provence and into the Southwest. As a major component of blush wines, Cinsaut adds flavors of tart berry and cherry fruit with spice and notes of black tea and watermelon. Tavel's qualities are emulated by many dry rosé wines around the world (with the exception of *vin gris* wines, specifically the lighter "gray" bleed from Pinot Noir, which are elegant, less weighty, and unquestionably less fruit-driven).

PAIRING WITH FOOD

Because good red Cinsaut can be hard to find, I focus mostly on rosé styles. As a red, Cinsaut has a meaty and spicy character without the charm and assertive black pepper of Mourvèdre or the overtly grapey charm of Grenache. It pairs best with spicy and ethnic fare, from North African couscous and *tagine* to rustic stews and daubes or even a hearty bowl of Creole red beans and rice. Although it matches nicely with most grilled meats, a more regal red wine will show off your marbled beef better.

As a rosé with food, Cinsaut rocks. Indulge me while I extol the merits of good, dry blush wines. Most wine consumers do not take rosé seriously. It's seen as maybe suitable for a picnic or a beach party, but not for the dinner table. These people are missing out. Rosé is loved by winemakers, who appreciate its unique white-wine structure, its light red-wine flavor, and its affinity with food. It's a great alternative to beer and a change from drinking chewy reds.

Dry rosé is brilliant with seafood of all kinds. If it has a shell or fins, it will go with dry rosé—grilled tilapia or tuna, steamed mussels or clams, salty anchovies or sardines, and sashimi of any color or texture. At the Asian table, a good Tavel pairs beautifully with dim sum, Indian biryani, Japanese yakitori, and Singaporean chicken rice. Dry rosé is also very good with many dishes from the Caribbean, ranging from Jamaican jerk chicken to a good Cuban pressed-pork sandwich or one of those wonderful seafood concoctions from Martinique, Barbados, or Antigua. And if you want a great wine for gumbo or paella, look no further. I could go on and on, but I have to save a few other tablemates for Grenache.

Cinsaut goes well with:

- Composed tuna salads (as a rosé). Tavel with salade niçoise is timeless, but so is a plate of lightly dressed white beans and chopped red onion, topped with grilled tuna or a quickly seared piece of soy-marinated tuna, served with a tomato vinaigrette on a bed of spring greens.
- Rustic stews and braises (as a red). Whether you're serving braised lamb shanks or Texas chili, a red-wine blend containing Cinsaut will match up to the rich texture of these rib-sticking recipes.
- Chinese food (as a rosé). Okay, now you know my go-to wine. If I'm not taking a break from wine and sucking down a Tsingtao beer, I'm likely to open a bottle of dry blush to unify the range of flavors in a family-style Chinese dinner, where dishes are shared and people are eating a range of tastes and flavors.
- Flavorful rice dishes (as a rosé). While a classic Grenache rosé is a time-honored match with Spanish paella, a Cinsaut-based blush is a fine substitute. The spicy elements of the wine pair nicely with a New Orleans gumbo or a risotto of mussels, fennel, diced tomatoes, and a touch of pesto.
- Ratatouille (as a rosé or red). I love this classic Provençal preparation, and it's especially good with Cinsaut-based rosé wines as well as local reds with Cinsaut in the mix. The combination of diverse flavors brings out the spicy best in the reds and melds harmoniously with the rosés.

Cinsaut isn't good with:

- Overly spicy food (as a rosé or a red). The relatively high alcohol level of Cinsaut clashes with ultraspicy foods. Although rosé is often a great choice with hot food, Cinsaut isn't the best choice: but go for a wine with lower alcohol and a kiss of sweetness (something from the Loire Valley or California). The same goes for reds.
- Most fish (as a red). The meaty character you find in the best varietal versions (from Lebanon, Morocco, and South Africa) clashes with most fish. And if the fish is pungent and oily, then, as they say in New York, "fuggetaboutit."
- Fine cuts of red meat (as a red). For cuts like prime rib and well-marbled rib-eye steak, a wine like Cabernet Sauvignon will bring out their flavors to the fullest. Most Cinsaut-based red wines won't be bad, but they won't add any magic. And with the price of prime beef these days, I want my world rocked a little when I serve it.
- Overtly salty foods (as a red). Saltier dishes, from tangy, hot Buffalo wings with blue-cheese dressing to a plate of fried clams, exaggerate what little tannin the wine has, accentuate its meaty character, and flatten the fruit.

- Desserts (as a rosé). People often assume that because it's pink, all rosé is brilliant with fruit. And although off-dry blush wines certainly can be, the drier styles come off as tart in the presence of ripe red fruit—strawberries, raspberries, and the like. Cinsaut works better with fruit that is underripe to tart (strawberries out of season, pomegranate seeds, and red plums are great and readily available examples).

THE CHEESE PLATE

FRESH	Burrata (Italy, U.S.A.), fresh chèvre (many countries)—rosé
SEMI-SOFT	Monterey Jack (U.S.A.), Saint-Nectaire (France)—rosé
SOFT-RIPENED	Brie (France, U.S.A.), Mount Tam (U.S.A.)—rosé
SEMI-HARD	Asiago (Italy), Gruyère (Switzerland, U.S.A.)—dry red

cinsaut | DUCK BASTEEYA

MOURAD LAHLOU   Aziza, San Francisco, California

Makes 4 to 6 first-course servings

4 whole duck legs
Kosher salt and freshly ground black pepper
1 tablespoon grape seed oil
2 tablespoons olive oil
1/2 pound yellow onions, thinly sliced
4 tablespoons unsalted butter
Leaves from 1/2 bunch flat-leaf parsley, chopped
1/4 cup loosely packed fresh cilantro leaves, chopped
1 cinnamon stick, about 3 inches long
1/4 teaspoon Spanish saffron threads
1/2 teaspoon ground ginger
1/4 teaspoon ground turmeric
2 1/2 cups duck stock, chicken stock, or water
1/2 pound blanched almonds
6 large eggs, lightly beaten
1 1/2 teaspoons orange blossom water (optional)
1/2 cup clarified butter, melted and cooled
1/4 cup granulated sugar
1 1/2 teaspoons ground cinnamon, plus more for sprinkling
12 *feuilles de brik* or phyllo sheets (see note)
1/2 pound arugula
1/4 cup extra virgin olive oil
4 teaspoons fresh lemon juice or red wine vinegar
Confectioners' sugar for dusting

Sprinkle the duck legs on both sides with salt. Heat a heavy sauté pan over medium-high heat until hot. Add the grape seed oil and tilt the pan to coat the bottom evenly. In batches if necessary to avoid crowding, add the duck legs and sear, turning once, until golden brown on both sides, about 5 minutes on each side. Transfer to a plate and set aside.

In a Dutch oven or other heavy pot large enough to hold the duck legs in a single layer, heat the olive oil over medium heat. Add the onions and cook, stirring occasionally, until softened and translucent, 8 to 10 minutes. Add the 4 tablespoons butter, the parsley, cilantro, cinnamon stick, saffron, ginger, turmeric, 1 tablespoon salt, and $1\frac{1}{2}$ teaspoons pepper and cook, stirring occasionally, until the butter melts, about 1 minute.

Place the duck legs, skin side up, in the pot. Raise the heat to medium-high, pour in the stock, and bring to a boil. Reduce the heat to medium-low, cover, and simmer until the duck is tender, about $1\frac{1}{2}$ hours.

About 30 minutes before the duck is ready, preheat the oven to 375°F. Spread the almonds on a rimmed baking sheet, place in the oven, and toast, stirring once or twice, until they have a nutty fragrance and are golden, about 10 minutes. Pour onto a plate and let cool to room temperature. Raise the oven temperature to 400°F.

When the duck legs are ready, remove from the pot and set aside. Remove and discard the cinnamon stick. Bring the sauce to a boil over high heat and boil until very thick and almost all of the liquid has evaporated. Reduce the heat to medium-low, add the eggs, and stir constantly until the eggs are scrambled and the mixture starts to separate, about 5 minutes. Once the curds are firm, drain the egg mixture in a colander or large sieve, discarding the juices. Let the solids cool.

Meanwhile, pull the meat off the duck legs and discard the bones and skin. Cut the meat into bite-size chunks and set aside.

In a food processor, pulse the cooled almonds until coarsely ground. Transfer to a large bowl, add the orange blossom water, $\frac{1}{4}$ cup of the clarified butter, the granulated sugar, and the $1\frac{1}{2}$ teaspoons cinnamon, and mix well. Add the duck meat and cooled eggs and stir to distribute evenly.

Place the stack of pastry sheets on a flat, dry work surface, and cover with plastic wrap and then a damp kitchen towel to prevent them from drying out. Have ready the remaining $\frac{1}{4}$ cup clarified butter, a pastry brush, and a rimmed baking sheet. Remove 1 pastry sheet from the stack and lay it flat, with a short side facing you, on the work surface. Brush the sheet with a generous amount of the clarified butter, then place $\frac{1}{2}$ cup of the duck mixture about $1\frac{1}{2}$ inches in from the edge nearest you and 2 inches in from each side. Fold the edge nearest you over the filling and then roll up the sheet about halfway. Fold in both sides and finish rolling up the sheet. Place the roll, seam side down, on the baking sheet. Repeat until all of the duck mixture is used.

Bake the rolls until golden brown, about 10 minutes. Remove from the oven and let cool for 5 minutes.

Meanwhile, place the arugula in a bowl. In a small bowl, whisk together the olive oil, lemon juice, and salt and pepper to taste to make a vinaigrette. Drizzle over the arugula and toss to coat evenly.

Using a serrated knife, cut a thin slice off both ends of each roll (so they will stand upright), then cut each roll in half on the diagonal. Using a fine-mesh sieve, dust the roll halves on all sides with confectioners' sugar, then sprinkle with cinnamon.

Divide the arugula evenly among individual plates, arranging a mound in the center of each plate. Stand 4 to 6 warm roll halves around each salad. Serve at once.

NOTE *Feuilles de brik* are paper-thin pastry sheets used in Moroccan kitchens. They can be found in shops selling North African foods. Greek phyllo sheets, which are carried in both Middle Eastern grocery stores and many well-stocked supermarkets, may be substituted. If the pastry sheets are purchased frozen, thaw them overnight in the refrigerator.

MOURAD: *I love basteeya, and it works so well with Cinsaut treated as a rosé wine. The fruity character of the wine is enhanced by the sweetness and cinnamon, which take it right to the edge while not making the wine taste sour. The texture of the duck is perfect for a full-bodied wine.*

EVAN: *Mourad is one of the most creative North African chefs I have ever met. Although many people might pigeonhole Aziza as a Moroccan restaurant, it is much more. As Floyd Cardoz has taken India as an inspiration for his food at Tabla in New York, Mourad has taken Moroccan inspiration and bridged it with Western cuisine. And although he doesn't drink alcohol, Mourad understands how to marry wine with food. Indeed, many of the best wine waiters I have ever worked with are nondrinkers. They focus on aroma, and, as we know, smell and taste are tightly interrelated.*

Basteeya is more traditional than many of the menu items you find at Aziza, but it's a great choice with the wine. As you cook and sample the dish and the wine, you may want to go lightly on the sugar if you find it takes too much out of the wine. Overall, the rich and crunchy texture pairs well with Cinsaut: the cinnamon is a great bridge spice, and the duck works with a fuller Cinsaut-based rosé. You could also serve this dish with a Cinsaut-based red blend—something from North Africa or southern France rather than South Africa, Lebanon, or Italy.

RECOMMENDED PRODUCERS

EVERYDAY	PREMIUM	SPLURGE
Altyd Somer Coastal Region, South Africa	Barreto Cellars Southern Central Coast, California	Château Musar Bekaa Valley, Lebanon
Azzaro Languedoc, France [R]	Foggo Wines McLaren Vale, South Australia [R]	Domaines Ott Provence, France [R]
Château Ksara Bekaa Valley, Lebanon	Frick Sonoma County, California	
Domaine d'Aupilhac Languedoc, France	Preston Sonoma County, California	
Domaine des Terres Falmet Languedoc, France		
Les Jamelles Languedoc, France [R]		

R = Rosé

dolcetto

dohl-*cheht*-oh | dohl-*cheht*-uh

The word *authenticity* has been abused to the point where it's almost meaningless. But Dolcetto is about authenticity. With the exception of a few winemakers who seek to make the grape into something it isn't, Dolcetto, by and large, is an honest, direct, and completely unpretentious grape that delivers on its promise: a juicy, grapey, and almost Zinfandel-like variety that provides great pleasure when enjoyed fresh and young.

Dolcetto is one of the light, bright reds that flexibly play at the table and pair up as happily with many fish and "white wine" dishes as with classic "red wine" meals. While Barbera's screaming acidity has to be accounted for with the food, Dolcetto matches up easily with many of the same dishes but is also drinkable and fun on its own. A couple of bottles of Dolcetto are regular features in my monthly wine box.

Alternative Names Ormeasco (Liguria, Italy)

Styles Light-medium- to medium-full-bodied red

Sometimes Blended With Barbera, Nebbiolo, Rossese (Italy), various grapes (U.S.A.)

Flavor Lexicon *Fruit/vegetable:* Blueberry, cherry, plum, porcini, raspberry ▪ *Floral:* Anise, orange blossoms, rose petals ▪ *Earth:* Graphite, mineral ▪ *Wood:* Coffee

Similar Sips Rich Beaujolais, fruit-forward Merlot, easy-drinking Zinfandel

Where It's Grown Australia (Victoria), Italy (Liguria; Piedmont: Alba, Dogliani, Ovada), U.S.A. (California: Central Coast, Mendocino County, Napa County, Sonoma County [Dry Creek Valley, Russian River Valley]; Maryland; New Mexico; Oregon: southern Oregon, Umpqua Valley; Pennsylvania; Washington: Columbia Valley)

Italy's "little sweet one," the Piedmontese translation of Dolcetto, makes you smile when you drink it. Lacking the sharpness of Barbera and gifted with explosive fruit and generous, dark color, Dolcetto is a staple wine in its home region of Piedmont, but it is enjoyed all over northern Italy. Like Barbera, it is a helpful grape for winemakers to have around while they wait for the impenetrable Nebbiolo-based wines that Piedmont is renowned for to soften up. It is grown all over Piedmont but is at its best in the northwest of the region, especially in the districts of Alba, Dogliani, and Ovada. Just over the mountains that separate Piedmont from Liguria, Dolcetto (here called Ormeasco) also performs well and is often blended with the local Rossese grape. Although it may be just a matter of time, not much Dolcetto is grown outside Italy. And what is often thought to be Dolcetto under a pseudonym actually isn't: Charbono in the United States and Bonarda in Argentina are often referred to as Dolcetto, but they are actually different grapes with similar characteristics.

A few hundred acres of genuine Dolcetto planted in California were likely brought over with Barbera by Italian immigrants in the 1800s. Most plantings are in Sonoma County (primarily in the Russian River Valley), Napa, Mendocino, and the Central Coast. In California it comes off as a denser, less sprightly wine, often oaked and with surprisingly bright acidity considering the climate. In Oregon, it's found mostly in the south, specifically in the Umpqua Valley, the state's hub for any grape that isn't Pinot Noir or Pinot Gris. Dolcetto can also be found in small amounts in Washington's Columbia Valley. And although I haven't sampled any, I'm told that Dolcetto is being grown in Pennsylvania, Maryland, and New Mexico.

Dolcetto hasn't taken off in Australia yet either, but there are more than twenty wineries in Australia making Dolcetto, mostly in Victoria.

Vintner's Choices Oak vs. no oak, single variety vs. blend, traditional vs. modern approach

Dolcetto is an early-ripening red grape that is made for enjoying both with and without food. It's a pretty straightforward variety that poses relatively few challenges to the grower. To avoid conflicts with its jovial and drinkable image, vintners make an effort to keep any bitter, gritty tannin in check.

On matters of style and interpretation, however, arguments can be heated. For traditionalists, the hallmarks of Dolcetto are the purity and honesty of the fruit, its succulence and softness on the palate, and the almost sweet (*dolce*) quality of ripeness. Like Gamay, it is meant to be consumed soon after bottling and is therefore made in a clean, unoaked, and vibrant style. Some consultants and flying winemakers are encouraging producers to make Dolcetto into serious, oak-aged, cellar-worthy stuff. To me the effort seems forced and detracts from the inherent charm of the grape.

Most Dolcetto is unblended, and why not? Its charm is in its singularity. Moreover, blending it with other grapes takes a deft hand to retain that charm. In Piedmont, local blends of Barbera and Dolcetto can be found, as Dolcetto is used to cut Barbera's sharpness. An occasional effort to blend lesser-quality Nebbiolo with Dolcetto tends to be less successful. In Liguria, much of the local Dolcetto is blended into enjoyable wines that are best consumed locally.

Finally, in the United States, some winemakers work within the letter of the law regarding varietal wines: to qualify for the varietal label, a wine must typically contain at least 75 percent of the specified grape, but that leaves room for blending experiments.

PAIRING WITH FOOD

Dolcetto is silver-bullet stuff, easygoing and versatile. Although it can be overwhelmed by some dishes, it pairs up with a remarkable range. Because it's relatively low in acid, it can't be used as effectively to cut the fat or texture of rich dishes. This low acidity also means that it can pair delightfully with hors d'oeuvres and many appetizers, but salads are not a good match unless they have a soft, creamy dressing, based on light amounts of yogurt, or perhaps buttermilk, that won't hurt the wine. Say yes to a plate of salumi or a simple bowl of gnocchi in light tomato sauce tempered with a kiss of cream, and no to acidic antipasti (including pickled vegetables) and marinated fish.

Dolcetto is also not a wine that's meant to accompany fine cuisine. Burgers, grilled sausages, simple quiche, and roasted chicken are tasty with Dolcetto, but traditional French *blanquette de veau*, with its rich cream sauce, or braised rabbit in mustard cream sauce are too rich and, in my opinion, too polished for a basic Dolcetto. It pairs best with more rustic fare, wholesome but not flashy.

Dolcetto is another red wine that can break the rule and pair with fish. Choose sweeter, milder fish and shellfish for the best results. Halibut, butterfish (black cod), salmon, trout, shrimp, and scallops are all great candidates to pair up with a Dolcetto when prepared simply and in a red-wine vein—with a little tomato, perhaps a bit of meat (pancetta, sausage, or ham), or a judicious use of mushrooms or black olives. A fillet of fish served with an uncomplicated sauce of olives, ripe summer tomato, sautéed onions, reduced red wine, and julienned prosciutto would be a nice pairing.

PAIRING POINTERS

Dolcetto works well:
- By itself. More than most red wines, Dolcetto is great for drinking alone or before a meal. Great conversation, great friends, and several glasses of Dolcetto are a delightful combination.
- With simple, everyday foods. A good burger, a roast chicken, and a straightforward pizza Margherita are all fine with a nice bottle of Dolcetto.
- With sandwiches of all shapes and sizes. If only Subway offered Dolcetto as a beverage option, I'd be much happier taking the kids out for a quick lunch. Whether the sandwich is roast beef and Swiss or a classic tuna melt, Dolcetto's an excellent choice.

- With pâté, salumi, and assorted sausages. Though the "cut" of Barbera can also be a sublime foil to cured meats, I often prefer Dolcetto's softness with milder country pâté, mortadella, prosciutto, or serrano ham. And if you prefer fiery *coppa,* peppery salami, or piquant Spanish chorizo, the wine will be just as happy.
- Served slightly chilled. While chilling works for red wines such as Gamay, Barbera, and many fruit-forward Pinot Noirs, none is as nice as a slightly chilled Dolcetto. Its bright fruit, soft tannin, and low acidity make it a prime candidate for chilling to serve at a picnic or an alfresco dinner on a warm evening.

Dolcetto isn't good:
- With subtle, nuanced dishes. It's not that the wine fares poorly (indeed, Dolcetto gets along with almost everything), it's just that its simple charm might not tease out the layers of flavor in a complex dish.
- With really rich main courses. Dolcetto's lower acidity means that it can't handle the richness of cream and butter sauces and thick, rich stews as effectively as wines that have more acid (which will cut) or more tannin (which will bind with the fat). Forget trying to pair it with duck, goose, or pork belly.
- If you want a big, powerful wine. Though Dolcetto is far from wimpy, if your heart is set on a big, chewy, and tannic red wine, you'll probably be disappointed.
- When it's older. Dolcetto is made to be consumed within five years of its release. It's definitely at its best within the first two to three years. Don't cellar this stuff; drink it!
- When you need tannin. Got steak? Or prime rib? If you need the counterbalance of tannin to provide a foil to a richer protein, pick a wine with more tannin.

THE CHEESE PLATE

FRESH	Mozzarella, ricotta (Italy, U.S.A.)
SOFT-RIPENED	Boursault (France), Brie (France, U.S.A.)
SEMI-HARD	Fontina (Italy), Gouda (Holland)
WASHED-RIND	Morbier (France), Taleggio (Italy)

dolcetto | WILD SALMON WITH DOLCETTO WINE SAUCE, CHANTERELLES, AND BRUSSELS SPROUT LEAVES

PAUL BARTOLOTTA Bartolotta Restaurants, Bartolotta Ristorante di Mare, Las Vegas, Nevada

---

Makes 4 main-course servings

DOLCETTO WINE SAUCE BASE

6 tablespoons unsalted butter

1 pound salmon bones, rinsed and cut into small pieces

10 shallots (about 6 ounces total weight)

$\frac{1}{2}$ cup finely diced yellow onion

$\frac{1}{4}$ cup finely diced, peeled carrot

$\frac{1}{4}$ cup finely diced celery

3 bay leaves

1 tablespoon fresh thyme leaves

1 tablespoon cracked black peppercorns

6 tablespoons tomato paste

2 tablespoons red wine vinegar

$2\frac{1}{4}$ cups Dolcetto or other medium-bodied red wine

2 cups chicken stock

TO FINISH DOLCETTO WINE SAUCE

1 tablespoon red wine vinegar

2 tablespoons balsamic vinegar

$\frac{3}{4}$ cup Dolcetto

2 tablespoons tomato paste

Sea salt and freshly ground black pepper

2 tablespoons cold unsalted butter, cut into 4 pieces

SALMON

4 (7-ounce) skinless wild salmon fillets

Sea salt

$\frac{1}{4}$ cup extra virgin olive oil

4 shallots, cut in half

6 tablespoons unsalted butter, cut into 6 pieces

4 fresh thyme sprigs

4 bay leaves

4 tablespoons unsalted butter
5 ounces chanterelles, trimmed and cut into ½-inch pieces
5 ounces porcini or other wild mushrooms or cremini mushrooms,
trimmed and cut into ½-inch-thick slices or pieces
10 ounces Brussels sprouts, leaves separated
Sea salt

To make the sauce base, preheat the oven to 450°F. In a roasting pan, melt the butter over medium heat. Add the salmon bones and stir to coat them with the butter. Place the pan in the oven and roast until the bones are golden brown, about 20 minutes.

Remove the pan from the oven, then remove the bones and set aside. Reduce the oven temperature to 400°F.

Return the roasting pan to the stove top over medium heat. Add the shallots and cook, stirring occasionally, until caramelized, about 5 minutes. Add the onion, carrot, celery, bay leaves, thyme, and peppercorns and cook, stirring occasionally, until the vegetables are tender and golden brown, 5 to 8 minutes. Stir in the tomato paste and vinegar and cook briefly until the vinegar evaporates.

Pour in the wine and return the salmon bones to the pan. Stir well and continue cooking until the wine is reduced by three-fourths, 8 to 10 minutes. Raise the heat to medium-high, add the stock, and bring to a boil. Reduce the heat to maintain a steady simmer and cook, uncovered, for 20 minutes. Remove from the heat and pass through a fine-mesh sieve into a small saucepan. You should have about 1½ cups. Place over medium heat and bring to a simmer.

To finish the sauce, in a small saucepan, reduce the red wine vinegar over medium heat until almost dry. Add the balsamic vinegar and reduce until almost dry. Finally, add the wine and tomato paste and reduce by three-fourths.

Raise the heat under the strained sauce base to high and bring to a rapid boil. Then bring the wine reduction to a boil. Very slowly add the sauce base to the reduction while whisking constantly. When the mixtures are combined, continue to cook over medium heat until reduced to 1 cup, about 5 minutes.

Season the sauce with salt and pepper, and then whisk in the butter, a piece at a time. Pass the sauce through a fine-mesh sieve, and keep warm until serving.

To prepare the salmon, season both sides of each fillet with salt. In an ovenproof sauté pan large enough to accommodate the salmon fillets without crowding, heat the olive oil over high heat. Add the fillets and shallots and cook until the fillets are golden brown on the first side, about 3 minutes. Turn the fillets over and add the butter, thyme, and bay leaves to the pan. Place the pan in the oven and roast until the salmon is almost opaque throughout, about 4 minutes. (If you prefer your salmon opaque in the center, roast for 7 minutes.)

Begin cooking the vegetables at the same time you put the salmon on the stove top. In an ovenproof sauté pan, melt the butter over medium heat. When the butter begins to brown, add the mushrooms and Brussels sprout leaves, season with salt, and stir to coat. Place the pan in the oven and roast the vegetables until tender, about 5 minutes.

To serve, divide the vegetables evenly among 4 warmed plates, arranging them in the center of each plate. Spoon the warm Dolcetto sauce around the vegetables, then place a salmon fillet on top of each mound of vegetables. Spoon the fragrant butter-oil mixture from the pan over the salmon, glazing it. Garnish each serving with 2 roasted shallot halves, a thyme sprig, and a bay leaf and serve right away.

PAUL: *Even though salmon is not in my lexicon of Italian seafood, I thought its pairing with one of my favorite Italian varieties, one that often goes unnoticed, would result in a surprisingly happy marriage. I hope you will agree that Dolcetto, whether a traditional version—light and fresh, grapey and tart— or a more contemporary world-beat version—concentrated and fruity, lush, and in some cases with a touch of new oak—matches very well. The richness of the pan-roasted salmon, perfumed with caramelized shallots and thyme on a bed of nutty mushrooms and earthy Brussels sprout leaves, pairs beautifully with the intensity of the Dolcetto wine sauce.*

EVAN: *There's an adage that a chef's food comes straight from his or her personality. Many tactical chefs create precise and technically correct food, while those who are more fanciful bring their whimsy to the plate. Paul is authentic, pure, and thoughtful in life and in the kitchen. Few have mastered seafood as well as he has, and his love of fish and skill in preparing it made me eager to place this variety in his capable hands.*

The pairing of salmon (or Arctic char) and Dolcetto is high on the list of successful pairings of red wine with fish (along with salmon paired with Pinot Noir, and Merlot with tuna). Using a wine sauce to link the two is natural and effective. Here the mix of chanterelles and porcini is a bridge to the red wine that picks up on a flavor people associate with many Piedmontese reds—porcini. If your Dolcetto is an oaky, modern interpretation, choose a very mild-fleshed salmon and perhaps go a little lighter on the Brussels sprout leaves, which may bring out the tannins in the oak.

RECOMMENDED PRODUCERS

EVERYDAY	PREMIUM	PREMIUM
Cavalier Bartolomeo Piedmont, Italy	Abacela Southern Oregon	Giacomo Ascheri Piedmont, Italy
Gianfranco Alessandria Piedmont, Italy	Bargetto Santa Cruz Mountains, California	Giuseppe Cortese Piedmont, Italy
Giribaldi Piedmont, Italy	Bonny Doon Ca' del Solo Santa Cruz, California	M. Cosentino Lodi, California
Marcarini Piedmont, Italy	Domenico Clerico Piedmont, Italy	Roberto Voerzio Piedmont, Italy

gamay

Gamay is the butt of far too much ridicule. As a person who loves the grape, I'm tired of jokes about how it's just Hawaiian Punch on steroids or Kool-Aid with a kick. Yes, most Gamay is made into that often-bland wine called Beaujolais Nouveau, but this single interpretation does not tell the full story of this unique grape.

Furthermore, there's confusion about the "real" Gamay grape, which is Gamay Noir au Jus Blanc ("black Gamay of clear juice"). It is not the same grape as Napa Gamay (Valdeguié), Gamay Beaujolais (a strain of Pinot Noir), Gamay du Rhône, or Gamay Saint-Laurent (the last two of which have been correctly identified as another grape, Abouriou).

Even outside Beaujolais in France, where the top crus (Moulin à Vent, Morgon, and Régnié) can be rich, succulent, and capable of aging up to ten years or so, Gamay makes perfumed and enjoyably fruity wines that please wine lovers who appreciate it for what it is.

Alternative Names Gamay Noir au Jus Blanc (France)

Styles Light-medium to medium-full-bodied dry red, light-medium-bodied rosé (not widely available)

Sometimes Blended With Pinot Noir (France, Switzerland)

Flavor Lexicon *Fruit:* Banana, blackberry, cherry, cranberry, raspberry, strawberry ▪ *Earth:* Graphite, mineral ▪ *Other:* Bubble gum, cotton candy

Similar Sips Fruit-forward Dolcetto or Pinot Noir, less-earthy and less-sharp Barbera

Where It's Grown Australia (New South Wales: Hunter Valley; Tasmania; Victoria: Mornington Peninsula, Yarra Valley), Canada (British Columbia: Okanagan Valley; Ontario: Niagara), Croatia, France (Burgundy: Beaujolais; Loire Valley: Anjou, Touraine), Serbia, Switzerland, U.S.A. (Oregon: Willamette Valley)

Gamay is celebrated for its universal appeal and the fact that you don't have to be a wine expert to enjoy it. Melding low tannins and bright red fruits, it displays a distinct pale-red color with blue hues. Carbonic maceration, a style of winemaking that brings out fruit and color while softening tannin and acidity, adds notes of banana and bubble gum and turns the color an almost neon purple.

Gamay is native to France, specifically to the southern Burgundy region of Beaujolais, the largest winemaking area of Burgundy proper. Beaujolais wines, which take their name from the northern Beaujolais village of Beaujeu, can range in style from those simply labeled as Beaujolais, which are easygoing cranberry- and raspberry-scented wines from the southern portion of the region, to Beaujolais Villages, which are wines coming from any of more than three dozen towns known for their high-quality fruit. In the northern part of the appellation, with its distinctive granitic slopes, you find the ten Crus Beaujolais (wines from single towns or vineyard areas) that represent the best of Gamay: racy but with a broad palate, ample texture, and often some wood aging. Although carbonic maceration is all the rage in the south, it's rarely employed in the north. Instead producers use partial carbonic or some whole-cluster fermentation and, at times, techniques that treat the wine like Pinot Noir. In the north, the flavor profile includes ripe raspberry and sour cherry and can also include a layer of spice, mineral, and herbal notes. Gamay Noir au Jus Blanc is also grown in the Loire Valley, in the Anjou and Touraine, where it makes lighter and very enjoyable wines, and it is also grown in small quantities in other parts of France (such as the Savoie).

A cool-climate grape, Gamay of any variety is not widely grown in North America, and it is rare to find "real" Gamay. In Canada, British Columbia's Okanagan and Ontario's Niagara Peninsula offer nice examples. The best U.S. efforts seem to be in Oregon (Amity's is worth seeking out in the Willamette Valley). Intriguingly, the grape is scattered across a broad range of climatic bands in Australia, from cool, southern Tasmania and the Mornington Peninsula near Melbourne in Victoria to the warmer Yarra Valley (also in Victoria), the Hunter Valley (in New South Wales), and the Granite Belt (in Queensland). Rarely exported, these wines are nevertheless quite enjoyable.

Although it is rarely found beyond local markets, Gamay is also an important grape in central Europe, and fairly sizable plantings exist in countries such as Croatia and Serbia. Finally, it is also found in Italy, but not in significant quantity.

Vintner's Choices Carbonic maceration vs. traditional red fermentation, oak vs. no oak, red vs. rosé, single variety vs. blend, soil type (granite, limestone, clay, or alluvium), young vs. old vines

The single most important decision made by makers of Gamay is the choice of fermentation technique. Red wines are made traditionally by picking fruit, crushing it, and creating must (a combination of seed, pulp, and skins), that is then allowed to ferment. After fermentation and some maceration, the wine is separated from its solids. With carbonic maceration, the fruit is carefully picked in whole, unbruised clusters and stacked in stainless steel tanks that create an environment rich in carbon dioxide, a byproduct of fermentation. As the weight of the grapes crushes the fruit at the bottom, fermentation begins. But, as most of the grapes are whole, fermentation occurs inside them, and the resulting wines are vibrant in color, exploding with sweet-tart berry fruit. They contain almost no perceptible tannin and have low acidity (Gamay is pretty sharp stuff when fermented by traditional techniques). This is how Beaujolais Nouveau is made. These wines have a very short shelf life, about six months, and are famed for being the first wines sold in France in the "new vintage," on the third Thursday in November. Some wines made by traditional fermentation methods are augmented with clusters of whole fruit: these techniques are often referred to as partial-carbonic or partial-whole-cluster fermentations. This approach, which offers the best of both worlds if it's done right, is employed in northern Beaujolais for cru wines and also in wines like Pinot Noir, Dolcetto, some styles of Tempranillo, and even Zinfandel.

Gamay is partial to granite and limestone soils, which add sinew and muscle. A comparison of a basic Beaujolais Villages and a cru wine from the north make this difference clear. Within the ten crus, some are "bigger" than others, and much of this difference is again due to soil composition. The difference in intensity between a flowery and light Saint-Amour or Fleurie and a more concentrated Moulin à Vent or Morgon is obvious. Producers also claim that vine age is important with Gamay and that the best and most consistent wines come from vines that are more than fifty years old. Gamay is rarely aged in oak, much less small oak, though the ampler cru wines are made identically to a Pinot Noir and aged in small *barriques;* they bear the designation *tradition* to reflect this style of winemaking. However, most wines are produced in stainless-steel and glass-lined cement vats.

Complexity in Gamay is achieved through blending not different grapes but the products of different vineyards that may have slightly different strains of Gamay. There are two exceptions. From Burgundy, mostly from the Mâconnais, comes a wine called Passe Tout Grains, which is a blend of at least one-third Pinot Noir with Gamay. It's enjoyable, easy to drink, and not super-expensive. In Switzerland, the appellation wine of Dôle is also a blend of Pinot Noir and Gamay, in similar proportions. It's considered Switzerland's best red wine. Another variation is Beaujolais rosé, which is made in a dry style that, when made well, is redolent of light strawberry and watermelon fruit.

PAIRING WITH FOOD

With its low tannins, bright acidity, and light (if any) oak, Gamay has broad appeal and pairs nicely with most foods. It is considered the classic red wine to pair with fish. Given the range of Gamay available, from everyday wines to the more sophisticated Beaujolais crus, along with the dry rosé styles, there's a Gamay for every meal and occasion.

Because of its higher acidity, Gamay lends itself to drinking early in the meal. Pairing with composed salads (especially those with creamier, textured dressings) is a practical approach, and Gamay with charcuterie, from duck-liver mousse to rustic country pâté, is a time-honored match. The acidity of the wine is a nice foil for the richness of these pâtés and terrines, and the soft tannins work well with their meatiness. Cold-meat plates are wonderful with Gamay: slices of flank steak on a bed of arugula, room-temperature roast pork loin served with honey mustard and a rice salad, or half a cold roast chicken served with a three-bean salad. And the wine rocks with the leftovers when served as sandwiches.

The wine's lower tannins make it friendly to fish. Meatier fish, from shark to swordfish, are obvious choices; white flaky fish like cod and snapper also work well. But this is a red wine that can handle strong-flavored fish if you select one of the minimally tannic crus or even a rosé. From a bowl of steamed clams and sausage to a mussel-and-potato salad, the matches can be enjoyable. And there's no better red wine to go with a tuna-salad sandwich or Baja fish tacos!

Released on the third Thursday of November, Beaujolais Nouveau arrives in the United States just in time to work its magic at the Thanksgiving table. It can pair with nachos, chips and dip, and Buffalo wings as well, making it a great choice for football fans who don't fancy beer or soda with their TV snacks. Chill it down and serve it alongside a spicy Thai or Malaysian curry, and you've got bliss.

PAIRING POINTERS

Gamay goes well with:
- Just about everything. It's a good bet for meals requiring a versatile wine—from potlucks to smorgasbords to cruise ship buffets. Few wines can cover a broad gamut of ingredients and styles of food like Gamay.
- Most sandwiches. Heaven is a well-made BLT and a glass of Beaujolais. Or roast pork with chutney, sliced turkey with avocado and Havarti, or a classic ham and Swiss. Even a PB&J, heavy on the peanut butter, could be okay! And burgers—well, do I really have to explain?
- Pâté, charcuterie, and cured or sliced deli meats, especially if you are just snacking. Add bread, crackers or croutons, a bit of mustard, and a few cornichons. And this wine can be great with hot dogs while you're watching a ball game.
- A good steak. Really. Pull out a good, gutsy Moulin à Vent or Morgon, and you've got a wonderful pairing. After all, French Charolais beef comes from the land of Beaujolais. And with steak tartare—heavenly!
- A slight chill on it. As with Dolcetto, chilling a Gamay wine lightly brings out the fruit and freshness, making it a fine accompaniment for spicy food and a nice picnic wine—especially the Nouveau.

Gamay isn't good:
- If you expect too much. Gamay, apart from the complex crus, is meant to be easy, appealing, and unintellectual. It's better to enjoy it at a party or ballgame alongside a buffet or tailgate than expect too much with an elaborate meal at a fine restaurant.

- If you select the wrong style. There's a big difference between the readily drinkable Nouveau, the easy and enjoyable Beaujolais Villages, and the rich and complex cru wines, especially those that are oak-aged. Match the wine to the occasion and fare.
- With *all* spicy food. Although I suggest above that Gamay is a good match for things like Thai curry, it doesn't work with all hot dishes. A chilled Nouveau is wonderful with spice but can be so grapey that it overwhelms the flavors of the dish. A lightly chilled basic Gamay is probably a better choice, but again it depends on the recipe. Finally, a rich oak-aged cru wine would be better than a Cabernet Sauvignon or Syrah with New Orleans barbecued shrimp, but a basic Beaujolais would be better still.
- With subtler dishes. Gamay is versatile, but it still has its own personality. Delicate flavors and intricate sauces and marinades can be blown out by the extroverted nature of Gamay.
- With sweet foods. If your wine is ripe and fruit-forward, using sweetness as an accent in the food makes a good link—ketchup on a burger, peanut sauce on a chicken satay, or cranberry sauce with turkey. But, as always, the pairing is not successful when the dish is sweeter than the wine, and Gamay is definitely not good with dessert, except perhaps something like a bowl of ripe strawberries served alone or with a little crème fraîche (but hold the brown sugar).

THE CHEESE PLATE

FRESH	Burrata (Italy, U.S.A.), chèvre (many countries)
SEMI-SOFT	Havarti (Denmark), Port Salut (France)
SOFT-RIPENED	Humboldt Fog goat cheese (U.S.A.), Pierre Robert (France)
SEMI-HARD	Cheddar (U.K., U.S.A.), Manchego (Spain)
WASHED-RIND	Chaumes (France), Taleggio (Italy)

gamay | SALAD OF CORNISH GAME HEN
WITH SHIITAKE MUSHROOM VINAIGRETTE

CHARLIE TROTTER   Charlie Trotter's, Chicago, Illinois, Restaurant Charlie, Las Vegas, Nevada

Makes 4 first-course servings

CORNISH GAME HENS
2 Cornish game hens
Sea salt and freshly cracked black pepper
2 tablespoons extra virgin olive oil

VINAIGRETTE
1 clove garlic, minced
1 shallot, minced
2 tablespoons extra virgin olive oil
6 ounces shiitake mushrooms, stems discarded and coarsely chopped
$\frac{1}{2}$ cup mushroom or vegetable stock, or as needed
2 tablespoons light soy sauce
1 tablespoon fresh lemon juice
Sea salt and freshly ground black pepper

$\frac{1}{2}$ pound organic salad greens
Freshly ground black pepper
$\frac{1}{2}$ cup dried cranberries

To prepare the hens, preheat the oven to 425°F. Dry the hens, then season with salt and pepper and rub thoroughly with the olive oil. Place the hens, breast side up, on a rack in a small roasting pan.

Place in the oven and roast for 10 minutes. Reduce the oven temperature to 325°F and continue roasting until the juices run clear when a thigh joint is pierced with a knife tip, 35 to 45 minutes longer.

While the hens are roasting, make the vinaigrette. In a small sauté pan, combine the garlic, shallot, and olive oil and sweat over low heat until softened and translucent, about 5 minutes. Raise the heat to medium, add the mushrooms, and cook until the mushrooms soften, 4 to 6 minutes. Add the $\frac{1}{2}$ cup stock and cook until the liquid is reduced by half, about 2 minutes. Remove from the heat and stir in the soy sauce and lemon juice.

Transfer the contents of the sauté pan to a blender and process until a silky smooth vinaigrette forms, thinning with more stock if necessary to achieve the correct consistency. Season with salt and pepper.

When the hens are ready, remove from the oven and let rest for 5 minutes. Split each hen in half lengthwise to create 4 servings.

To serve, place the salad greens in a large bowl, drizzle with ¼ cup of the vinaigrette, and toss to coat evenly. Place a hen half to one side of each plate. Place one-fourth of the salad on the opposite side of each plate. Drizzle the remaining vinaigrette over the salad greens and around the hens. Finish with a sprinkle of pepper and a scattering of cranberries. Serve at once.

CHARLIE: *The springlike characteristics of this recipe, united by the creamy mouthfeel of the mushroom vinaigrette, create a lovely salad to be enjoyed with a vibrant Gamay. The acid from the fresh fruit combined with a delicate protein, such as Cornish game hen, allow the fruitiness and lightweight component of the wine to star. The slight tartness from the red fruit in the wine is accented by the dried cranberries. The striking black-pepper notes of the wine are balanced in the salad with crushed black pepper and sea salt.*

EVAN: *To sommeliers and wine-loving waitstaff, Charlie is an icon. From the day he opened his eponymous restaurant, he has been committed to understanding the interactions of wine with food. The short list of sommeliers that have worked with Charlie is phenomenal and includes several Master Sommeliers. Because his food-and-wine sense is so finely tuned, I had no fear in asking Charlie to create a salad course to accompany a red wine.*

The dressing is structured for red wines of Gamay's style: a bit minerally and earthy, with foresty overtones. Whether you're pairing it with a basic Beaujolais Villages or a more sophisticated cru, the slightly emulsified texture of the dressing, the slight sharpness, and the sweet-earth note from the shiitakes make this match work well.

RECOMMENDED PRODUCERS

EVERYDAY	PREMIUM
Château Thivin Beaujolais, France	Amity Vineyards Willamette Valley, Oregon
Domaine Manoir du Carra Beaujolais, France	Domaine des Nugues Beaujolais, France
Georges Duboeuf Beaujolais, France	Hubert Lapierre Beaujolais, France
Jean-François Mérieau Loire Valley, France	Jean-Paul Brun Beaujolais, France
Joël Rochette Beaujolais, France	Louis Jadot Beaujolais, France
Mommessin Beaujolais, France	Paul Janin Beaujolais, France

grenache

gruh-*nahsh*

The word *pangkarra* in Aborigine means "sense of place," similar to the concept of *terroir* but more ephemeral and hard to pin down. I prefer the Aborigine word, though outside Australia it's virtually unknown. I've heard it used most often there with reference to Grenache, for which soil and climate are especially important. Australian Grenache, the country's number two grape (after Shiraz), makes and contributes to many of the country's best red wines.

Grenache has many homes and faces. It can make extraordinary varietal wines, as the rich examples of Australia, Spain, France, and the United States all demonstrate. It blends magnificently, as anyone who enjoys a great bottle of Châteauneuf-du-Pape, a GSM (Grenache-Shiraz-Mourvèdre), or well-balanced Rioja can attest. It makes formidable rosé wines around the world, and you could argue that the great VDNs *(vins doux naturels)* coming from Banyuls, Rasteau, and Maury demonstrate Grenache's ability to yield a full-flavored and complex dessert wine. There are also a white version of the grape, Grenache Blanc, and a "gray" version, Grenache Gris, which I do not cover in this chapter. And although sparkling Grenache is available, it takes a back seat to sparkling Shiraz.

Alternative Names Alicante, Carignane Rousse, Roussillon (France), Cannonau (Italy), Garnacha, Garnatxa (Spain)

Styles Medium- to full-bodied red, medium-bodied dry rosé, full-bodied fortified red dessert

Sometimes Blended With Carignan, Cinsaut, Counoise, Mourvèdre, Syrah, and other grapes from southern France (France); grapes from the Cabernet family, Carignan, Tempranillo (Spain); Cinsaut, Counoise, Mourvèdre, Syrah (other countries)

Flavor Lexicon

RED   *Fruit:* Blackberry, cherry, grape, raspberry, tomato ▪ *Floral:* Violet ▪
        Earth: Loam, minerals, potting soil ▪ *Other:* Black or white pepper

ROSÉ   *Fruit:* Orange, red apple, sour cherry, strawberry, tangerine, watermelon

Fruit: Candied citrus peel, dried cherry, dried fig, raisin ▪ *Wood:* Caramel, coffee, dark chocolate

Similar Sips Full-flavored Gamay, juicy Zinfandel or Syrah

Where It's Grown Algeria, Australia (South Australia: Barossa Valley, McLaren Vale), France (Rhône Valley: Châteauneuf-du-Pape, Gigondas, Rasteau, Tavel, Vacqueyras; Languedoc-Roussillon: Banyuls, Maury), Italy (Calabria, Sardinia, Sicily), Morocco, Spain (Catalonia: Priorat; Navarra; Rioja; Valencia: Utiel-Requena), U.S.A. (California: Central Valley, Sierra Foothills [El Dorado], Sonoma County, Southern Central Coast [Paso Robles]; Washington: Columbia Valley)

Grenache is the world's most widely planted red wine grape. It is thought to have originated in Spain, where it remains hugely popular and extensively grown; but it's just as important over the border in France.

In France, the majority of Grenache is planted in the Southwest, in Languedoc-Roussillon, where it is second only to Carignan. Grenache is blended with a variety of other grapes, most notably Cinsaut, Syrah, and Mourvèdre. Many dry red wines contain varying percentages of Grenache, though most are led by other grapes, with Grenache in a supporting role. In the appellations of Banyuls and Maury on the Spanish border, however, Grenache makes exquisite VDN wines that are both age-worthy and splendid with food. Concentrated with cherry, dark chocolate, coffee, and raisin tones, these exquisite dessert wines can be sublime. Though less majestic, the dry red of Banyuls—Collioure—can also be enjoyable. Moving east, the wines of the Rhône Valley demonstrate the strength of Grenache as a table wine. Grenache performs well in arid conditions like those of the southern Rhône. Everyday Côtes du Rhône wines consume the lion's share of the Grenache harvest, and most of them are pleasant wines that put forward grapey, jammy fruit with a touch of peppery spice. In several southern Rhône appellation wines, Grenache achieves stardom: in Châteauneuf-du-Pape, where it can be blended with as many as twelve other grapes but is generally the lead player, and in other quality appellations such as Gigondas, Vacqueyras, Valréas, and finally Rasteau, where a VDN-style red is made. In the southern Rhône, yields are restricted dramatically both by Mother Nature (the stony vineyards of Châteauneuf contain virtually no soil) and by vintners who restrict vine yields to concentrate the fruit. Usually coupled with Syrah, which adds a peppery bite and more structure, these grapes make wonderful, rich wines exuding ample blackberry fruit. Grenache also accounts for much of southern France's rosé, from the basic Côtes du Rhône bottlings to more interesting examples in Tavel, Lirac, and Provence.

Garnacha, as it's known in Spain, is ubiquitous but found mostly in the north and east. It is a key element of wines from Rioja, Navarra, Campo de Borja, Costers del Segre, La Mancha, Penedès with its DOCa *(denominación de origen calificada)* of Priorat and the adjacent Monstant, and Somontano, Tarragona, and Utiel-Requena. In Priorat and Montsant, Garnacha is at its peak—inky dark, with spicy black licorice, black plum, black fig, and dried herbs. Pure or blended with a little Cariñena (Carignan) or other red grapes, the grapes from these century-old, gnarly vines produce many great wines. Elsewhere Garnacha is blended: in Rioja, it adds flesh and ripe fruit to Tempranillo's brighter, sharper character. In neighboring Navarra, it makes wonderful basic table wines but is most noteworthy for its vibrant, ripe, and fleshy watermelon-scented *rosado*, which sets the standard for a classic dry blush wine. Elsewhere in Spain it adds character to many a wine and can be surprisingly good when yields are held in check, as with the new offerings from Utiel-Requena.

In Italy, Grenache is known in Sardinia as Cannonau and is important for the island's reds, both rich table wines and dessert wines. The grape is also grown in Calabria and Sicily. Across the Mediterranean, it's grown in Algeria and Morocco for both reds and rosés.

Australia is a source of delicious Grenache, especially the wines from low-yielding old vines. Grenache in Australia is dense with black plum, blackberry, dark cherry, and a soft, herbal, eucalyptus-like character. It achieves greatness both on its own and as an integral part of GSM. Many wineries make lovely wines under this acronym, especially in the Barossa Valley and McLaren Vale regions of South Australia.

Sadly, in the United States, much of California's great old-vine Grenache ends up in generic wines—rosés, ports, and reds. The Rhône Ranger movement* has successfully salvaged some of these great old vineyards and used their fruit for varietal wines, red and rosé, and for adding to red Rhône blends. These can be first-rate, especially the rosés and the blends. Farther north, as the Rhône movement has solidified, we've seen a similar commitment to the variety in Washington's Columbia Valley, where the wines are quite good even though the vines are young.

Vintner's Choices Balanced vs. high yield, oak vs. no oak, red vs. rosé vs. dessert, single variety vs. blend, young vs. old vines

Left to its own devices in a warm and dry climate, Grenache would take over the world. Its productivity has made it the world's most widely cultivated red-wine grape. It ripens and ripens, yielding grapes with lots of fruit and a high sugar content, and it's not unusual to have wines of more than 15 percent alcohol. But if it grows unrestrained, it produces alcohol without much grace, leading to blowsy wines. As the vines mature, they regulate their own fruit production: indeed, the world's greatest varietal Grenache wine, Château Rayas in Châteauneuf-du-Pape, yields less than one ton of fruit per acre (two to three tons being standard for quality

---

* This movement was pioneered by Randall Grahm of California's Bonny Doon Winery. Grahm believed that California's climate favored Rhône grapes and began producing wines from Rhône varieties, which met with wide acclaim. Grahm is pictured on the cover of the *Wine Spectator* in April 1989 wearing a Lone Ranger's mask and cowboy hat.

wines and six to eight, or even more, for high-volume wines). The great wines of Australia's Barossa, France's Rhône Valley, and Spain's Priorat all come from older vines.

The desired wine style is the vintner's biggest decision. The requirements of a rosé differ immensely from those of a red wine, which also differ from those of a dessert wine. Many grapes for rosé or *rosado* wines are cultivated and harvested for those specific uses; but, especially in the New World, Grenache rosé is often produced by bleeding off the juice early in the fermentation process of a red wine. The bled wine is made into a dry rosé, leaving a more concentrated product from which to produce a Grenache red. Grenache destined for dessert wine is allowed to ripen late into the season and even to begin to desiccate on the vine.

Despite its jammy character, Grenache that's aged in new oak tastes like . . . new oak! As a result, many producers avoid newer or smaller oak barrels, which can easily dominate the wine and mask much of its fruit-driven charm. When other varieties are up front in the mix (like Syrah), more new oak can be employed.

PAIRING WITH FOOD

The red wines, rosé wines, and fortified dessert wines pair very differently with food, so I discuss them one at a time.

Red Grenache is distinguished by a rich, velvety texture, opulent berry and black-grape fruit, and soft, mild tannins. In these respects it resembles Gamay, but Grenache has more alcohol and significantly lower acidity. Pure varietal Grenache is soft and quite flexible, but it won't pair well with foods that require tannin in the wine to stand up to their protein, such as thick steaks, peppery stews, or heavy pastas. If it's blended with Syrah, Grenache can engage those types of dishes too, as with a good Vacqueyras or Châteauneuf-du-Pape. Unblended Grenache is magnificent with poultry, especially milder birds like poussin, game hen, turkey, and quail. As a blend, it will stand up to gamier squab, duck, or pheasant. It pairs well with a range of cheeses, and the less tannic styles can be a delightful match with fish. I've enjoyed light Grenache-based reds with seafood paella, cioppino, and even bouillabaisse, all of which also pair well with Grenache rosé or *rosado* wines.

A balanced *rosado* from Navarra is my first choice with seafood in Spain when I've tired of dry whites or dry sherry but am not in the mood for a red. Like their counterparts around the world, these Grenache blush wines are perfect with a pepper-crusted tuna, prosciutto- or *jamón*-wrapped snapper, or a straightforward *gambas a la plancha* (prawns sautéed quickly with parsley, garlic, and smoked paprika, or *pimentón*). It's equally delightful with roast pork, including Asian *char siu;* egg dishes such as quiche and frittatas; and basic charcuterie—from a platter of *saucisson sec* to chorizo-stuffed dates. And most dry rosés are magic with picnic fare, sandwiches, and Fourth of July burgers, hot dogs, and barbecue.

Dark chocolate may have no better friend than a good Banyuls, Maury, or Rasteau. The darker the better: these Grenache-based fortified wines are not as sweet as port, the other great chocolate wine. Opt for treatments of chocolate that pick up on other clues in the wine—raisins (there's no better wine to go with Raisinettes!), citrus (as in an orange-scented chocolate crème brûlée), or dark dried cherries (try adding dried cherries to a chocolate bread pudding). Fortified Grenache can be lovely with fruit compotes using either fresh or reconstituted dried fruit, and it is exquisite with baked figs.

PAIRING POINTERS

Grenache goes well with:
- Alfresco fare (as a rosé or lighter red). Served with a slight chill, a crisp rosé or a light Côtes du Rhône can be excellent with cold roast chicken, mixed cold cuts and sandwiches, potato salad and coleslaw, and anything on the grill—hot dogs, burgers, grilled corn, and juicy spareribs.
- Simple preparations of shellfish (as a rosé). When I think of Grenache rosé, I am drawn to crab simply boiled with a peppery rouille, or scallops or prawns sautéed in fruity olive oil with garlic, a little pepper, parsley, and chorizo. Even lobster, grilled ever so quickly over hardwood, is a great match with a Grenache-based blush wine.
- Lamb dishes (as a red). Richer Grenache-led blends (such as Châteauneuf-du-Pape or Priorat) are excellent with lamb. The addition of peppery Syrah or spicy Carignan to Grenache's generous, velvety texture provides a tasty backdrop for a rich stew, juicy chops, or a roasted six-rib rack.
- A range of cheeses (as a red or fortified wine). The red wines are especially tasty with lightly aged soft and semi-hard cheeses; blue cheeses are best with the fortified examples.
- Chocolate (as a fortified wine). A rich fortified Grenache such as Banyuls is sublime with dark chocolate mousse, a plate of chocolate-covered macaroons, or dark-chocolate bread pudding with dried cherries.

Grenache isn't good:
- If it's too old (this applies to both reds and rosés). With the notable exception of some Spanish Priorat wines, most Grenache blends are meant to be enjoyed young. Their low acidity and tannins prevent them from aging well. Even Châteauneuf-du-Pape loses its charm after five to seven years, and it begins to turn brown in color even sooner than that. As for the rosés, drink them within a year or so of release.
- With raw oysters and clams (as rosé). I was disappointed when trying out various blush wines with platters of raw mollusks, as the wines tasted sour and lost all their charming fruit. With cooked shellfish, however, they fared much better (baked clams casino and fried-oyster poor boys being especially tasty).

- With dishes that need tannin and acid (as a red). It's difficult to pair pure Grenache reds with steaks, roasts, and rich stews, although Grenache blended with other grapes can work. The less Grenache, the better when matching the wine to a dish like cassoulet. Keep your spices balanced and not too hot so as to avoid popping the naturally high alcohol.
- With green and cruciferous vegetables (as a red). Unless your Grenache is part of a blend that's dominated by green, unripe fruit, like Cinsaut, Syrah, Carignan, or Mourvèdre, it's likely to be too ripe and jammy to go with broccoli, Brussels sprouts, leafy greens, or asparagus. Making adjustments to sweeten and mellow the vegetables (adding bacon to Brussels sprouts or grilling your asparagus) will help make the match more palatable, but it's still a stretch.
- With fresh white summer stone fruit and tropical fruit (as a fortified wine). I find it challenging to pair classic Banyuls with ripe peaches, nectarines, or plums, or passion fruit, guava, or papaya.

THE CHEESE PLATE

FRESH	Chèvre (many countries), mascarpone (Italy)—rosé
SEMI-SOFT	Boursin (France), teleme (U.S.A.)—rosé
SOFT-RIPENED	Brie (U.S.A., France), tetilla (Spain)—red, rosé
SEMI-HARD	Comté (France), pecorino romano (Italy)—rosé
HARD	Aged Cheddar (U.K., U.S.A.), aged Mahón (Spain)—dessert
BLUE	Fourme d'Ambert (France), Gorgonzola (Italy)—dessert
WASHED-RIND	Morbier (France), Taleggio (Italy)—red, dessert

grenache | ROASTED CHICKEN WITH FINGERLING POTATOES AND FAVA BEAN AND CIPOLLINI ONION SALAD

LAURENT MANRIQUE   Café de la Presse, Rouge et Blanc Wine Bar, San Francisco, California

Makes 4 main-course servings

WINE AND STOCK REDUCTION

1¹⁄₂ teaspoons unsalted butter

1¹⁄₂ shallots, chopped

1¹⁄₂ cups Grenache or other medium-bodied dry red wine

4 cups chicken stock

Sea salt and freshly ground black pepper

CARAMELIZED CIPOLLINI ONIONS

1 tablespoon unsalted butter

¹⁄₂ pound small cipollini onions (about 1 inch in diameter)

¹⁄₂ cup water

Sea salt and freshly ground black pepper

4 tablespoons unsalted butter, at room temperature

1 tablespoon plus 1¹⁄₂ teaspoons chopped fresh flat-leaf parsley leaves

1¹⁄₂ teaspoons chopped fresh thyme leaves

³⁄₄ teaspoon chopped garlic

Sea salt and freshly ground black pepper

1 (3¹⁄₂-pound) chicken

1¹⁄₂ pounds fingerling potatoes

2 tablespoons extra virgin olive oil

3 ounces bacon, in a single piece

¹⁄₂ pound young fava beans

¹⁄₂ cup cherry tomatoes, stemmed and halved

4 tablespoons mixed chopped fresh herbs such as flat-leaf parsley,
   chervil, tarragon, and chives, in any combination

1 small head frisée, torn into bite-size pieces

To make the reduction, in a saucepan, combine the butter and shallots and sweat over low heat until the shallots are softened and translucent, about 5 minutes. Raise the heat to high, add the wine, and cook until reduced by three-fourths, about 5 minutes. Add the stock and cook until reduced by one-half and the mixture coats the back of a wooden spoon, about 10 minutes. Season with salt and pepper. Remove from the heat and set aside. You should have about 2 cups sauce.

To prepare the cipollini onions, in a sauté pan, melt the butter over medium heat until it foams. Add the onions and cook, stirring occasionally, until lightly browned on all sides, about 5 minutes. Add the water and continue to cook over medium heat until the liquid has evaporated and the onions are nicely browned on all sides and tender when pierced with a knife tip, about 5 minutes. If any liquid remains in the pan and the onions are not fully browned, pour off the liquid and cook and stir the onions until they are browned. Season with salt and pepper and remove from the heat. Let cool, then cut in half through the root end and set aside.

Preheat the oven to 350°F. Put the butter in a small bowl. Add 1 tablespoon of the parsley, the thyme, and the garlic and mix them into the butter with a rubber spatula until they are uniformly distributed and the mixture is smooth. Season with salt and pepper.

Place the chicken, breast side up, on a work surface. Starting from the cavity end, slide your fingers under the skin, gently separating the skin from the breast meat and extending your fingers down to the sides of the breasts and the tops of the thighs. Be careful not to tear the skin or separate the skin at the neck end. Slide the herb butter between the skin and the flesh, distributing it evenly over the flesh, then gently press the skin back into place. Season the chicken on all sides with salt and pepper.

Place the potatoes in the bottom of a roasting pan in which they fit in a single layer. Drizzle with 1 tablespoon of the olive oil, season with salt and pepper, and toss to coat evenly, then spread evenly in the pan. Put the chicken, breast side up, on the potatoes.

Place the pan in the oven and roast the chicken until an instant-read thermometer inserted into the thickest part of a thigh away from bone registers 160°F, about 1 hour.

While the chicken is roasting, cut the bacon into slices $1/4$ thick. Divide the slices in half, and then neatly stack each half. Cut each stack crosswise into lardoons $1/4$ inch wide. (The rectangular strips should be a uniform $1/4$ inch on each side.) Heat a sauté pan over high heat for 1 minute. Add the bacon and cook until browned and crisp, 3 to 4 minutes. Using a slotted utensil, transfer to paper towels to drain.

Shell the fava beans. Bring a small saucepan filled with salted water to a boil. Add the fava beans and blanch for about 30 seconds. Drain immediately and immerse in cold water to cool completely. Squeeze each bean to free it from its tough outer skin. Set the beans aside.

When the chicken is ready, remove the roasting pan from the oven. Transfer the chicken to a large cutting board, tent loosely with aluminum foil, and let rest for 15 minutes. Transfer the potatoes to a large bowl, add the remaining $1 1/2$ teaspoons parsley, and toss to mix. Taste and adjust the seasoning with salt and pepper. Keep warm.

In another bowl, combine the caramelized onions, bacon, fava beans, cherry tomatoes, mixed herbs, frisée, and the remaining 1 tablespoon olive oil. Toss well, then season with salt and pepper and toss again.

Cut the chicken into serving pieces. Gently reheat the reduction sauce, and pour it into a warmed sauceboat. Arrange the potatoes on a large warmed platter, top with the chicken pieces, and serve at once. Pass the onion salad and the sauce at the table.

LAURENT: *When I was thinking of a recipe to be paired with Grenache, I was trying to think of what matches well. First, considering the earthiness of the wine, I started to think about food that comes from the ground. I immediately thought of potatoes, and what's better than roasting a chicken over them? I added the bacon for smokiness to complement the wine's peppery elements. The red-wine reduction made with Grenache adds a velvety element. This is a classic dish that has been changed a little bit but is still very easy to make at home.*

EVAN: *I met Laurent when he was working at Campton Place in San Francisco years ago and putting out tasty and inspired food that was true to his French roots. Having dined at Michel Rostang in Paris several days before, I asked about a dish that reminded me of Rostang's cuisine, only to be greeted by a big smile. I learned that the recipe I was asking about had been inspired by Rostang. Quel petit monde! Among Laurent's great strengths are purity and restraint, two keys to showing off a great Grenache-based blend.*

Roast chicken and Grenache is a favorite combination for me, whether the chicken is served warm or near room temperature. The bacon is a nice bridge for a Grenache that is naturally piquant, but it also works for blended wines, like GSMs, that have peppery elements from Mourvèdre (which adds a cracked-black-pepper character) and Syrah (bringing a penetrating black-spice note). The potatoes' waxy texture works seamlessly with Grenache's richness. It's a straightforward and effective pairing that is equally delightful with Garnacha from Spain and North American "Rhône Ranger" blends. It's scrumptious with a rosé style, too. Magnifique!

RECOMMENDED PRODUCERS

EVERYDAY	PREMIUM	SPLURGE
Bodegas Julián Chivite Navarra, Spain [R]	Adelaida Cellars Southern Central Coast, California	Château de Beaucastel Rhône Valley, France
La Vieille Ferme Rhône Valley, France	Anglim Southern Central Coast, California	Clarendon Hills McLaren Vale, South Australia
Tres Ojos Calatayud, Spain	Château d'Aqueria Rhône Valley, France [R]	M. Chapoutier Rhône Valley, France [Sw]
	Craneford Barossa, South Australia	
	Mas de la Dame Provence, France	
	Pasanau Priorat, Spain	

R = Rosé   Sw = Sweet

malbec

mahl-*behk*

As is the case with several other grapes, Malbec has proved to be more successful as an expat grape than in its homeland. Carmenères from Chile are much better than anything left in France. With Malbec, the wines coming from Argentina are outclassing most of the wines from France's Southwest—including Cahors, where Malbec is renowned. A gifted Argentinean winemaker told me that Malbec makes great wines anywhere in the country. There may be regional differences, but the results are always good. Judging from my tastings across the country, he's right.

Alternative Names Auxerrois, Cot (France), Malbech, Malbeck (Italy)

Styles Medium- to full-bodied dry red, medium-bodied dry rosé

Sometimes Blended With Bonarda, Cabernet Sauvignon, Syrah (Argentina), Cabernet Franc, Cabernet Sauvignon, Gamay, Merlot, Petit Verdot, Tannat (France), Cabernet Franc, Cabernet Sauvignon, Merlot, Petit Verdot (U.S.A.)

Flavor Lexicon *Fruit:* Blackberry, black cherry, black olive, black plum, cassis, mulberry ▪ *Floral:* Tobacco ▪ *Earth:* Mineral ▪ *Wood:* Chocolate, mocha, vanilla ▪ *Other:* Black licorice

Similar Sips Approachable and low-tannin Cabernet Sauvignon, ripe Cabernet Franc, dense, juicy Merlot

Where It's Grown Argentina (Mendoza, Patagonia, Salta, San Juan), Australia, Chile (Colchagua Valley, Curicó Valley, Maipo Valley), France (Bordeaux; Loire Valley; Southwest: Cahors), Italy (northeast), New Zealand, South Africa, U.S.A. (California: Central Valley [Lodi], Napa County, Sonoma County; New York: Long Island; Oregon; Washington: Columbia Valley)

Ask any wine geek about Malbec and they will mention Cahors, the "black wine of the Southwest," which was known for its classic—and notorious—interpretation of the grape. Though there are some excellent Cahors wines, others testify to the accuracy of the grape's name, which is said to have been derived from the colloquial *mal bec,* "bad mouth." Many of the wines are hard, angular, sour, and tannic. Historically, they were renowned for their intense color and austere structure, which were reinforced by blending with the even more impenetrable Tannat grape. This style has since fallen out of favor, and Cahors is very much in transition. Some producers are making dedicated efforts to apply New World techniques, including use of new wood and micro-oxygenation, to this noteworthy variety.

Bordeaux is the other home of Malbec, and here it's usually a supporting player in the classic Médoc blends, fourth in importance after Cabernet Sauvignon, Merlot, and Cabernet Franc. (Petit Verdot is also important in small quantities in blends, where it adds dense color, backbone, and a unique inky character.) In Bordeaux, Malbec adds color, fat (or texture), and structure (a combination of acid and tannin) to blends. In the Loire Valley, to the northeast, Malbec is frequently blended with Cabernet Franc and Gamay in appellation wines for the same reasons; it never stars on its own.

In the United States, results from Malbec have been variable. It crops irregularly in California, and though there are a few varietal Malbec wines made, some of which are quite good, it is used primarily as a blending grape in Bordeaux-style blends and in varietal wines like Cabernet Sauvignon and Cabernet Franc. The California style falls somewhere between the austerity of France and the generosity of Argentina, with distinctive notes of black licorice, black cherry, and conifer saplings. The limited plantings in the Columbia Valley in Washington and Oregon are mostly employed in a similar way, mainly in blends. Long Island has a little Malbec planted, but only one winery (Raphael) currently makes a varietal wine.

The true home of Malbec today is in Argentina, where it is made successfully in a range of styles, produced as both blends and varietal wines, including a wonderful rosé style. These are sometimes known as the wines of Icarus (because the grapes are grown at high altitudes, much closer to the sun). If purple had a smell and taste, it would be Argentinean Malbec. The largest (and best) appellation is Mendoza, where the grape flourishes particularly in subareas of Luján de Cuyo and the Uco Valley. Exploding with rich round plum, blackberry, and blueberry, Mendoza Malbec tends to have more sinew and structure than the wines from farther north in San Juan, which are round, full, and almost Grenache-like. Indeed, many San Juan wines tasted blind could be confused for quality southern Rhône wines. Bottles from Patagonia and the appellations of Rio Negro and Neuquén tend to be lighter in pigment, but, being from a cooler climate, they are racier in the mouth, with as much red fruit as black. Argentinean Malbec is delightful on its own and can be quite complex, but it can also be magic when blended with Cabernet Sauvignon or even Bonarda (the number-two grape in Argentina, after Malbec). I suspect this grape will be the next big thing in the United States, as it delivers the powerful and dense fruit that Americans crave in a rich and not overly tannic package. Coupled with Malbec's moderate alcohol levels, these traits add up to a formula that promises great success.

Chile, quietly and with less fanfare, is also producing ample amounts of Malbec, with most varietal bottlings coming from Colchagua. Chilean Malbec offers wonderful wines at great values. Across Australia, more than eighty wineries are using Malbec, though mostly for blending. A few plantings are found in New Zealand and South Africa as well as Italy's northeast.

Vintner's Choices Choice of clone or selection, micro-oxygenation vs. traditional tannin management, oak vs. no oak, old oak vs. new oak, red vs. rosé, single variety vs. blend, small barrels vs. casks

For all varieties of grape, the clone or selection of grape is important. Within any grape variety, vines exhibit slight variations that can be exploited to the winemaker's advantage. Viticulturalists regularly cultivate cuttings from selected vines that promise to enhance such characteristics as pigment, flavor, and tannic structure. These are known as selections. Clones are genetically identical copies of a "mother" vine, carefully isolated and propagated to avoid cross-fertilization. "Clonal selection," which is different from simply taking cuttings from a successful vineyard, has led to vast improvements in the quality of Malbec, especially in Argentina. Nobody has done more for this grape than Argentina's Nicolas Catena, the proprietor of the Catena Zapata winery.

A winemaker may choose to produce Malbec as a varietal wine or as a component of a wide range of blends. Many 100 percent Malbec wines are good, but they can be augmented with a small amount of other grapes while still qualifying for the varietal label. In Argentina, Cabernet Sauvignon may be added to expand the palate. Classic Cahors from France must be at least 70 percent Malbec. A movement is afoot in Cahors to adopt a New World style in order to make the wines appeal to a larger global audience: examples of this approach include toning down tannins by micro-oxygenation, reducing the maceration time, and blending with more Merlot to make rounder and more approachable wines. Another trend is the use of small, new French oak barrels, which increases the sweet, toasty oak components, with their coffee, chocolate, vanilla, and mocha tones. When oaking is done with a deft hand, Malbec can handle it without being overwhelmed. Using barrels of varying age and size is another way to calibrate the oak's influence on the wine.

PAIRING WITH FOOD

Because Malbec is a minor grape in Bordeaux, my comments here are tailored more to pure Malbec and Malbec-driven blends than to Bordeaux-style wines. Most dishes that demand "big" reds will pair nicely with these wines.

In Argentina, if you're not eating pasta and pizza, you are likely eating *asado,* the traditional slow-grilled, grass-fed beef served with *chimichurri* sauce. Many red wines will pair nicely with this simple, tasty dish, but ample Argentinean Malbec and Malbec-based wines can be especially successful. The inky intensity and rich fruit complement the character of Argentinean beef, which has a stronger, "beefier," more savory character than the corn-fed beef typically found in the United States. Accompanied with classic *chimichurri*—a sauce of garlic, oregano, olive oil, vinegar, and a little chile—it's both traditional and tasty. This is not to say that you must have Argentinean beef or even grass-fed beef to make Malbec sing. Most cuts of red meat, from a juicy rib-eye steak to a textured hanger or flank steak, are good, whether grilled over wood or with gas. Plates of sausage, marinated pork chops . . . you catch the drift.

Malbec pairs very well with other gamy flavors, too: lamb, squab, and even venison. The tannic, sharper versions from France hang in there with rich stews, daubes, and even cassoulet, a specialty of southwestern France, as well as with dishes from elsewhere that feature rich meats, beans, and sausage: American chili, Italian fennel sausage and white beans, and Portuguese bean soup flecked with ham.

You might guess from these pairings that Malbec isn't stellar with most fish, shellfish, and delicate dishes, and you'd be right, though a Malbec rosé could pair well with fish. Regardless of country and appellation of origin, Malbec makes full-flavored wines and wines that simply demand more traditional red-wine pairings. Even chicken and lighter cuts of veal and pork can be overmatched by Malbec's robust character.

PAIRING POINTERS

Malbec goes well with:

- Big slabs of beef. If you don't happen to travel regularly to Argentina for *asado,* grilling your own steaks and chops at home will be just fine. Mixed grills of sausage, meat, and offal (liver, sweetbreads, and the like) are delicious with Malbec.
- Rib-sticking stews. Traditional Gascon cassoulet with a wine from nearby Cahors is as classic a pairing as *asado* is with Argentinean Malbec. For the more tannic Cahors, opt for dense, thick stews and meal-in-a-bowl soups. For riper and smooth Argentinean and Chilean versions, full-flavored but not so thick dishes are fine.
- Game and other flavor-packed meats. I love Malbec with venison, pheasant, partridge, and woodcock (which I sampled at the London restaurant of the chef whose recipe follows). And Malbec with lamb or a rich preparation of rabbit is fantastic.
- Rich root vegetables, or dried fruit with meat. A savory, meaty cassoulet is great, but you can also accentuate the ripe fruit in a Malbec with a slow-cooked dish incorporating carrots, parsnips, and rutabagas. Also, the deft addition of chopped or puréed prunes to a stew enhances richness and sweetness.

- Blue cheese. Don't ask me why, but these wines seem to contradict the rule that powerful wine is not good with powerful cheese. Cahors is "mean" enough to hang in there with Roquefort, and a Gorgonzola dolcelatte is lovely with a ripe, fruit-forward Argentinean Malbec. This wine is still not great with a strong Époisses or Alsatian Munster, but it works better than many.

Malbec isn't good:

- On its own. The French interpretations and most other Malbec wines, although smooth, still need a little something to accompany them—a plate of charcuterie, authentic Central American empanadas, or even pizza. Some of the very light styles can be enjoyed on their own, but even they are better with a nosh or two.
- With fish. Even the traditional regional dish of eel with prunes doesn't hold up to a Cahors. And forget fishy fish or subtle white fish. If you want to serve Malbec with fish, select a rosé, or one of the many other wine options.
- With cream-based sauces. Ouch. Yes, the tannins are softened, but pairing dairy, aside from cheese, with these wines makes them taste disjointed.
- With most Asian fare. There are some meaty Asian dishes that do rock with Malbec, especially the New World styles: Korean short ribs, Chinese lacquered duck, and beef teriyaki. But there are far more recipes that don't, like shrimp with lobster sauce or spicy kung pao chicken. Opt for easier reds, off-dry whites, or rosés instead.
- With delicate white meat and mild poultry. The pairing can be okay, but most Malbecs will overwhelm your typical sautéed chicken, pork or veal scaloppine, or oven-roasted quail. New World Malbec may go down easily, but it packs a punch and can easily overshadow milder dishes.

THE CHEESE PLATE

SEMI-SOFT	Port Salut (France), teleme (U.S.A.)—red, rosé
SEMI-HARD	Lancashire (U.K.), raclette (France)—red, rosé
HARD	Asiago (Italy), aged Jack (U.S.A.)—red
BLUE	Gorgonzola dolcelatte (Italy), Roquefort (France)—red
WASHED-RIND	Morbier (France), Taleggio (Italy)—red

 | **BRAISED SHANK OF BEEF**

FERGUS HENDERSON St. John, London, United Kingdom

Makes 4 to 6 main-course servings

2 tablespoons rendered duck fat or unsalted butter
1 (6- to 7-pound) whole beef shank
Salt and freshly ground black pepper
12 shallots, peeled but left whole
12 cloves garlic, peeled but left whole
8 carrots, peeled and cut into ½-inch-thick slices
1½ cups dry white wine
Bouquet garni of 6 fresh thyme sprigs, 3 fresh rosemary sprigs,
   ½ bunch fresh flat-leaf parsley, and 2 bay leaves, tied in a cheesecloth bundle
About 2 quarts chicken stock

Preheat the oven to 275°F. In a large skillet, heat the duck fat over medium heat until hot. Season the whole shank with salt and pepper and add to the skillet. Brown, turning as needed, until well browned on all sides, about 10 minutes. Remove from the heat.

Select a baking dish or Dutch oven deep enough to accommodate all of the ingredients, including stock almost to cover. Assemble the ingredients in the dish in the following order: shallots, garlic, shank, carrots, wine, and bouquet garni. Add enough stock to reach iceberg level—in other words, the ingredients more covered than exposed—and cover tightly.

Place in the oven and cook for 6 hours, then check for doneness by stabbing the flesh with a knife tip. It is ready if the tip meets no resistance. If it is not ready, return it to the oven for 15 to 30 minutes longer, and test again.

Remove from the oven, season with salt and pepper, and serve. Don't worry about carving etiquette—just attack!

FERGUS: *The reasoning behind this pairing was simple: the unctuous slow-braised meat might encourage this sometimes harsh-seeming wine to show its more velvety side.*

EVAN: *Fergus is a great chef. He's taken on the noble and patriotic task of showing the world just how delicious traditional English cuisine can be. His cookery is pure, honest, and ingredient-driven: it makes you want to lick every last finger. His wine sensitivity, like his sense of humor, is eclectic, and I thought that despite the history of international tensions, it would be fun to bring England and Argentina together at the table.*

Pairing beef with Malbec may not come off as daring, but serving it braised, rather than grilled or barbecued (as in asado), is less traditional. The success of this dish depends entirely on the quality of the ingredients: good meat, fresh herbs (buy a new jar of bay leaves if yours are as old as I suspect they may be), and the smallest, sweetest carrots you can find. All Malbecs shine with this dish, whose simplicity is intended to show off the wine. Serve the beef with potatoes—roasted or mashed—to complete this tasty pairing. Choosing an accompanying green vegetable is up to you.

RECOMMENDED PRODUCERS

EVERYDAY	PREMIUM	SPLURGE
Alamos Mendoza, Argentina [R]	Bodega Colomé Salta, Argentina	Achaval-Ferrer Mendoza, Argentina
Clos la Coutale Cahors, France	Bodega Goulart Mendoza, Argentina	Alta Vista Mendoza, Argentina
Humberto Canale Patagonia, Argentina	Doña Paula Mendoza, Argentina [R]	Catena Zapata Mendoza, Argentina
Valentín Bianchi Mendoza, Argentina [R]	Kaiken Mendoza, Argentina	Château du Cedre Cahors, France

R = Rosé

mencía

mehn-*cee*-ah

About fifteen years ago, I first tasted Mencía as a basic *joven,* a young and unoaked wine, in a café near Cambádos in Spain's Galicia region. I was being entertained by a friend who owns a few wineries in the Rías Baixas, and we enjoyed a casual lunch of fish, seafood, and plenty of Albariño, the local white wine. He went on to order *cocido,* a rich, meaty stew that doesn't work with crisp Albariño, and with it a carafe of this wine. I was mesmerized. It was so tasty, exploding with ripe black raspberry fruit, black spice, and distinctive earth notes, and framed by a pronounced flavor of laurel. I became an instant convert to Mencía.

Almost two decades later, I'm delighted that this grape is now being appreciated by international wine consumers, led by fans in the United States, which is the biggest export market for the wines of Bierzo, Mencía's best-known appellation. It's a unique red grape that makes inimitable red wines, and curious and open-minded wine drinkers often fall in love with it on the first sip. Although it's not yet planted outside the Iberian Peninsula, the future appears bright for this food-friendly and very tasty variety.

Alternative Names Jaen (Portugal)

Styles Medium- to medium-full-bodied dry red

Sometimes Blended With Garnacha, Godello (Spain), Alfrocheiro, Touriga Nacional, Trincadeira (Portugal)

Flavor Lexicon *Fruit:* Blackberry, blackcurrant, raspberry, red currant ▪ *Floral:* Bay leaf, chicory ▪ *Earth:* Graphite, mineral ▪ *Wood:* Smoke, spice

Similar Sips Exotic Cabernet Franc, light, earthy Merlot, herb-scented Barbera

Where It's Grown Portugal (Dão), Spain (Castilla-León: Bierzo; Galicia: Monterrei, Ribeira Sacra, Valdeorras)

Mencía—which is not related to Cabernet Franc, as was once believed—has been planted for a long time in Spain. It is grown throughout Bierzo, in the greater León region adjoining Galicia, and there are anecdotal claims that it arrived in the region with religious pilgrims traveling to Santiago de Compostela, most of whom passed through Bierzo. It is also grown in Galicia proper, in Monterrei, Ribeira Sacra, and Valdeorras (which is actually most celebrated for the white Godello grape). In Valdeorras, Mencía is often blended with Godello to make tasty, quaffable red wines like the one I had at lunch that day. Ribeira Sacra is renowned locally for Mencía but does not (yet) have an international reputation or consistently high quality. Its terraced vineyards (recalling Porto's steep Douro valley) can make for exquisite grapes and wines, with deep color, red to black raspberry fruit, and a pronounced mineral and herbal personality. Again, fun blends are made for daily consumption that incorporate Garnacha (Grenache) and Godello. However, it is in Bierzo that the most exciting wines are being made. The old vines that abound in the region, when well cared for, make for intense, full wines. Some wine experts feel that ultimately, given the necessary expertise, Ribeira Sacra may produce better wines. It's a good debate to have over a bottle of Mencía!

The Portuguese grape Jaen, found in the Dão region, is identical to Mencía. Jaen is most often blended with other grapes, including Touriga Nacional, to make full-bodied red wines. Before the arrival of dry Douro (port) reds about a decade or so ago, Dão red wines were acclaimed as Portugal's "big reds."

Vintner's Choices Low altitude vs. high-altitude vineyards, old oak vs. new oak, single variety vs. blend, traditional vs. modern approach, young vs. old vines

Northwestern Spain and Mencía are a perfect pairing of terrain and vine. The soil here is characterized by *llicorella*, a licorice-colored black slate, similar to that of Catalonia's Priorat region, where intense Grenache-based wines are made. This soil, along with the steep terrain, naturally restricts yields. Growers here believe that the higher the concentration of *llicorella* and the steeper the slopes, the better the wine. Also important to quality is vine age. Some vineyards have vines that are a century old or more, and these highly sought-after vineyards (*pagos* in Spanish) indeed make the most interesting wines.

The lion's share of wine made for the domestic market is fruit-forward, enjoyable wine that can be pure but may well be blended, sees no oak, and is served in unassuming carafes in bars and restaurants (like the one where I sampled my first glass). More ambitious wines are likely to be unblended and produced with some oak to add nuances, along with cleaner winemaking techniques (including use of stainless steel tanks and more highly controlled vinification) consistent with a New World style. Finally, there are those who use extensive new wood to create chocolate-berry bombs that are captivating but less typical. This grape's charm lies in the honesty of its varietal character, which can be well set off with a deft kiss of oak but killed with too much wood.

PAIRING WITH FOOD

Mencía is very good with food. It tends to produce wines of ample acidity (the cooler northern climate is better known for whites than for reds) and moderate levels of alcohol. The tannins are not excessive, and when the oak is kept in check, you have the profile for a food-friendly grape and wine style. Marinades and sauces stressing thyme, marjoram, and rosemary are very effective. Given the grape's green nature (with inherent bay leaf and green olive signature flavors), it can be quite good with dishes ranging from stuffed peppers to eggplant parmigiana to ratatouille. Also successful are most red meat dishes, especially lamb and other stronger-flavored meat, stews and braises, and less sexy but tasty items like oxtails and shanks. Texturally, it pairs well with medium-bodied soups; with borscht it picks up nicely on the sweet, earthy quality of the beets. Pastas and rice dishes that incorporate meat and poultry, as well as tomato or meat *sugo* bases, are equally successful.

Curiously, this is a great wine to have with dishes cooked in wine. It's a nice alternative to classic Pinot Noir with coq au vin or boeuf bourgignon or paired with lamb served with a jus and red-wine reduction sauce. And with squab, cooked any way, Mencía is terrific. It's on my top twenty list! It goes with roast duck, too.

PAIRING POINTERS

Mencía goes well with:

- Vegetable recipes. The grape has a naturally green edge that is brought out by its distinct earth tones. Stuffed peppers, dolmas, eggplant lasagna, pasta primavera, and a tomato and zucchini casserole are all brought into focus with a good bottle of Mencía-based wine.
- Rich stews and braises. From lamb shanks to beef stew, these dishes pair well with Mencía's naturally higher acidity, balanced tannins, and rich texture.
- Fresh and dried herbs. Quality Mencía has inherent notes of thyme, marjoram, bay leaf, and occasionally rosemary. Herbal marinades, *salsa verde,* herbal vinaigrettes drizzled over a piece of meat, and branches of herbs in the grill or smoker complement the wine.
- Combinations of green and red. Okay, this sounds odd. But grill up a plate of asparagus, make up a quick dressing of pomegranate molasses, a little lemon juice, a bit of light olive oil, and a kiss of soy and serve it as a side dish with Mencía. The same thing can be done with sautéed Chinese long beans, stir-fried broccolini, or grilled zucchini.
- Stronger-flavored meat and fowl. I love Bierzo wines with squab, lamb, and dark turkey meat. With a tapenade made from black olives and herbs, you have a super meal to serve with Mencía. And paired with piquant Spanish chorizo or *morcilla,* a blood sausage, it is perfection.

Mencía isn't good:

- If you pick the wrong one. Many of these wines, sadly, are oak bombs. If you find yourself with an example like this, play to the oak by choosing grilled or smoked foods, appropriate spices, roasted nuts, and the like. The less oaked or *joven* (unoaked) styles tend to be the most flexible.
- With briny seafood. I must have tried this a half dozen times when in Spain, only to be disappointed each time. Paired with oysters, mussels, clams, or sea snails, these wines lose all their charm.
- With very spicy food. The wines hang in there with their moderate alcohol levels, but all the pretty fruit vanishes. And those oakier bottlings simply taste like spicy oak.
- With pizza and burgers. Unlike the easy-drinking carafes you get in Spain, juicy and exploding with fruit, earth, and spice, most exported Mencía-based wines call for more serious food.
- With slightly sweet appetizers. Most Mencía wines are refreshing enough to enjoy early on in a multicourse meal. Because of their mineral and herbal personality and higher acidity, though, they are often challenged with slightly sweet appetizers. Asian dumplings or pot stickers with plum or hoisin sauce, foie gras served with fig jam or confit of quince, and caramelized onion tart are three examples.

THE CHEESE PLATE

SEMI-SOFT	Chèvre (many countries), tetilla (Spain)
SOFT-RIPENED	Brie (France, U.S.A.), robiola (Italy)
SEMI-HARD	Gouda (Holland), Petit Basque (France)
HARD	Mimolette (France), Roncal (Spain)

mencía | SEARED TUNA WITH BRAISED CABBAGE AND ROASTED MUSHROOMS

DOUGLAS KEANE Cyrus and Healdsburg Bar and Grill, Healdsburg, California

Makes 4 to 6 main-course servings

SPICE MIX
2 teaspoons black peppercorns
2 teaspoons fennel seeds
1 teaspoon brown mustard seeds
1 teaspoon juniper berries
1 teaspoon caraway seeds
3 allspice berries
3 bay leaves

1 head red cabbage, about 1½ pounds, cored, halved, and thinly sliced
Salt and freshly ground black pepper
1 teaspoon sugar
2 tablespoons unsalted butter
½ cup finely diced bacon (about ¼ pound)
2 shallots, finely minced
1 clove garlic, finely minced
¼ cup finely minced, peeled green apple
1 cup Mencía or other dry red wine
½ cup red wine vinegar
1 tablespoon unsalted butter
¾ pound cremini mushrooms, trimmed and quartered (about 2 cups)
2 teaspoons canola oil
2 pounds ahi tuna fillets, trimmed of any blood lines and sinew

To make the spice mix, in a small, dry skillet, combine the peppercorns, fennel seeds, mustard seeds, juniper berries, caraway seeds, allspice, and bay leaves over low heat and toast, shaking the pan occasionally, until fragrant, 3 to 5 minutes. Pour onto a plate and let cool, then grind in a spice grinder to a fine powder. Measure out 1 tablespoon for seasoning the cabbage. Transfer the remainder to an airtight container and store in a cool cupboard for up to several weeks for use in other recipes.

Preheat the oven to 350°F. In a large bowl, toss together the cabbage, 1 tablespoon salt, and the sugar, mixing well. Set aside.

In a large sauté pan or Dutch oven, melt 1 tablespoon of the butter over low heat. Add the bacon and cook, stirring, until it renders some of its fat, about 3 minutes. Add the shallots, garlic, and apple and cook, stirring occasionally, until the shallots and apple are soft, about 5 minutes. Add the 1 tablespoon spice mix, stir well, and cook until fragrant, 2 to 3 minutes. In batches, lift the cabbage with your hands, squeeze to remove any excess moisture, and add to the pan. Stir in the wine and vinegar, mixing well.

Cover the pan, transfer to the oven, and braise until the cabbage is soft to the bite and all the excess liquid has evaporated, about 1 hour.

About 10 minutes before the cabbage is ready, in a sauté pan, melt the remaining 1 tablespoon butter over medium-high heat and heat until lightly browned, about 30 seconds. Add the mushrooms, season with salt and pepper, and place in the oven until the mushrooms are tender, about 5 minutes.

When the cabbage is ready, transfer it to a warmed serving dish large enough to accommodate the fish, and place the cooked mushrooms on top. Cover to keep warm while you cook the fish.

Just before serving, in a large, heavy skillet, heat the canola oil over high heat until very hot. Season the tuna on both sides with salt and pepper, add to the hot pan, and cook, turning once, until seared on both sides and still rare in the center, 1 to 2 minutes on each side. Transfer to a cutting board and cut into slices across the grain.

Arrange the tuna slices on top of the cabbage and mushrooms and serve at once.

NOTE The cabbage can be cooked up to several hours in advance and reheated in a 350°F oven for about 15 minutes before serving.

DOUGLAS: *Tuna is one fish that can carry a red wine with almost no problem; the earthiness of the cabbage and mushrooms blend harmoniously with the Mencía.*

EVAN: *Doug's greatest strength is his range—from simple comfort food to haute cuisine. In the heart of Sonoma's wine country, chefs need to be up on their wine, and Doug certainly is. I challenged him to demonstrate Mencía's ability to work with fish, and of course he rose to the occasion.*

Tuna is meaty enough to get along with most red wines. The mushrooms and bacon provide a link to the earthy and mineral character of most Mencía-based wines, while the cabbage subtly connects with the wine's greener notes. The mixture of spices is very effective with those wines that have seen oak, even the oak-laden examples so popular in the marketplace. The recipe is understated but very effective.

RECOMMENDED PRODUCERS

EVERYDAY	PREMIUM	SPLURGE
Adria Bierzo, Spain	Bodegas Estefanía Bierzo, Spain	Bodegas y Viñedos Gancedo Bierzo, Spain
Bodegas del Abad Bierzo, Spain	Dominio de Tares Bierzo, Spain	Descendientes de J. Palacios Bierzo, Spain
Bodegas y Viñedos Luna Beberide Bierzo, Spain	Luzdivina Amigo Bierzo, Spain	Paixar Bierzo, Spain
Val da Lenda Ribeira Sacra, Spain	Mencías de Dos Bierzo, Spain	Ucedo Bierzo, Spain

mourvèdre

moor-*veh*-druh

Because most wine lovers know this grape by its French name, I chose to title this chapter Mourvèdre rather than Monastrell (as it is known in Spain) or Mataro (a name used in California and Australia). Overlooked but interesting regardless of what you call it, this grape offers up peppery fruit and an edgy earthiness. It is gaining favor far and wide.

Grown in Spain and southern France for centuries, Mourvèdre has experienced renewed popularity in France, but sadly it has been losing ground in Spain, where it competes with traditional grapes like Tempranillo and Garnacha and international varieties like Cabernet Sauvignon, Merlot, and Syrah. But thanks to the Rhône Ranger movement in the United States, its future is bright in the New World.

Alternative Names Monastrell (Spain), Mataro (Australia, U.S.A., Spain, Portugal)

Styles Medium- to full-bodied dry red, medium-bodied dry rosé (*rosado*)

Sometimes Blended With Cabernet Sauvignon, Cariñena, Garnacha, Merlot, Tempranillo (Spain); Cabernet Sauvignon, Cinsaut, Counoise, Grenache, Merlot, Syrah (France); Grenache, Shiraz (Australia); Rhône varieties (Cinsaut, Counoise, Grenache, Syrah), Petite Sirah, Zinfandel (U.S.A.)

Flavor Lexicon *Fruit:* Blackberry, black plum • *Floral:* Herbs (basil, cilantro, fennel seed, tarragon) • *Earth:* Mineral, stone • *Wood:* Spice • *Other:* Anisette, black pepper, game

Similar Sips Peppery Zinfandel, Petite Sirah, Syrah

Where It's Grown Australia (South Australia: Barossa Valley, Clare Valley, McLaren Vale), France (Languedoc-Roussillon, Provence, Rhône Valley), Portugal, South Africa, Spain (Murcia: Jumilla, Yecla; Valencia: Alicante), U.S.A. (California: Central Valley [Lodi], Napa County, Northern Central Coast [Contra Costa County], Sierra Foothills; Oregon: Umpqua Valley)

Spain is the ancestral home of Mourvèdre, which is the fourth most widely planted red-wine grape in the country. Grape sleuths have tracked its origin to Valencia, specifically to the town of Murviedro. Interestingly, there's also a municipality called Mataro near Barcelona. Origins aside, Mourvèdre/Monastrell is grounded in the region of Murcia and its *denominaciónes de origen* (or DO, the Spanish equivalent of the French AOC or Italian DOC) of Jumilla and Yecla, and in Valencia, where it thrives in Alicante. Although it has traditionally been used to boost volume rather than quality, some growers are experimenting with reducing the yields. In Murcia, where many vineyards are very old, the fruit is capable of making excellent wines full of black fruit, rich dark spice, fresh green herbs, and a leathery gaminess. Local Monastrell-based *rosado*s are also very good, but they're hard to find in the United States.

France's Mourvèdre is a wonderful interpretation of the grape. It's planted across the southern swath of the country, from the Languedoc, not far from the Spanish border, west to Provence and specifically Bandol, where it is at its best. In the western Languedoc, Mourvèdre's chief role is as a blending grape with Cinsaut, Carignan, and similar grapes that dominate the vineyard landscape. Mourvèdre produces inky-dark wines, and its depth can supplement qualities lacking in the main varieties of the region. Its success as a blending wine has motivated many producers to produce varietal Mourvèdre wines, which can be quite good and exceptional values. Farther east, in the heart of the Rhône Valley, the variety plays a similar role in Côtes du Rhône blends, though it's not widely planted; it plays a larger part in Châteauneuf-du-Pape blends, where it's thought to add a specific structure and spice to the mix of thirteen grapes. It's in Provence, though, that Mourvèdre, under the label of Bandol, makes the most interesting wines. It may not always comprise 100 percent of the cuvée, but it's usually far more than the minimum percentage required for the appellation, and its signature notes of cracked black pepper, gamy meat, spice, and scented black fruit are unmistakable. It makes a similar, though lower-key contribution in the rosé wines from the same appellation and is, of course, a component of most red and rosé wines labeled Côtes de Provence.

In the United States, Mourvèdre, often called Mataro, is a beloved grape, though the acreage planted to it is not vast. In California, where it is most widely planted, it is said to lack some of the structure and pigment for which it is known in Europe, but nevertheless it makes very good wines both on its own and in Rhône-style blends (Ridge Vineyards has made a tasty Mataro for years). The American wine shows more fruit and less pepper and spice than its European cousins, although promising new plantings in eastern Washington have more in common with the Old World bottlings. Australia's Mourvèdre (or Mataro) is concentrated in South Australia and is an integral part of several popular GSM (Grenache-Shiraz-Mourvèdre) blends. Sadly, a lot of the older Mataro vineyards have been ripped up and planted with other varieties, to the detriment of Rhône-style blends Down Under. There's no significant quantity of Mourvèdre grown in the rest of the world, although it can be found in both South Africa and Portugal, and undoubtedly in small quantities elsewhere, too.

Vintner's Choices Harvested when ripe vs. less ripe, choice of clone or selection, single variety vs. blend, red vs. rosé

Above all, Mourvèdre requires ample sun and heat to ripen fully, which is why it is more widely grown in Spain than in France, and more in Southern California than the north. Because it's a late ripener, Mourvèdre has a greater risk of weather damage than other grapes, and when it does crop, it's not prolific. It's said that Châteauneuf-du-Pape is as far north in France as Mourvèdre can ripen and perform reliably. Ironically, it also struggles if the climate is too hot and dry. California's Central Coast appears to provide ideal conditions in the United States; the Barossa is best in Australia; and Murcia in Spain and Provence in France are the most suitable spots in Europe. There are several clones of Mourvèdre but no consensus as to which are the best, so most preferred vineyards are created from a bevy of different clones.

Winemaking philosophies for Mourvèdre are diverse. Deep, forceful, and concentrated, this grape can achieve magic on its own, as anyone who has had a pure Mourvèdre from Bandol, Jumilla, or Alicante can attest. Indeed, many of the most interesting reds coming from France's Languedoc-Roussillon region are 100 percent Mourvèdre. Offerings from California and Washington are often 95 percent to 100 percent pure, and a favorite Mourvèdre out of South Africa, Spice Route, is 100 percent Mourvèdre. But blends can also be excellent: a GSM from McLaren Vale or a Châteauneuf-du-Pape that includes Mourvèdre is a compelling wine. Though representing less than 6 percent of plantings in Châteauneuf, Mourvèdre's role is clearly to add richness and concentration to the fruitiness of Grenache, the sinew of Syrah, and the finesse and soft flesh of Cinsaut. In Spain, Monastrell is successfully blended with the traditional Cariñena (Carignan), Tempranillo, and Garnacha and with Bordelais reds like Cabernet Sauvignon and Merlot. Mourvèdre is also an important part of many lovely rosé wines in Provence and the Rhône Valley and (as *rosado*) in Murcia, where it offers pink peppercorns, raspberry, and tangerine flavors.

PAIRING WITH FOOD

There are three distinct categories of Mourvèdre: two red and one pink, or reds that are powerful and usually pure, those that are easy-drinking (and likely blended), and rosés. For the fuller-styled wines, rich red-wine fare is the ticket. Red meat, rich poultry, and game are all classic matches, as are rustic stews, sausages, and anything from the grill. Ample spicing, especially pepper, rosemary and other strong flavors that often overwhelm other wines, can go well with Mourvèdre. Grilled eggplant, roast squab, and steak au poivre are seamless with this style of the grape. With the lighter reds, tone down the intense spice and pick up on the fruit: try duck with thyme and olives for the Bandol, and Peking duck with a fruity blended Monastrell-Grenache wine from Jumilla. Tomato sauces also pair easily with these softer interpretations, whereas they make the robust wines taste metallic and sharp. Herb-marinated meat en brochette is an excellent tablemate, especially accompanied by grilled vegetables. Actually, almost anything flavorful en brochette is good with red Mourvèdres, though fish and some lighter poultry pair better with rosés.

The rosé wines are excellent with flavorful fish preparations. The Provençal appetizer spread of warm *brandade* (salt cod and potato), chunky tuna crostini, or a plate of sardines marinated in olive oil are flavorful, harmonious matches. Salmon, stuffed trout, a simply prepared chicken breast on the bone, and ratatouille would pair nicely with most Mourvèdre-driven rosé blends.

PAIRING POINTERS

Mourvèdre goes well with:

- Duck, squab, and wild pheasant (as a red). Rich and flavorful birds are at home with Mourvèdre. Choose sweeter, smokier preparations for the medium- to full-bodied blends and coarser and spicier dishes for the bigger wines. Duck with sausage or the classic Provençal duck with olives is great for the ample wines, while Peking or tea-smoked duck may be better with a Spanish or fruit-forward California version.
- Dark mushrooms (as a red). Mourvèdre seems to pair well with morels, porcini, and even reconstituted Chinese dried black mushrooms. Use them as an accent rather than as a dominant flavoring, and note how they bring out the intense spice and mineral tones in the Mourvèdre.
- Peppery dishes (as a red). To me, the classic flavors you find in Mourvèdre, regardless of origin, are pepper and meatiness. Pick up on the pepper and the meat together, and you have great matches. Beef carpaccio with a heavy dose of cracked black pepper, lemon, and Parmesan; traditional steak au poivre; or a filet mignon with a green peppercorn, Cognac, and cream sauce are all good choices.
- A *fritto* of fish and shellfish (as a rosé). I'm a sucker for almost anything that's taken from the water, battered, and then rolled in a little egg and flour before finding its ultimate gastronomic destiny in a deep fryer. Top it with a little Spanish *romesco* sauce or a Provençal rouille and serve with a bottle of Mourvèdre rosé, and you'll have a wonderful afternoon or evening.
- Fish and light poultry (as a rosé). From a turkey kebab (see below) to swordfish served with olives, rosemary, capers, and tomato *concassé,* the blush interpretations are flexible with recipes that the bigger reds might steamroller.

Mourvèdre isn't good:

- By itself (as a red). This is a variety that demands food alongside. It needs only a bowl of fried olives, a plate of chorizo, or a selection of tapas as an accompaniment, but it's less interesting and pleasant when drunk solo.

- With most white meat (as a red). The subtle sweetness of pork and veal tend to get lost behind the ample red versions of Mourvèdre. They're not terrible matches, but I like the delicacy of a roast pork loin, a light Asian pork stir-fry, or an unadorned veal chop, and I don't want to have to work too hard to enjoy them through the wine's commanding presence.
- With seafood (as a red). Some people argue that meaty fish can hold its own with these rich red wines. I find that unless you specifically cook to the wine (grilling and serving the fish with bridging sauces), the wine doesn't make the fish taste better, and the fish doesn't make the wine taste better, so why bother?
- With many sauces (as a red). This result is peculiar, and there are exceptions: Mourvèdre-based wines are good with either peppery and spicy sauces or with meat dishes drizzled with olive oil or served with a compound butter with garlic and herbs. But keep these wines away from sauces that are mildly sweet, tart, or hot.
- When it's too old (as a red or rosé). Like the grapes with which it is often blended, Mourvèdre is most charming in its youth. Aging a Châteauneuf-du-Pape, a GSM, or a Spanish Jumilla for as long as a bottle of Cabernet Sauvignon or red Bordeaux makes no sense. It holds up but loses many of the attributes of its younger self.

THE CHEESE PLATE

FRESH	Chèvre (many countries), fromage blanc (France)—rosé	
SEMI-SOFT	Crescenza (U.S.A.), Saint-Paulin (France)—rosé	
SOFT-RIPENED	Camembert (U.S.A., France)—red, rosé	
SEMI-HARD	Fontina (Italy), Idiazábal (Spain)—red, rosé	
WASHED-RIND	Taleggio (Italy), vacherin Mont d'Or (France)—red, rosé	

mourvèdre | BARBECUED TURKEY SKEWERS WITH CARAMELIZED SAGE ONIONS

CINDY PAWLCYN Mustards Grill, Cindy's Backstreet Kitchen, and Go Fish, Napa Valley, California

Makes 4 main-course servings

TURKEY

4 cups water
$\frac{1}{2}$ cup pomegranate molasses (see note)
$\frac{1}{2}$ cup firmly packed dark brown sugar
5 fresh thyme sprigs
2 cloves garlic, peeled
1 tablespoon coarsely ground black pepper
1 tablespoon chile paste
4 cups ice cubes
2 turkey thighs (2$\frac{1}{2}$ pounds total weight)

BARBECUE SAUCE

$\frac{1}{2}$ cup ketchup
$\frac{1}{2}$ cup pomegranate molasses
$\frac{1}{2}$ cup mirin
$\frac{1}{2}$ cup jam, any kind

SAGE ONIONS

2 tablespoons unsalted butter or extra virgin olive oil
$\frac{1}{2}$ cup water
6 to 8 radishes, thinly sliced
12 to 16 cipollini or large pearl onions (about 1 inch in diameter), sliced
6 to 8 shallots, sliced
2 or 3 fresh sage sprigs, minced
Sea salt and freshly ground black pepper

SERVING SAUCE

Reserved barbecue sauce
1 to 2 teaspoons unsalted butter
2 to 4 tablespoons Mourvèdre

To prepare the turkey, in a saucepan, combine the water, pomegranate molasses, sugar, thyme, garlic, pepper, and chile paste and bring to a boil over high heat, stirring to dissolve the sugar. Reduce the heat to medium and simmer for 5 minutes to blend the flavors. Remove from the heat and pour into a large heatproof bowl. Add the ice cubes and let stand until cooled to room temperature. Add the turkey thighs, turn to coat well, cover, and refrigerate for at least 3 hours or up to overnight.

When you are ready to grill the turkey, make the barbecue sauce. In a bowl, combine the ketchup, pomegranate molasses, mirin, and jam and mix well. Set aside. Have ready 4 bamboo or metal skewers. If using bamboo skewers, soak in cold water to cover for about 30 minutes, then drain.

Remove the turkey thighs from the bowl and discard the liquid. Using a sharp knife, cut the meat from the bone in large pieces. Remove the skin, if desired, then cut the meat into $1^1/_2$-inch cubes. Don't worry that they are not uniform in shape. Divide the turkey cubes evenly among the 4 skewers. If you have left the skin on, make sure it is always facing the same way, for easier grilling. Also, leave some space between the cubes to ensure more even cooking. Divide the barbecue sauce in half, and set aside half for making the serving sauce. Thoroughly coat the cubes with some of the remaining barbecue sauce and set the skewers aside to marinate while the grill heats.

Prepare a charcoal or gas grill for direct grilling over a medium fire. (Or, preheat a stove-top grill pan over medium heat.)

While the grill is heating, make the sage onions. In a sauté pan, combine the butter, water, radishes, onions, shallots, and sage and sprinkle with salt and pepper. Place over medium heat, cover, and cook for 10 minutes to blend the flavors. Uncover, raise the heat to high to evaporate the liquid, and cook, stirring occasionally to prevent burning, until the onions are caramelized, 3 to 4 minutes. Remove from the heat and keep warm.

Arrange the skewers on the grill and cook, basting occasionally with the remaining barbecue sauce and turning often so the meat caramelizes nicely on all sides and does not burn. It should be cooked through and nicely browned in 8 to 12 minutes.

To make the serving sauce, in a small saucepan, combine the reserved barbecue sauce, the butter, and 2 tablespoons wine, stir well, and bring to a boil. Cook until reduced and thickened enough to coat the turkey lightly, adding up to 2 tablespoons wine if needed to achieve a good consistency.

Remove the skewers from the grill and arrange on a warmed platter or individual plates with the sage onions. Drizzle some of the serving sauce over the skewers and pass the remaining sauce at the table.

NOTE If you cannot find pomegranate molasses, use $1/_4$ cup each unsulfured light molasses and pomegranate juice, such as POM brand.

CINDY: *I love these skewers, whether done over hot coals on a cold night or on the barbecue next to the pool on a summer evening. This barbecue with Mourvèdre is a great combination. The tartness of the pomegranate molasses doesn't destroy the flavor of the wine the way a vinegar would. The smokiness and brightness of the sauce balance with the intensity of the wine. Wild rice would make a flavorful accompaniment.*

EVAN: *Cindy is one talented chef. Working in the Wine Country attunes you to cooking with and for wine, consciously or not. When Cindy opened up Mustards in 1983, she opened the door for serious food in the Napa Valley, an area long renowned for its wines but less so for its food. Because of her skill, I could have asked her to devise a recipe for any of the wines in this book, but her talent for making comfort food led me to suggest turkey, and from there we went to pairing it with Mourvèdre.*

I was wrong in my first pairing ideas for this dish. My initial thought was that the dish would work great with rosé wine and the lightest of reds. Grilling and Mourvèdre work well together, and anything on a skewer stands a chance, but I worried that the most robust styles of wine would overwhelm the turkey. But to my surprise, the dish works with all three styles of Mourvèdre. The brine makes the turkey more assertive, the tang of pomegranate molasses in the sauce is sheer brilliance, and the sage-infused onions pull it all together.

RECOMMENDED PRODUCERS

EVERYDAY	PREMIUM
Bodegas Agapito Rico Jumilla, Spain	Château de Pibarnon Provence, France [DR, R]
Cline Southern Central Coast, California	d'Arenberg McLaren Vale, Australia
Domaines Bunan Provence, France [R]	Domaine Begude Provence, France [DR, R]
Juan Gil Jumilla, Spain	Domaine Tempier Provence, France [DR, R]
Montgó Yecla, Spain	McCrea Columbia Valley, Washington
	Spice Route Swartland, South Africa
	Tablas Creek Southern Central Coast, California

DR = Dry red   R = Rosé

nebbiolo

neh-b'*yoh*-loh

If I were asked to name a variety that isn't at the tip of everyone's tongue but can rank among the longest-lived, greatest red wines in the world, it would likely be Nebbiolo. Possibly the finest grape of Italy, red or white, Nebbiolo offers soft versions as well as the prolific age-worthy bottlings of Barolo and Barbaresco in Piedmont. The best Barolo and Barbaresco are must-have bottles in any collector's cellar and can improve for thirty years or more in great vintages. But not all Nebbiolo wine is made in these two esteemed regions: Nebbiolo is also found in other Piedmontese districts and outside Italy.

No other classic red grape has had so much trouble defining itself outside its native area. While Cabernet Sauvignon, Pinot Noir, and Syrah have achieved worldwide success, and other grapes that had a difficult time establishing themselves, like Tempranillo, have now adapted to foreign soils, the character of Nebbiolo seems to depend heavily on its home *terroir* of northeastern Italy.

Alternative Names Chievannasca, Picutener, Spanna (Italy)

Styles Medium- to full-bodied dry red

Sometimes Blended With Barbera, Bonarda, Freisa, Neyret (Italy)

Flavor Lexicon *Fruit:* Black cherry, raspberry, red cherry ▪ *Floral:* Anise, rose, violet ▪ *Earth:* Truffles ▪ *Wood:* Chocolate, smoke ▪ *Other:* Black licorice, leather, tar

Similar Sips Rustic Cabernet Sauvignon, refined Mourvèdre, spicy Syrah, full-flavored Xinomavro

Where It's Grown Argentina, Australia (South Australia: Adelaide Hills, McLaren Vale; Queensland: Granite Belt; Victoria: Bendigo, Heathcote, King Valley, Nagambie Lakes; Tasmania), Chile, Italy (Piedmont: Barbaresco, Barolo, Carema, Gattinara, Ghemme; Lombardy: Valtellina [Inferno, Sassella, Sforzato]; Valle d'Aosta: Donnas), New Zealand, Uruguay, U.S.A. (California: Napa County [Carneros, Rutherford], Southern Central Coast

[Paso Robles, Santa Barbara, Santa Ynez Valley]), Oregon (Rogue Valley), Washington (Red Mountain)

Nebbiolo, which takes its name from the Italian word *nebbia*, meaning "fog"—for the heavy late-summer mist that creeps into local vineyards—gives Piedmont its fame as one of the great European red wine–producing regions, alongside Bordeaux and Burgundy in France and Rioja and Ribera del Duero in Spain. In truth, this variety makes up barely 3 percent of all the wines produced in Piedmont. There are twice as many acres planted with Dolcetto and ten times as many planted with Barbera. But if you come across an amazing Barolo or captivating Barbaresco, you'll understand why the grape makes Piedmont's great reputation. The success of Barolo and Barbaresco is very site-specific. The best sites, known as crus, are recognized for their amazing complexity, like the great vineyards of Germany's Rheingau and Mosel or Burgundy's Côte d'Or. Traditionally, the best sites have been known as *sori*—vineyards with good southern exposure—and *bric* or *bricco*, a Piedmontese term for the highest part of the terrain or vineyard. A new official system is being implemented to categorize these sites, but it is provoking heated debate.

Barbaresco, which produces generally easier-drinking wines than Barolo, is made up of three adjoining communes—Barbaresco, Treiso, and Neive—which are in turn subdivided into more than sixty subzones. Barolo, situated in the Langhe region surrounding the town of Alba, is made up of the communes of Barolo, Castiglione Falletto, La Morra, Monforte, and Serralunga. Within Barolo, La Morra and Barolo tend to produce lighter, smoother, and more luscious wines, while those coming from Serralunga and Monforte tend to be more austere, robust, chunkier wines that have great aging potential. Wines from Castiglione Falletto are said to be in the middle, possessing both perfume and structure. A number of other Nebbiolo-based wines are also produced in Piedmont, ranging from the easy-drinking Nebbiolo d'Alba or Nebbiolo delle Langhe to Ghemme and Gattinara, which can be excellent wines and superb value for money. To the far north is the region of Carema, which sits on the border of Valle d'Aosta. Its wines, which are produced in smaller quantities, are known for their floral and earthy perfume and can age quite well.

Across from Carema is the Valle d'Aosta zone of Donnas, a very stony region producing rich and often very powerful red wines, similar in style to Barolo. But it's in Valtellina, in the northern region of Lombardy, that Nebbiolo makes its most noteworthy appearance outside Piedmont. Here the wines take on names that are representative of the difficult terrain and circumstances in which they are produced—Inferno (hell), Sassella (little rock), and Sforzato (forced, or strained). With Grumello, Valgella, and Maroggia, they represent the wines of Valtellina Superiore, which are characterized by rose petals, saddle leather, and black truffles. Less full-bodied than those wines of Piedmont, they are more elegant and stylish. If you're heading off to the store in search of inky wine, remember that Sforzato has the biggest structure and flavor.

Despite many sporadic efforts by California's Cal-Ital movement, the Italian counterpart of the Rhône Rangers, Nebbiolo is not yet a mainstream variety in the United States. The best efforts so far have been the Central Coast appellations of Paso Robles and the Santa Ynez Valley; as better clones are selected and vines mature, the wines are improving. Tasty as they are, they face an uphill battle for market share, as much of the wine-drinking public is only now becoming comfortable with Italy's benchmark wines. In any case, California's best examples taste very different from the Italian wines. Some limited plantings of Nebbiolo can be found in eastern Washington (Red Mountain) and southern Oregon (the Rogue Valley). Experiments in other states have not yet produced anything noteworthy.

In Australia, more than seventy producers are incorporating Nebbiolo and coming up with award-winning bottles. Various styles of wines, both blended and single variety, are being made in Murray Darling, the Adelaide Hills, Rutherglen, Geographe, and King Valley. Not as widely available in the United States, the Nebbiolos can be worth trying if you are in Australia and tired of Shiraz, Grenache, and Mourvèdre either separately or blended into GSM. There are plantings of Nebbiolo in Argentina's Mendoza region and a smattering in New Zealand, Chile, and Uruguay.

Vintner's Choices Choice of clone or selection, low vs. high altitude sites, micro-oxygenation vs. traditional tannin management, old oak vs. new oak, single variety vs. blend, small barrels vs. casks, traditional vs. modern approach

Nebbiolo performs best at higher elevations with ample sun (in the Northern Hemisphere, that means south-facing slopes). In Piedmont's Barolo and Barbaresco regions, the controversial effort to certify the best sites has produced a ranking system. It replaces traditional terms like *sori* and *bricco* with the term *vigna,* the equal of "single vineyard," with many restrictions on yields, vineyard registration, and prohibitions on the use of the colloquial and long-used names that always follow these *sori* and *bricco* terms. The new system is confusing and may not catch on, but it does officially recognize the hierarchy of vineyards. The best sites include Conterno's Francia (Barolo), Cannuba (sourced by Chiarlo, Prunotto, Scavino, and other estates in Barolo), Rabaja in Barbaresco (sourced by Giacosa, Rocco, and Cortese, among others), and Vigna Rionda in Barolo (a great vineyard for Pira, Canale, and Massolino).

Two of the other decisions pertinent to Nebbiolo include choice of clone (there are many for Nebbiolo and a handful that are preferred) and tannin management. Though few vintners are using micro-oxygenation, they do implement other measures, such as shorter maceration periods and use of riper fruit, to attenuate the astringency that can plague this grape. Nebbiolo (and Barolo in particular) has traditionally been a gamble, often characterized as much for its drying tannin, volatile and dried-out fruit, and coarse winemaking as by its potential complexity. When new vintages were released, most producers would shrug and encourage you to wait at least ten years. Then you'd be rewarded with either a fabulous bottle or, more likely, a very dry, tea-colored wine that reminded you of dirty desiccated plums, black figs, and dried flowers. The best traditionalists, those wineries capable of making this wine into something brilliant, include the Conternos (Aldo and Giacomo), Giuseppe Mascarello, and Bruno Giacosa. The rest of the pack's poor showings encouraged a younger group of vintners, led by Elio Altare, Roberto Voerzio, and Domencio Clerico, to take a more modern approach. Defined by the use of small, new oak (versus large, old casks), shorter but more intensive macerations, and shorter vinification, this fresher, more opulent style of wine attracted a new generation of wine drinkers. While some scoff at this "internationalization" of a classic wine, others embrace it as a demonstration of Nebbiolo's true pedigree and a justification of its ranking among the great modern reds. I encourage you to explore both styles and decide for yourself which you prefer.

Although quality Nebbiolo is almost always 100 percent pure, some regions are known for their adept blending (Gattinara, for example, for its deft touch with Bonarda, and Carema for its skillful use of the local Freisa, among other grapes).

PAIRING WITH FOOD

When I think about serving Barolo, Barbaresco, Gattinara, and Valtellina Superiore Sforzato, it's generally with main courses leading to a cheese plate. For a simpler Nebbiolo delle Langhe or other straightforward wine, I am happy to opt for pasta, a mixed selection of antipasti, or its foreign equivalents—Spanish tapas or Middle Eastern meze.

Nebbiolo loves meat, especially beef, and lamb, and the traditional local dish of *brasato al Barolo,* a rich version of braised beef, is perfect Nebbiolo fare. The bigger wines handle these preparations well: braised shanks (osso buco), rich stews and casseroles, and basic grilled lamb all shine with this grape. I enjoy preparations that incorporate smoked bacon or ham as an accent, as they bring out the wine's smoky character, as well as its fruit and naturally spicy elements. Valtellina is a solid pasta wine, as are the lighter Piedmontese interpretations. *Pasta alla bolognese,* noodles served with traditional meat sauce, and full-flavored lasagna are also tasty pairings.

Mushrooms, especially Piedmont's famous white and black truffles, are splendid with Nebbiolo. And no, you don't need to pay a small ransom for them. An accent added through the judicious use of truffle oil or truffle salt can be enough to link the dish with the wine. Of course, if you do have fresh truffles, you are in for a real treat.

Older Nebbiolo requires two things in the food it is paired with: simplicity, to bring out the wine's intricacies, and juiciness, since the wine's fruit becomes drier over time. For the latter, rare meat can work, as can incorporating tomato paste or some fruit, such as prunes or raisins, into the dish. I often sneak a little purée of prune into a stew or sauce to pick up on the wine's character and add texture. This trick, often used to add moisture and texture to those nonfat muffins you get at Starbucks, can be very effective.

One oddity that is worth enjoying if you get the chance is the acclaimed Barolo Chinato. This unique wine, a Barolo digestive infused with over two dozen different herbs and spices (including quinine!), can be fun with dessert, especially one that includes chocolate and mint. It's also good with rhubarb tarts and clafoutis. It makes a change from port and Banyuls!

PAIRING POINTERS

Nebbiolo goes well with:

- Truffles and porcini. Barolo and Barbaresco are the quintessential truffle wines: the wine and the intoxicating fungi complement one another to bring out a heady earthiness in each. Again, truffle salt or oil can do the trick if you aren't feeling flush. Porcini, earthy and savory brown mushrooms, are also magic with Nebbiolo, as are morels.
- Stews and slow braises. Nebbiolo's tannins and richness are the perfect foil for these rich meat dishes, from the classic *osso buco alla milanese* to a rich preparation of lamb shanks cooked slowly in a rich stock.
- Simple preparations of quality meat. Young Nebbiolo is a great partner for a roast leg of lamb, a perfectly cooked hanger steak, or grilled lamb chops.
- Veal. This is a bit of a surprise match given the subtle flavor of veal, but an easy-drinking Nebbiolo—say a Ghemme, Gattinara, or one of the many Valtellina appellations—is a nice match with tasty milk fed veal.
- Rich pasta, risotto, and polenta. These dishes are perfect with most Nebbiolo-based wines. Make certain there's some protein to latch onto those tannins (braised meat *sugo*, pancetta or sausage, or perhaps melted cheese or cream); and of course a little bit of truffle or porcini won't hurt!

Nebbiolo isn't good with:

- Cheese. Though many cheeses can pair brilliantly with Nebbiolo wines, especially as they get older, a big, brawny Barolo doesn't pair well with most cheeses, especially the strong varieties. The classic *fonduta,* however, a Fontina cheese fondue usually studded with truffles in the Piedmontese tradition, can be sublime with a Barbaresco or a rich Ghemme, Spanna, or Valtellina.
- Fish. The bigger wines—no way. The lighter wines are a stretch. And shellfish—don't even think about it.
- Spicy food. The combination of the wine's mouth-ripping tannin and bold flavor with the capsaicins in hot peppers is a disaster drama waiting to happen. A couple of red pepper flakes can be an effective accent, but if the food is spicy enough to make you grab for the bread or the water jug, avoid these ample red wines.

- Lighter recipes. Nebbiolo demands some backbone in the dishes it accompanies. Duck, yes; chicken and quail, no. Beef and lamb, yes; lighter preparations of pork, no. Eggplant, yes; sweet spring peas, no.
- Lots of salt. Because Nebbiolo emphasizes oak and tannin, very salty dishes can be troublesome. Country ham, salt-and-pepper prawns, strong feta cheese, and the like are all tough on these wines.

THE CHEESE PLATE

SEMI-HARD	Comté (France), Fontina (Italy)
HARD	Cantal (France), aged pecorino toscano (Italy)
WASHED-RIND	Durrus (Ireland), Taleggio (Italy)

nebbiolo | BRAISED DUCK LEG IN RAGÙ
WITH CHESTNUT POLENTA AND GREEN OLIVES

NATE APPLEMAN   Pulino's Bar and Pizzeria, New York City, New York

Makes 6 main-course servings

6 whole duck legs
Salt
2 tablespoons extra virgin olive oil

¼ pound pancetta, in a single piece
1 red onion, chopped
1½ cups Nebbiolo or other dry red wine
1 (28-ounce) can San Marzano tomatoes with juice
1 cup green olives, preferably Castelvetrano

POLENTA
1 cup polenta, preferably Anson Mills brand
6 cups water
Salt
1 cup chestnut flour

Extra virgin olive oil for serving

To prepare the duck legs, season them well with salt, cover, and refrigerate for 24 hours.

The next day, preheat the oven to 275°F. In a Dutch oven, heat the olive oil over medium heat. In batches if necessary to avoid crowding, add the duck legs, skin side down, and cook until the skin is well browned and some of the fat has rendered, about 5 minutes. Do not let the fat turn black. Turn the legs over and sear on the second side for a minute or two. Remove the pan from the heat. Transfer the duck legs to a plate.

Cut the pancetta into slices ¼ inch thick. Neatly stack the slices. Cut the stack crosswise into lardoons ¼ inch wide. (The rectangular strips should be a uniform ¼ inch on each side.) Pour out half of the fat from the Dutch oven and place the pan over medium heat. Add the onion and pancetta and cook, stirring, until the onion is soft, about 5 minutes. Do not allow the pancetta to become crispy. Add the wine, raise the heat to high, and cook until reduced by half, about 5 minutes. Crush the tomatoes with your hands and add to the pan along with their juice. Return the duck legs to the pan and add the olives.

Cover the pan, transfer to the oven, and braise the duck legs until they are tender but the meat is not falling away from the bone, about 1½ hours.

Once the duck legs are in the oven, begin making the polenta. In a heavy 2½-quart saucepan, combine the polenta and water and stir to combine. Season with salt, place over medium-high heat, and bring to a simmer. Cook, stirring constantly with a wooden spoon, until the first starch takes hold, 5 to 8 minutes. Reduce the heat to low and continue cooking, stirring frequently, until the grains are soft and hold their shape on a spoon, about 1 hour. Add the chestnut flour and continue to cook, stirring frequently, until the flour has lost its raw taste, about 10 minutes. Taste and adjust the seasoning with salt. Remove from the heat, cover, and keep warm until the duck legs are ready.

Just before serving, check the polenta and add a little hot water if it has become too stiff. Then divide the polenta among warmed soup plates. Top each polenta serving with a duck leg and some sauce, including some olives. Finish with a generous drizzle of olive oil and serve at once.

NOTE Look for chestnut flour imported from Italy in Italian delicatessens and specialty-food stores. If you cannot find the flour, cook plain polenta, using a total of 1½ cups.

NATE: *Slow braising is my favorite way of preparing duck: it produces an almost velvety texture. Italian chestnuts have a smoky quality that comes from the practice of burning fallen leaves to keep bugs out of the trees. That smokiness, combined with the duck, tomato (for acidity), and olives, brings out the berry fruit and cedar smoke that are often associated with Nebbiolo.*

EVAN: *Nate's understanding of* la cocina italiana *comes from deep within his soul. He becomes passionate in discussions about real* porchetta *or the nuances of chestnut flour. I had expected him to take a southerly approach to this pairing, given his prior tenure at San Francisco's A16 and SPQR, but this dish has a northern Italian ethos.*

Nebbiolo requires rich, tannin-canceling food. Duck fits the bill. Slow braises are a good match with these wines, and the chestnuts add richness, with their natural sweetness amplifying the wine's fruit. The olives create a perfect bridge to the wine. The dish can accompany a full range of Nebbiolo-based wines, though it is most successful with younger bottlings. Bravissimo!

RECOMMENDED PRODUCERS

PREMIUM	SPLURGE
Caven Valtellina, Italy	Aldo Conterno Piedmont, Italy
Giovanni Almondo Piedmont, Italy	Angelo Gaja Piedmont, Italy
Luciano Sandrone Piedmont, Italy	Bruno Giacosa Piedmont, Italy
L'Uvaggio di Giacomo Southern Central Coast, California	Marchesi di Barolo Piedmont, Italy
Martin & Weyrich Southern Central Coast, California	Prunotto Piedmont, Italy
Renato Corino Piedmont, Italy	Roberto Voerzio Piedmont, Italy

petite sirah

peh-*teet* sih-*rah*

I field three questions about grape varieties more often than any others. The first is the difference between Sauvignon Blanc and Fumé Blanc (none; it's the same grape). The second is the difference between Syrah and Shiraz (none; it's same grape). The third is the difference between Syrah and Petite Sirah. Okay, pull up a chair. Often confused with "real" Syrah, "real" Petite Sirah is actually a grape called Durif—named for the Dr. Durif who, in the 1800s, discovered this cross of the prized Syrah with the less-prized Peloursin—which originated in France's Rhône Valley. Ironically, there's almost no Durif and little Peloursin left in France. And what we think is Petite Sirah is often something else again. But regardless of its pedigree or the way it's blended, Petite Sirah in California and Australia has turned out some very good bottles over the years.

Petite Sirah has a devoted niche following. Some people love it for its sheer volume, the way it coats your entire mouth (and leaves your teeth stained a deep purple). Others embrace its rustic edge, which calls out for red meat and rib-sticking fare. Others just like to cheer for the underdog. Check out the website "PS (Petite Sirah), I love you" (www.psiloveyou.org).

Alternative Names Durif (France, Australia, Argentina)

Styles Medium-full- to full-bodied dry red

Sometimes Blended With Barbera, Grenache, Syrah, Zinfandel (U.S.A.); Shiraz, other red grapes (Australia)

Flavor Lexicon *Fruit/vegetable:* Beetroot, blackberry, black currant, black raspberry ▪ *Wood:* Chocolate, clove, mocha, toffee, vanilla ▪ *Other:* Black licorice, black pepper

Similar Sips Intense Zinfandel or powerful and spicy Rhône Syrah-based blends

Where It's Grown Argentina, Australia (Queensland: Granite Belt; Victoria: Rutherglen), Brazil, Israel, Mexico (Baja California), U.S.A. (California: Amador County, Central Valley [Lodi], Mendocino County, Napa County, Northern Central Coast [Livermore Valley], Sonoma County [Dry Creek Valley, Russian River Valley], Southern Central Coast [Paso Robles])

Petite Sirah is most closely associated with the United States, especially California. It's amazing that this French grape is now so rare in its native country, where it was once prevalent in the Isère and Ardèche regions of the Rhône Valley and in Palette, a tiny appellation in Provence. Just as Zinfandel left Croatia and took off in California, Petite Sirah has also spread its wings abroad. To complicate matters, it's been revealed that although a majority of the Petite Sirah plantings in California are Durif, a few are actually Peloursin. Because Petite Sirah was mentioned as early as the 1880s in California, when Durif was only beginning to be expanded as a variety in France, some suspected that what we call Petite Sirah in the United States may never have been exclusively Durif. Over the years, research has demonstrated that vines thought to be Petite Sirah have turned out to be several different grapes, including true Syrah, Alicante Bouschet, and Carignan. These findings are validated by most growers, who refer to Petite Sirah as a field blend (four to six grapes grown, harvested, and vinified together) that includes Durif. It's safe to say that almost all the wine labeled Petite Sirah in California is of mongrel ancestry. What is consistent is the wine's ability to deliver intense pigment, full body, ample peppery black and purple fruit, and plenty of tannin. Pockets of great old-vine Petite Sirah vineyards fleck the state, but they are concentrated in Sonoma's Dry Creek and Russian River valleys, Mendocino, Napa, Lodi, Livermore, Amador, and the Central Coast, from Paso Robles south. The appellations worth singling out are Dry Creek Valley, Mendocino, Lodi, and Paso Robles.

Australia is the only other country that has truly welcomed Petite Sirah. Starting in Victoria's Rutherglen, more and more producers have embraced the grape, which in Australia has been conclusively identified as Durif and not Peloursin or something else, and it's being planted around the country, from the high-volume growing tracts of the Riverina area to the smaller, quality-focused areas of the Granite Belt in Queensland and the Hunter Valley of New South Wales. It can be found as a varietal wine but is more often blended with Shiraz. Petite Sirah is planted in pockets of Mexico's Baja California peninsula, in Argentina and Brazil, and in Israel, where it's usually blended with Syrah and Cabernet Sauvignon.

Vintner's Choices Single variety vs. blend, traditional vs. modern approach, young vs. old vines

Petite Sirah's strength is also its weakness. Its intensity and pigment seem to be expressed well even when it's overcropped and in young, less-established vineyards. As a result, producers in both California and Australia have tended to emphasize volume and overextend the vines, creating a lot of mediocre but not truly terrible wine that shortchanges the grape's finer qualities. However, the older the vines, the more interesting the fruit. Old vines and restricted yields make for intense, powerful, and deeply pigmented wines. The tannins also appear to soften as the vines get older. This discovery has led to myriad uses of the grape, both on its own as a varietal wine (often unblended), and as a blending grape in wines ranging from Rhône-style blends to Zinfandels, where a few percentage points of Petite Sirah add peppery complexity and a tannic backbone. It's a discreet way to prop up more-classic varietal wines that may be a bit lacking. Petite Sirah is at its most exciting as a spice in a Zinfandel or a synergistic addition to a Syrah, Carignan, or Grenache blend.

Varietally labeled Petite Sirah is no new phenomenon. Since I began enjoying wine in the late 1970s, I've seen these wines on shelves and in restaurants. Bottlings from Freemark Abbey, Concannon, Souverain, and Stags' Leap Winery have been of great importance in California's wine evolution. These early wines shared an old-school interpretation: they were colossal wines with massively coarse and astringent tannins that would dry up your mouth, take the skin off your gums, and stain your teeth a dark purple color that would alarm your dentist. Today's wines are far tamer, and many producers have adapted techniques to calm the wild tannic beast, bring out the ripe, peppery fruit, and balance the wine's rustic charm with the modern preference for rich, round, supple, less chewy wines. You can still find examples made in the old-school style, along with 'tweeners and modern-style wines, which have ripe, smooth tannins and the obligatory dollops of new oak. As a variety, Petite Sirah, often called "Pets" by its many devotees, can handle the intensity of new oak better than most other red varieties and without losing its varietal character.

PAIRING WITH FOOD

Petite Sirah's bold personality makes it relatively straightforward to pair with food. The grape craves big red-wine fare: meat, meat, and more meat. From slow-cooked brisket to smoked sausages, rich braises and stews, and charcoal-grilled steaks, dishes for carnivores will nearly always please the Petite Sirah drinker. Boldly flavored meats are especially good, from Mongolian barbecue to tandoori lamb kebabs, as are dishes that can pick up on the grape's peppery character and ripe fruit. A coconut curry that's not too sweet or hot and slow-smoked southern pork shoulder that's peppery but not flamethrower hot are both superb with Petite Sirah. Burgers, pot roast, and even meat loaf can find a happy dining partner among the modern interpretations of the grape.

Game and strong-flavored meat dishes pair especially well with this variety, as do many strongly flavored Asian grilled dishes, Mexican and Latin American moles and *asados,* and North African couscous and grilled lamb *mechoui.* Petite Sirah with a ripe-fruit profile can also pair well with a surprisingly wide range of cheeses, including mild blue-veined offerings. Some of the wines actually come off as sweet, so they can work with cheeses when drier versions do not. Finally, the modern, round styles can pair up with some bitter-chocolate preparations: not only Mexican mole but also dark-chocolate desserts that are not overly sweet.

PAIRING POINTERS

Petite Sirah goes well with:

- Meat. From burgers to steaks, shish kebab to short ribs, Petite Sirah handles most red meats well. Treatments with a sweet edge, like American barbecue or teriyaki, are especially good with ripe and round styles of the wine. The more austere, old-school styles work better with classic grilled and roasted fare.
- Thick stews, braises, and hearty meals in a bowl. If you want a wine to pair with a rich dish— French cassoulet, American bean and beef chili, Mexican chili verde, or Brazilian *feijoada*— this is it. Gauge the body of the wine and match the weight of the dish to that. Since most Pets range between medium-full- and full-bodied, the dishes served should also be on the full side.
- Barbecue. Yum. Petite Sirah works with all styles, especially mustard based (from Georgia and the Carolinas) and molasses based (from Kansas City and Oklahoma). When the barbecue style leans toward the sweet (as in Texas), a modern, ripe version of the wine is better than the big, tannic wines.
- Slightly spicy foods. These work specifically with the modern interpretations of the wine: juicy, with vivid fruit and minimal tannins. Many southwestern dishes and mildly hot Asian preparations are lovely with a lightly chilled Petite Sirah, as are sandwiches, hot dogs, burgers, and most other picnic fare.
- Many cheeses. This is a bit of a surprise given the larger-than-life personality of Petite Sirah, but its ripe fruit and sweetish tones give it the flexibility to pair with anything from mild blues to semi-hard cheeses. The portlike, sweeter versions with moderate tannin can even hold their own with some boldly flavored runny cheeses.

Petite Sirah isn't good:

- By itself. As with many powerhouse reds, there's no pleasure in drinking Petite Sirah without something to munch on.
- With fiery-hot food. This combination can actually be painful in the mouth, given the tannin and alcohol content of most Petite Sirahs.
- With delicate food. It's simply not fair to the food to be overshadowed by such a bold personality.

- With most fish. It's too tannic, too powerful, too much. And the fuller-bodied the wine, the more difficult the match.
- When it's too old. This is a matter of opinion, but most people consider Petite Sirah at its best when it's flavor packed, young, and explosive. An aged Petite Sirah will react very differently with food, more like an aged Zinfandel or Syrah.

THE CHEESE PLATE

SOFT-RIPENED	Camembert (U.S.A., France), robiola (Italy)
SEMI-HARD	Emmentaler (Switzerland, U.S.A.), São Jorge (Portugal)
HARD	Aged Cheddar (U.K., U.S.A.), aged Jack (U.S.A.)
BLUE	Cambozola (Germany), Point Reyes Blue (U.S.A.)
WASHED-RIND	Chaumes, Morbier (France)

petite sirah | MIXED GRILL

CHRISTOPHER GROSS   Christopher's and Crush Lounge, Phoenix, Arizona

Makes 4 main-course servings

VINAIGRETTE

¼ cup minced oil-packed sun-dried tomatoes
2 cloves garlic, minced
3 tablespoons balsamic vinegar
¾ cup extra virgin olive oil
1½ teaspoons coarsely ground mixed black and white peppercorns
Salt

SALAD

½ head Savoy cabbage
2 cups mixed salad greens
1 tomato, peeled and quartered

4 lamb chops
4 skinless, boneless chicken breast halves
½ pound beef tenderloin or flank steak, in a single piece
Olive oil for brushing
Salt and freshly ground black pepper
4 *merguez* or other sausages of choice
1 large russet potato, about 4 inches long
Canola oil for deep-frying

To make the vinaigrette, in a small bowl, whisk together the sun-dried tomatoes, garlic, and vinegar. Slowly whisk in the olive oil until emulsified. Season with the pepper and with salt to taste and set aside.

To make the salad, bring a saucepan filled with salted water to a boil. Add the cabbage and blanch until tender-crisp, about 3 minutes. Drain well, immerse in cold water to halt the cooking, and drain again. Cut the cabbage half into 4 equal wedges, pat the wedges dry, and set aside with the salad greens and tomato quarters.

Prepare a charcoal or gas grill for direct grilling over a medium fire. Lightly brush the lamb chops, chicken breasts, and beef tenderloin on both sides with olive oil. Season with salt and pepper. Set aside with the sausages.

Peel the potato and cut lengthwise into slices $\frac{1}{4}$ inch thick. Cut each slice lengthwise into strips $\frac{1}{4}$ inch wide. Place in a bowl, add water to cover, and let stand for about 5 minutes to remove excess starch, then drain and pat dry.

To fry the potato strips, pour canola oil to a depth of about 2 inches into a deep, heavy saucepan and heat to 375°F on a deep-frying thermometer. Add the strips to the hot oil and fry, stirring occasionally to prevent them from sticking together, until golden brown, about 8 minutes. Using a wire skimmer, transfer to paper towels to drain. Keep warm.

Arrange the meats, chicken, and sausages on the grill rack. Grill the lamb chops, turning once, for 3 to 5 minutes on each side for medium, depending on their thickness. Grill the chicken breasts, turning once, until opaque throughout when tested with a knife tip, 3 to 5 minutes on each side. Grill the beef tenderloin, turning once, for 2 to 3 minutes on each side for medium-rare. If using flank steak, grill for about 4 minutes on each side. Grill the sausages, turning as needed to cook evenly, until cooked through when tested with a knife tip, about 8 minutes.

To serve, place a cabbage wedge in the center of each dinner plate. Place one-fourth of the salad greens and a tomato quarter atop each wedge. Cut the beef tenderloin into 4 equal pieces. Or, if using flank steak, slice the steak across the grain. Divide all of the grilled meats evenly among the plates, laying them atop the salad. Garnish with the fried potatoes and serve immediately. Pass the vinaigrette at the table.

NOTE Blanching the cabbage is important because it softens it slightly so it will absorb the vinaigrette better, but it is still crisp enough to provide a contrast to the salad greens. Or, you can skip the salad completely and fry a big batch of potatoes. If you want to serve this dish for a dinner party without a lot of last-minute cooking, grill the meats an hour or so before serving, then arrange them on a baking sheet and reheat them in a preheated 350°F oven for about 5 minutes just before serving.

CHRISTOPHER: *When I worked in London, this was a popular item and one I enjoyed eating, too. It's a very versatile dish that you can adapt depending on the ingredients you have on hand. It can work well as a main course for lunch or dinner. With a small salad, it can be used as a lighter summer lunch that is easy to prepare; it could even be served cold. It goes very well with many styles of Petite Sirah, ranging from the light to the more robust. Keep your seasonings for this dish simple: use a salad dressing that's milder than the wine so as not to overpower it. Add a strong French mustard to serve on the side.*

EVAN: *Christopher has been a pioneer and a beacon in the Southwest since I met him, more than a dozen years ago. Bringing a little unexpected southwestern flair to French traditions has always been a hallmark of his, and perhaps it's the meeting between France (Durif) and the U.S.A. (Petite Sirah) that inspired this recipe!*

This match is simple and just right for the wine. I love meat with dressed salad, and the juices from the meat and chicken cut the vinegar and neutralize any perceptible sharpness. The varied proteins stand up to the wine's tannins. Adjusting the seasoning as Christopher recommends is an effective strategy that adds range and depth to this marriage.

RECOMMENDED PRODUCERS

EVERYDAY	PREMIUM	PREMIUM
Big House Southern Central Coast, California	EOS Southern Central Coast, California	Foppiano Sonoma County, California
Bogle Multiple appellations, California	Girard Napa Valley, California	Norman Vineyards Southern Central Coast, California
De Bortoli Southeastern Australia	Nugan Estate Southeast Australia	Parducci Mendocino, California
Vinum Cellars Lodi, California	Peltier Station Lodi, California	Rosenblum Multiple appellations, California

pinotage

pee-noh-*tahj*

The variety that seems to take the most bashing from my wine-geek friends is Pinotage. Sadly, it's the wine they love to hate. South Africa's pioneering cloning of Pinot Noir and Cinsaut has yielded a widely misunderstood wine. If the Pinotage of today resembled the wines of even just a decade ago, the drubbing would be justified. In the days of apartheid, South Africa's somewhat isolated wine market led consumers and producers to start taking pleasure in the quirky flavors and faults of the only wines that they could get or make—a phenomenon known as "cellar palate." (Yes, flavors like rubber tire and roadkill are considered faults.) But modern Pinotage has come a long way.

Pinotage, distinguished by dark, rich fruit, tastes nothing like Pinot Noir, nor is it exactly like Cinsaut. As there are no Old World benchmarks for its winemakers, opening a Pinotage is always an adventure. Many winemakers have labeled Pinotage the Zinfandel of South Africa, but Pinotage is more than that. It is successfully grown in New Zealand and a few other parts of the world, and it has a devoted international following. Indeed, there's a Pinotage Producers Association, funded research on the grape, an annual Pinotage Top 10 competition, and a good website devoted to the cause: www.pinotage.co.za.

Alternative Names None

Styles Medium- to medium-full-bodied dry red wine, medium-bodied dry rosé wine, fortified red dessert wine (not widely available), and one token sparkling wine

Sometimes Blended With Cinsaut, Merlot, Syrah (South Africa); Cabernet Sauvignon, Merlot (New Zealand)

Flavor Lexicon *Fruit:* Banana, blackberry, plantain, plum ▪ *Floral:* Anise ▪ *Earth:* Farmyard, parched earth ▪ *Other:* Acetone (nail polish), black pepper, burnt rubber, game/animal

Similar Sips Rustic Zinfandel, earthy Mourvèdre, Cinsaut

Where It's Grown New Zealand (Auckland: Kumeu, Gisborne, Hawke's Bay), South Africa (Breede River Valley: Robertson; Coastal Region: Paarl, Stellenbosch), U.S.A. (California: multiple appellations), Zimbabwe

Pinotage was created in South Africa in 1925 by Abraham Izak Perold, the first professor of viticulture at Stellenbosch University. He was attempting to combine the best qualities of Cinsaut, a vigorous grape with a reliable history, with Pinot Noir, which had been problematic despite its great potential. Since Cinsaut is known as Hermitage in South Africa, he gave it the hybrid name of Pinotage.

Initial winemaking efforts with the grape were hit-and-miss, and the inconsistency and the flaws were exacerbated by South Africa's isolation. When Pinotage entered onto the international stage with the end of apartheid, it met with a harsh reception: the wines were ridiculed for odd flavors and other deficiencies. Time and tough love are great teachers, however, and the advocates and producers of this variety have learned their lessons. If you haven't sampled Pinotage before or haven't done so in a long time, it's worth a try now. The best examples have always come primarily from the large Cape Region, especially the renowned district of Stellenbosch. Other noteworthy efforts emanate from Paarl and on occasion from outside the Cape Region, in locations like Robertson in the Breede River district. The unique dark fruit and earthy, gamy signature, combined with improved use of oak and reduced yields from established older vineyards, are resulting in distinctive and delicious wines.

Pinotage has, alas, not gained much traction outside South Africa, though it is planted successfully in small quantities in Zimbabwe and has crossed the ocean to New Zealand, where it has also taken root successfully in wine-producing areas like Auckland (Kumeu), Gisborne, and Hawke's Bay. Some of the best Pinotage-based wines I have tasted are Kiwi in origin. New Zealand is said to be the second largest producer of Pinotage and has more than four decades of experience in making it. California is the lone home of Pinotage in the United States, with a few efforts by wineries in the North Coast region, though there are also said to be some experimental efforts in New York and Virginia.

Vintner's Choices Dry vs. sweet, old oak vs. new oak, red vs. rosé, single variety vs. blend, younger vineyards vs. older vineyards

Like many other grapes, Pinotage is made in a range of styles. It can be quaffable, light, and fruity, like Gamay; deep and rich, like a Grenache-based Rhône blend or a Zinfandel; or elegant, age-worthy, and restrained, like Bordeaux. There are also rosé wines and fortified wines (like port). Successful wines require a winemaker who knows the idiosyncrasies of the grape.

Pinotage is very susceptible to a spoilage yeast called *Brettanomyces*, which is found in a majority of South African vineyards and wineries. Brett, as it's called colloquially, also occurs in many other parts of the winemaking world, but much as some strains of influenza are more virulent than others, South African brett is very pungent and has to be kept in check.

Lab analysis of old-school Pinotage wines that earned the unfortunate descriptors of rubber tires, roadkill, and horse sweat has shown them to be full of brett. Today, brett is being much better managed. Experimentation and research have shown that fermentation at temperatures that were too low was the cause of the additional nail-varnish or paint-thinner flavor that plagued earlier bottlings.

One key to Pinotage's success seems to be using grapes from established vineyards. Old-vine Pinotage is among the most expensive of grapes in the South African harvest, fetching a significant premium over other Pinotage. Along with more modern approaches toward the grape has come a better understanding of oak, and the use of new oak with old-vine grapes is producing wines that delight Pinotage lovers. Fortunately, these wines haven't suffered from the overoaking that has plagued so many other wines.

An increasingly common sight on labels in South Africa and the U.K. is the term "Cape blend." This generally refers to a red blend of Cabernet, Shiraz, Merlot, and Pinotage, which makes up 25 to 50 percent of the wine.

PAIRING WITH FOOD

Despite its occasionally odd flavor profile, Pinotage is a very good food wine, to the surprise of many of my friends, validating my theory that wines that are the best with food are not necessarily enjoyable on their own. This grape's structure is firm but round, a testament to what happens when the tannins of Cinsaut and Pinot Noir combine.

Ask South African locals what to pair with Pinotage, and you'll get a list of dishes and ingredients that will make you scratch your head. One is *snoek* (pronounced "snook"), a firm-fleshed fish with a texture similar to pike but a stronger flavor, more like mackerel. It's said to be great with Pinotage. The other de rigueur regional match is biltong—dried, salted meat from antelope, boar, or ostrich that is the nation's favorite snack. I couldn't get biltong, but pairing Pinotage and beef jerky was very good. These pairings tell us two interesting things. One is that Pinotage can go with fish. Softer in tannin, and a bit gamy, it can match well with strong-flavored fish, from herring to sturgeon and from sardines to *snoek*. And Pinotage, and many Pinotage-heavy Cape blends, is wonderful with strongly flavored game and meat like lamb, venison, dry-aged beef, squab, pheasant, and liver.

Styles do vary, and you should adjust accordingly. A Pinotage that's easy-drinking and more like Beaujolais can be treated the same way you would pair with a Gamay. A version that's more rustic, like a Rhône wine, may find happiness with the same kinds of partners as Mourvèdre or Grenache, while the more Cabernet-like wines can follow classic Bordeaux pairings. The Pinotage Association website lists arrays of desserts that pair well with Pinotage, from chocolate pancakes (crepes?) to chocolate truffle cake. Ouch. Maybe one of the dessert-style interpretations of Pinotage could work, but those are hard to find outside South Africa. I'd stick with savory dishes and meaty or strong flavored recipes.

PAIRING POINTERS

Pinotage goes well with:

- Grilled foods, especially meat. South Africa's version of the Argentinean *asado* or American barbecue is the *braai,* a large open-air grill. It's a perfect excuse for fun with Pinotage. Try grilled beef, lamb, venison, sausages, and stronger-flavored fowl like squab and duck (watch out for the dripping fat). Classic American barbecue sauce is good, but anything simply grilled over mesquite or other charcoal would still be more interesting than meat cooked over a gas grill, as the wood adds a smokiness that works well with the wine.
- Indian food. Here the styles come into play. The lighter versions, served slightly chilled, are great with vindaloo and other powerful dishes, while the richer Rhône or Zinfandel-like styles are super with milder curries, butter chicken, and chicken *tikka masala.* Both the red and rosé styles will go nicely with filled breads like *pakoras* and samosas and rice dishes like *biryani.*
- Rich stews and braises. Pinotage pairs well with many interpretations of a basic full-flavored stew, with or without meat, whether Indian curries or classic European recipes. Pinotage can handle combinations of meat, vegetables (textured items like potatoes, parsnips, turnips and fennel are really nice in the mix), and greens. It works especially well with kale, chard, and dandelion greens added to stews for color and punch.
- Flavorful fish. It's not often that you find a red wine that can pair with a strong fish without tasting metallic or off. The best Pinotage and fish matches are with the more traditional styles of wine (made with less oak, balanced alcohol, and fruit that is not overripe), and the more pungent Pinotage wines are happy with more fishy fish.
- Strongly flavored foods. Along the same lines, the more rustic versions of Pinotage seem to work in pairings where other wines can fail. Pinotage works with pungent Asian food and quickly sautéed calves' liver, and it is one of the few wines I've found that goes with that classic Taiwanese dish of "stinky tofu" and anything including Vegemite—really.

Pinotage isn't good with:

- Sushi. I bring this up because some people seem to love this combination. It might work with barbecued eel (*unagi*) or some of the mushroom plates, but it's not the wine to pair with *toro, uni,* or *amaebi!* If you want to try *snoek* sashimi, of course, be my guest.
- Rich cream sauces. Pinotage's softer tannins and distinctive flavor profile don't pair well with the classic European dishes typically served with cream-based sauces. Pinotage blends are much better with a simple dish like grilled pork chops with whole-grain mustard.
- Oysters, clams, and mussels. It's interesting that a wine that pairs nicely with many fish doesn't have as good a time at a shellfish party. Cooked shellfish with Pinotage is slightly more successful than enjoying Pinotage at a raw bar, but I'd opt for other wines with my bivalves.

- Less savory dishes. Despite the advice of the Pinotage Association, this wine really doesn't go with chocolate pancakes, nor does it go well with sweet-and-sour pork, apricot-glazed pork loin, stir-fried chicken with candied walnuts, or macadamia-crusted mahimahi served with mango salsa. A light and fruit-forward version might solve this culinary dilemma, but it's a stretch for most classic Pinotage.
- Mild-flavored poultry. Although Pinotage can pair with squab, duck, pheasant, goose, and ostrich, it's a bit too much for milder birds like chicken, Cornish game hen, quail, and poussin.

THE CHEESE PLATE

SEMI-SOFT	Havarti (Denmark), Port Salut (France)—red, rosé
SOFT-RIPENED	Brebiou (France), Camembert (U.S.A., Canada)—red
SEMI-HARD	Cheddar (England, U.S.A., especially Vermont), Comté (France)—red, rosé
HARD	Aged Mahón (Spain), mimolette (France)—red

pinotage | ROASTED PORK SHOULDER WITH PAN-ROASTED CARROTS

MICHAEL LEVITON Lumière, Newton, Massachusetts

Makes 6 main-course servings

1 bottle (750 ml) Pinotage or other dry red wine
Grated zest and juice of ½ orange
5 cloves garlic, crushed
10 fresh thyme sprigs
½ fresh bay leaf or 1 whole dried bay leaf
1 cinnamon stick, about 3 inches long
4 juniper berries, crushed
2 whole cloves
1 (2½- to 3-pound) boneless pork shoulder roast, rolled and tied
Kosher salt and freshly ground black pepper
Olive oil for roasting pan

PAN-ROASTED CARROTS
5 tablespoons unsalted butter
2 pounds carrots (about 10 medium), peeled and cut into ½-inch chunks
Salt and freshly ground black pepper
3 tablespoons nonpareil capers, rinsed and drained
3 tablespoons golden raisins,
    soaked in hot water to cover for 10 minutes and drained
3 tablespoons pine nuts, toasted
2 tablespoons minced fresh chives

2 cups rich chicken stock
Red wine vinegar (optional)
1 tablespoon unsalted butter (optional)

Select a shallow glass dish or other nonreactive vessel large enough to hold the pork roast. Add the wine, orange zest and juice, garlic, thyme, bay leaf, cinnamon stick, juniper berries, and cloves to the dish and mix well. Add the pork roast and turn several times to coat well. Cover and marinate in the refrigerator for 2 days, turning the roast occasionally.

Preheat the oven to 500°F. Remove the roast from the marinade, scraping off any clinging marinade ingredients, and reserve the marinade. Dry the roast well, then season liberally with salt and pepper. Select a roasting pan just large enough to hold the roast, and lightly oil it with olive oil. Place the roast, fat side up, in the pan.

Roast the pork for 30 minutes. Reduce the oven temperature to 300°F and continue to roast until an instant-read thermometer inserted into the thickest part of the roast registers 175°F, $2^1/_2$ to 3 hours.

While the pork is roasting, strain the reserved marinade through a fine-mesh sieve into a small saucepan. Bring to a boil over medium heat, reduce the heat to a steady simmer, and simmer until reduced to $^1/_3$ to $^1/_2$ cup, 30 to 40 minutes. Set aside.

To prepare the carrots, in a sauté pan large enough to hold half of the carrots in a single layer, melt 2 tablespoons of the butter over medium-high heat. When it begins to turn brown, add half of the carrots and cook, stirring frequently, until they are nicely browned around the edges and are tender when pierced with a knife tip, 4 to 5 minutes. If the edges are browned but the carrots are not yet tender, reduce the heat to low and cook for another minute or two, adding a couple tablespoons of water to aid the cooking. Season with salt and pepper, then drain the carrots in a large sieve or colander and set aside. Rinse the pan and repeat with the remaining carrots and 2 tablespoons of the butter. Rinse the pan again and set the carrots and pan aside to finish the dish just before serving.

When the pork roast is ready, remove it from the oven. Transfer the roast to a cutting board, tent loosely with aluminum foil, and let rest for about 15 minutes. Pour the contents of the roasting pan into a 1-quart measuring cup, let stand for a few minutes, and then skim off the fat with a large spoon.

In a small saucepan, combine the reduced marinade, the defatted pan juices, and the chicken stock, place over medium-high heat, bring to a boil, and boil until reduced by half, 10 to 15 minutes. Taste and adjust the seasoning with salt and pepper. If the sauce needs a sharper flavor, add a little vinegar. For a richer sauce, whisk in the butter. Keep warm.

To finish the carrots, heat the sauté pan over medium heat and add the remaining 1 tablespoon butter. Add the carrots, capers, raisins, and pine nuts and cook, stirring occasionally, until hot. Taste and adjust the seasoning with salt and pepper, then stir in the chives. Transfer to a warmed serving dish.

Snip the string on the roast, cut into slices, and arrange the slices on a warmed platter. Pour the sauce into a warmed sauceboat. Serve the pork at once with the sauce and the carrots.

MICHAEL: *The challenge in pairing food with Pinotage can be the harsh tannins, so I've marinated the shoulder in red wine, garlic, thyme, fresh bay, a little orange zest and juice, and some cinnamon, clove, and juniper. This is essentially a traditional game marinade, whose flavors will combine with the richness of the pork shoulder to provide a nice counterpoint to the intensity of the Pinotage.*

EVAN: *Michael and I worked together in the 1980s at Square One, when I was host and sommelier and he was one of the lead cooks on the line. He was passionate about food, and you could tell by that gleam in his eye, contagious smile, and sense of humor that he'd be a star. (If I had laid a bet on that in Vegas, I could have retired by now.) Michael always made an effort to attend my daily talk on the restaurant's wine line-up. I knew from the start that he'd be in the mix of this book, that I could throw him a variety like Pinotage and he wouldn't flinch. And of course he has excelled.*

While this pairing is successful with several styles of Pinotage, I especially enjoyed it with the increasingly popular modern interpretations, with ample, ripe fruit, balanced oak, and spice without too many rustic or gamy notes. The slow cooking of the meat makes a perfect match for the rich but soft tannins of Pinotage, and the spice in the marinade and seasoning picks up on the wine's many brown spices and notes of sweet citrus. If you have a gamier style of wine, make sure you have a pungent accompanying vegetable to help balance the wine's earthy intensity.

RECOMMENDED PRODUCERS

EVERYDAY	PREMIUM
Bellevue Estate Stellenbosch, South Africa	Babich Hawke's Bay, New Zealand
Fairview Coastal Region, South Africa	J Sonoma County, California
Fleur du Cap Coastal Region, South Africa	Kanonkop Stellenbosch, South Africa
Graham Beck Robertson, South Africa [R]	Muddy Water Waipara, New Zealand
Nederburg Western Cape, South Africa	Simonsig Stellenbosch, South Africa
Stormhoek Western Cape, South Africa	Warwick Stellenbosch, South Africa

R = Rosé

tannat

tah-*nat*

The name *Tannat* is derived from the word *tannin*. No wine could be more aptly named and perhaps, in its own way, more onomatopoetic—*Tannat* even sounds harsh as it rolls off the tongue. It's a brute of a grape that, unless carefully managed, can leave your mouth feeling as if it had been rubbed with a sheet of coarse sandpaper. Fortunately, Tannat today is better understood, as contemporary winemakers have worked to soften its rough nature, bringing out its inky-dark fruit while taming its astringency.

The grape that gives substance to the wines of Madiran, the neighbor of Bordeaux and home of Armagnac, Tannat is mouth-drying, thick, and intriguing. It's a favorite variety of "big red" wine lovers and one that demands to be served with food. Sipping a glass of Tannat while watching the clouds float by is not a concept.

Alternative Names Madiran, Mostroun, Moustrou (France), Harriague (Uruguay)

Styles Medium- to full-bodied dry red, medium-full-bodied dry rosé

Sometimes Blended With Cabernet Franc, Cabernet Sauvignon, Courbu Noir, Fer, Manseng Noir (France); Merlot (Uruguay)

Flavor Lexicon *Fruit:* Blackberry, black raspberry, red raspberry ▪ *Floral:* Herbs (parsley, tarragon, thyme), lavender, violet ▪ *Earth:* Charcoal ▪ *Wood:* Baking spice ▪ *Other:* Black licorice, red licorice

Similar Sips Mourvèdre, Nebbiolo, Petite Sirah, Zinfandel

Where It's Grown Argentina (Salta: Cafayate), Australia (New South Wales: Hunter Valley; Queensland: Granite Belt; South Australia: Barossa Valley), France (Southwest: Béarn, Côtes de St.-Mont, Irouléguy, Madiran, Tursan), Uruguay (Canelones: Colorado, Juanicó, Las Violetas; Cerro Chapeu; San José), U.S.A. (California: Central Valley [Lodi], Southern Central Coast [Paso Robles]; Virginia: Monticello)

Tannat is most strongly associated with France and is thought to be Basque in origin; it likely migrated inland to Madiran and Côtes de St.-Mont from the area around Irouléguy. However, it is in Madiran that the grape has achieved its reputation for the best wines. Tannat is known for being big: it has big black-raspberry and blackberry fruit, ample and occasionally overpowering acidity, and, of course, big and often mouth-scorching tannins. It has historically been softened by blending it with other, less powerful grapes and by keeping the wines for more than two years in oak to soften the edges and add texture. The success of these methods is variable, so in 1990 the Madiran winemaker Patrick Ducournau experimented with adding controlled amounts of oxygen to the wine during fermentation, essentially creating the process we now know as micro-oxygenation. It has worked wonders for Madiran and is helping reshape the local industry in a world where wine drinkers want rounder and more approachable wines. Because of this success, micro-ox has now been adopted by winemakers for different grapes all over the world. The intense reds of Irouléguy and Côtes de St.-Mont can be equally powerful, though without the sheer raw power of Madiran.

Imported to Uruguay with Basque settlers in the 1800s, Tannat has become the most important red-grape variety in the country, frequently going by the name Harriague (after Don Pascual Harriague, one of the fathers of modern winemaking in that country). Representing more than one-quarter of all plantings in Uruguay's eighteen official winegrowing regions, Uruguayan Tannats are not as massive as those of France and don't show as much austerity and dryness. They are rustic (Uruguay is still learning what the global palate prefers) and not squeaky clean. My tastings turned up wines that varied widely in style and flavor, but all showed a clear match of region with variety and had amazing potential. Like Malbec in Argentina, Tannat does well in different parts of Uruguay and helps the country's wines stand out in a Chardonnay- and Cabernet-dominated world. The largest wine region, Canelones, is the home of Las Violetas, Colorado, and Juanicó, an important subregion that gives its name to Bodega Juanicó, one of the country's biggest and most successful wineries. Cerro Chapeu, near Brazil's southern border, is known for its warmer climate and "bigger" wines. Some Tannat is also found in Argentina, especially in Cafayate, a valley that spans three different provinces (Salta, Tucuman, and Catamarca). Here the wines coming from older, developed vineyards are very exciting, albeit hard to find outside Argentina.

Approximately two dozen producers in Australia are working with Tannat, which seems to do quite well in warmer climates. It has been made in Queensland's Granite Belt, New South Wales's Hunter Valley, and South Australia's Barossa Valley to increasing critical acclaim. Although most Tannat is employed in blends, a few estates are making varietal wines, which are becoming increasingly popular. Full-bodied and extracted, this Tannat is tannic but does not have the astringency and austerity of the European wines, and it is often accompanied by the crowd-pleasing pop of New World oak. In California, Tannat is still relatively new and scarce, but be on the lookout for bottlings from Lodi and Paso Robles that satisfy the American craving for massive red wines. In Virginia, Tannat has been planted in the state's AVA (American viticultural area) of Monticello and in the Shenandoah Valley and the Blue Ridge Highlands.

Vintner's Choices Micro-oxygenation vs. traditional tannin management, old vs. new oak, red vs. rosé, single variety vs. blend, young vs. old vines

Tannat's charm, and curse, is its intensity. Even the most ardent wine lover acknowledges that it can be overbearing on its own. Tannat is almost never found in the Old World as a pure varietal wine. By law in most places it must be blended to soften the wine's raw nature—which also adds complexity. In Madiran and the Côtes de St.-Mont, wines are typically blended out at 40–60 percent Tannat, some Cabernet (Sauvignon or Franc), and a small quantity of a local variety or two. In Irouléguy similar blends are rounded out with the local Fer and Courbu Noir, with the Tannat still prominent. Other ways of making the wines more elegant include picking only the most mature grapes (and often concentrating the fruit by green harvesting), keeping the stalks out of the fruit (indeed, destemming is mandatory in Madiran), handling the fruit gently, and using new oak to add sweetness and roundness to the wines. Taste any wine from Montus Bouscassé in Madiran, produced by the committed and visionary Alain Brumont, to sample Tannat at its very best. Brumont's contributions to the appellation and the grape itself have been stellar. Vine age is important for most grapes, and it certainly seems to be a significant consideration for Tannat. Many of the best Tannat-based wines come from vines more than half a century old.

Finally, don't think that this grape is capable of making only rough and tough reds; there are many rich, spicy rosés made in Irouléguy and some hard-to-find examples from Béarn and Tursan. They are hard and fuller in body than most rosés, and explode with ample, spicy berry fruit.

PAIRING WITH FOOD

Tannat just isn't very flexible with food. It's a massive wine, in spite of micro-oxygenation and other tricks of the trade, that calls for a focused approach to pairing. In its home region of Madiran, in Gascony, this wine is drunk with two classic main dishes: duck confit and cassoulet. Both are very rich, full-flavored, and ample in texture and fat. The sheer magnitude of a Tannat-based wine is the perfect foil to these delicious and filling meals. However, most of us don't live on a diet of duck and cassoulet (at least not for long). For alternatives that don't quack, don't clog your arteries, and don't take days to prepare, look at other rich stews and braises.

Tannat loves lamb, in all shapes and presentations. Although a traditional leg of lamb might show more range with a classic Cabernet Sauvignon or Bordeaux blend, it is certainly enjoyable with Tannat. So is a great steak (T-bones and rib-eye steaks are among my favorites) or venison roast. I encountered the best beef I have ever eaten while in Montevideo, which was total bliss with an ample and tasty Uruguayan Tannat! My own preference with Tannat is for rich braises (oxtails, shanks, and other off-cuts) and slow-cooked stews. Earthy, country-style cooking seems to suit Tannat, which doesn't have the refinement of Cabernet or the Rhône-style reds. It's in a class by itself, somewhere between a brawny Barolo and a full-flavored (but not overly alcoholic) Zinfandel. Root vegetables, sturdy pastas, and hearty soups are also candidates, though with those selections I'd look for an easier-drinking bottling (they do exist).

Tannats from Uruguay are a bit tamer but still somewhat coarse and rustic. Many examples are blended with other grapes, and these can be easier on the mouth and more flexible with food. Most French wines wouldn't pair well with a roast chicken, for example, whereas a Uruguayan example would not be too overwhelming.

The challenge with Tannat is typically that the naturally high acidity is accompanied by profound bitterness or astringency (tannin is also an acid). So pairing the wine with sharp ingredients or sauces is not an option. If you really want to punish dinner guests, serve a green salad vinaigrette and a plate of strong cheese with a Tannat at the end of a meal and watch them pucker up. Tannat's high acid requires food to cut it—rich, thick, fatty preparations. And fish with Tannat—well, you've been warned.

PAIRING POINTERS

Tannat goes well with:

- Traditional southwestern French fare. There's no gainsaying the amazing traditional pairing of Tannat with duck confit or cassoulet. Other rich birds like goose and wild pheasant (as opposed to the mild, domesticated kind) are also very tasty.
- Red meat. Another conventional no-brainer, but it works. A rack of lamb, a grilled flank steak, and braised short ribs are all good alongside a bottle of Tannat. If you can locate some Uruguayan beef, go for it! Accompany the meat with a dish of hearty beans, polenta, or a gratin of potatoes and fennel for a real treat.
- Stews and off-cuts. Tannat is often my wine of choice for traditional stews, lamb shanks, or oxtail because such rich dishes need to be "cut" with tannins and acid.
- Pungent and wild flavors. Venison, wild boar, and other strong-flavored meats are tamed and happy when served with most Tannat-based reds.
- Mild but rich cheeses. Follow your natural inclination to avoid intense, pungent blue cheeses. Rich but mild triple-cream cheeses, young surface-ripened cheeses like Brie and Camembert, and even young, sharp cheeses like a high-acid chèvre pair well with many Tannat-based wines.

Tannat isn't good:

- On its own. This is not a cocktail wine. Unless you are into genuine pain, have something meaty to go with it. If you must sip it while you chat with friends, put out a plate of selected cheeses and meats. Rosés are an exception—they are just fine solo.
- With simple and mild dishes. The wine simply has too much personality: it will overwhelm basic dishes. Avoid white-fleshed birds (chicken, quail, turkey) and most white meat (pork and veal) unless the preparation really calls for a big red wine, or you plan to serve a less intense example (such as a wine from Uruguay).
- With sharp foods. Despite the grape's high acidity, it's not happy with sharp recipes that accentuate its often bitter and astringent tannins. A drizzle of balsamic vinegar on your steak is one thing, but a sharp, citrusy sauce or a pickled vegetable medley would be far less enjoyable.
- With fish. Tannat is the quintessential example of why you don't pair many red wines with fish, as it causes the classic "sucking on a penny" reaction with even slightly oily fish. With milder, meaty fish, it simply bullies and overpowers them.
- With Asian and other international fare. Tannat seems at its best and most versatile with traditional Western food pairings. Most exotic spices, from cardamom to five spice, seem disjointed with Tannat-based wines. Intense combinations of heat, salt, and sugar aren't great for the wines.

THE CHEESE PLATE

FRESH	Chèvre (many countries), feta (Greece, Bulgaria)—red, rosé
SOFT-RIPENED	Brie (France, U.S.A.), Saint-André (France)—red
SEMI-HARD	Gruyère (Switzerland), Idiazábal (Spain)—red, rosé
HARD	Aged Cotija (Mexico), aged Mahón (Spain)—red
WASHED-RIND	Butterkäse (Germany), Chaumes (France)—red

tannat | RUSTIC BEEF STEW WITH PRUNES AND GUAJILLO CHILE SAUCE

ROBERT DEL GRANDE RDG + Bar Annie, Houston, Texas

Makes 4 main-course servings

1 (2½-pound) boneless beef chuck roast
2 quarts water

GUAJILLO CHILE SAUCE
6 guajillo chiles, stemmed and seeded (see note)
¼ cup golden raisins
4 cloves garlic, peeled but left whole
½ small fennel bulb, trimmed and coarsely chopped
3 cups broth from cooking beef
½ cup pine nuts, toasted
⅓ cup smoked almonds
1 tablespoon red wine vinegar or other mild vinegar
1 teaspoon salt
¼ teaspoon freshly ground black pepper

2 tablespoons unsalted butter
12 prunes, pitted

GARNISHES
½ cup pine nuts, toasted
⅓ cup smoked almonds, coarsely chopped
2 tablespoons fresh tarragon leaves, or 4 fresh tarragon sprigs
Coarse sea salt

In a deep, 5-quart Dutch oven, combine the beef roast and water over medium-high heat. Bring just to a boil, skimming any scum that forms on the surface. Cover, reduce the heat to medium-low, and simmer gently until the beef is almost done, about 2 hours. The beef will finish cooking in the sauce.

Remove the beef from the broth and set aside to cool to room temperature. Bring the broth to a gentle boil over medium heat and cook, uncovered, until reduced to 3 cups, about 15 minutes. Remove from the heat, let stand for 5 minutes, and then, using a large spoon, skim off the fat from the surface. Set the broth aside to use for making the chile sauce.

When the beef is cool, trim away any fat and tendons, then cut into 1-inch cubes. Set aside.

To make the chile sauce, preheat the oven to 350°F. Arrange the chiles on a rimmed baking sheet and place in the oven to toast until lightly browned, about 15 minutes. Do not allow them to darken too much.

Transfer the chiles to a bowl, add warm water to cover, and let soak until soft, about 30 minutes. Drain well, chop coarsely, and set aside.

In a saucepan, combine the raisins, garlic, fennel, and the 3 cups broth and bring to a boil over high heat. Reduce the heat to medium, cover, and simmer until the garlic and fennel are soft, 20 to 30 minutes. Remove from the heat and let cool to room temperature.

In a blender, combine the cooled broth mixture, chiles, pine nuts, almonds, vinegar, salt, and pepper and process until smooth. Set the sauce aside.

Return the pot used for cooking the beef to medium-high heat, add the butter, and heat until it foams. Add the beef cubes and prunes and cook, stirring occasionally, until the beef is lightly browned on all sides and the prunes are nicely sautéed, about 5 minutes. Carefully add the chile sauce (it will spatter) and bring to a gentle simmer. Adjust the heat to maintain a very slow simmer and cook, uncovered, until the beef is tender, 30 to 40 minutes. If the sauce becomes too thick, add a little water to adjust the consistency.

To serve, spoon the stew onto warmed plates, dividing the beef, prunes, and sauce evenly. Garnish with the pine nuts, almonds, and tarragon. Finish each plate with a little coarse sea salt and serve at once.

NOTE The guajillo is one of Mexico's most popular dried chiles. If you cannot find guajillo chiles, substitute 6 New Mexico red or 4 ancho chiles.

ROBERT: *I am most at home cooking rustic foods with great earthy flavors, and I enjoy wines that are deep and rustic in style. When pairing wine and food, I first try to understand what flavors and textures will give the wine room to expand and evolve and bring out its hidden qualities. Because Tannat can be very dense, deep, tannic, and rich, I developed this rustic beef stew with a sauce that is not too deep and dense but rather toasty and aromatic, with a soft touch of fruitiness. While the rich, meaty texture of the beef is excellent with the wine alone, the sauce acts like an open canvas for the wine's flavors to spill onto. The toasty nature of the sauce (from the nuts) provides a great space for the aromatics of the wine to develop. The prunes in the sauce absorb the flavors of the beef and take on an almost winelike character that acts as a bridge between the sauce, the beef, and the wine. Here, salt is the key to keeping the tannins in the wine and the fruity flavors of the sauce and garnish in balance. When in doubt, add a little extra salt or garnish each plate with a little coarse sea salt.*

EVAN: *When I was cutting my teeth as a sommelier in the early 1980s, I had the pleasure of meeting Robert (and his wife, Mimi) at several food conferences, and I was impressed by his knowledge of wine and food. Later, when I had the opportunity to dine at Cafe Annie, I realized how lucky Houston is to have such an expert on both. Robert excels at rich, rustic fare, so Tannat seemed a good match for him.*

Robert's introductory comments explain perfectly why this match is successful. The ratio of salt to tannin is something you may want to experiment with, as salt exaggerates both alcohol and hard tannin. The more tannic your wine, the more cautious you'll want to be initially. You can always add more salt at the end, so start low and add more later. The prunes work well with Tannat's black-fruit nature in a very subtle way, and the nuts work wonders with oak, especially if the wine is in the New World sweet style. This is a tasty dish you'll come back to with or without Tannat.

RECOMMENDED PRODUCERS

EVERYDAY	PREMIUM	PREMIUM
Bodega Ariano Hermanos Canelones, Uruguay	Bodegas Carrau Canelones, Uruguay	Montus Bouscassé Southwest France
Bodega Juanicó Canelones, Uruguay [DR, R]	Domaine Arretxea Southwest France	Pisano Canelones, Uruguay
Domaine Monte de Luz San José, Uruguay	Domaine Berthoumieu Southwest France	Tablas Creek Southern Central Coast, California
Michel Torino Salta, Argentina	Domaine Etxegaraya Southwest France	
Quara Salta, Argentina		

DR = Dry red   R = Rosé

tempranillo

tem-prah-*nee*-yoh

When I'm asked which is my favorite wine, I usually reply in one of two ways: it's like your kids—it depends what day; or, as long as it's balanced, varietally correct, and true to its specificity of place, I'm happy. But at the end of the day, I suppose I'm a Pinot Noir guy and—a Tempranillo guy. I love Pinot Noir because of its seductive charm, intoxicating complexity, and amazing peacock's tail of flavor (when it's at its best). But Tempranillo I rate equally high because of its incredible food-friendliness, range of styles, and unique character.

The most important grape of Rioja, Spain, Tempranillo has rich red to black fruit, signature *balsamico* flavors (see below), and an ability to age gracefully. Like Tuscany's Sangiovese, which it resembles in some ways, Tempranillo is wonderful on its own and in blends. It varies from easy-drinking to age-worthy and serious, and is made according to so many classifications (in Spain) that the wine lover has a wide range of age and flavor profiles to choose from.

Alternative Names Cencibel, Tinto Fino, Tinto del Pais, Tinta del Toro, Ull de Llebre (Spain), Aragonez, Arauxa, Tinta Roriz (Portugal)

Styles Light-medium to full-bodied dry red, medium-bodied dry *rosado*

Sometimes Blended With Mazuelo/Carignan, Garnacha/Grenache, Graciano, Viura, Cabernet Sauvignon, Merlot, Monastrell/Mourvèdre (Spain), Touriga Nacional, Touriga Franca, Trincadeira (Portugal), Bonarda, Malbec (Argentina)

Flavor Lexicon *Fruit/vegetable:* Black olive, dried cherry, fennel, fresh cherry, red plum ▪ *Floral:* Herbs (dill, marjoram, mint, oregano, thyme), laurel, patchouli, tobacco ▪ *Earth:* Dust ▪ *Wood:* Cinnamon, cocoa, masala mix, vanilla

Similar Sips Pinot Noir, Sangiovese, lighter-style Syrah

Where It's Grown Argentina (Mendoza), Australia (South Australia: Adelaide Hills, McLaren Vale), Chile, Mexico, Portugal (Alentejo, Dão, Douro), Spain (Castilla–La Mancha: Valdepeñas; Castilla-León: Ribera del Duero, Toro; Catalonia: Penedès; Navarra; Rioja),

Uruguay (Canelones), U.S.A. (California: Central Valley [Lodi], Sierra Foothills, Sonoma County [Green Valley], Southern Central Coast [Paso Robles]; Oregon: Umpqua Valley; New Mexico)

For wine lovers, Tempranillo is Spain, and Spain is Tempranillo. Though the grape is grown in other parts of the world, Spain is its geographic and spiritual home. It's planted all over the country, but it's at its best in the northern and central areas. *Temprano* means "early," and the grape ripens well before most of the varieties that it is usually blended with, in Rioja as well as other regions.

Any conversation about Tempranillo must begin in Rioja, easily Spain's best-known region for table wine. Here Tempranillo shines in blended wines. It plays the role of Cabernet Sauvignon in Bordeaux, an important and complex varietal that nevertheless can appear more interesting and complex in the company of its siblings, Graciano, Mazuelo (Carignan), and Garnacha (Grenache). Rioja blends of Tempranillo are elegant and complex, like a great Burgundian Pinot Noir, rather than powerful. This complexity is expressed in the multiple classifications of Spanish wine, including *joven* (unoaked and easy to drink), *crianza* (with some oak and some bottle aging), *reserva* (with more oak and longer bottle aging), and *gran reserva* (even more oak and aging: these wines can't be sold until the sixth year after harvest). Tempranillo in Rioja has a unique flavor called *balsamico*. It was explained to me as a combination of flavors that include the herbal (marjoram, cilantro, oregano, and rosemary), the exotic (sandalwood, incense, curry, and hyssop), and the especially distinctive (thyme, lemon thyme, peppermint, chocolate mint, and spearmint).

In contrast to the elegant wines from Rioja, those from Ribera del Duero and Toro are all about power and purity. In Ribera del Duero, Tinto del Pais (Tempranillo's local alias) makes wines that are chunky, powerful, and complex—arguably the best big red wines of Spain, where they go by the classification Vino de la Tierra de Castilla y León. (*Vinos de la tierra* are table wines made by producers who want to create wines like these but bypass the strict rules governing them.) Ribera del Duero, the home of Spain's famous and fabulous Vega Sicilia winery, produces wines that show a plummier black fruit, more vanilla-scented oak, and a dusty earthiness, along with faint notes of *balsamico*. Toro's wines can be even bigger. This region makes wines that fit the name (*toro* means "bull") and can be heady. Toro's hot climate produces wines with high levels of alcohol and significant richness and concentration. Made from very old vines with low yields, these wines are ample and brooding. In Spain's other regions, Tempranillo is a staple grape either on its own or blended according to local tradition, still delivering quality, a distinctive signature, and (once you leave Rioja, Toro, and the Ribera del Duero), great value. Indeed, many of the best values in Spain today are Tempranillo-based wines coming from Valdepeñas, Utiel-Requena, Penedès, and especially Rioja's neighbor Navarra, where Tempranillo planted at higher altitudes makes exquisite wines.

As you cross the border from Spain into Portugal, the Duero River changes its name to the Douro River. Here Tempranillo, now known as Tinta Roriz, is an integral part of port wines (to which it adds spice and rusticity) and dry Douro red wines. In the Alentejo, it's blended with Trincadeira for an enjoyable drink, and in the Dão it's again part of a red-wine blend.

It makes sense, given the historical connection, that Tempranillo has made its way to Argentina. Here, especially in Mendoza, it can be a lovely wine and a tasty change of pace from Malbec. Alas, it's often underachieving, blended off into nice but not stellar bottles. The situation in Chile and Uruguay is pretty much the same.

In the United States, California has long grown a grape called Valdepeñas, though no definite connection has been established between it and Tempranillo. Given California's Mediterranean climate, this grape ought to perform well, but it's new on the scene, and a true style has yet to be established. Efforts led by winemakers in the Lodi and Paso Robles regions appear promising, and the best bottles have that hallmark *balsamico* character. Abacela Winery, in Oregon's Umpqua Valley, is leading the way in the Northwest, and there are plantings in other spots, from New Mexico to Mexico proper. Tempranillo is now challenging Sangiovese as the rising star among red varietal wines in Australia. Plantings have exploded of late. Stay tuned.

Vintner's Choices Aged vs. not aged, old oak vs. new oak, red vs. rosé (*rosado*), single variety vs. blended, traditional vs. modern approach

Much as I love Tempranillo, it's not a perfect grape. In spite of ripening early, it has comparatively low acidity. This means it can be vibrant in youth but may not age well on its own. Thus winemakers often blend it with other grapes. Even so, some wines that are pure or almost pure Tempranillo do very well. Toro, arguably the biggest and most age-worthy of all Tempranillo wines, must be at least 75 percent Tempranillo and is often 100 percent. The same is true of some of the better wines from the Ribera del Duero and Castilla-León.

The judicious use of oak, most often American, is important to these wines. The debate over traditional versus modern approaches that swirls around Nebbiolo in Italy is also taking place with Tempranillo in Spain. Some winemakers favor the traditional approach: longer time in oak, more oxidative character, and later release dates on their *reserva* and *gran reserva* wines. In Rioja, they include Faustino, La Rioja Alta, and Marqués de Arienzo. The unabashed modernists include Martínez Bujanda, Cosme Palacio y Hermanos, and Roda. The traditionalists are more likely to use a little older oak for an accent, whereas the modernists use ample new wood. There's more middle ground between these styles in Spain than in Italy. Generally these producers make individual cuvées that lean toward the traditional, such as Marqués de Riscal's Baron de Chivel and Cune's Contino.

The age-based classification system also influences wine styles. Wines labeled *crianza, reserva,* and *gran reserva* must spend different minimum periods in the cask (barrel) and in the bottle before they are released for sale. *Reserva* and *gran reserva* wines are generally made only in exceptional years: the extended aging requirements call for only the best fruit, which can handle aging without drying out. The personality of a *gran reserva* is shaped by its time in oak: it will have more bouquet, more development, and a more fruit-forward character than younger wines that have seen minimal oak (*crianza*) or no oak (*joven*), and it is likely to be more suited to immediate consumption. The strict requirements governing these wines have led many producers, especially in the Ribera del Duero, to opt out of the system: they simply name their wines in a proprietary manner and label them as table wine. Something similar happened earlier in Tuscany with the advent of the Super Tuscan category, proprietary blends of the local Sangiovese and other grapes, mainly Cabernet Sauvignon and Merlot, which produce world-class red wines such as Tignanello, Sammarco, and Sassicaia. The new cuvées from Rioja are also the product of this movement.

In addition to red-wine Tempranillos, wonderful rosés (or *rosados*) produced in many parts of Spain contain Tempranillo. *Rosados* from Rioja are exceptional: they are usually made from Tempranillo in concert with varying amounts of Garnacha and sometimes a little white Viura grape. Refreshing and full of spicy strawberry, tangelo, and watermelon flavors, they are lighter than many of the other blush styles I've discussed.

PAIRING WITH FOOD

Tempranillo's versatility at the table derives from its wide range of styles, from easy-drinking Rioja to bruising Toro; from the age classifications, which result in varying ranges of tannin; from the variety of flavor profiles (over time, its fruit becomes a more secondary than primary flavor); and from the grapes with which it has been blended.

Most Tempranillo-based wines go with red meat, especially the lamb and pork that are so popular in Spain. I joked on a trip to Rioja that it seemed like we were eating lamb for breakfast, lunch, and dinner. Tempranillo-based wines have a magical synergistic relationship with lamb, from a basic roast to a rare cut of leg to a slow-simmered stew. It goes well with an equally broad range of pork dishes, from chorizo and other dried, cured, and uncured sausages to *jamón* (dry ham, like prosciutto) and *cochinillo,* roast suckling pig. Pork pairs well with Rioja, Navarra, and other elegant styles of Tempranillo, and lamb is marvelous with the bigger offerings from Toro and the Ribera del Duero. The baby roast lamb cooked in a wood-burning oven at the Casa Florencio in Aranda de Duero, the capital village of Ribera del Duero, with a good bottle of local wine is a memorable meal. Though beef isn't consumed widely throughout Spain, it goes quite well with Tempranillo-based wines, as any Argentinean pairing demonstrates. Try it with a rib-eye, marinated with fresh herbs and garlic, on your grill at home.

Speaking of herbs, the inherent *balsamico* character of Tempranillo makes a great bridge between the wine and herbal preparations. Using herbal marinades or sauces, tossing a few branches of rosemary onto your coals when grilling, and serving herb-roasted potatoes all make for a pleasurable experience. Mint, fennel, laurel, dill, and lemon verbena will reveal the corresponding notes in the wine. Tempranillo also has an exotic side that the right recipe can bring out. Savory curries, a veal chop served with a fresh tomato and mint salsa, or slow-cooked ribs with a glaze of balsamic vinegar and fennel all play to this side of the grape.

The more elegant versions of Tempranillo are great with fowl, from a simple herb-roasted chicken to chorizo-stuffed quail or Cornish game hens served with a dried-fruit compote. The bigger bruisers can hold their own against rich pastas, venison, duck, and dishes featuring beans and lentils.

Rioja *rosado* (rosé) is one of my house staples. Delightful on its own, it's also enjoyable with tapas, dim sum, fish, lighter meat dishes, and shellfish. Plus it's flexible with cheese, and I always finish with cheese!

PAIRING POINTERS

Tempranillo goes well:

- With lamb. Try an easy-drinking *joven* or *crianza* wine with a lamb burger at lunch, or a basic rack of lamb with a more ample wine for dinner. Accompany the rack with herb-roasted potatoes and peas with onions and mint, and it's a great match. And while Tempranillo works magic for lamb, it goes well with beef, too.
- With herbal treatments and preparations. The *balsamico* character of Tempranillo makes for an easy match with food. Sauces, marinades and dishes incorporating oregano, rosemary, thyme, and cilantro are naturals with this grape, from basil pesto to a classic *salsa verde*.
- Throughout the meal. Start with a refreshing young Tempranillo-based *rosado* before dinner, then move on to a soft, easy wine with your first course, followed by a more ample bottle for your main dish. Not many grapes have this much range. You can weave in different styles and age classifications as you like.
- With vegetarian dishes. This is particularly true of more traditional styles and wines that are light on the new oak. Again, the herbal character lends itself to many dishes incorporating vegetables. I enjoy Tempranillo with ratatouille, grilled vegetable brochettes, a vegetarian lasagna, or risotto with roasted vegetables.
- When you play the "wine age game." My friend Josh Wesson first explained this to me almost twenty years ago, and it hasn't let me down: the rarer the meat, the older the wine you can serve with it. Serve the aged *gran reserva* wines with rarer cuts of meat, simply prepared to allow the wine's nuances to come through while allowing the meat's juices to supplement what time has taken away from the wine. Pair stews and longer-cooked cuts with the succulent young *joven* and *crianza* wines.

Tempranillo isn't good:

- When you pick the wrong one. Although versatile, these wines are not completely interchangeable. Don't choose a big wine from Toro to go with your simply sautéed chicken breast, or opt for an easy-drinking, unoaked style for a roast leg of lamb. If you are unsure, pick a style somewhere in the middle.
- With very bitter foods. Endive, unpeeled eggplant, escarole, chard, and other bitter vegetables bring out a mean streak in most Tempranillo wines and suffocate the fruit. If you must serve these vegetables, temper the bitterness with other ingredients or cooking techniques such as slow-roasting or long braising that mellow the flavors.
- With strongly flavored fish and shellfish. Even the easy-to-drink unoaked styles are hurt by these pairings, and the more ample wines really don't work at all. Opt for a *rosado*, or serve a mild fish with one of the gentle, less tannic bottlings.
- With salads and sharp dishes. Because it's not high in acidity or sharpness, Tempranillo has a hard time pairing with dressed salads. Avoid vinaigrettes altogether, and stay away from pickled items, asparagus, citrus, and sharp dairy dressings (yogurt or sour cream).
- With blue cheeses. I thought for sure when I was going through the range of wines that I'd find some happiness here. But sadly, I didn't find a single blue cheese that didn't hurt the wine. If you really want to have a blue, opt for a mild and less salty cheese, such as a Castello, Montbriac, or Cambozola, and choose a light red or *rosado* wine. Those can be great pairings.

THE CHEESE PLATE

FRESH	Burrata, chèvre (many countries)—rosé
SEMI-SOFT	Saint-Nectaire (France), tetilla (Spain)—red, rosé
SOFT-RIPENED	Pierre Robert (France), robiola (Italy)—red, rosé
SEMI-HARD	Manchego (Spain), São Jorge (Portugal)—red
HARD	Dry or aged Jack (U.S.A.), aged Mahón (Spain)—red
BLUE	Cambozola (Germany), Castello (U.K.), Montbriac (France)—rosé

tempranillo | ROAST RACK OF LAMB WITH CREAMY RICE WITH PARSNIPS

DAN BARBER Blue Hill, New York City, and Blue Hill at Stone Barns, New York

Makes 4 to 6 main-course servings

CREAMY RICE
1 cup basmati rice
2 cups water
1½ teaspoons canola oil
½ pound parsnips (2 small), peeled and cut into ½-inch chunks (about 1 cup)
Salt and freshly ground black pepper
2¾ cups vegetable stock, or as needed
Chopped fresh chives for garnish

LAMB
Canola oil for searing
2 (8-bone) lamb racks
Salt and freshly ground black pepper

Preheat the oven to 425°F for the lamb, then begin cooking the rice. In a saucepan, combine the rice and water and bring to a simmer over medium heat. Reduce the heat to low, cover, and cook until the water has been fully absorbed and the rice is tender, 17 to 20 minutes. Remove from the heat and set aside. You should have about 3 cups cooked rice.

In another saucepan, heat the oil over medium heat. Add the parsnips, season with salt and pepper, and sauté gently until beginning to soften, about 10 minutes. Do not allow the parsnips to color. Add 1½ cups of the stock and bring to a simmer. Cook, uncovered, until the parsnips are tender and the stock has reduced by about half, 5 to 10 minutes.

Transfer the parsnips and their cooking liquid to a blender and process until smooth. If the purée is too thick to flow freely, add a little more stock. You should have about 1 cup purée. Set aside.

Begin roasting the lamb while the rice is cooking. Film the bottom of a large skillet with the canola oil and place over medium-high heat until hot. Season both sides of the lamb racks liberally with salt and pepper. When the oil is hot, place the racks, fat side down, in the pan and sear until golden brown on the first side, 3 to 4 minutes. Turn and sear on the second side until browned, about 4 minutes. Transfer to a rimmed baking sheet, place in the oven, and roast for 20 minutes for medium-rare, or until done to your liking.

Remove the racks from the oven, transfer to a cutting board, tent lightly with aluminum foil, and let rest for 10 to 15 minutes.

To finish the rice, in a saucepan, combine the 3 cups cooked rice and the remaining $1\frac{1}{4}$ cups stock over medium heat and bring to a simmer. Add the 1 cup parsnip puree, stir well, and heat until piping hot. Taste and adjust the seasoning with salt and pepper. Transfer to a warmed serving dish.

Cut the racks into individual chops, divide among warmed plates, and serve at once. Sprinkle the chives over the rice and pass at the table.

DAN: *Just as the Tempranillo grape absorbs the rich fruity notes of its terroir, a grass-fed lamb takes on the flavor and ecology of the pasture. Together, the combination is earthy and fragrant—and perfect with the creaminess of the parsnips.*

EVAN: *Dan is a gifted chef, dedicated to preserving the integrity of the ingredients in his dishes. Anyone who has eaten his food can attest to his keen sense of pairing textures and tastes and generally seducing the palate. He ranks high on my mom's list of amazing chefs, and her opinion carries a lot of weight with me! I specifically requested a lamb recipe to go with Tempranillo, as most of us can't eat at Casa Florencio in Spain very often, and he came up with this delightful recipe.*

I could eat the rice side for breakfast, lunch, and dinner—with Tempranillo, of course. Its sweet richness brings out the fruit in the wine and tames those young versions of Tempranillo with sharper acid. If you like your lamb rare, this is a great dish to show off an aged reserva *or* gran reserva; *if you prefer longer-cooked chops, younger wines that display ripe fruit (*joven, crianza, *or New World examples) may be better partners.*

RECOMMENDED PRODUCERS

EVERYDAY	PREMIUM	SPLURGE
El Coto Rioja, Spain [DR, R]	Alberto Furque Mendoza, Argentina	Carmelo Rodero Ribera del Duero, Spain
Finca Antigua La Mancha, Spain	Alejandro Fernandez Ribera del Duero, Spain	Numanthia-Termes Toro, Spain
Marqués de Caceres Rioja, Spain [DR, R]	Emilio Moro Ribera del Duero, Spain	Quinta do Crasto Douro, Portugal
Viña Izadi Rioja, Spain	La Rioja Alta Rioja, Spain	Roda Rioja, Spain

DR = Dry red   R = Rosé

touriga nacional

too-*ree*-gah nah-syoo-*nahl*

Portugal's wine industry has always found market conditions challenging in the United States. First, the Portuguese language can intimidate consumers, and some of Portugal's native grapes have tongue-twisting names. Second, Portugal lacks most of the household-name grape varieties that many of us latch on to as we are learning about wine. Finally, Portuguese wines have been overshadowed for years by those of neighboring Spain. However, anyone who has been to Portugal knows how wonderful its wines are, and how special the people and cuisine make this country. Bread still tastes like bread, wine still tastes like wine, and Portugal's winegrowing regions have been spared much of the glitz, snobbery, and marketing hype that have marred so many winegrowing areas in other parts of the world.

The brightest star in Portugal's wine-grape galaxy is unquestionably Touriga Nacional. Lovers of sweet wines know it as the most complex red grape of great port, but Touriga Nacional can also make exceptional dry red table wine. Like Cabernet Sauvignon in Bordeaux, Touriga Nacional is capable of yielding high-quality wines, both dry and sweet, on its own, but blending it with other grapes can bring out its regal qualities. New dry red wines incorporating this grape are scoring surprisingly well in the rankings of prominent wine critics.

Alternative Names Touriga (Portugal)

Styles Medium-full- to full-bodied dry red, dry rosé, full-bodied fortified dessert

Sometimes Blended With Alfrocheiro Preto, Aragónez, Castelão, Jaen, Moreto, Tinta Barocca, Tinta Cão, Tinta Roriz, Touriga Franca, Trincadeira (Portugal), Shiraz, Zinfandel (Australia)

Flavor Lexicon

DRY *Fruit:* Blackberry, black cherry, black fig, black plum ▪ *Floral:* Jasmine, lavender, violet ▪ *Earth:* Loam, mineral ▪ *Wood:* Bitter chocolate, carob ▪ *Other:* Black or white pepper, gingerbread

SWEET   *Fruit:* Acorn or butternut squash, black plum, prune ▪ *Wood:* Baking spice, caramel, chocolate, coffee, mocha ▪ *Other:* Black licorice, persimmon pudding

Similar Sips Dry or dessert-style Petite Sirah or Zinfandel

Where It's Grown Australia (South Australia: Barossa Valley), Portugal (Alentejo, Dão, Douro Valley, Estremadura, Tejo), South Africa, U.S.A. (California: Amador, Central Valley [Lodi], Sierra Foothills, Sonoma County, Southern Central Coast [Paso Robles]; Georgia; Texas: Texas Hill Country)

Despite its reputation for its role in port, Touriga Nacional represents a mere 2 percent of Douro vines. In fact, it wasn't until a few decades back that the best vine selections were identified and propagated throughout the Douro's most respected districts, the Cima Corgo and the Douro Superior, by Miguel Corte Real at Cockburns and his colleagues in the Port Wine Commission. These collective efforts to identify the best vine selections (now clones) and weed out the poorer strains have brought Touriga Nacional into the limelight. Twenty grapes are officially allowed in port production today, but five are commonly known as the best: Touriga Nacional (sometimes simply called Touriga), Touriga Franca, Tinta Roriz, Tinta Cao, and Tinta Barroca. Touriga Nacional is capable of making great port on its own, but blending with these other four grapes produces much better results in all styles, from vintage to single *quinta* (estate), and from late bottle vintage (LBV) to fine aged tawny, as well as for the emerging high-quality red table wines for which the Douro is becoming increasingly known.

Once exclusively available as the amazing Barca Velha of Ferreira (a Douro wine equal to the historic Vega Sicilia in Spain's Ribera del Duero), table reds from this region are meeting with more and more acclaim. They now represent more than 50 percent of the Douro's red-wine production. Port is known for its fiery power, concentrated black fruit, peppery spice, deep texture, and rich cocoa- and dark-chocolate-scented finish, along with a balanced but present sweetness. The dry reds, by contrast, are marked by black raspberries, blue flowers (violet and lavender), black cherry, spicy earth, and round but present tannins. Yet few people know much about them. Please, please go out and pick up a few bottles of these delightful, great-value wines.

Farther south, in the region of Dão, Touriga Nacional is more widely grown. It generally constitutes at least 20 percent of most bottles of red Dão wine. Here it is blended with Tinta Roriz (known in Spain as Tempranillo), as in the Douro, but also with other local grapes, including Jaen (known in Spain as Mencía) and Alfrocheiro Preto. Long considered among the finest of Portugal's ample reds, Dão wines from the best producers can also be great value. In the Tejo and the Estremadura regions, Touriga is also used to make blended reds.

Surprisingly, this superb grape hasn't yet caught on much outside Portugal. In California, where it was first cultivated by producers of port-style wines, winemakers are discovering it as a great grape (used judiciously) for adding oomph and spice, much like Petite Sirah, to richer red blends. I was delighted to find some in the Barossa Valley in Australia, where it is added to fun blends with Shiraz and also made into port-style wines along with other rich red grapes. I suspect we'll be seeing more of it from Down Under, as it does well in warm climates. Strapping, inky and black, Touriga in small amounts can add a lot to a wine. It's also rumored to be grown in South Africa, though I had no luck tracking down any to taste.

Vintner's Choices Fortified vs. not fortified, old oak vs. new oak, red vs. rosé, sweet vs. dry

The best Touriga Nacional from the best vineyards makes it into the best wines, whether they are high-quality vintage ports or premium red table wines. The lesser fruit is likely to end up in a less exalted port or in a red or rosé table wine for local sale. Regardless of the quality of fruit that is used, in the world of port, the critical style decision comes about two years into the winemaking process, when the winemaking team decides whether the wine is destined to become a fine aged tawny, a vintage port, or a basic ruby. The tawny then spends up to thirty years in a barrel, while the last two are bottled earlier, resulting in quite dissimilar wines. A gorgeously nutty and toffee-nuanced twenty-year-old tawny port is a completely different animal from a bold, plummy, spicy, opaque, ruby-colored vintage bottling.

With the dry wines, house style often dictates treatment choices. Some winemakers choose to produce very traditional wines that show the rustic character and *terroir* of the Douro, using older and larger oak, while others may go for a modern style showcasing forward fruit and new oak.

PAIRING WITH FOOD

The two styles of Touriga Nacional, the dry reds and the sweeter fortified wines, have to be discussed separately; there are few common threads or magic ingredients that work for both styles.

On the dry side, pairings really depend on the weight and style of the wine. Most of the Dão wines, as well as more traditional styles from the Douro, are best treated like a rustic Bordeaux blend. They tend to be earthy, redolent more of red fruit than of black, and work well with traditional red-wine fare. With their earthier edge and medium body, they can also pair nicely with fowl, white meats, and tamer offal, like sweetbreads. I enjoy Dão with rustic Western foods rather than Asian, especially lamb dishes, beef daubes, and coq au vin. It's delicious as a change from a full-flavored Tempranillo or Sangiovese and pairs quite well with many of the same dishes. The bigger, bolder styles of Touriga, with ample oak, ripe black fruit, and present but round tannins partner best with dishes you'd enjoy with a rich Cabernet Sauvignon–Shiraz blend or a riper Bordeaux red: roast duck, flank steak, standing rib roast, or rack of lamb. If the oak is strong and lends a deep, almost sweet mocha or chocolate note, play it up—use a cocoa or coffee rub on your meat or serve a mole sauce with the dark meat of a chicken. A richer black-fruit compote or dark fruit chutney with your meat can pick up on Touriga's inherently sweet plum or prune character. The wine can overwhelm subtle recipes. Avoid anything from the sea, except perhaps with a fleshy rosé.

More people drink Touriga as a dessert wine than as a table wine, so dessert pairings merit careful exploration. As with all sweet pairings, remember my one hard-and-fast rule: *the wine's sweetness must match or exceed that of the food,* or the wine will taste sour and unappealing.

With tawny port, the wine's wood (oak) flavors will be more pronounced. Successful pairings include recipes with vanilla, caramel, or sweet spice flavors. For example, dishes featuring butterscotch, caramel, toffee, or crème brûlée are good pairings, as are desserts with custard, pastry cream, and crème anglaise. These ports will often have a golden-raisin (sultana) flavor that accentuates the same ingredients and recipes while also inviting pairings with dishes that use dried fruit—reconstituted or otherwise.

The other genres of port—vintage, late bottled vintage, single *quinta,* and even a good basic ruby—are happy playmates for chocolate. Bring out the fruit notes of the Touriga by including fruit in your chocolate dessert: cherry and berry jam spread between layers of a chocolate cake, or cherry sauce drizzled over a dark-chocolate pot de crème can be sublime.

PAIRING POINTERS

Touriga Nacional goes well with:
- Dark mushrooms (as a dry red). I enjoy a balanced, earthy, Touriga-based wine (especially a good Dão) with morels, Chinese black mushrooms, or portobellos—grilled, baked, or stuffed. These earthy, dark mushrooms have the texture of meat and can be paired easily with wines that include Touriga.
- Foods or treatments that pick up on the wine's oak (as a dry red). These are especially successful with modern-style dry reds from the Douro. Grilling, smoking, and plank-roasting mirror the oak's characteristics. The incorporation of toasted or roasted nuts (pumpkin seeds are especially good) or a charred soy or teriyaki glaze on meat will echo similar tastes in the wine.
- Caramel, nougat, and toffee (as a sweet wine). A balanced tawny port is a slam-dunk with desserts that incorporate caramelized sugar, toffee, and caramel, or some combination with nougat. The choice can be as straightforward as a toffee pudding or as nuanced as a *tarte Tatin,* with its caramelized top making a nice bridge to the wine. Classic apple is great in the tart, but you could substitute pear or even bananas, as they do at Union Square Café in Manhattan. Anytime cooked or burnt sugar is involved, it's a call for tawny port.
- Some form of dried or dense fruit (in both dry and sweet styles). All Touriga-based wines have a dark-fruit character that can range from plum, black fig, and sweet prune in the dry styles to dark raisins, dried cherry, or prune and persimmon pudding in the sweet styles.

Working this angle with your recipes is always a safe strategy. Chutneys and dark-fruit relishes can be sublime with drier wines, while any rich dark-fruit dessert is an obvious call for pairing with port.

- Blue cheese (as a sweet wine). If ever a wine were designed for blue cheese, it's port. From the legendary pairing of port with Stilton to a tawny with a creamy, mild Montbriac from France, the combination of the sugar and the salt, with the pungency of the cheese working with the wine's tannins, is close to perfection. Throw in some dried fruit (apricots, pears, or dates) and a few walnuts, and you're locked and loaded.

Touriga Nacional isn't good with:

- Fish and shellfish (as a dry red). A rosé made from Touriga might work well, so don't throw the baby out with the seawater. But most creatures with fins or shells have a hard time pairing with the rustic and powerful reds made from Touriga Nacional.
- Less robust dishes (as a dry red). Touriga demands full attention. Pairing the wine with a subtle and understated dish is at best a neutral strategy and generally one that will make the food an afterthought to the wine.
- Hot peppers (all wines). Serving Touriga with searing hot peppers isn't wise. The trendy idea of adding cayenne or pepper to chocolate when paired with port can set your mouth (or your stomach) on fire. As for the dry wines, many are high in alcohol and will react harshly with peppery heat.
- Berries (as a sweet wine). Berries alone are not at their best with fortified wines, as their inherent acidity seems to cut into the wine. That's why spring and summer berries are most often served with sparkling wines, which are less sweet. When berries are used only as an accent, pairings can be more flexible. For example, berries served alongside a molten chocolate cake or with a chocolate mousse, or puréed and served as a sauce, will work much better.
- Chocolate (as a sweet wine). The subtle, dry ports will be overpowered by intense chocolate, so choose a vintage or ruby port. The darker the chocolate the better. Be careful with mocha as well: you'll want to balance the bitterness of the coffee with the chocolate (especially if your recipe calls for espresso), as too much bitterness will make the wine taste off.

THE CHEESE PLATE

SOFT-RIPENED	Brillat-Savarin (France), Camembert (France, U.S.A.)—dry red
SEMI-HARD	Pecorino romano (Italy), Petit Basque (France)—dry red, rosé, port
HARD	Aged Beemster (Holland), aged Cheddar (U.S.A., U.K.)—dry red, port
BLUE	Gorgonzola (Italy), Montbriac (France), Stilton (U.K.)—port

touriga nacional | GRILLED PORK CHOPS WITH DRIED CHERRY, BACON, AND VIDALIA ONION CONSERVE

BEN BARKER   Magnolia Grill, Durham, North Carolina

Makes 4 main-course servings

4 (¾-pound) pork rib chops, preferably from pasture-raised pork
2 cloves garlic, halved
Kosher salt

DRIED CHERRY, BACON, AND VIDALIA ONION CONSERVE
½ cup dried sour cherries
1½ cups Touriga Nacional or other fruity red wine
¼ pound slab bacon, in a single piece
2 (6-ounce) Vidalia or other sweet onions, thinly sliced
2 bay leaves
2 tablespoons unsulfured light molasses,
     or ¼ cup pomegranate molasses
¼ cup balsamic vinegar
Kosher salt and freshly ground black pepper

1 teaspoon aniseeds or fennel seeds,
    coarsely ground in a mortar or spice grinder
1 teaspoon coriander seeds,
    coarsely ground in a mortar or spice grinder
1 teaspoon freshly cracked black pepper
¼ cup olive oil

Trim away any excess fat from the pork chops, then dry the chops well. Rub the chops all over with the cut side of the garlic cloves, and then sprinkle lightly on both sides with salt. Cover the chops and refrigerate for at least 2 hours or up to overnight. Remove the chops from the refrigerator about 30 minutes before grilling.

To make the conserve, in a small saucepan, combine the cherries and wine over medium heat and bring to just below a simmer. Remove from the heat and let cool to room temperature. Drain the cherries through a sieve placed over a bowl, and set the cherries and the wine aside separately.

Cut the bacon into slices ¼ inch thick. Divide the slices in half, and then neatly stack each half. Cut each stack crosswise into lardoons ¼ inch wide. (The rectangular strips should be a uniform $\frac{1}{4}$ inch on each side.) In a heavy saucepan, fry the bacon over medium heat until browned and tender, 3 to 5 minutes. Using a slotted spoon, transfer to paper towels to drain.

Pour off all but $\frac{1}{4}$ cup of the fat from the pan, and return the pan to medium heat. Add the onions and bay leaves and cook, stirring, for 2 minutes. Reduce the heat to very low, cover, and cook, stirring occasionally, until the onions are soft and translucent, about 20 minutes. Add the molasses and vinegar, raise the heat to medium, and bring to a boil. Add the reserved cherry-soaking wine, bring to a simmer, and cook, stirring occasionally, until most of the wine has been absorbed, about 10 minutes. Stir in the reserved bacon and cherries and season with salt and a generous amount of pepper. Remove from the heat and keep warm.

While the conserve is cooking, prepare a charcoal or gas grill for indirect grilling over a medium fire. In a small bowl, mix together the aniseeds, coriander, pepper, and olive oil. Rub the chops on both sides with the spice-oil mixture.

Oil the grill rack. Arrange the chops on the grill rack directly over the fire and grill for 2 minutes. Rotate the chops 90 degrees to create attractive grill marks and grill for 2 minutes longer. Transfer the chops to a cooler part of the grill, cover the grill, and cook for 6 to 8 minutes for medium, or until done to your liking. Transfer the chops to a wire rack, tent loosely with aluminum foil, and let rest for 4 to 5 minutes.

Reheat the conserve over low heat if necessary, and transfer to a warmed serving bowl. Place the chops on warmed plates and serve at once. Pass the conserve at the table.

NOTE You can prepare the conserve except for stirring in the bacon a few hours ahead of serving. Stir in the bacon just before serving.

BEN: *I love pork in all its forms. Chops are especially quick to prepare and adaptable to a broad range of flavors and therefore wine pairings. Whenever we're matching wine with food, we look at the dominant flavor profile of the variety or blend and try to either echo that or contrast it with the food. Touriga Nacional expresses plummy, dried-cherry elements, with hints of licorice, pepper, and smoke, so we present a little sweet-spice inflection on the chop, smoky grill flavors, and a fruity, sweet onion conserve accented with bacon and dried cherries. Serve this with creamy stone-ground grits and sautéed bitter greens, such as escarole or broccoli rabe.*

EVAN: *Ben's command of savory dishes has created an ideal pairing. I guess I could have theoretically asked him for different recipes for the two branches of the Touriga family, one entrée and one dessert, but in the end I decided to be more daring and present a recipe suited to the dry red table wines. Ben's decision to match a recipe evoking southern cooking to a decidedly non-southern wine style led to some great discussion as the recipe was developed.*

    Throughout the testing, this match was a favorite of mine. Keep the sweetness in check (ingredients do vary: if the cherries, for example, seem especially sweet, maybe cut back on the molasses). Finally, although the wine is served here with pork, I had a little left over and tried it with quail—yum! The bird's slightly gamy character paired brilliantly with Touriga's more rustic personality. Squab too would work well.

RECOMMENDED PRODUCERS

EVERYDAY	PREMIUM	SPLURGE
José Maria da Fonseca Multiple appellations, Portugal [DR]	Cockburns Douro, Portugal [P]	Niepoort Douro, Portugal [DR, P]
Quinta da Alorna Tejo, Portugal [R]	Duas Quintas Douro, Portugal [DR]	Quinta do Noval Douro, Portugal [P]
Quinta da Aveleda Bairrada, Portugal [DR, R]	Quinta dos Roques Dão, Portugal [DR]	Symington Family Estates Douro, Portugal [DR]
Sandeman Douro, Portugal [P]	Quinta do Vallado Douro, Portugal [DR]	Taylor Fladgate Douro, Portugal [P]

DR = Dry Red   P = Port   R = Rosé

Xinomavro

k'zee-*noh*-mah-vroh | xee-*noh*-mah-vroh

How can a grape whose name means "acid black" and reads like line 4 of the eye test at your optometrist's office be a rising star on the American wine scene? American understanding of Greek wines is limited mostly to retsina, which is white; few have heard of Mavrodaphne, the luscious dessert wine. Ask most folks about Greek reds, even the better-known Agiorghitiko, and you'll elicit a blank stare. So it's fitting that the last wine grape to be addressed in this book is perhaps the most obscure of all.

Grown only in Greece, Xinomavro is unique in both flavor and personality, fascinating, and very food-friendly. My dear friend Sofia Perpera, Greece's leading enologist and the driving force behind the All About Greek Wine website, tells me that Xinomavro is her favorite red for serving with food, for cellaring, and for general enjoyment.

Alternative Names Kozanis, Mavro Goumenissas, Mavro Naoussis, Mavro Xino, Niaoustiano, Popolka (Greece)

Styles Medium- to medium-full-bodied dry red, medium-bodied dry or off-dry rosé, dry white (not widely available), sparkling

Sometimes Blended With Cabernet Sauvignon, Merlot, Negoska, Syrah

Flavor Lexicon *Fruit/vegetable:* Fresh cherry, dried cherry, green or black olives, rhubarb, strawberry, tomato ▪ *Floral:* Herbs (oregano, tarragon) ▪ *Earth:* Parched dirt ▪ *Wood:* Spice ▪ *Other:* Black pepper, game

Similar Sips Old World Pinot Noir, lighter Nebbiolo or Barbera

Where It's Grown Greece (Macedonia: Amyndeo, Goumenissa, Naoussa; Thessaly: Rapsani)
Xinomavro is planted all over northern Greece and as far south as the foothills of Mount Olympus in Thessaly, where Rapsani is made. The soul of Xinomavro is, however, in Macedonia (the region of central Greece, not the independent republic), where it is the predominant variety. Laden with bright, zesty acidity reminiscent of Italian Barbera or Nebbiolo, Xinoma-

vro is almost always light in color and body and can remind you of Pinot Noir. Its palate is exotic, ranging from strawberry and rhubarb to fresh tomato or tomato jam, and punctuated with a leathery character and a hint of cracked peppercorn and black olive. It can be bracingly tannic when young, yet can age for decades and reward the patient wine drinker with its amazing staying power and peacock's tail of complexity. In addition to making super red wines, it's made into a rosé and even into a white wine in the cooler district of Imathia in northern Macedonia. Xinomavro is also used as a base for sparkling wine in the high-altitude vineyards of Amyndeo, an area so cool that the grape can produce aromatic whites, delightful, crisp rosés, and superior sparkling wines, as the bottlings of XM (the brand name of Xinomavro wines from the Karanika winery) attest.

Vintner's Choices Old oak vs. new oak, red vs. rosé vs. white, single variety vs. blended, still vs. sparkling

Both law and style often determine whether a wine is blended. To be labeled Naoussa, the wine must be 100 percent Xinomavro, from the everyday bottlings to the Reserve and Grand Reserve, which have mandatory minimum aging periods in the cask (oak) and the bottle, much like Tempranillo wines in Rioja in Spain. Xinomavro can handle these longer prerelease aging regimens, with six months in the barrel and a minimum of three years aging. In other appellations, blending with other native grapes is typical: Negoska is blended with Xinomavro in Goumenissa. And some producers have been experimenting successfully with blends incorporating so-called international varieties, like Merlot and Syrah. Xinomavro can be blended with other varieties without losing its personality. In Imeros, a regional bottling from Imathia, Xinomavro is usually little more than 50 percent of the local blend.

The other winemaking debate today concerns old versus new wood, which can be regarded as a facet of the nearly ubiquitous debate over traditional and modern styles. Greek red wines have historically been harsh, tannic, and, in Xinomavro's case, acidic, and different producers, especially in Naoussa, have different ideas of how Xinomavro should be interpreted. Traditionalists don't want to lose the leather and earthy fruit behind too much sweet new oak, but others argue that the time has come for Naoussa to compete on the global stage and cater to international tastes. A great example of the modern, oakier style is the wine from Alpha Estate, which is rich, plummy, and succulent. These styles are currently in the minority, but time will tell which style prevails. Blends of Xinomavro with more popular grapes like Syrah and Merlot are also signs of the modernist movement.

PAIRING WITH FOOD

Xinomavro, in its most readily available and purest form from Naoussa, is a very flexible food wine. When young, it's best enjoyed like other hard, young tannic reds, with red meats, grilled meats and vegetables, and the like. As it ages and softens, it is still fine with the same dishes, but you can be subtler. Opt for simple roasts rather than wood-grilled chops or steaks. Greek wines do work with Greek food. The grape has an inherently gamy personality that works well with Greece's trademark lamb dishes. Yogurt, feta cheese (which is naturally sharp), and lemon, three other core elements of Greek cuisine, can play havoc with most wines because of their acidity, but Xinomavro can stand up to them.

Xinomavro's bright acid and unique flavors worked well with vegetables, too—not just the predictable eggplant and the classic Greek dish moussaka of which it is the essential element (though moussaka and Xinomavro are quite nice together), but also grilled vegetables of all sorts (peppers, zucchini, and even asparagus), as well as mixed greens sautéed in a little garlic and olive oil. Even salads hang in there if the dressing is more citrusy than vinegary. And yes, Greek salad is a nice match. So are grape-leaf dolma, whether served alone, with yogurt, or drizzled with lemon.

I was surprised at how well the wine paired with many seafood dishes. Octopus is a staple of Greece, and its sweet fleshy, chewy character pairs well with rosé and whites made from Xinomavro, as well as with some of the lighter, more traditional reds. Tomato is both high in acid and a flavor component of Xinomavro, so the incorporation of tomatoes anywhere—as a sauce, tossed in salad, or quickly sautéed with a little butter and oregano—is almost always successful.

PAIRING POINTERS

Xinomavro goes well with:
- Greek food, and not just because the food and wine are geographic neighbors. Lamb (with gamy flavors that can handle tannin), lemon, yogurt, olives, and feta (all sharp, matching the wine's acidity) are all good ingredients to pair with this grape.
- Shellfish. Though it's safest to go with a solid rosé wine or even a white or sparkling wine that's based on the grape, Xinomavro is essentially medium-bodied and high in acid, so it can pair with shellfish. If the wine is very tannic, avoid the stronger-flavored bivalves, like assertive mussels and clams. Shrimp and scallops can also be good matches, and so can other sea creatures, like squid and octopus.
- Salads. Salads with dressings based on creamy yogurt or sour cream are actually quite nice with most Xinomavro, as long as you avoid the oak bombs.
- Vegetables. Cabernet Franc, Carmenère, and Xinomavro are my usual choices of wine when I am serving vegetarian dishes. These grapes have high acid that sets off or matches the natural sharpness of the vegetables. The wine also partners nicely with grilling, a first-rate treatment for many kinds of produce.
- Milder cheeses. More aged and developed Xinomavro can range well across an array of cheeses, not just feta. Just avoid the stronger blues and washed-rind types. If the wine is older, serving dried fruit and nuts can pick up on those elemental similarities.

Xinomavro isn't good:

- By itself. Xinomavro is a food wine, not a cocktail wine. Choose a sparkling or a rosé version for chatting; most reds are less pleasant flying solo.
- With fiery heat. Anything that burns the lips will burn out Xinomavro's elegance, especially that of the delicate aged wines like the Reserves and Grand Reserves.
- With bold recipes. Xinomavro is medium-bodied and not too extroverted, and a full-flavored dish that commands too much attention can easily overshadow it.
- With overly rich sauces and dishes. Despite its moderate tannins, the elegance of most Xinomavro-based wines won't stand up to lashings of cream, butter, and thick, mayonnaise-based sauces. Remember, match the weights of your dish and your wine.
- With sweeter dishes. These wines can be lean and sharp. Dishes that are sweet or have a sweet edge to them exaggerate the wine's inherent acidity, which will work against the dish. With this wine, opt for tart rather than sweet.

THE CHEESE PLATE

FRESH	Feta (Greece, Bulgaria, U.S.A.)—rosé
SEMI-SOFT	Gouda (Holland), Port Salut (France)—rosé, red
SOFT-RIPENED	Camembert (France, U.S.A.), Nevat (Spain)—rosé, red
SEMI-HARD	Comté (France), Gruyère (Switzerland), kasseri (Greece)—red
HARD	Kefalograviera (Greece), Parmesan (Italy)—red, sparkling
WASHED-RIND	Young Livarot (France), young Taleggio (Italy)—rosé, red

xinomavro | GRILLED LAMB SKEWERS WITH XINOMAVRO AND HONEY GLAZE

TOM DOUGLAS Dahlia Lounge, Palace Kitchen, and Lola, Seattle, Washington

Makes 4 to 6 main-course servings

MARINADE AND LAMB
2 teaspoons minced garlic
2 teaspoons dried Greek or other oregano
1 teaspoon grated lemon zest
½ teaspoon kosher salt
½ teaspoon freshly ground black pepper
⅓ cup extra virgin olive oil
2 pounds boneless lamb from leg, cut into 1-inch chunks

XINOMAVRO GLAZE
1 tablespoon unsalted butter
2 tablespoons minced shallots
3 cups Xinomavro
2 tablespoons plus 1 teaspoon honey
Kosher salt and freshly ground black pepper

PARSLEY SALAD
1½ cups fresh flat-leaf parsley leaves
¼ lemon
1½ teaspoons extra virgin olive oil
Kosher salt and freshly ground black pepper

Have ready 4 to 6 bamboo or metal skewers. If using bamboo skewers, soak them in cold water to cover for 30 minutes, then drain.

To make the marinade, in a bowl, combine the garlic, oregano, lemon zest, salt, and pepper. Whisk in the olive oil.

Thread the lamb chunks onto the skewers, and place in a shallow baking dish. Pour the marinade over the lamb, and turn the skewers to coat the meat evenly. Cover and marinate in the refrigerator for at least 6 hours or up to overnight.

To make the glaze, in a small saucepan, melt the butter over medium-high heat. Add the shallots and sauté until lightly browned, about 3 minutes. Add the wine, raise the heat to high, and boil until the wine is reduced and syrupy. This will take 20 to 30 minutes, depending on the intensity of the heat. Watch carefully, as once the mixture becomes syrupy, it can burn easily. You should have about $^1/_3$ cup. Whisk in the honey, season with salt, and add 5 or 6 grinds of pepper. Cook the glaze for 1 minute longer to melt the honey, then remove from the heat and let cool completely. (The glaze can be made up to 2 days in advance, covered, and refrigerated. Bring to room temperature before using.)

Prepare a charcoal or gas grill for direct grilling over a medium fire. Remove the dish holding the skewers from the refrigerator and bring the lamb to room temperature.

Remove the skewers from the marinade, shaking off the excess marinade, and season the meat with salt and pepper. Place the skewers on the grill rack and grill, turning the skewers frequently to ensure even cooking, for 7 to 8 minutes for medium-rare, or until done to your liking. When the lamb is almost ready, brush the pieces on all sides with the glaze and turn the skewers to caramelize the glaze lightly.

While the lamb is on the grill, make the parsley salad. Put the parsley in a bowl, squeeze the lemon quarter over the top, drizzle with the oil, and toss to coat evenly. Season with salt and pepper and toss again.

Remove the skewers from the grill and pile them on a warmed platter. Top with the parsley salad and serve at once.

TOM: *I like the flavor of red wine with lamb, but a red-wine marinade can break down the texture of the meat and make it mealy, and it also tends to muddle the flavor of the wine. So instead I decided to brush charcoal-grilled lamb skewers with a bright, intense Xinomavro glaze made by reducing the wine to a syrup.*

Xinomavro is not as fruit-forward as the red wines I usually use for cooking, like Cabernet or Syrah, but by reducing the Xinomavro, I intensified the flavor of the wine, and I then added honey for a little sweetness. Don't forget the pepper grinder! Freshly ground pepper in the glaze plays to the peppery characteristics of the wine.

I often like to balance rich, meaty flavors with a crisp, fresh salad. In this case I topped the wine-glazed lamb skewers with a simple parsley salad, which also helps point up the green and herbal qualities of the Xinomavro.

EVAN: *Tom's cooking has been a favorite of mine since Dahlia Lounge opened in the 1980s. Each of his restaurants brings out a different facet of his culinary skills. A meal at Lola will show you that this is a chef who understands Greece and Greek food. I knew that Tom would respect the classic nature of this pairing while placing his own signature on the recipe.*

Some aspects of this pairing and recipe are conservative—serving lamb with Xinomavro, using the same variety as the basis of the glaze—but there's nothing stodgy about the seamless way its elements work together. Balancing the honey (and its sweetness) may be challenging with some wines; feel free to try a bite of lamb with the glaze just before you serve it, and adjust the amount of honey you add at the final moment accordingly. The parsley salad is brilliant and delicious with the wine.

RECOMMENDED PRODUCERS

EVERYDAY	PREMIUM	PREMIUM
Megapanos Macedonia, Greece	Boutari Macedonia, Greece	Alpha Estate Macedonia, Greece
Stelios Kechris Macedonia, Greece	Chrisohoou Macedonia, Greece	Amyntaion Macedonia, Greece
Tsantali Macedonia, Greece	Katogi & Strofilia Macedonia, Greece	Ioannis Hatzis Macedonia, Greece
Vaeni Macedonia, Greece	Kir-Yianni Macedonia, Greece [DR, R, Sp]	Pavlou-Kagas Macedonia, Greece

DR = Dry red   R = Rosé   Sp = Sparkling

ABOUT THE CHEFS

Nate Appleman is a partner in Pulino's Bar and Pizzeria in New York City, where he moved after many years as the executive chef and co-owner of San Francisco's A16 and SPQR. He was nominated by the James Beard Foundation for Rising Star Chef in 2007 and 2008; in 2009, he won the award and was also honored as one of *Food & Wine* magazine's Best New Chefs. He is the coauthor, with Shelley Lindgren, of *A16: Food + Wine*.

Dan Barber is the chef and co-owner of Blue Hill and Blue Hill at Stone Barns. As a board member of the Stone Barns Center for Food and Agriculture, Dan works to bring the principles of good farming directly to the table. Blue Hill and Blue Hill at Stone Barns have both received Best New Restaurant nominations from the James Beard Foundation. The foundation named Barber Best Chef: New York City in 2006 and Outstanding Chef in 2009. Also in 2009, *Time* magazine featured him in its Time 100, an annual list of the world's most influential people.

Ben Barker, with his wife and partner, Karen, has operated Magnolia Grill in Durham, North Carolina, for twenty-three years. Barker was named a Rising Star Chef by *Esquire* in 1992 and one of the Ten Best New Chefs in America by *Food & Wine* in 1993. In 1996 Magnolia was elected into the *Nation's Restaurant News* Fine Dining Hall of Fame. He was the 2000 James Beard Southeast Regional Chef of the Year, and Magnolia Grill was nominated in 2007 for the James Beard Outstanding Restaurant award.

Paul Bartolotta became the first Italian chef to win the James Beard award for Best Chef: Midwest in 1994, and in 1997 he earned the prestigious Insegna del Ristorante Italiano del Mondo. Under Bartolotta's direction, as chef and managing partner from 1991 to 2000, Chicago's Spiaggia earned every major national fine-dining award. In 2005 his Bartolotta Ristorante di Mare, at Wynn Las Vegas, was named one of the Best New Restaurants in America by *Esquire*, and in 2006 it received a Best New Restaurant nomination from the James Beard Foundation.

Michelle Bernstein won the James Beard Award for Best Chef: South in 2008. Her restaurant Michy's was named one of the Top Fifty Restaurants in the Country by *Gourmet* magazine and

Best New Restaurant 2006 by *Food & Wine* magazine. In 2009 she opened the "small plates" restaurant Sra. Martinez in Miami. Bernstein has been recognized as a Top Latina in the Nation by *Latina* magazine and one of the Top Ten Jewish Women in America by the Jewish Women International Federation, and she received an honorary doctorate from Johnson & Wales University for her work in hospitality. Her first cookbook, *Cuisine à Latina*, was published in 2008 with Houghton-Mifflin. Bernstein also creates the entrées for Delta First Class and BusinessElite.

Floyd Cardoz is the executive chef and co-owner of Tabla, where he celebrates the sensual flavors and spices of his native land with his pioneering New Indian cuisine. Tabla has received numerous accolades, and *Bon Appétit* named Cardoz as one of the Innovators in its 2003 Restaurant Edition. He has received four nominations from the James Beard Foundation for Best Chef: New York City (2004 through 2007).

Robert Del Grande was the executive chef and owner of Cafe Annie in Houston until 2009, when the restaurant moved to a nearby location and reopened as RDG + Bar Annie. Del Grande has won the James Beard Foundation award for Best Chef: Southwest and the Silver Spoon award from Food Arts, and he has been inducted into the Beard Foundation's Who's Who of Food and Beverage. Cafe Annie was featured in many national publications, including *Food & Wine*, *Food Arts*, *Saveur*, *Gourmet*, and *Bon Appétit*.

Tom Douglas, with his wife and partner, Jackie Cross, owns five Seattle restaurants: Dahlia Lounge (nominated for Best Restaurant by the James Beard Foundation in 2006), Etta's, Palace Kitchen (nominated for Best New Restaurant by the James Beard Foundation in 1997), Lola, and Serious Pie. In 1994 he won the James Beard award for Best Chef: Northwest. Douglas is also the author of three cookbooks: *Tom Douglas' Seattle Kitchen*, which won a James Beard award for Best Americana Cookbook; *Tom's Big Dinners*; and *I Love Crab Cakes*.

Suzanne Goin worked at Chez Panisse in Berkeley and Arpège in Paris before returning to her hometown of Los Angeles in 1998 and, with her business partner, Caroline Styne, opening Lucques—named the number one restaurant in the city by *Los Angeles* magazine in 2008. Goin was honored as one of *Food & Wine*'s Best New Chefs in 1999, and in 2002 Goin and Styne opened their second restaurant, A.O.C. In 2006, the James Beard Foundation voted Goin Best Chef: California and named her *Sunday Suppers at Lucques,* coauthored with Teri Gelber, Best Cookbook from a Professional Viewpoint. In 2005 she opened her third restaurant, the Hungry Cat, which was followed by Tavern in 2009. In 2008 she was nominated for the James Beard Foundation Outstanding Chef award.

Joyce Goldstein is a teacher and consultant to the restaurant and food industries. For twelve years she was chef and owner of the groundbreaking Mediterranean restaurant Square One in San Francisco, which won numerous awards for food, wine, and service. In 1993 she received the James Beard award for Best Chef: California. Goldstein is the author of many cookbooks, including *The Mediterranean Kitchen*; *Back to Square One,* which won both the Julia Child and James Beard awards for Best General Cookbook of 1992; *Italian Slow and Savory*, which was a James Beard and International Association of Culinary Professionals Cookbook award nominee for 2004; and, most recently, *Tapas* and *Mediterranean Fresh*. Goldstein also contributed the recipes for *Perfect Pairings,* written by her son, Evan Goldstein, and published by University of California Press in 2006.

Christopher Gross was named one of America's Best New Chefs by *Food & Wine* in 1989, and in 1997 he received the Robert Mondavi Culinary Award of Excellence. In 1995 Perrier-Jouët and the James Beard Foundation named him Best Chef: Southwest. Gross opened Christopher's, named Best New Restaurant by the *Chicago Tribune* and *Esquire*, and Christopher's Bistro in 1990 in Phoenix. In 1998 Gross opened Christopher's Fermier Brasserie and Paola's Wine Bar, which was named America's Best Restaurant: Phoenix and Scottsdale by *Gourmet* in 2002; Best French Restaurant: Best of Phoenix 2002 and 2003 by the *New Times;* and Best Lunch: The Rep's Best in 2002 by the *Arizona Republic*. Gayot.com named Christopher's Restaurant and Crush Lounge—which opened in 2008 and serves American cuisine with a French accent—one of the Top Ten New Restaurants in the United States.

Fergus Henderson opened St. John with Trevor Gulliver in 1994, and in 2003 they launched St. John Bread and Wine. Recognized by *Time Out London* as Best British Restaurant in 2006, St. John has also been named one of *Restaurant* magazine's World's Top Fifty Restaurants since 2003 and was awarded its first Michelin star in 2009. Henderson received an André Simon Award in 1999, an MBE in 2005, and more recently the *Food Observer Monthly*'s Outstanding Achievement Award and the Global Gastronomy Award from the Sweden-based *White Guide*. He is the author of *Nose to Tail Eating* and *Beyond Nose to Tail Eating*.

Gerald Hirigoyen and a partner opened Fringale, a modern French bistro, in 1991. With his wife, Cameron, he opened Piperade in 2002 and Bocadillos in 2004. Hirigoyen was named one of *Food & Wine*'s Best New Chefs in 1994, *San Francisco* magazine's San Francisco Chef of the Year in 1995 and Best Chef of the Bay Area in 2003, and a James Beard award nominee for Best Chef: California in 2006. He is the author of *Bistro; The Basque Kitchen*, which won the Versailles Award for Best Regional Cookbook; and *Pintxos: Small Plates in the Basque Tradition*.

Philippe Jeanty was born in the Champagne region of France. He came to California in 1977 with a team from Épernay, France, to open the Chandon Restaurant in Yountville, where he became executive chef in 1978. In 1998 he opened Bistro Jeanty, named that year as Best New Restaurant in the Bay Area by the *San Francisco Chronicle*, and chosen as one of four nominees for Best New Restaurant in America by the James Beard Foundation.

Douglas Keane worked at the Four Seasons restaurant in New York and under Gray Kunz at Lespinasse before moving to San Francisco's Jardinière, where he was honored by the *San Francisco Chronicle* as a Rising Star Chef. In 2002 Keane opened Cyrus and has since been named *Esquire*'s Chef of the Year in 2005, *Food & Wine*'s Best New Chef in 2006, and *San Francisco* magazine's Best Chef in 2006. Cyrus was named one of *Gourmet*'s Top Fifty Restaurants in the United States and received two stars in the *Michelin Guide*. In 2009 Keane was honored with the James Beard award for Best Chef: Pacific Region.

Hubert Keller runs Fleur de Lys in San Francisco and Las Vegas; Burger Bar in Las Vegas, St. Louis, and San Francisco; and Sleek, his first steakhouse, in St. Louis. In addition to winning the James Beard award for Best Chef: California in 1993, Keller was elected into the Who's Who of Food and Beverage by the James Beard Foundation in 2003. In 1998 *Wine Spectator* named Fleur de Lys in San Francisco as the second best restaurant in the world. Keller is also the host of the national public television series *Secrets of a Chef*.

Loretta Keller is the owner of COCO500, which opened in 2005 and was named one of the *San Francisco Chronicle*'s Top One Hundred restaurants in 2007. Keller started her career with Susan Spicer in New Orleans and cooked for many years at Jeremiah Tower's acclaimed Stars Restaurant. In 2008 she partnered with Charles Phan of the Slanted Door to open the Academy Café and the Moss Room in San Francisco's new California Academy of Sciences to critical acclaim, receiving three stars from the *San Francisco Chronicle*. In 2009 Loretta was nominated for the James Beard Award for Best Chef: California/Hawaii.

David Kinch opened his highly acclaimed restaurant, Manresa, in Los Gatos in 2002. Manresa has been named one of America's Top Fifty Restaurants by *Gourmet*, awarded two Michelin stars for three consecutive years, 2007–2009, and received four stars from the *San Francisco Chronicle*, the *San Jose Mercury News*, and the *Mobil Travel Guide*. In 2008 and 2009, Kinch was nominated for the James Beard award for Best Chef: Pacific Region, and in 2009 he was a winning contestant on Food Network's *Iron Chef America*.

Evan Kleiman opened Angeli Caffe, the first modern Italian café in Los Angeles, in 1984. It became one of the most widely imitated restaurants in the city. In 1998 Kleiman began hosting the radio show *Good Food* on KCRW and kcrw.com. She is the author or coauthor of six cookbooks, including *Cucina Fresca*, *Pasta Fresca*, and *Cucina Rustica*.

Mourad Lahlou is the chef and owner of Aziza in San Francisco, which serves modern interpretations of traditional Moroccan dishes. In 1998 the *San Francisco Chronicle* named Lahlou a Rising Star Chef, and in March 2009 he beat Cat Cora in an episode of *Iron Chef America* on the Food Network. Aziza has been recognized as one of the *San Francisco Chronicle*'s Top One Hundred Restaurants annually since 2002, and in 2010 the restaurant was awarded a Michelin star. Lahlou will be featured in his own PBS show in 2010.

Michael Leviton opened Lumière in his hometown of Newton, Massachusetts, in 1999. Leviton and Lumière have been recognized with numerous awards, including Best New Restaurant from *Bon Appétit* in 1999; Best New Restaurant and Best New Chef from *Boston* magazine in

1999; and Best Restaurant in America from *Gourmet* in 2002. Leviton has been nominated by the James Beard Foundation for Best Chef: Northeast every year from 2005 to 2009.

Emily Luchetti moved to San Francisco in 1984, where she was part of the opening team of Stars Restaurant. In 1987 she moved on to become the executive pastry chef at Farallon, and today she is also the executive pastry chef at Waterbar and Nick's Cove restaurants. She received a Food Arts Silver Spoon award in 2003 and was named Outstanding Pastry Chef by the James Beard Foundation in 2004. Luchetti has written several cookbooks, including *Stars Desserts*, an International Association of Culinary Professionals cookbook award nominee; *Four Star Desserts*, nominated for a James Beard Foundation cookbook award in 1995; *A Passion for Desserts*; and *A Passion for Ice Cream*. She is also a cohost on the PBS series *The Holiday Table*.

Laurent Manrique has worked as executive chef at Le Grand Comptoir; the Waldorf Astoria's Peacock Alley, where he was named *Bon Appétit*'s Rising Star Chef; San Francisco's Campton Place, which was ranked in *Gourmet*'s Top Ten Best Restaurants in the Bay Area and *Food & Wine*'s Fifty Best Hotel Restaurants; and the Michelin-starred Fifth Floor. For six years he was corporate executive chef at Aqua, which earned two Michelin stars, a three-and-a-half-star ranking in the *San Francisco Chronicle*, and a third-place ranking on the *Wine Spectator*'s list of Best San Francisco Restaurants. Manrique owns Café de la Presse and Rouge et Blanc Wine Bar.

Lachlan M. Patterson, with master sommelier Bobby Stuckey, opened Frasca Food and Wine in Boulder, Colorado, in 2004. The following year, Patterson was named one of *Food & Wine*'s Best New Chefs, and in 2006 he became the first-ever James Beard Rising Star Chef nominee from Colorado. Frasca was cited on the 2006 *Condé Nast Traveler* Hot List and *Gourmet*'s list of Top Fifty Restaurants in the United States. In 2008, Patterson won the James Beard award for Best Chef: Southwest.

Cindy Pawlcyn opened Mustards Grill, her first of more than a dozen restaurants, in 1983. Today she co-owns Mustards Grill, Cindy's Backstreet Kitchen, and Go Fish, all in the Napa Valley. She has written four cookbooks: *Fog City Diner Cookbook*; *Mustards Grill Napa Valley Cookbook*, with Brigid Callinan (a James Beard Foundation award winner); *Big Small Plates*, with Pablo and Erasto Jacinto; and *Cindy Pawlcyn's Appetizers*. She has received two nominations for a James Beard Foundation award for Best Chef: California.

Anne S. Quatrano is co-chef and co-owner of Bacchanalia, Quinones, Star Provisions, and Floataway Cafe, all in Atlanta. In 2006 Bacchanalia was named one of *Zagat*'s Top Ten Restaurants in the country, and it has been ranked the number one restaurant in Atlanta for eleven consecutive years. Quatrano was named one of *Food & Wine*'s Best New Chefs in 1995 and won the James Beard Foundation award for Best Chef: Southeast in 2003. Along with her husband, Clifford Harrison, she was honored as James Beard Discovery Chef of the Year.

Michael Romano became the executive chef at Union Square Cafe in 1988, which received three stars from the *New York Times* in 1989 and was named the James Beard Outstanding Restaurant of the Year in 1997. Romano was nominated for the James Beard Foundation's Best Chef: New York City seven times and won in 2001. In 1991 he was selected as one of *Food & Wine*'s Best New Chefs, and in 2000 he was inducted into the James Beard Foundation's Who's Who of Food and Beverage in America. Romano and partner Danny Meyer collaborated on two cookbooks, *The Union Square Cafe Cookbook* and *Second Helpings*.

Susan Spicer, with Regina Keever, opened Bayona in 1990 in the French Quarter of New Orleans. Bayona was one of *Restaurants and Institutions*' Ivy Award winners in 1996 and was named to the *Nation's Restaurant News* Fine Dining Hall of Fame in 1998. In 1993 Spicer received the James Beard award for Best Chef: Southeast, and in 1995 she was chosen for the Robert Mondavi Culinary Award for Excellence. Her cookbook *Crescent City Cooking: Unforgettable Recipes from Susan Spicer's New Orleans* was published in 2007.

Frank Stitt is the chef and proprietor of the celebrated Highlands Bar and Grill, Bottega, and Chez Fonfon restaurants in Birmingham, Alabama. Most recently, Highlands Bar and Grill was nominated for the 2009 James Beard Foundation award for Outstanding Restaurant. Stitt was honored by the foundation as Best Chef: Southeast in 2001 and nominated for James Beard Outstanding Chef in 2008. He is involved with many organizations promoting sustainable agriculture, including the local Slow Food chapter and the Alabama Governor's Advisory Board of Farmer's Markets.

Craig Stoll is the chef and coproprietor, with his wife, Anne, of Delfina in San Francisco's Mission District, which they opened in 1998; Pizzeria Delfina, opened in 2005; and Pizzeria Delfina–Pacific Heights, opened in 2009. In 2000 Stoll was named Rising Star Chef by both the *San Francisco Chronicle* and *San Francisco* magazine. In 2008 he won the James Beard Foundation's award for Best Chef: Pacific Region.

Ethan Stowell, *Seattle* magazine's 2005 Chef to Watch and a *Food & Wine* Best New Chef for 2008, is the chef and co-owner of four Seattle restaurants. Union, opened in 2003, was named one of *Esquire*'s Best New Restaurants in 2004 and listed in *Food & Wine* as one of the Top 376 Restaurants in the World in 2006. Tavolàta and How to Cook a Wolf opened in 2007; the former was named one of the Ten Hottest New Restaurants by *Bon Appétit* magazine. Anchovies and Olives, opened in 2009, is his newest venture with business partners Patric Gabre-Kidan and Angela Stowell.

Charlie Trotter is the owner and chef of a namesake restaurant that was inducted into the esteemed Relais and Châteaux luxury hotel alliance in 1995. It has received five stars from the *Mobil Travel Guide* and five diamonds from the American Automobile Association. *Wine Spectator* named Charlie Trotter's the Best Restaurant in the World for Wine and Food in 1998 and America's Best Restaurant in 2000. Trotter has garnered ten James Beard Foundation awards, including Outstanding Chef in 1999 and Outstanding Restaurant in 2000. He is the author of fourteen cookbooks and two management books and hosts the award-winning PBS cooking series *The Kitchen Sessions with Charlie Trotter.* In 2008 he opened Restaurant Charlie in Las Vegas.

Larry Tse is the chef and owner of The House, an Asian American restaurant in San Francisco's North Beach that opened in 1994. The restaurant has been featured in the *San Francisco Examiner, San Francisco Chronicle,* and *Asian Week,* as well as the San Francisco version of the popular PBS program *Check, Please!* In 1995 Tse was named a Rising Star Chef by the *San Francisco Chronicle.*

Richard Vellante has been with Legal Sea Foods for twelve years, developing menus and overseeing the culinary staff of more than thirty restaurants. Vellante was voted Menu Strategist of the Year by *Restaurant Business* magazine. He has appeared on the Food Network shows *Food Nation* and *Sara's Secrets,* and his credits include *Chef on a Shoestring, Healthy Kids, The Rosie O'Donnell Show,* multiple cooking demonstrations in the about.com video series, and two Days of Taste children's seminars for the American Institute of Food and Wine.

Vikram Vij was born in India and studied hotel management in Salzburg, Austria. He moved to Canada in 1989 and opened Vij's Restaurant in 1994. Vij's won *Vancouver* magazine's Gold Award for Best South Asian Restaurant in 1995 and from 1997 through 2002 was listed in the Top Five Vancouver Restaurants in *Gourmet*'s annual restaurant awards. Vij's has been featured on the Food Network and CNN and in the Toronto *Globe and Mail,* the *New York Times,* the *Washington Post, Travel and Leisure, Food & Wine, Bon Appétit,* and *Sunset.*

Kate Zuckerman was the pastry chef at New York's Chanterelle for ten years, until the restaurant closed in 2009. The *New York Times* described eating her desserts as a "life-changing experience," and she was named one of the Ten Best Pastry Chefs in America by *Pastry Art and Design* in 2005. She is the author of *The Sweet Life: Desserts from Chanterelle.*

SUMMARY OF WINE STYLES

If you've read faithfully through all the chapters of this book and now find your head spinning—and you don't think it's from sampling one too many of the wines—here's a cheat sheet that summarizes the main characteristics of the varieties discussed. Of course, successful pairings depend on much more than check marks and numbers, so if you're using these charts as a guide to pairing with food, I urge you to go back and review the pairing recommendations for the relevant varieties before settling on a choice. And if you're devising a match for a special occasion, it always pays to sample both the wine and the recipe ahead of time.

WHITE WINES

VARIETY	ACIDITY	SWEETNESS	TANNIN	OAK	ALCOHOL	SPARKLING STYLE	DESSERT STYLE
Albariño	9	1	0	0–2	3–5	✓	
Arneis	8	1.5	0	0–1	4		
Assyrtiko	8.5	2–8	0	0–1	3–7.5		✓
Chenin Blanc	8.5	.5–8	0	0–2.5	3–8	✓	✓
Garganega	8	1.5–7	1	0–2	2–8		✓
Grüner Veltliner	9	1	0	0–1.5	3		✓
Marsanne	6.5	3	2.5	0–5	7	✓	•
Muscat	7	1–8	1	0–3	3–8	✓	✓
Pinot Blanc	8	1.5	0	0–2	6	✓	✓
Prosecco	7	3.5	0	0–1	5	✓	✓
Roussanne	6.5	3	2.5	0–5	8	•	
Sémillon	7.5	2–8	1	0–5	3–8	•	✓
Torrontés	4.5	3	1	0–2	5		
Trebbiano	8	1–7	0	0–1.5	4		✓
Txakoli	9.5	1.5	0	0–1	2	✓	
Verdejo	7.5	2.5	2	0–3	6		
Vermentino	8.5	1.5	0	0–2	3		

The scale used in these tables ranges from 0 to 10, with 0 being low and 10 being high.

✓ Generally available in the U.S.

• Limited availability in the U.S.

RED WINES

VARIETY	ACIDITY	SWEETNESS	TANNIN	OAK	ALCOHOL	ROSÉ STYLE	SPARKLING STYLE	DESSERT STYLE
Aglianico	6	1.5	7–9	4–7	8	•		
Barbera	7	2	5–6	0–8.5	6–8	•	✓	
Cabernet Franc	7.5	1.5	6–7	3–8	5–8	•	•	✓
Carignan	7.5	1.5–7	5–7	0–6	4–8	✓		✓
Carmenère	7.5	1.5	4–8	3–9	7			
Cinsaut	8	2–3	3–6	0–4	5–7.5	✓		
Dolcetto	7	2.5	3–5.5	0–2	4–6			
Gamay	8	3	3–5	0–7	3–6.5	•		
Grenache	6	2.5–7	3–6.5	0–8	4–8.5	✓		✓
Malbec	7.5	2.5	4–8	0–9	7–8	✓		
Mencía	8	1.5	4–7	2–8	5–7			
Mourvèdre	7.5	2	4–8	3–8.5	5–7.5	✓		
Nebbiolo	7	1.5	6–9.5	3–9.5	5–8.5			
Petit Sirah	6.5	3	5–9	4–8	6–9			
Pinotage	7.5	2	4–7	0–8	5–8	✓	•	•
Tannat	7.5	1.5	4–9.5	3–8.5	5–8.5	✓		
Tempranillo	8	1.5–2.5	4–8	0–8.5	4–8	✓		
Touriga Nacional	7	2–8	4–8.5	3–8.5	5–8.5	✓		✓
Xinomavro	7.5	2	3–7	0–7.5	4–7	✓	•	

SHOPPING FOR WINE

A number of the wines I discuss in this book are not easy to find and may require some legwork to track down. I wouldn't walk into a Safeway or Publix and expect to find an array of Grüner Veltliners or Mencías. But you may be surprised by what you can buy locally: Grenache, Chenin Blanc, and Petite Sirah, for instance, are reasonably widely distributed. My advice for acquiring the best wines is as follows:

- *Unusual wines are easier to find in fine wine stores than in grocery or big-box stores.* Depending on where you live, you may be pleasantly surprised at the range of wines available to you in your local market. And of course high-end grocers like Whole Foods, Dean & Deluca, and even Trader Joe's carry some of the more esoteric varieties. But for many of the less common varieties, and for guidance in choosing among them, you're better off shopping at a specialty store.

- *If you don't see what you want on the shelf, ask.* Less popular wines may be tucked away somewhere or can be ordered for you if you're a regular customer.

- *Online shopping rules!* One of the best ways to find anything you want these days is to shop on the Internet. The world of wine is no different. I highly recommend Wine Searcher (www .wine-searcher.com) as a great site for finding and comparing prices on wines. In addition, many premium retailers nationwide have online stores and often (in states where shipping wine to customers is legal) competitive pricing on these hard-to-find bottles.

RECOMMENDED IMPORTERS

The vast majority of the wines in this book are imported. Indeed, several of them are not produced in the United States. Selecting among unfamiliar foreign labels can be daunting. Selecting from producers whose names you may not even be able to pronounce is downright scary. It's been claimed that there are some thirteen thousand different wines available at retail. So where to begin? Choosing reliable importers and import companies is a start. Although there are hundreds of importers bringing wines into the United States, a few display a special talent for finding great producers and importing their best wines; they act essentially as prepurchase sommeliers. One of these importers' names on the label, while not a guarantee of quality, will guide you toward wines that are more than calculated risks.

All-Around
Broadbent Selections
Clicquot, Inc.
Dreyfus Ashby
European Cellars (Eric Solomon)
Frederick Wildman
Hand Picked Selections (Dan Kravitz)
Kobrand
Kysela Père et Fils
Michael Skurnik
Moët Hennessey
Palm Bay Imports
Pasternak Wine Imports
Paterno
Robert Chadderdon
Vineyard Brands
Wilson Daniels
Wine Sellers, Ltd.
W. J. Deutsch

Australia
Australian Premium Wine Collection
Grateful Palate
Negociants USA
Old Bridge Wine Cellars
Southern Starz

France
Arborway Imports
Boisset America
Classic Wine Imports
Diageo Chateau & Estates
Ideal Wines
Kermit Lynch
Maison Marques et Domaines
Martine Saunier
North Berkeley Imports
Robert Kacher Selections
Rosenthal Wine Merchant (Neal Rosenthal)
Weygandt-Metzler
Wines of France (Alain Juguenet)

Germany and Austria
International Wine Cellars (Rudi Wiest)
Terry Theise/Michael Skurnik
Vackenberg
Vin Divino
Winemonger

Greece
Athenee Importers
Diamond Importers
Hellas Imports, Ltd.
Vina Mediterranean/Sotiris Bafitis Selection

Italy
Domaine Select
Empson Selections
Marco di Grazia
Vinifera
Winebow

New Zealand
Negociants USA
Robert Bath Selections
Via Pacifica

South Africa
Cape Classics

South America
Billington Imports
Southern Starz
TGIC Importers
Vine Connections

Spain
CIV USA
Classical Wines of Spain
Fine Estates from Spain (Jorge Ordoñez)
Grape Moments
Vinos and Gourmet

GLOSSARY

Acid adjustment Manually adding acidity to a wine to increase its sharpness and balance. Usually added in the form of tartaric acid, when well done it is effective, but when poorly executed, wines will taste painfully sharp and noticeably disjointed (overly acidulated) on the finish.

Acidity The level of acid in the wine. A wine's acidity is reflected by the perception of tartness or sharpness. It's critical to the wine's structure and balance and to the wine's ability to pair with food. Acidity is the ultimate contrast to foods that are fatty, rich, salty, greasy, or mildly spicy. Additionally, it brings out the taste of quality ingredients, acting as a vinous highlighter pen.

AOC *Appellation d'origine contrôlée* This term refers to geographical indications for wines and other agricultural products, including cheeses and butters, whose certification is managed by the government bureau Institut National des Appellations d'Origine (INAO). For wines, AOCs also prescribe specific yields, recognized grapes, viticultural practices, and the like.

Appellation The geographical area from which a wine comes, which is usually identified on the label, such as the Napa Valley or Champagne. In countries where the use of appellation names is legally restricted, a wine using the name may have to contain a certain minimum percentage of a particular variety, be made from grapes grown in a specific area, or conform to other requirements.

Astringency The puckery sensation in the mouth often associated with the tannins in red wines. Bitterness suggests the same flavor sensation but without the puckering, mouth-drying effects.

Austerity A term often used to describe wines that are lean and sharp in nature. Although sometimes unpleasant to drink solo, such wines can be remarkable with food and often provide a needed contrast to a rich dish.

AVA American viticultural area A legal certification, the American equivalent of a French AOC or Italian DOC. Unlike their European counterparts, however, AVAs only specify physical boundaries and do not mandate expected or obligatory winemaking and viticultural practices and limitations.

Balance The quality all winemakers strive for: the sense that all the components—acidity, tannin, oak, alcohol, and sweetness—are present in appropriate proportions. If one characteristic seems to dominate the rest, the wine may be described as being out of balance. Balance can be achieved not only in the wine itself but also by judicious pairings of wine and food.

Barrel fermentation Alcoholic fermentation of wine that takes place inside an oak barrel. Using barrels rather than stainless steel tanks for this process adds different flavors and textures: typically a toastiness, a butterscotch or toffee flavor, and a rounder, creamier consistency. Although barrel fermentation is most often associated with white wines, many reds today are also barrel-fermented.

Barrique The French term for barrel, used to describe the small coopered barrels (holding about sixty gallons) universally employed by the wine industry. The classic choice of wood is oak.

Bleeding This term is used in winemaking as a translation of the French *saigné*. Bleeding is the process of removing some of the fermenting must (pulp, juice, and skins) in red wines partway through alcoholic fermentation to concentrate the remaining wine. Often this "bled" wine, pinkish in hue, is fermented dry and made into a rosé wine called *vin gris* (gray wine).

Body The weight and texture of the wine as it appears in the glass when the wine is swirled, and as it tastes and feels in the mouth. Body is directly related to the alcohol content of the wine and is described as ranging from light to full.

Botrytized Refers to grapes that have been affected by the "noble rot," *Botrytis cinerea,* which affects grapes in conditions of alternating warm and wet weather with dry afternoons. *Botrytis* mold settles on the skins of the grapes and punctures small holes in them, allowing water to escape without affecting the fruit's flavors or inherent acidity. It is easily recognizable in a wine by its signature flavor of honey.

Bouquet The spectrum of scents associated with a wine as it ages and develops. Younger, fruity smells are often described as aroma rather than bouquet.

Clarity The absence of any debris or haze in a wine. A clean-looking wine is a well-made wine, although the flavor may or may not be to your liking and the degree of clarity has no effect on wine and food pairings.

Clone An isolated, heat-treated, and disease-free selection of a specific grape variety. Each clone is assigned a unique name or code: Chardonnay clones, for example, include UC Davis 05, 06, and 07 and the French clones 124, 131, and 133. *Clone* is often used interchangeably with *selection* (see below), but they are not synonymous.

Cold soaking Also known as *macération pelliculaire:* the maceration of the unfermented grape must (pulp, juice, and skins) before alcoholic fermentation to extract more fruit flavors and create a deeper color. Chilling the must prevents fermentation, because yeasts are not active at lower temperatures. Once the maceration period is over, the temperature is raised to allow fermentation to proceed. This process is most commonly used for Pinot Noir and some whites.

Color The hue of the wine, determined first by the grapes (red or white) and then by the winemaking process. White wines can be made from red grapes: most of the pigment is in the skins, and the color of the wine depends in part on the length of time the juice is in contact with the skins. One person's ruby is another's purple, so descriptors are highly subjective. Color gives some indication of age: red wines lighten and turn brown as they mature, whereas white wines and rosés gain color.

Complexity The presence of multiple layers of flavor and aroma. The more tastes you can perceive in the wine, the more complex it is said to be. While complex wines can be fabulous with food, they are often best savored on their own, as their subtleties can be lost behind complicated recipes.

Cru A term for a high-quality wine from a designated appellation (e.g., *premier cru* in a Burgundian AOC) or for certain as-yet undesignated areas seeking to emulate cru systems established elsewhere (e.g., in Italy's Piedmont).

Cuvée The blending (or, in French, *assemblage*) of many wines from different years, varieties, or vineyards.

DO and DOCa *Denominación de origen* and *Denominación de origen calificada* These are the classifications for the highest-quality Spanish wines. As with French AOC wines, regional governing bodies oversee the laws concerning such matters as minimum and maximum yields, oak and bottle aging, and grape varieties. DOCa is a recently added designation for the most limited and celebrated wines.

DOC *Denominação de origem controlada* This is the Portuguese equivalent of the Spanish DO and the French AOC wines. They are likewise tightly regulated and must adhere to strict controls on grape varieties, alcohol content, maximum yields, and, in some cases, winemaking practices.

DOC and DOCG *Denominazione di origine controllata* and *Denominazione di origine controllata e garantita* The Italian equivalent of the French AOC and Spanish DO systems. DOCG wines are the most restricted and considered among the best in Italy.

Dryness The amount of residual sweetness in a wine. Dryness is not the same as fruitiness, the level of fruit presence in a wine. Although ripe-fruit aromas may suggest sweetness, the wine may still be dry—without perceptible sweetness—to the taste.

Earthiness Flavors suggesting the earth—dust, earth, mineral, slate, gravel, forest floor, humus, and even barnyard. Many wines, especially those from western Europe, exhibit earthiness.

Eiswein Literally "ice wine," made from grapes that are harvested and pressed while frozen. While the best of these are made from grapes naturally frozen by cold weather, this process can be replicated by freezing grapes artificially (a process called cryoextraction).

Finish Also referred to as *persistence* or *length,* this is a measure of how long the taste of the wine can be detected in the mouth. The longer the finish, the better the wine—assuming you like the flavor!

Flabby A term for wine whose weight is not balanced by sufficient acidity or tartness. A dessert wine that doesn't have adequate sharpness to foil the sweetness will be at once flabby and cloying.

Frizzante The Italian term for a light sparkle (similar to French *pétillant*) that tickles the palate.

Fruity The term for a wine that has abundant fruit flavors other than grape. A Torrontés may suggest citrus or tropical-fruit flavors in its aroma. A Petite Sirah may exhibit a strong aroma of blackberries or black raspberries. The younger the wine, the fruitier it's likely to be. *Fruity* is not synonymous with *sweet.*

Grassy A term for many of the "green" flavors associated with wine. It may refer to the varietal character of a Verdejo or the underripe nature of an Arneis or even a Cabernet Franc.

Green harvesting The practice of intentionally cutting off unripe grape bunches during the ripening stage to concentrate the flavors of the remaining fruit on the vine. The vine puts more nutrients and energy into the remaining fruit, resulting in more flavorful grapes and a smaller yield per vine.

GSM A red wine consisting of a blend of Grenache, Syrah (Shiraz), and Mourvèdre.

Ice wine See *Eiswein.*

Late harvest(ed) A term for wine made from grapes picked late in the year and at higher levels of sugar, so that they are often left with some residual sugar after fermentation. Most are dessert wines.

Length See *Finish.*

Malolactic fermentation Often referred to by the abbreviation ML, this process is used to transform some of the sharp malic acid (such as that found in green apples) in a wine to a softer lactic acid (such as that in yogurt or sour cream). In the process, a by-product called diacetyl is released that adds a strong buttery or buttered-popcorn flavor. ML decreases the perception of tartness in a wine, adds a rounder, softer texture, and can make it less susceptible to spoilage.

Méthode traditionnelle The term used in France to describe sparkling wines made using the so-called Champagne method (secondary fermentation occurring in the bottle) but practiced outside the appellation of Champagne. The term *méthode champenoise,* referring to the same process, is limited by law to use in the region of Champagne in France. Also called the *traditional method* in the United States.

Micro-oxygenation The process of injecting precise, minuscule amounts of oxygen into red wine during its production. This can be done during or after fermentation. Its objectives are to soften tannins, bring out flavor, and contribute to or modify texture. While generally practiced with bigger and more tannin-rich grape varieties, this process is increasingly being implemented for red-wine grapes as a matter of course.

Monovarietal wine A wine made from a single grape variety and not blended with any other grapes. Pure 100 percent Arneis, Verdejo, and Mencía, for example, are monovarietal wines.

Must The combination of grape juice, pulp, and skins that is fermented into wine. In making white wines, the skins, if present in the must at all, are removed after a short period of macerating with the pulp and juice.

New World A term used in the wine industry to refer collectively to North and South America, Australia, New Zealand, and South Africa.

Oak The wood of choice for the production of wine barrels. The age and size of the oak barrels affect the wine: younger oak contributes much more powerful, assertive flavors than older, previously used oak. Using larger oak barrels, which results in a smaller surface area of wine coming in contact with the wood, results in less oak flavor. The level of char (toasting of the wood) used in making the barrel also affects the wine. Too much oak on a wine makes it unbalanced and hard to match with food.

Off-dry A term for wines that have some sweetness but are not as sweet as dessert wines; it is more commonly used than *semi-sweet* among wine professionals.

Old World A term used in the wine industry to refer to the traditional winegrowing regions of Europe, from Spain and Portugal east to the Balkans.

Overcropping The practice of allowing too much fruit to ripen on a vine. Although this practice increases yield, it dilutes the fruit's flavors. Removing some of the fruit during the growing season (see *Green harvesting* above) concentrates flavor in the remaining grapes.

Oxidation (1) In winemaking, the natural process of oxygen coming into contact with the wine in the tank or barrel. (2) The process that causes wine to age and eventually lose character and flavor. As a wine develops, it oxidizes as minute amounts of oxygen in the bottle react with chemical compounds in the wine. (3) The natural incorporation of air into wine when it is poured into the glass, which makes the aromas and flavors more apparent.

Passito A style of Italian wine made from intentionally desiccated grapes. Amarone is a well known example of a *passito*-styled wine.

Pétillant A term used to describe a sparkling wine with a light effervescence. *Pétillant* wines prickle the palate very gently.

Qualitätswein mit Prädikat A term from the German wine law, literally meaning "quality wines with attributes." The terms for these attributes, used to designate different categories of wines, represent increasing levels of ripeness: *Kabinett, Spätlese, Auslese, Beerenauslese* (BA), *Trockenbeerenauslese* (TBA), and *Eiswein.*

Recioto An Italian term that originally referred to the "ears," or the fattest and ripest clusters of grapes on a bunch. Today the term has come to mean a selection of high-quality fruit that has been made into *passito* wines that are usually, though not always, sweet.

Reserve A term frequently understood to imply high quality but which, in the United States, has no legal meaning. At its best, it refers to wines that are produced from the finest lots and the best vineyards and treated with extra care, resulting in superb wines. At its worst, it's exploited by disingenuous wineries that prey on the consumer's belief that *reserve* must mean better. The European terms *reserva* (Spanish) and *riserva* (Italian) are, however, legally binding and have to do with aging requirements in the barrel and bottle.

Residual sugar The amount of sugar that is left in a wine after alcoholic fermentation.

Selection A cutting from an existing vine selected for propagation in new vineyards to produce fruit with the desired characteristics of the original vine. The term *selection* is often used interchangeably with *clone* (see above), but they are not synonymous.

Semi-sweet See *Off-dry.*

Skin contact The process of fermenting grapes with their skins. In red wines this step is critical, as all of the flavor, color, and tannins are in the skins. The juice may also be left in contact with the skins either before or after alcoholic fermentation.

Soft A term suggesting an approachable wine. In the positive sense, *soft* suggests a gentle elegance that can match splendidly with food. In the negative sense, it implies that the wine is lacking in character and apt to be easily dominated by a dish.

Spiciness The suggestion of spice aromas in a wine. They can be inherent to the grape type (as pepper is to Mourvèdre and cardamom to Gewürztraminer), but more often they come from extended oak aging. Sweet spices (such as cinnamon, nutmeg, clove, and vanilla) are easily detected in many oak-aged wines.

Spumante The Italian word for "sparkling."

Structure The overall sense of weight and texture in a wine; a direct function of the levels of alcohol, tannin, acidity, and other essential characteristics.

Sweetness The amount of sugar perceived in a wine. Sweetness can range from nonexistent or imperceptible (in dry wines) to slightly sweet (in off-dry or semi-sweet wines) to very sweet (in dessert wines).

Tannins Naturally occurring, bitter-tasting and astringently acidic compounds in wine that are extracted from the skins, stems, and seeds of the grapes. Although tannins are most often associated with red wines, which are fermented with their skins, white wines also can be tannic if fermented in contact with the grape skins. Wines that spend time in oak may also pick up tannins from the barrels. Tannins enable red wines to age well and must be taken into account in wine and food matching.

Taste The perception in the mouth of the basic components of a food or wine. Basic components of flavor—salt, sweet, tart, bitter, and umami—can be measured; the aromas and bouquet suggested by olfactory perception cannot.

Terroir A term referring to the characteristics of a wine contributed by the place where the grapes are grown. It is a combination of soil composition, aspect, rainfall, drainage, and exposure to sunlight, among myriad other characteristics. Wines that have a distinctive minerality or earthiness to them, especially Old World wines, are said to demonstrate a strong sense of *terroir*. Often referred to as the "taste of the earth."

Thin A term applied to both foods and wines that lack character or flavor. A thin wine may come off as dilute or simply vapid. Thin (light, uninteresting) foods can be very difficult to match with wine because they are so easily dominated.

Variety A specific strain of grape; also used to designate types of wine. Carignan and Grenache are both varieties. When a wine tastes distinctively of the specific grape it is made from, it is said to exhibit strong varietal character. Whereas many New World wines are labeled by variety, most European wines are labeled by geographic region of origin. Another term for grape type is *cultivar*.

VDN *Vin doux naturel* A dessert wine made by adding a neutral spirit to the fermenting wine (a process known as *mutage*) to stop the fermentation, thus preserving some of the natural (residual) sugar while increasing the alcohol content of the wine to somewhere between 15 and 18 percent.

Vinsanto, Vin Santo In Greece, where it originated, Vinsanto is a barrel-aged dessert wine produced from late-harvested Assyrtiko and Aïdani grapes. In Italy, Vin Santo (two words) is traditionally produced from late-harvested Trebbiano and Malvasia grapes.

Vintage The year that the grapes were harvested and the resultant wine made, a significant determinant of flavor and quality. Vintages vary around the globe: a good year in California may not equate to a good year in Bordeaux. Vintage can also be used to describe the actual grape harvest. Wines labeled as vintage in America must contain at least 95 percent wine from the stated year, though it varies from country to country (compare Australia's 85 percent and Chile's 75 percent).

Whole-cluster fermentation The use of clusters of grapes rather than must (see above), leaving all the berries and stems in one piece. The use of a combination of grape must and some whole clusters is called partial whole-cluster fermentation.

RESOURCES

RECOMMENDED BOOKS

Dorenburg, Andrew, and Karen Page. *What to Drink with What You Eat*. New York: Bulfinch Press, 2006.

Fletcher, Janet. *Cheese and Wine: A Guide to Selecting, Pairing, and Enjoying*. San Francisco: Chronicle Books, 2006.

Herbst, Ron, and Sharon Tyler Herbst. *The New Wine Lover's Companion*. 2nd ed. New York: Barron's Educational Series, Inc., 2003.

Jenkins, Steve. *The Cheese Primer*. New York: Workman Publishing, 1996.

Johnson, Hugh, and Jancis Robinson. *The World Atlas of Wine*. 6th ed. London: Mitchell Beasley, 2007.

Robinson, Jancis. *The Oxford Companion to Wine*. 3rd ed. New York: Oxford University Press, 2006.

Stevenson, Tom. *The Sotheby's Wine Encyclopedia*. New York: DK Publishing, 2007.

———. *Wine Report 2008* and *2009*. New York: DK Publishing, 2008 and 2009.

Werlin, Laura. *Laura Werlin's Cheese Essentials: An Insider's Guide to Buying and Serving Cheese*. New York: Stewart, Tabori & Chang, 2007.

ONLINE RESOURCES

WINE-RELATED SITES

There are hundreds of wine websites, but here are a few that consistently deliver useful and accurate information.

***Decanter* online** www.decanter.com The website for one of the most respected wine magazines in the world. Includes articles, news, and tasting notes.

eRobertParker.com The subscription-only site of perhaps the world's best-known wine critic offers tasting notes, articles, vintage charts, reviews, and other useful information.

JancisRobinson.com This website, much of which is accessible only to subscribers, is a wonderful combination of tasting notes, news, food information, and opinion from possibly the most influential wine journalist in the world.

National Grape Registry http://ngr.ucdavis.edu A great resource for amateurs, providing information on grapes of all colors, shapes, and sizes.

***Wine and Spirits* online** www.wineandspirits magazine.com Much of the valuable, well-researched information on this site is available to subscribers only. A useful alternative to the *Wine Spectator* and Robert Parker.

Wine Anorak www.wineanorak.com This U.K. site offers information from the elementary to the esoteric, including sections on wine travel and industry controversies.

Wine Communications Group, Inc. www .winebusiness.com My home page. Geared to wine-industry professionals, this site includes wine news from around the globe and listings for jobs, real estate, and sales of bulk grapes and wine.

Wine Lovers Page www.wine-lovers-page.com This site claims to be the "oldest, largest and most popular independent wine-appreciation site on the World Wide Web." Includes everything from feeds from Wine Library TV to online chat boards to a thirty-second e-mail bulletin.

Wine Pages www.wine-pages.com A distinctly Eurocentric website run by Tom Cannavan that brings together valued opinions on wine. It's been around since 1995 and includes thousands of pages of content.

Wine Release newsletter www.winerelease .com Updated regularly, this website lets you know when new wines are being released and provides links to winery websites.

Wine Spectator online www.winespectator .com The website of the industry's most widely read print publication. Features thousands of archived tasting notes along with informative articles, travel tips, opinions from industry experts, and blogs by regular columnists and guests. A paid subscription gives you access to even more material.

FOOD-RELATED SITES

Asia Society's Asia Food www.asiafood.org A great resource for fans of Asian cuisine, offering feature stories, a comprehensive glossary, and a library of recipes.

BBC Food www.bbc.co.uk/food As you'd expect from the BBC, this website is rich, easy to navigate, and full of recipes, information on techniques and ingredients, and instructional videos.

Chow www.chow.com The parent site of Chowhound, Chow is hip and comprehensive. It includes recipes, feature stories, regular columns, videos, and foodie news from all over.

Chowhound http://chowhound.chow.com Whenever I want restaurant recommendations, I turn to Chowhound. This large and diverse forum attracts serious foodheads who love to share their experiences. Its strict rules for posting seem to ensure quality contributions.

Cook's Illustrated Recipe Resource www .cooksillustrated.com Like the popular print magazine it's affiliated with, this site is exceptionally practical, well thought-out, and cleanly designed. Leaning toward traditional American cuisine, it provides everything from cooking tips to reviews of equipment and ingredients—and boatloads of thoroughly tested recipes.

John Mariani's Virtual Gourmet www.john mariani.com John is a bon vivant with exquisite taste. I consult his site for advice on all my travels. It includes links to websites by others who share his passions and to articles he writes on food, drink, and culture for publications like *Esquire*.

Tablehopper www.tablehopper.com This site, run by Marcia Gagliardi, is a must for everybody interested in things epicurean in San Francisco. It has restaurant reviews, weekly updates on the comings and goings of chefs and restaurants, and information on bars, wine, and clubbing.

Saveur online www.saveur.com One of the best of the monthly food magazines, *Saveur* has an equally compelling website, with solid coverage of food and wine.

Surprisingly, there's not much good information online about pairing wine and food, but here's a sampling of the best sites.

Albariño to Zinfandel http://recipes.albzin .com This Australian website includes recipes and wine pairings, categorized and cross-referenced by grape variety, key ingredients, and course.

***Food & Wine* online** www.foodandwine.com This behemoth is the online presence of the print magazine. From recipes and menus to dining guides and entertaining tips, it's all there. The wine and food section offers advice on pairing for both readily available and more obscure grapes.

Matching Food and Wine www.matchingfood andwine.com One of my favorite food-and-wine people is Fiona Beckett, the food correspondent for *Decanter* magazine. Her website (with premium content accessible only by subscription) is a must for anyone who's serious about food and wine pairing.

Alltop www.wine.alltop.com This site is the ultimate aggregation, listing virtually every wine blog. There are also sister sites covering beer and food.

Dr. Vino www.drvino.com Tyler Coleman, alias Dr. Vino, is an articulate, thoughtful, and provocative wine writer and a columnist for the *New York Times.*

Fermentation www.fermentation.typepad.com Tom Wark shoots from the hip. In addition to his own posts, which are well organized and easy to search, he includes a comprehensive list of other blogs, which will provide hours of surfing time (be warned!).

***New York Times* Pour Blog** http://thepour .blogs.nytimes.com Eric Asimov is a thoughtful and judicious writer on wine, spirits, food, and restaurants.

Vinography www.vinography.com This site, run by Alder Yarrow, offers everything from wine and sake reviews to restaurant discussion and criticism, book reviews, and a calendar of special events.

The Wine Knows http://community.winepress nw.com Andy Perdue is one of the most highly regarded wine writers in the Pacific Northwest and the force behind the respected *Wine Press Northwest.* His blog, which includes news and opinion, is a nice complement to his print and online magazine (www.winepressnw.com).

Podcasts, whether audio or video, are a useful alternative for those of us who absorb information better by watching or listening than by reading.

Full Circle Wine Solutions www.winecouch .com Full disclosure: I'm a partner in this wine-education company. As part of our outreach program, I present weekly videocasts on various wine topics. The site also features travelogues, a blog, and a Q and A column.

Grape Radio www.graperadio.com A pioneer in the medium, this outstanding website has won multiple awards, including a James Beard Foundation award. It broadcasts interviews with everyone from winemakers and growers to restaurant people and sommeliers.

TasteTV Networks www.tastetv.com Perhaps the most diverse of the video websites, this site has pages tailored to different regions (San Francisco, Chicago, Los Angeles, and global). Among its features are sections that connect wine with aspects of food and lifestyle, such as "cool drinks," "cool restaurants," and "cool cooks."

Wine Library TV www.winelibrarytv.com The online home of the controversial Gary Vaynerchuk. Gary has rocked the wine-appreciation world by attracting a younger and hipper audience with his irreverent style. Whether you like him or hate him, he's a force to be reckoned with, and his shows have a strong following.

ONLINE SHOPPING

WINE

BevMo www.bevmo.com Retailer with a wide selection of wines from around the world and a presence in many states.

CellarTracker www.cellartracker.com Offers community tasting notes and wine cellar management software.

Ferry Plaza Wine Merchant www.fpwm.com The expert staff of this San Francisco company select wines based on style, grape variety, and vineyard location. If you want something that's off the beaten track, they can find it.

Wine.com www.wine.com This online-only retailer ships to multiple states.

The Wine Club www.thewineclub.com My local store in San Francisco, the Wine Club (which has several California locations) offers lots of good wines at reasonable prices.

Wine-Searcher www.wine-searcher.com This site is amazing: it can search the Web for any wine you want, list sources, and compare prices. If you're looking for a specific wine, vintage, or producer or you have a rare wine and want to know what it's worth in today's market, this is the best place to start.

Zachys www.zachys.com A large New York company that offers a broad assortment of wines and terrific service and advice. Also a leader in the increasingly popular wine-auction market.

FOOD

A.G. Ferrari Foods www.agferrari.com My source for all good things Italian.

EthnicGrocer www.ethnicgrocer.com This is a mecca for foodstuffs from the world's most popular cuisines, searchable by country or by product. The site has a very cool gifts section, and I'm always scouring the specials page.

Formaggio Kitchen www.formaggiokitchen .com Another nice Italian shop.

The Spanish Table www.spanishtable.com Although I love to visit this company's Berkeley and Mill Valley stores for helpful and knowledgeable advice, you can just as easily browse online. It's a one-stop shop for Spanish and Portuguese wine, food, cooking equipment, ceramics, and music.

Tienda.com Tienda is all about Spain. It has a great selection of cheeses, *jamón,* chorizo, and wine.

Zingerman's www.zingermans.com This company, based in Ann Arbor, Michigan, is an amazing source of extraordinary breads, cookies, oils, vinegars, and cheeses.

GENERAL INDEX

Names of wine producers recommended in this book are flagged with an asterisk.

crème brûlée, 54, 295
crescenza, 48, 101, 108, 117, 247
Crianza Castilla la Vieja, Bodegas*, 147
Criolla Chica, 121–122
Crios de Susana Balbo*, 127
critics and ratings, 4, 11
Croatia, 212, 261
Croatina, 167
Crocker Starr*, 179
Crozes-Hermitage, 72, 106
cru, defined, 322
Crus Beaujolais, 212, 213
Cune*, 286
cured meats. *See* charcuterie and antipasti
Currado, Luca, 168
curries, 67, 74, 288
  coconut, 55, 73, 100, 151, 262
  mild, 123, 271
  spicy, 13, 47, 107, 214
custards, 54, 83, 115, 295
cuvée, defined, 322
Czech Republic, 65, 90

D
Damilano*, 44
Dão, 237, 286, 293, 294–295, 299
d'Arenberg*, 111, 250
De Bortoli*, 120, 267
De Conciliis*, 165
Del Grande, Robert, 281, 309
Derenoncourt, Stéphane, 5
Descendientes de J. Palacios*, 242
Desiderio Bisol & Figli*, 104
desserts, 24
  cakes and tortes, 13, 60, 84, 176, 184, 270, 295
  candies, 131, 295
  cheesecake, 84
  chocolate, 84, 176, 183, 184, 223, 255, 263, 295
  cookies, 116
  custards, 54, 83, 295
  fruit, 54, 55, 60, 82, 83, 84, 115, 116, 130, 295, 296
  honey, syrups, and sauces, 54, 83, 84, 130
  mousses, 55, 82, 83

nut, 83, 130
puddings, 84, 295
tarts, 54, 55, 60, 83, 115, 184, 255, 295
dessert wines. *See* fortified wines; sweet and off-dry wines
De Trafford*, 57
Di Majo Norante*, 165
dim sum, 138, 196, 288
D. Kourtakis. *See* Greek Wine Cellars
DO, DOCa (Spain), defined, 322
DOC (Portugal), defined, 322
DOC, DOCG (Italy), defined, 322
Dogliani, 204
Dolcetto, 252
  about, 203–205
  in blends, 168
  pairing with, 205–206
  recipe, 207–209
  recommended producers, 210
  summary of wine style, 317
Dôle, 213
dolmas, 41, 47, 302
domain. *See individual domain names*
Domenico Clerico*, 210, 254
Dominio de Tares*, 242
Doña Paula*, 235
Doniene*, 141
Donnas, 252
Douglas, Tom, 304, 309
Douro, 285–286, 291, 293, 294–295, 299
Douro Superior, 293
Drama, 46
dried fruits, 24, 83, 107
  See also prunes; raisins
Dry Creek Valley, 167, 181, 261
Dry Creek Vineyard*, 57
dryness, defined, 322
Duas Quintas*, 299
duck, 36, 73, 222, 288
  charcuterie, 213
  confit, 278, 279
  grilled, 271
  with olives, 245, 246
  Peking, 245, 246
  roast, 83, 238, 294
  with sausage, 246

Ducournau, Patrick, 277
Durif, 260, 261
  See also Petite Sirah
Durrus, 256

E
E. & M. Berger*, 70
earthiness, defined, 322
Eberle*, 111
Edam, 145
Edelzwicker, 90
Edna Valley, 38
egg dishes, 60, 61, 205, 222
eggplant, 100, 190, 238, 245, 302
Egypt, 80
eiswein, defined, 322
El Coto*, 291
Elena Fucci*, 165
Elio Altare*, 172, 254
Elysium, 87
Emilia-Romagna, 167
Emilio Moro*, 291
Emmentaler, 75, 264
enchiladas, 176
Entre-Deux-Mers, 113
EOS*, 267
Epcot Food and Wine Festival, 7
Époisses, 67, 85, 108
Ermitage, 72
Estefanía, Bodegas*, 242
Est! Est! Est!, 129
Estremadura, 293
Etchart, Bodegas*, 127
Etxegaraya, Domaine*, 283
Evharis, Domaine*, 50
exotic and ethnic foods, 107, 123, 196, 262, 263
  See also specific cuisines
Éxplorateur, 36, 93, 108, 117

F
Fairview*, 275
falafel, 41
Falesco*, 135
Farnese*, 135
Fattoria di Felsina*, 135
Faustino*, 286
Favorita, 149
  See also Vermentino

Fer, 278
fermentation methods and processes, 321, 323, 324, 325
Ferreira*, 293
feta
  reds and rosés with, 280, 302, 303
  whites with, 48, 61, 93, 101, 117, 139, 145
Feudi di San Gregorio*, 165
figs, 115, 223
Finca Antigua*, 291
Finca Jakue*, 141
finish, defined, 322
fish, 18, 19, 138
  broiled, 130
  cakes, 100
  fillet, 40, 60, 151, 205
  fried, 92, 137
  grilled, 47, 60, 92, 124, 144, 151, 169
  mild, 41, 54, 169, 190, 197, 205
  oily or strong, 12, 35, 36, 66, 123, 271
  raw, 20, 36, 150, 151
  smoked, 91
  soups and stews, 116, 123, 191
  tacos, 47, 91, 214
  See also specific types
Fitou, 181, 182
flabbiness, defined, 322
flavor profiles. See wine flavor
flavors, vs. tastes, 10, 11
Fleur du Cap*, 275
Fleurie, 213
Foggo Wines*, 202
foie gras, 54, 115
Folle Blanche, 137
Fontanafredda*, 44
Fontina
  reds and rosés with, 206, 247, 255, 256
  whites with, 42, 61, 108, 132
Fontsainte, Domaine de*, 187
food characteristics, 18–21
Foppiano*, 267
fortified wines
  Carignan-Grenache, 183
  Madeira, 142
  Málaga, 83

Muscat, 79–80, 81, 82, 83, 84, 85, 88
Pinotage, 269, 270
port, 23, 292, 293, 294, 295, 296, 299
  See also sherries; VDN wines
Fourme d'Ambert, 93, 117, 224
fowl. See poultry; specific types
France
  Cabernet Franc, 173, 174, 175, 179
  Carignan, 180, 181, 182, 187
  Carmenère, 189
  Chenin Blanc, 52, 53, 57
  Cinsaut, 194, 195, 196, 197, 198, 202
  Gamay, 211, 212, 218
  Grenache, 219, 220, 221–222, 228
  Malbec, 229, 230, 231, 232, 233, 235
  Marsanne, 71–77
  Mourvèdre, 243, 244, 245, 250
  Muscat, 78–80, 81, 82, 88
  Petite Sirah, 260, 261
  Pinot Blanc, 89, 90, 96
  Roussanne, 105–111
  Sémillon, 112, 113, 114, 116, 120
  Tannat, 277, 278, 279, 283
  Trebbiano, 128, 129, 130
  Vermentino, 149, 150
Frascati, 129
Freemark Abbey*, 262
Freisa, 3, 254
French food. See specific dishes and ingredients
Frick*, 187, 202
fried food, 12, 20, 36, 92, 151
  chicken, 100
  fish, 137
  seafood, 83, 91, 138, 197
frittatas. See egg dishes
Friuli–Venezia Giulia, 90, 96, 174
frizzante, defined, 322
fromage blanc, 55, 108, 247
Fronsac, 174
fruit, 60, 100, 123, 131
  with chocolate, 41, 223, 295
  compote, 41, 55, 85, 223
  crisps and cobblers, 84, 85
  dried, 24, 83, 223, 296
  stone, 54, 82, 83, 116

summer, 83
tarts, 55
tree, 54, 82, 116
tropical, 83, 115
  See also specific types
fruitiness, defined, 322
fruit-meat combinations, 24
Fumé Blanc, 260
  See also Sauvignon Blanc
F. X. Pichler*, 70

G
Gaia Estate*, 50
Gaiter, Dorothy J., 4
Gaja, Angelo, 168
Gaja Winery*, 259
Galicia, 33–34, 38, 122, 237, 242
Gallura, 149, 150, 155
Gamay
  about, 211–213
  in blends, 230
  pairing with, 213–215
  recipe, 216–217
  recommended producers, 218
  summary of wine style, 317
Gamay Beaujolais, 211
Gamay du Rhône, 211
Gamay Saint-Laurent, 211
game. See specific types
game hens, 40, 54, 123, 222, 288
Gancedo, Bodegas*, 242
Garganega
  about, 58–60
  pairing with, 60–61
  recipe, 62
  recommended producers, 63
  summary of wine style, 316
garlic, as "magic" ingredient, 19
Garnacha, 220–21
  See also Grenache
Garrotxa, 67, 177
Gattinara, 252, 254
Geelong, 189
Georges Duboeuf*, 218
Germany, 90, 319, 324
Getariako Txakolina, 137, 141
Gewürztraminer, 123, 149
Ghemme, 252
Giacomo Ascheri*, 44, 210
Giacomo Bologna*, 168, 172

online wine shopping, 318
Ontario, 175, 179, 212
Orange Muscat, 81
Oregon, 2, 3
    reds, 204, 210, 212, 218, 230, 253, 286
    whites, 38, 40, 53, 90, 96
Ormeasco, 204
    See also Dolcetto
Orvieto, 129, 130
osso buco, 161, 170, 254, 255
Ostertag, Domaine*, 88
Ott, Domaines*, 202
Ottavianello, 195
Ovada, 204
overcropping, defined, 323
Owen Roe*, 179
Oxford Companion to Wine (Robinson), 27, 59
oxidation, defined, 323–324
oysters, 47, 54, 55, 91, 115, 116, 138

P

paella, 35, 196, 197, 222
pairing guidelines (general)
    cheeses, 28–29
    cooking with wine, 21–23
    dining out, 21
    overview, 9–11
    quick reference, 24–25
    understanding foods, 17–21
    understanding wine flavors, 11–17
Paixar*, 242
Pala*, 155
Palacios, Alvaro, 5
Palmina*, 44, 172
Palomino, 143
panettone, 60
Pangeon, 50
Pantelleria, 80
Pape Johannou*, 50
Paradise Ranch*, 96
Parducci*, 267
Parker, Robert, 4
Parmesan, 55, 101, 117, 139, 177, 184, 303
parsnips. *See* root vegetables
partridge, 232
Pasanau*, 228
Pascual Toso*, 127

Paso Robles
    Aglianico, 160
    Barbera, 167
    Nebbiolo, 253
    Petite Sirah, 261
    Roussanne, 106
    Tannat, 277–278
    Tempranillo, 286
Passe Tout Grains, 213
passito, defined, 324
pasta, 54, 123, 130, 150, 176, 279
    with butter or cream sauce, 74, 92, 107, 115, 143, 151, 161, 183, 288
    with lemon zest, 40, 60, 115
    with meat sauce, 162, 190, 238, 254, 255
    with mushrooms, 169
    primavera, 131, 238
    with seafood, 35, 60, 68, 115, 151
Patagonia, 230, 235
pâté, 91, 206, 213–214
Patras, 79, 82
Patrimonio, 149, 150, 155
Patterson, Lachlan M., 43, 312
Paul Jaboulet*, 88
Paul Janin*, 218
pavé d'affinois, 42, 61, 67, 152
Pavia, Agostino, 168
Pavlou-Kagas*, 306
Pawlcyn, Cindy, 248, 312
Pazo de Señorans*, 38
peaches, 23, 82, 83, 84, 115
pears, 55, 82, 115
pecorino, 48, 132, 162, 170, 224, 256, 296
Pedro Ximénez, 79, 80
Peking duck, 245, 246
Peller Estates*, 179
Peloponnese, 46
Peloursin, 260, 261
Peltier Station*, 267
Penedès, 174, 220–221, 285
pepper (spice), 183, 222, 245, 246, 262
    alcohol accentuated by, 16
    to counterbalance tannin, 24
peppers/chiles, 61, 66, 137, 143, 176, 238, 302
Perera, 99
Perold, Abraham Izak, 269

Perpera, Sofia, 300
Pertinace*, 44
pesto, 60, 61, 100, 144, 197, 288
Peter Lehmann*, 120
pétillant, defined, 324
Petit Basque, 184, 239, 296
Petit Courbu, 137
Petite Sirah, 294
    about, 260–262
    pairing with, 262–264
    recipe, 265–266
    recommended producers, 267
    summary of wine style, 317
Petit Manseng, 137
Petit-Suisse, 108
Petit Verdot, 188, 189, 230
Peynaud, Émile, 142–143
pheasant, 222, 232, 246, 270, 279
Philippe Alliet*, 179
Piave, 85, 170
Pibarnon, Château de*, 250
Pichot, Domaine*, 57
pickles, 47, 61, 138
picnic foods, 60, 92, 206, 214, 222, 223, 263
Piedmont
    Arneis, 39, 44
    Barbera, 166–167, 168, 172, 252, 255
    Dolcetto, 203–204, 210, 252
    Favorita/Vermentino, 149
    Muscat, 80, 81–82, 83
    Nebbiolo, 251, 252, 253–254, 259
Pieropan*, 63
Pierre Robert, 215, 289
Pierre Soulez*, 57
Pierre Sparr*, 96
Pigato, 149
    See also Vermentino
Pinotage, 27
    about, 268–270
    pairing with, 270–272
    recipe, 273–274
    recommended producers, 275
    summary of wine style, 317
Pinot Bianco, 90
    See also Pinot Blanc
Pinot Blanc, 11
    about, 89–91
    pairing with, 19, 91–93

recipe, 94–95
recommended producers, 96
summary of wine style, 316
Pinot Blanco, 53
See also Chenin Blanc
Pinot Gris, 90
Pinot Noir, 90, 196, 213, 268, 269, 270, 284
Pio Cesare*, 172
Pisano*, 283
pizza, 169, 205
Plantagenet*, 120
Point Reyes Blue, 264
polenta, 99, 100, 107, 124, 255
Pomerol, 174
Ponzi*, 40, 44
popcorn, 54
porcini, 99, 255
pork, 143, 150, 161, 196, 287
  casseroles, 35
  chops, 183, 232
  ham, 107, 206
  loin, 11, 115, 214
  marinated, 107, 176, 232
  roast, 47, 60, 115, 123, 169, 214, 222
  shoulder, 190, 262
  smoked, 54, 262
  stews and braises, 35, 36
  sweet and sour, 66, 123
port, 23, 292, 293, 294, 295, 296, 299
Port Salut, 93, 124, 215, 233, 272, 303
Portugal
  Albariño/Vinho Verde, 33, 34, 38, 137
  Jaen, 237
  Muscat, 80–81
  Tempranillo, 285–286, 291
  Touriga Nacional, 292–299
  Verdelho, 142
poultry, 18, 19, 54
  See also specific types
pound cake, 60
poussin, 222
Prager*, 70
prawns, 47, 54, 83, 91, 190, 222, 223
  See also shrimp
Preston*, 202
Primitivo, 148

Priorat, 181, 220, 221, 222, 223, 228, 237
producer recommendations, criteria for, 29
Prosecco
  about, 97–99
  pairing with, 99–101
  recipe, 102–103
  recommended producers, 104
  summary of wine style, 316
Prošek, 98
Provence
  Cinsaut, 196, 202
  Grenache, 228
  Mourvèdre, 244, 245, 250
  Petite Sirah, 261
  whites, 106, 129, 149
provolone, 93, 124, 145, 191
prunes, 23, 183, 232, 254
Prunotto*, 172, 253, 259
PX (Pedro Ximénez), 79, 80

Q
Quady Winery*, 87
quail, 40, 54, 222, 288
Qualitätswein mit Prädikat, defined, 324
Quara*, 283
Quarts de Chaume, 52, 57
Quatrano, Anne S., 49, 312
Queensland, 261, 277
queijo de Évora, 36
queso fresco, 132
quiche. *See* egg dishes
quince, 55
quinta. *See individual quinta names*
Qupé*, 3, 77

R
Raats*, 57
rabbit, 232
raclette, 48, 85, 233
radicchio, 190
raisins, 130, 131, 223, 254
Rapel, 193
Raphael*, 230
Rasteau, 220, 222–223
ratatouille, 197, 238, 246, 288
ratings and critics, 4, 11

raw foods, 20, 36, 92, 150, 151
  See also sashimi
Rayas, Château*, 221–222
reblochon, 132
recioto, defined, 324
Recioto di Soave, 60, 61, 63
recommended producers, criteria for, 29
Red Hawk, 117, 184
red meats. *See specific types*
Red Wine with Fish (Rosengarten and Wesson), 10–11
Régnié, 211
Renato Corino*, 259
reserve wines, defined, 324
residual sugar, defined, 324
retsina, 46
Rhône
  Cinsaut, 194, 195, 196, 197, 202
  Grenache, 220, 222, 228
  Marsanne, 71–77
  Mourvèdre, 244, 245
  Muscat, 80, 88
  Petite Sirah, 261
  Roussane, 105–111
  Trebbiano, 129
Rhône Rangers, 221, 243
Rhône-style wines
  in California, 3, 72, 106, 195, 221, 243
  Petite Sirah in, 262
rhubarb, 255
Rías Baixas, 33–34, 38
Ribeira Sacra, 237, 242
Ribeiro, 122
Ribera del Duero, 285, 286–287, 291
rice, 115, 131, 197, 238
  See also paella; risotto
ricotta, 36, 55, 85, 124, 132, 206
ricotta salata, 42
Ridge Vineyards*, 244
Riesling, 3, 33, 51
Rieussec, Château*, 120
Rinaldi, Giuseppe, 168
Rioja, 181
  Carignan, 182
  Grenache, 219, 220, 221
  Tempranillo, 284, 285, 286–287, 291

Rio Negro, 230
Rios do Minho, 33, 34, 38
risotto, 60, 123, 168, 255
  with butter or cream sauce, 74,
    92, 107, 115, 116
  meat, 131, 162, 176
  seafood, 47, 74, 116, 150, 197
  vegetable, 288
Rive della Chiesa*, 104
Riverina, 261
Rivesaltes, 79–80, 84
Roberto Voerzio*, 210, 254, 259
Robertson, 269
Robinson, Jancis, 4, 27, 59
robiola, 67, 124, 170, 239, 264, 289
Rocca*, 155
Rocca delle Macie*, 135
Rocchetta Belbo, 167
Roda, Bodegas*, 286, 291
Rodríguez, Telmo, 5
Roero, 39
Rolland, Dany, 5
Rolland, Michel, 5
Rolle, 72, 149
Romano, Michael, 178, 312–313
Roncal, 145, 162, 239
root vegetables, 54, 73, 107, 123,
    150, 232, 279
Roque Eizaguirre*, 141
Roquefort, 85, 116, 117, 233
Roques, Quinta dos*, 299
Roques Mauriac, Château*, 120
Rosenblum*, 77, 267
Rosengarten, David, 10–11
rosé wines, 16
  Aglianico, 160
  Barbera, 168
  Beaujolais rosé, 213
  Cabernet Franc, 174
  California Rhône-style, 221
  Carignan, 180, 183
  Cinsaut, 194, 195, 196, 197, 198, 202
  Gamay, 213
  Grenache, 220, 221, 222, 223, 224,
    228
  Malbec, 230, 233, 235
  Mourvèdre, 244, 245, 246, 247, 250
  Pinotage, 269, 272, 275
  Prosecco, 100
  Tannat, 280, 283

Tempranillo, 287, 288, 289, 291
Touriga Nacional, 294, 295, 296
Xinomavro, 301, 302, 303, 306
Roussane
  about, 105–107
  and Marsanne, 71, 72
  pairing with, 19, 107–108
  recipe, 109–110
  recommended producers, 111
  summary of wine style, 316
Roussanne du Var, 106
Roussette, 106
Roussillon, 78–80, 81, 82, 187,
    195
  See also Languedoc-Roussillon
Rudi Pichler*, 70
Rueda, 142–143, 147
Ruggeri & Co.*, 104
rutabagas. See root vegetables
Rutherglen, 261
Rutherglen Estates*, 77, 80

S

Saint-Amour, 213
Saint-André, 101, 117, 280
Saint-Nectaire, 198, 289
Saint-Paulin, 247
salads, 19
  composed, 41, 66, 92, 115, 184, 213
  Greek, 144, 302
  mixed green, 12, 47, 144, 302
  seafood, 92, 143, 151, 197
  Waldorf, 123, 131
salmon, 18, 94, 205, 246
  raw, 36, 150
  smoked, 54, 91
salsa verde, 40, 131, 144, 190, 238,
    288
Salta, 122, 127, 235, 277, 283
salt cod, 35, 73, 138, 246
salty foods, 25, 35, 100, 138, 151
  alcohol accentuated by, 16, 24
salumi, 99, 151, 169, 206
Samos, 79, 82
Sandeman*, 299
sandwiches, 92, 137, 205, 214, 222,
    223, 263
Sangiovese, 286
San José, 283
San Juan, 167, 230

Santa Barbara, 3, 106, 167
Santa Cruz, 88, 210
Santa Cruz Mountains, 210
Santadi, Cantina di*, 187
Santa Isabel*, 127
Santa Julia*, 127
Santa Rita*, 193
Santa Ynez Valley, 253
Santi*, 63
Santorini, 46, 50
Santo Stefano Belbo, 167
São Jorge, 264, 289
sardines, 92, 196, 246
Sardinia, 148, 149, 150, 155, 187,
    221
sashimi, 74, 92, 150, 196
Sassella, 252
sauces and condiments, 20–21,
    22, 25, 161, 169, 176, 190
  See also creamy/buttery dishes;
    tomato sauces; wine sauces
Saumur, 52, 57
sausages, 67, 238, 245, 287
  assorted, 206, 232
  with duck, 246
  grilled, 169, 205, 271
  in pasta and risotto, 176, 183
  smoked, 262
  in stews and braises, 35, 66, 161
  See also charcuterie and antipasti
Sauternes, 112, 113, 114, 116, 120
Sauvignon Blanc, 46, 112, 113, 114,
    143, 174, 260
Savagnin, 34
Savatiano, 46
Savennières, 52, 57
Savoie, 106
Savona, 149
SBS wines, 114
scallops, 35, 60, 123, 302
  brochettes, 150
  with butter or cream sauce, 47,
    74, 107, 115
  in risotto, 116
  in salads, 41, 151
  sautéed, 223
  with tomato sauce, 205
Schiopetto*, 96
Schloss Gobelsburg*, 70
Scienza, Attilio, 159

sea bass, 116
seafood. *See* fish; shellfish; *specific types*
Seghesio*, 44
selection, defined, 324
  See also clone
Sella & Mosca*, 155
SemChards, 112, 113–14
Sémillon
  about, 112–114
  pairing with, 115–117
  recipe, 118–119
  recommended producers, 120
  summary of wine style, 316
Serbia, 212
Serra, 75, 85
Serralunga, 252
Serralunga d'Alba, 167
Setúbal, 80–81
Sforzato, 252, 254
SGN wines, 81
shark, 169, 214
shellfish, 12, 14, 19, 100, 138
  fried, 246
  mild, 40, 205
  oily or strong, 66
  raw, 151
  See also specific types
Shenandoah Valley, 278
sherries
  Muscat, 79, 80–81, 82, 83, 88
  Verdejo, 143, 144
Shiraz, 261, 270
  GSM blends, 219, 227, 244, 245
  See also Syrah
shopping for wine, 318–319
shrimp, 35, 54, 60
  with butter or cream sauce, 47, 74, 115, 123
  cocktail, 47
  fried, 12, 36, 91, 151
  in pastas and risottos, 74, 115, 150, 151
  reds with, 205, 302
  in salads, 99, 151
  in sandwiches, 91
  spicy, 40, 82
  See also prawns
Sicily, 80, 148
Sigalas, Domaine*, 50

Simonsig*, 275
Sitios de Bodega*, 147
skin contact, 122
  defined, 324
Slovenia, 90, 174
smoked foods, 20, 115, 295
  bacon, 254
  beef, 190
  fish, 54, 91, 190
  ham, 254
  pork, 190
  poultry, 123, 190
  snapper, 54, 214, 222
snoek, 270
Soave, 58–59, 63, 130
  Recioto di Soave, 60, 61, 63
softness, defined, 324
sole, 41, 92
Soltner, André, 123
Sommariva*, 104
sommeliers, 5–6
Somontano, 221
Sonoma
  reds, 167, 181, 202, 204, 261, 267, 275
  whites, 44, 57, 77
Sotheby's Wine Encyclopedia (Stevenson), 27
soups, 107, 116, 123, 144, 183, 238, 279
South Africa
  Cape blends, 270
  Chenin Blanc, 51, 52–53, 57
  Cinsaut, 195, 196, 202
  Mourvèdre, 245, 250
  Muscat, 81, 88
  Pinotage, 268–275
  Sémillon, 114, 120
South American wines, 53, 167, 319
  See also Argentina; Chile; Uruguay
South Australia
  reds, 168, 195, 202, 228, 244, 277
  whites, 149
Southeast Australia, 267
Southern Central Coast (California)
  Aglianico, 160, 165
  Barbera, 167
  Cinsaut, 202

Grenache, 228
Mourvèdre, 250
Nebbiolo, 259
Petite Sirah, 267
Tannat, 283
whites, 44, 77, 88, 96, 155
Southern Oregon, 204, 210, 253
Southwest France
  Cabernet Franc, 174
  Carignan, 180, 181, 182, 187
  Malbec, 229, 230, 231, 232, 233, 235
  Marsanne, 72
  Sémillon, 120
  Tannat, 277, 278, 279, 283
Souverain*, 262
Spain
  Albariño, 33–34, 35, 38
  Cabernet Franc, 174
  Carignan, 181, 182, 187
  Cava, 97–98
  Grenache, 219, 220–221, 222, 228
  Málaga, 80, 83
  Mencía, 236–242
  Monastrell/Mourvèdre, 243, 244, 245, 250
  Muscat, 79, 80–81, 82, 83, 88
  Tempranillo, 284–291
  Torrontés, 122
  Txakoli, 136–141
  Verdejo, 142–147
Spanish food. *See specific dishes*
sparkling and spritzy wines, 16
  Albariño, 34
  Barbera, 167, 168, 169
  Cabernet Franc, 175
  Cava, 97–98
  Chenin Blanc, 52, 53, 54, 55, 57
  Marsanne, 73, 75, 77
  Muscat, 79, 80, 81–82, 83, 84, 85, 88
  Pinotage, 268
  Pinot Blanc, 90, 91, 92, 93, 96
  Prosecco, 97–104
  Roussanne, 106, 108
  Sémillon, 113
  Txakoli, 137, 139
  Xinomavro, 301, 302, 303, 306
Spicer, Susan, 133, 313
Spice Route*, 245, 250
spices, sweet, 24, 66, 67, 74, 115, 123, 324

spiciness (in wine), defined, 324
spinach, 190
spirits, 128, 129
spumante, defined, 324
Spyros Hatziyiannis*, 50
squab, 190, 222, 238, 245, 246, 270, 271
squash, 75, 107
squid, 92, 138, 151, 302
SSB wines, 112, 114, 115, 116
Stags' Leap Winery*, 262
steak. *See* beef
Ste.-Croix-du-Mont, 113
Steen, 52
   See also Chenin Blanc
Stelios Kechris*, 306
Stellenbosch, 57, 275
Ste. Michelle, Chateau*, 120
St.-Émilion, 174
St.-Émilion grape, 128
Stevenot Winery*, 77
Stevenson, Tom, 27
stews and braises, 22
   beef, 161, 170, 183, 232, 238, 245, 255, 262, 263, 271, 279
   chicken, 35, 36, 115
   fish, 123, 191
   lamb, 161, 170, 197, 238, 255, 279
   pork, 35, 36
   sausage, 35, 66, 161
   veal, 36, 115, 183
St. George, 108
Stilton, 132, 296
Stitt, Frank, 192, 313
St.-Jean-de-Minervois, 80, 88
St.-Joseph, 72, 106
St.-Nicolas-de-Bourgueil, 174, 175
Stoll, Craig, 153, 313
Stormhoek*, 275
Stowell, Ethan, 62, 313
St.-Péray, 72, 73, 106
stracchino, 42, 61
strawberries, 84, 116
structure, defined, 324
sturgeon, 270
Styria, 90
Suavia*, 63
Sueño*, 147
sugar, residual, 324
Super Tuscan wines, 287

Susana Balbo*, 127
sushi, 35, 36, 74, 100, 138
Swartland, 250
sweet and off-dry wines, 16, 22, 24, 25
   Assyrtiko, 45, 46–47, 50, 325
   Cabernet Franc, 175, 176, 177, 179
   Carignan, 180, 184, 187
   Chenin Blanc, 52, 53, 54, 55, 57
   Garganega, 58, 60, 61, 63
   Grenache, 219, 220, 222–223, 224, 228
   Grüner Veltliner, 64, 65, 67, 70
   Marsanne, 72, 73
   Muscat, 79, 80, 81, 83, 84, 85, 88
   Pinotage, 268
   Pinot Blanc, 90, 93, 96
   Prosecco, 100
   Sémillon, 112, 113, 114, 115, 116, 117, 120
   Touriga Nacional (port), 292, 293, 294, 295, 296, 299
   Trebbiano, 128, 129, 130, 131, 135, 325
   See also VDN wines
sweet-and-sour dishes, 11, 66, 123
sweetbreads, 18, 116, 161, 232, 294
sweetness (in food), 13, 25
sweetness (in wine), 12–13, 24
   defined, 324
   summarized by wine style, 316–317
sweet potatoes, 54, 150
Swiss chard, 190, 271
Switzerland, 72, 73, 213
swordfish, 41, 60, 144, 169, 190, 214, 246
Symington Family Estates*, 299
Syrah, 3, 72, 189, 260
   and Grenache, 223
   and Petite Sirah, 261, 262
   and Xinomavro, 301
   See also Shiraz

T
tabbouleh, 41
Tablas Creek*, 3, 72, 155, 250, 283
Tahbilk*, 77
Talai-Berri*, 141

Taleggio
   reds and rosés with, 162, 191, 206, 215, 224, 233, 247, 256, 303
   whites with, 55, 85, 108, 117, 132
Tamari, Bodega*, 127
Tamellini*, 63
Tangent*, 38, 96
Tannat
   about, 276–278
   pairing with, 278–280
   recipe, 281–282
   recommended producers, 283
   summary of wine style, 317
tannic wines, 22, 24
tannins, 13–14
   defined, 324
   summarized by wine style, 316–317
Tanzer, Steve, 4
tapas, 41, 137, 138, 288
Tapeña*, 147
Tariquet, Domaine du*, 135
Tarragona, 221
tarts, 55, 60, 83, 115, 184, 255, 295
tastes, 10, 11
   defined, 325
Taurasi, Taurasi Riserva, 160, 161
Tavel, 194, 195, 196, 197, 198, 202
   See also Grenache
Taylor Fladgate*, 299
Tejo, 293, 299
teleme
   reds with, 224, 233
   whites with, 48, 55, 85, 101, 145
Telmo Rodríguez*, 147
Tempier, Domaine*, 250
Tempranillo, 3, 182, 251
   about, 284–287
   in blends, 221, 245, 293
   pairing with, 287–289
   recipe, 290–291
   recommended producers, 291
   summary of wine style, 317
Tenuta Garetto*, 168
Tenuta le Velette*, 135
Tenute Sella & Mosca*, 187
Terra Noble*, 193
Terre di Orazio*, 88
Terredora*, 165
Terres Falmet, Domaine des*, 202

RECIPE INDEX